LEGAL ISSUES

IN PEDIATRICS

AND ADOLESCENT

MEDICINE

LEGAL ISSUES

IN PEDIATRICS

AND ADOLESCENT

MEDICINE

Angela Roddey Holder, LL.M.

Member of the Bars of South Carolina
and Louisiana

Executive Director of the Program in Law,
Science, and Medicine
Yale Law School

Lecturer in Pediatrics
Yale University School of Medicine

Foreword by Howard A. Pearson, M.D.

A Wiley Medical Publication

JOHN WILEY & SONS, New York • London • Sydney • Toronto

iv

Library of Congress Cataloging in Publication Data:

Holder, Angela Roddey.
 Legal issues in pediatrics and adolescent medicine.

 (A Wiley medical publication)
 Includes bibliographical references.
 1. Pediatrics—Law and legislation—United States.

2. Fetus—Research—Law and legislation—United States.
3. Children—Law—United States. I. Title.
[DNLM: 1. Pediatrics. 2. Adolescence. 3. Legislation, Medical. 4. Human rights. WS100 H727L]
KF2910.P42H65   344'.73'041   76-41385
ISBN 0-471-40612-0

Printed in the United States of America

10 9 8 7 6 5 4 3 2 1

For John, as always, and, with gratitude and affection, for Jay Katz and Robert J. Levine, incomparable scholars and teachers and, most of all, supportive friends

FOREWORD

The courts, the law, and the legal process are terra incognita for most physicians. Interaction with the law evokes a great deal of uneasiness from the doctor—the same kind of reaction, I suspect, that lawyers experience when they become patients in a hospital! For both professions this is a consequence of being a professional exposed to an arcane system where unfamiliar ground rules operate. In both situations much of this uncertainty and fear can be dispelled by clear description, explanation, and candid discussion.

Angela Holder serves just this function in this book. She has used her considerable expertise and experience to describe and elucidate, for the pediatrician and child psychiatrist, legal issues that bear on the practice of medicine involving children and their families. She uses clear language and a minimum of legal terminology and jargon (thankfully, since Latin is no longer a premedical requirement).

The chapters encompass a broad spectrum of issues. The law that exists today is described; the law as it may evolve in the future is projected. Topics range from futuristic, Huxleyan considerations of in vitro fertilization and implantation—so-called test-tube babies—to practical, even pedestrian, problems involving the pediatrician as a school physician or Little League team physician.

Conflicts and controversies are vividly described. She elucidates laws that pertain to children both before and after birth, where ethics, morality, religion, and emotion interact and often conflict. She points out how some well intended laws for juveniles may deprive them of fundamental rights (felons may have more rights than children!). She describes how the powerful and fundamental rights of parents over the destiny of their children must on occasion, but only with due concern and process, be overruled by society and its laws.

The practice of pediatrics unavoidably interacts with the law and legal processes. This book will help to make that interaction more comprehensible and hopefully less intimidating for the pediatrician. It will be strongly advised reading for the pediatric house staff and faculty at the Yale–New Haven Hospital and can be highly recommended for all physicians who care for children.

HOWARD A. PEARSON, M.D.
Professor and Chairman
Department of Pediatrics
Yale University School of Medicine
Chief of the Pediatric Service
Yale–New Haven Hospital
New Haven, Connecticut

PREFACE

The medical profession in general is confronted with a variety of new legal problems, and the malpractice crisis has affected all specialties. Those physicians who work with infants, children, and adolescents are encountering even more complex legal issues peculiar to their patient population than are other specialists. The increasing concern over the rights of a child as an autonomous human being whose interests may conflict with those of his parents has resulted in new legal doctrines far removed from the days when a child was his father's chattel. The concept that a child has any rights at all when he is dealing with his teachers was unknown 20 years ago. The pediatrician is now in a position where he may feel that he needs to know almost as much about what the Supreme Court is doing as he does about advances in therapy. What is his responsibility when a seriously deformed child is born or when a 14-year-old girl asks him to arrange an abortion? What is his responsibility toward a runaway with a broken leg? The 10 chapters of this book discuss problems arising in pediatric practice today that were virtually unknown prior to the combined forces of a new legal climate for the child and his family in our society and the new therapeutic advances in medicine. In many of these issues the law has not yet found clear-cut solutions. To physicians, not only does the legal system move in mysterious ways, but it seems to do so with such glacial slowness that when answers are needed they are not available, and when the system finally makes answers available they are not responsive to the ever-evolving medical questions. I hope that the discussions in this book will be beneficial in solving as clearly as possible some of the new dilemmas of pediatric practice.

The majority of the issues in this book can be reduced to three questions: When is a fetus considered a human being? What are the limits of personal and family autonomy in our society? When does legitimate protection of what are conceived to be the best interests of a child who may not be able to protect his own interests become officious meddling or dehumanization? These questions can be answered, if at all, only with the help of philosophers and ethicists, but the legal system must try to solve the practical problems that confront our society while confessing its inabilities to answer the great questions to which mankind may never find clear answers. The examples in this book are actual cases. Each child was a human being, and in many of these situations his essential dignity was violated, usually with the best intentions. I hope that when the physician has read this book, he will be both less confused about his legal responsibilities and more aware that even the youngest child is entitled to respect for his humanity.

ANGELA R. HOLDER, LL.M.

New Haven, Connecticut
August 1976

CONTENTS

LEGAL ISSUES

IN PEDIATRICS

AND ADOLESCENT

MEDICINE

CHAPTER I

LEGAL ISSUES

AT CONCEPTION

AND DURING

THE PRENATAL

PERIOD

For the entire duration of human existence, babies have been conceived and born by one standard method—sexual intercourse followed by pregnancy and delivery. The old legal adage was "Motherhood is a matter of fact, fatherhood a matter of opinion." The "tried and true" method is now potentially capable of being supplemented by the clinical interventions, at least on an experimental basis, of physicians who have already succeeded in fertilizing and growing human ova in the laboratory for brief periods of time. At some point within the next few years, gestation of a fetus in the laboratory through its entire period of prenatal development will be possible. The legal issues inherent in these experiments have not been explored to any degree. Almost no one has even tried to establish a body of law that would serve as a practical guideline to provide solutions for physicians before the first legal issues involved in "the new biology" are presented to a court. Such a guideline would presumably be based on reasonable extensions of existing common-law principles for the disposition of the inevitable legal questions that will confront the courts within the next ten years.

There is a considerable body of thought to the effect that this research should be entirely prohibited. Objections range from the assertion that research in this area violates the "will of God" and dehumanizes people to fears that once artificial fertilization and gestation are possible, governments will create hundreds of beings with which they can control either their own citizenry or the world. The ethical issues in the discussion are of critical importance, but whether or not this type of research is a good thing, banning any form of research is probably futile as a practical matter. If, for example, the

1

American Medical Association's policy calling for a ban on in vitro research were to be followed by ethical and reputable physicians, who would be inclined to respect it, the field would be left to the unethical. Therefore, the assumption is made in this discussion that the research will continue as it has in the past few years to a point of successful conclusion regardless of ethical advisability.

THE STATE OF THE ART OF "THE NEW BIOLOGY"

In Vitro Fertilization and Implantation in the Same Woman

In 1959 Daniele Petrucci, an Italian scientist, announced that after more than 40 attempts he had fertilized a human egg in vitro and sustained the embryo alive in an artificial environment for 29 days. At that point, he terminated his experiment because, in his words, the embryo "had become deformed and enlarged, a monstrosity."[1] The Vatican took strenuous exception to Petrucci's experiments, and *L'Osservatore Romano,* the Vatican newspaper, called on him to terminate further experimental efforts in this area. After conferring with Vatican officials, Petrucci announced that he then considered that he might have committed two sins: creating human life in an unnatural way and destroying it. He therefore ceased his experiments. At the time he announced cessation of further work, however, he stated that he had kept one experimental female baby alive for a full 59 days before it died as the result of "a technical mistake."

As far as can be determined, Petrucci was only the first of several scientists who have succeeded in fertilizing a human ovum in the laboratory. In December 1970 R. G. Edwards and Ruth E. Fowler of Cambridge University reported on their successful efforts at fertilization of a human egg in a laboratory.[2] This article received enormous publicity and triggered extended comments in both lay and professional publications.

Shortly thereafter, Landrum B. Shettles of Columbia University reported that he had succeeded in aspirating a human ovum from its follicle and placing the ovum in a sterile petri dish.[3] A drop of the patient's husband's semen with a normal spermatozoa count was added to the preparation and the mixture was incubated for five days. At that point the ovum was in the blastocyst stage. The brief note of the procedure stated: "The grossly normal blastocyst of approximately 100 cells was not transferred in utero in that the patient was only five days post-multiple myomectomies. Otherwise there was no discernible contradiction for a successful transfer *in vitro* and continued developments." The note continued, however, that transfer "is scheduled for patients with ligated or excised Fallopian tubes who may want a child, with the ova obtained by culdoscopy or laparoscopy."

In 1973 a letter in *The Lancet* from the Department of Obstetrics and Gynecology of Queen Victoria Hospital, Victoria, Australia, signed by eight physicians, reported the management of "infertility due to tubal blockage" in a 36-year-old woman by transfer of an eight-cell embryo into the patient's uterine cavity.[4] She presented herself at the hospital requesting tubal repair but was informed that this type of surgery had only a 10 percent chance of success. She and her husband were then informed of research involving possible in vitro fertilization and volunteered for the research program "after being fully informed of the possible hazards." The letter points out that since the couple owned and managed a dairy farm, both husband and wife were "familiar with the techniques of animal husbandry." Sixty-seven hours after in vitro insemination an apparently healthy six- to eight-cell zygote was seen. It was decided at that time to transfer the zygote into the patient's uterine cavity. Unfortunately, the wound ruptured ten days after the operation, the abdominal incision was resutured under general anesthesia "but menstruation began on the third day after the wound was repaired." The conclusion was made that it might be advisable to give medication to support the viability of the corpus luteum after zygote transfer into the uterine cavity, but there was no indication except for the mishap after surgery that the experiment would not work.

In most articles on the subject it is apparently conceded that transfer to a "mother" for gestation of an ovum that has been fertilized in a laboratory will be an event of the very near future. One physician, in fact, claimed that he knew that this had been done. In July 1974 D. A. Bevis of the University of Leeds in Great Britain reported that three healthy children had been born from pregnancies initiated by in vitro fertilization.[5] The *New York Times* of July 16, 1974, included a story that "a gynecologist reported today that three babies born in Europe during the past eighteen months had been conceived in test tubes from ova removed from the would-be mother and placed in her womb."[6] This report originated at the annual scientific meeting of the British Medical Association. Bevis declared that apparently no abnormality could be detected in any of the babies. He declined to give details of the births, which he said had been kept secret for fear of the effects of publicity. The following day, however, the *New York Times* indicated in another story, titled "Doctors Dubious on Birth Report," that other physicians were very skeptical.[7] Critics included Patrick Steptoe, a pioneer in the field who stated: "This is not authenticated, it could be very distressing for the patients. Thousands of childless women who are waiting for the moment when this work can be made possible will be plunged into immediate states of anxiety." Steptoe continued that he was "astounded" by the report. Bevis denied that he himself had carried out the procedures but stated that he was in touch with the families and would remain so for some years to come.

On July 19, 1974, the *Times* continued this story by reporting: "Dr. Douglas Bevis, the British gynecologist, said today he was giving up research into the creation of test-tube babies. Dr. Bevis announced that he was sickened by the publicity given to the announcement and that he had decided to quit his research when a newspaper offered him $72,000 to reveal the identity of the doctors concerned in the birth."[8] The story also indicated that other British specialists in conception research had challenged Bevis to publish evidence in a scientific journal to corroborate his announcement, which he declined to do. According to a Congressional report to the House Committee on Science, there has been no publication by Bevis on the research so far.[9] Thus, there is still some doubt concerning the validity of the claims.

The research of Steptoe and Edwards, noted leaders in the field in Great Britain, and of Shettles in this country, has involved attempts to relieve childlessness in women who are unable to conceive because of medical problems involving their Fallopian tubes. Their research has been entirely devoted to situations in which the woman contributes her own eggs, which are fertilized in the laboratory, one being implanted in her uterus for gestation and birth. This procedure is delicately described by Shettles, who asked, "If the bridge is out, what's wrong with using a helicopter?"[10] In this procedure only three people are involved: the wife, whose Fallopian tubes are blocked or who cannot for some other reason ovulate but who does produce normal ova; her husband, whose sperm is used to fertilize the ova; and the gynecologist, who implants the fertilized ovum in her uterus from which time she will carry the child to term and deliver.

In Vitro Fertilization and Implantation in a Second Woman

Another use of the same clinical procedure would be to remove an ovum from the uterus of one woman, fertilize it in the laboratory, and implant it in the uterus of a second woman. This may involve two separate situations with very different legal consequences.

The usual thought discussed in medical journals at present is that this procedure would be performed on a woman who wants a child, who would then carry the child to term, deliver it, and be its "natural mother." This procedure would be done for women who cannot ovulate. The donee would presumably be considered the mother of the child, and the donor, whose ovary would have been removed for therapeutic reasons, would be no more a "relation" than the source of sperm donated in artificial insemination is considered to be the father of the resulting child. This process can be compounded legally and medically if a nonovulating woman and a sterile male are married and the donor's ova is fertilized in the laboratory with sperm donated by a noninvolved artificial insemination donor prior to implantation of the fertilized ovum into the uterus of the woman whose egg was used, because it is now clear that, unlike other forms of transplantation, the uterus does not set up rejection mechanisms, which are the most serious difficulties incurred with transplantations of other organs of the body such as hearts and kidneys.[11]

According to the June 1975 issue of *Good Housekeeping,* two United States physicians, Landrum B. Shettles and Wayne Becker, are prepared to perform the first embryo transplant, and the article reports "no lack of women" eager to undergo the process.[12] The article indicates that these physicians, associated with the New York Fertility Research Foundation, are prepared to implant a donor egg, obtained during surgical removal of an ovary, into the body of a donee woman to allow her to have a baby. Interviews with women who have applied for this procedure generally indicate that they either had had their tubes ligated and now think better of it or their ovaries were removed surgically. They based their decision to participate in large measure on the fact that fewer infants are now available for adoption.

Several claim that they were told that it would cost between $8,500 and $25,000 to obtain a healthy baby through private placement sources, sums that they could not afford. It does appear, if this article is any indication, that with the increase in the number of abortions, costs of the "gray market" in adoptions, if not the "black market," may be increasing the number of women willing to go through these procedures because they cannot have children of their own and cannot afford adoption. This, however, raises a question as to the economic aspects of these experiments. If the transplant procedure damages the ovum in some manner undetectable by normal diagnostic procedures and a deformed child is born, who will be responsible for the costs of care and treatment? It seems that since these women explicitly state that they think that the transplantation (and foreseeable consequences, it would appear) will be cheaper than adoption and since the physicians are thus doubtless aware that their patients are motivated to participate because they cannot afford higher costs, unless these patients have been made entirely aware of the costs of raising a deformed child, they have potentially excellent informed consent suits if anything goes wrong.

The second and even more legally complex question is the situation in which a woman who does not want to be pregnant would proceed to have her ovum fertilized in the laboratory (presumably by her husband's sperm), implanted in another woman who would carry the child to term, and then would retrieve the child from the gestating woman.[13]

The "rent-a-mother" possibility presents a basic problem of human exploitation totally unrelated to the morality of the fertilization process itself. It has already been established that some British physicians are prepared to pay the host-mother vast sums of money in order to induce her to carry another woman's child. For example, in 1970 a British embryologist at the University of Birmingham offered $4,800 to any woman who was willing to gestate a baby for another woman.[14] There was no follow-up story indicating whether or not he had any takers.

Although in theory the concept of the right of self-determination in a free market system would appear to indicate that there should be no restraints on a woman's right to be a host-mother if she so chooses, it is also arguable that only a woman who was so poor that she had no other way to survive would deliberately rent her body for nine months of pregnancy followed by labor and delivery. If poverty becomes the motivation for an agreement to serve as a host-mother, serious medical problems for the baby resulting from the host-mother's preexistant malnutrition, anemia, and other problems could also be reasonably predicted to occur. The resulting legal and moral questions of exploitation are not unlike those presented by experimentation in other areas of medicine, such as cases in which prisoners receive more humane treatment as the result of their participation in dangerous research. This situation, therefore, presents enormous ethical as well as legal difficulties.

In Vitro Gestation

There has not as yet been a report of any attempt to fertilize an ovum in a laboratory and to keep the product of the fertilization alive in the laboratory for any period of time approaching full-term gestation, but research is now underway to develop an artificial womb in which the developing child could be cared for and preserved until the time at which it would have been born in a normal pregnancy.[15] This development, however, appears to be at least a decade away. The artificial placentas that have been used thus far involved attempts to save or prolong the life of mid-trimester or later fetuses that have been aborted either spontaneously or deliberately. The longest time for which these experiments have been successful to date is 48 hours, because at this time there is no artificial womb with a placentalike mechanism to allow diffusion, thus carbon dioxide and other waste products quickly build to toxic levels and the fetus dies. In the near future perhaps a machine will be developed that can be used to save premature newborns and that thereafter can be modified and improved in order to permit the entire gestation of an infant to take place within it. Issues raised by laboratory gestation of a fetus are primarily those of "ownership." Does the physician serve as parent for purposes of decision-making if he wishes to terminate the experiment? Does a couple who has agreed to assume responsibility for the child have the right to order the physician to continue if he thinks termination should take place?

THE LAW TODAY

As Justice Oliver Wendell Holmes stated, "The life of the law is not logic but experience." Although the common law will have no easy answers to the problems generated by new methods of creating life, by analogy to existing principles in the areas of family law, constitutional law, and tort law some answers can presumably be found.

Adoption

Although adoption is entirely a creature of statute, the body of case law that is common to all jurisdictions in this country may be useful in determining which woman is the "mother" of a child in a situation in which a host-mother has had another woman's embryo implanted in her body, has carried the child to term, and has delivered but at that point refuses to return the child to the donor of the ovum. This situation would appear quite likely to occur eventually.

It is likely that these arrangements will be made by written contracts and payment for "services rendered" and medical expenses will presumably be made to the host-mother. To find an analogy, it should be noted that in most states, statutes impose criminal penalties for paying or receiving money in connection with the surrender of children for adoption. It is considered legal in most states to pay only the hospital and medical expenses of the natural mother of a child who is to be adopted, although at least one case holds that it is legal to pay other provable, necessary expenses, such as food and rent, incurred by the mother during pregnancy.[16] Some states, however, hold that even payment of the natural mother's hospital expenses is akin to the "sale" of the baby.[17]

In any case, the sale of children is illegal in all states; therefore, any contract by which a host-mother is paid a fee in excess of expenses to gestate the unborn child is likely to be held unenforceable as against public policy. That being the case, the "foster" or gestating mother would presumably be considered by most courts the natural mother of the child since she and not the donor-mother was willing to go through the inconvenience, discomfort, and dangers of pregnancy and childbirth.

It is highly unlikely that a judge, faced with a conflict between two women, one of whom has delivered the child and the other of whom "should" have done so by normal means but who was too busy or disinterested, would resolve the issue of which is the true mother in any way other than by awarding parental status to the host-mother, contracts to the contrary notwithstanding.

Second, by statute in many states any adoption release executed by the natural mother *before* the birth of a child is invalid.[18] Even in those states that do not declare prenatal surrenders to be absolutely void, courts appear to take a dim view of the validity of an adoption release signed prior to the birth of the child.

The burden of proving the validity of a prenatal adoption surrender rests on the litigant who wishes to uphold it, and the natural mother who wishes to revoke it is usually not required to submit evidence of actual coercion in order to have the surrender declared invalid. The courts that consider these cases are well aware of the implicit situational coercion that can occur when a penniless, distraught, unwed mother is promised food, shelter, and medical attention in return for surrender of her child.[19]

Where a physician undertakes to arrange a private adoption and makes consent to surrender the child a precondition of his attendance during childbirth, it is obvious that the surrender is invalid under normal principles of duress and fraud.[20]

Once the child is born, however, if the mother who has given birth voluntarily surrenders the child to the donor-mother in return for economic compensation, she probably cannot ask that the child be returned to her, since in most states selling a living child constitutes abandonment as a matter of law as well as subjecting the parent to criminal prosecution.[21]

This situation, involving a conflict between two "mothers," appears to be comparable to a situation in which a court is asked to invalidate an adoption surrender; the same principle of duress would seem to apply, particularly if the host-mother is desperately poor. It is likely that courts would be unwilling to enforce the terms of any contract that she made at the time the embryo was implanted (some two weeks after fertilization) to surrender the child which she would thereafter carry and to which she would give birth. It is possible that the "parent" who donated the ovum could sue the host-mother for damages for breach of contract, and if she has any money, which is unlikely, the "parent" might be able to collect a judgment. It seems, however, highly improbable, considering the care with which courts examine surrenders for adoption by natural mothers, that they will be at all eager to order specific performance (i.e., a delivery of the child) as long as the host-mother still has the child. Whereas a judge confronted with the first claim of this nature might have some sympathy for a woman whose child was gestated by a surrogate mother because the donor had a serious heart condition or some other medical problem that placed her at substantial risk if she went through with the pregnancy, most judges presumably would look with disfavor on a woman who simply couldn't be bothered to go through pregnancy in order to have a child.

In terms of the distribution of human sympathy as to the basic equities involved, it is highly improbable that the judge would award the "maternal interest" in the child to the woman whose sole contribution to the welfare of the child up to that point was to have a minor surgical procedure to extract ova. Contracts for surrogate gestation are likely to be held nonenforceable.

Another issue might arise if the donor-mother does not want the child when it is born. She may have simply changed her mind, the child may be defective and thus undesirable, she may have decided to get a divorce, or any number of other things may have happened. The law of adoption appears to indicate that although a final decree of adoption will be annulled only under the most extraordinary circumstances, usually involving willful fraud as to the condition of the child, an adopting couple may return the child at any time *prior* to entry of the decree.[22] Thus, it would appear that the host-mother would be responsible for care and nurture of the child. Since she is also the patient of the physician who implanted the ovum, if she has not been warned of this possibility she would appear to have an action against him for failure to obtain her informed consent, since this is a reasonably foreseeable material risk of the procedure.

The donor-mother might argue to the court that the host-mother is not analogous to the natural mother who surrenders her child for adoption but rather should be considered in the same legal context as the bailee of property in a storage warehouse, who is under a duty to preserve the goods and restore them to the bailor on request. This argument could arise either in a conflict between the two women over custody after the child is born or during the host-mother's pregnancy if she changes her mind and wants to abort. The Thirteenth Amendment, abolishing ownership of one person by another, has never been applied to a being in utero, but it is logical that courts would hold that whether or not a fetus is a person, it is demonstrably not a chattel to be covered by the law of bailment. The only logical principle for courts to follow in custody disputes, prenatal or postnatal, that may arise in in vitro host-gestation situations is that possession is ten points of the law and that she who has the child is to be considered the natural mother, excluding a situation involving removal by force.

Informed Consent

Legal standards of informed consent applicable to any experimental treatment will presumably be applied to these situations. It has been claimed that the women in in vitro experiments that have already been carried out probably did not give informed consent to the work. In Edwards's original article, it is stated that, "Our patients were childless couples who hoped that our research might enable *them* to have children," but it is obvious from the statement of the experiment in the same article that there was no intention whatever of implanting the blastocysts in the women involved.[23] Thus, there is a serious question that some women have been misled. In an article by Leon R. Kass, it is reported that Edwards stated at a scientific meeting in 1969, "We tell women with blocked oviducts that 'your only hope of having a child is to help us, then maybe we can help you.' " Kass remarks:

> It is altogether too easy to exploit, even unwittingly, the desires of a childless couple. It would be cruel to generate for them false hopes by inflated publicity of the sort that some of these researchers have promoted. It would be both cruel and unethical falsely to generate hope for example, by telling women that they by themselves rather than future infertile women might be helped to have a child in order to secure their participation in the experiments.[24]

Kass neglects to mention, however, that it would also subject the physician to a successful suit for failing to obtain the informed consent of his patients to the surgical removal of their ova if they were not told that implantation was not planned.

A woman, one of Edwards's patients, who had had an ovum extracted and fertilized with her husband's sperm, said in a news report that she "hoped the fertilized ovum would be implanted in her womb in the next two to six weeks and thus the world's first baby conceived in a test tube would be born by the end of 1970."[25] The implantation was never performed.

If a woman's ova are removed during ovarian surgery, presumably the law of informed consent would also apply to any donation of these ova. Use of her ova without her knowledge or consent would be sufficient to subject the physician to an action under the terms of the Uniform Anatomical Gift Act requiring adequate consent for transplantation donations by living donors.

It should be noted that the first suit has been filed presumably alleging lack of consent to destruction of a fertilized ova, although it is difficult to establish from press reports. The *New York Times* of August 20, 1974, carried a story stating, "A Florida couple filed a 1.5 million dollar damage suit in the United States District Court here yesterday alleging that a New York doctor last year 'had maliciously destroyed' the test tube culture from which they had hoped to have a baby."[26] The report continues that the complaint stated that ovarian tissue and eggs surgically removed from the woman and her husband's sperm were combined at the hospital in a mixture that was to have been implanted in the woman. However, the complaint added that before the implantation could take place, the physician destroyed the mixtures, citing a proscription by the National Institutes of Health against the fertilization method and the plaintiffs claim that the Institutes had no such ban." A further report on this action stated that two professors of obstetrics and gynecology had sought to treat the woman's infertility.[27] Her Fallopian tubes had been blocked and partially destroyed by disease. Eggs were obtained, bathed in follicular fluid that contained bits of tubal mucosa, and exposed to the husband's sperm. Before an egg could be implanted, one gynecologist claimed that his superior at the hospital confiscated the cultures and terminated the procedure.

In an interview, the chief of the gynecology staff made the distinction between in vitro fertilization and embryo transfer. He stated that the latter is "premature," and his conviction is that more work must be done in lower primates to establish whether the "number of malformations is acceptable." The would-be parents then filed a suit against him claiming that the termination of the procedure without their consent denied them their last chance to have a child. With regard to the objections raised by the physician, the woman said: "I can't see why some people believe that a baby conceived in this fashion isn't as sacred as a baby conceived in a normal fashion. There is even more care, more desire, more intent involved here, because so much time, energy and emotion had to be invested in its conception." Since her press statement was totally nonresponsive to the physician's to which it was supposedly an answer, serious questions may exist as to how much, if anything, she was told about risk of harm to the implant either before the in vitro fertilization or prior to its destruction. As far as can be established, this case has not yet come to trial, but the results will certainly be interesting.

Another aspect of informed consent would be the critical issue of disclosure of potential harm to the fetus and the possible difficulty in diagnosing deformities prior to birth. In recent *Good Housekeeping* interviews with patients who are awaiting donor implantations, several women said that they were told, "even with normal pregnancy there is some chance that the baby might be deformed or retarded."[28] This may not be a fair statement of the potential risk. The physician's statement to the author of the article was, "if damage does occur, the body is likely to reject the defective embryo through spontaneous abortion. This happens in natural pregnancy all the time." Thus, it does not appear from this article that particular effort was made to explain to these women that no one can possibly know what risks may occur in early human trials of any experimental procedure, especially one of this magnitude. Since, as noted above, several of these women chose implantation instead of adoption because they could not afford the latter, a situation in which they found themselves economically devastated by the costs of care of a deformed child might well provide an interesting case against the physicians on the subject of the materiality of an unknown risk.

It is quite clear from the jurisprudence in other experimental contexts that due care and requirements of informed consent require disclosure that the procedure is experimental and that, therefore, in addition to discussion of known risks, the patient must be told that unforeseen complications are possible.[29]

The mother of a 14-year-old boy consented to spinal surgery for him. Various risks were explained, but she was not told that the procedure had just been invented and that the defendant was the only surgeon in the world who had performed it. The child died of a sudden hemorrhage two weeks postoperatively, and it was clear that this could not have been anticipated. Liability was imposed because the mother had not been told of the experimental nature of the procedure.[30]

Normal rules of informed consent liability seem perfectly adequate to the task of confronting the new situations implicit in in vitro fertilization. The fact that some ethicists seriously question any procedure for which the conceptus itself cannot give informed consent appears to be beside the legal point. Where the desire of both physician and parent is to create a normal child, it is no more relevant to speak of the absence of consent by a conceptus conceived in a laboratory and placed, while too small to be seen by the naked eye, into the uterus of a woman than it is to speak of the right of consent of a "naturally" conceived newborn to come into the world.

Artificial Insemination by Donor (AID)

The current medical practice from which all in vitro experiments have been derived and which is the nearest legal analogy in attempting to devise some basic legal principles to use with these new procedures is AID.[31] One source estimates that by 1958, 100,000 children a year were being born after AID in this country.[32] The legal issues involved in AID have been the source of a number of decisions, four statutes, and numerous articles.

Assuming consent by the woman's husband as a prerequisite to legal performance of AID, four states have by statute declared that the child born of artificial insemination is considered to be the legitimate child of the woman's husband. In 1964 Georgia enacted a statute permitting only licensed physicians to perform artificial insemination and providing for the conclusive presumption of the legitimacy of a child born through AID provided that written consent of both husband and wife had been obtained.[33] Oklahoma's, in 1967, was next and includes the same wording.[34] Following the decision in *People v. Sorenson*,[35] holding that a consenting husband was criminally liable for failure to support a child born by artificial insemination during the marriage, the California legislature enacted a statute in order to conform all such cases to this ruling.[36] In 1968 Kansas enacted an AID statute providing that the child is legitimate as long as the husband's consent to the procedure is given in writing.[37]

The state of New York has no AID statute, but the city of New York has regulated the practice of AID since 1947 through the health code.[38] This ordinance is an attempt to protect couples from donations of sperm from anyone who is in poor health, but it does not make any attempt to regularize the role of an AID child in the family. It merely requires blood grouping, Rh testing, and a physical examination of donors.

Although most recent decisions tend to hold an AID child to be the "lawful issue" of a marriage, early decisions indicated that some courts considered the mothers adulterous and the children illegitimate.

The earliest AID case was a 1921 Canadian divorce decision, *Orford v. Orford.* [39] The judge, holding that adultery had taken place, granted the husband a divorce. Unfortunately, since *Orford* is widely cited as precedent that an AID child is illegitimate, the decision may prove only that the trial judge did not believe Mrs. Orford's testimony that artificial insemination had taken place and decided that the child was the product of old-fashioned adultery, not newfangled science.

The Orfords were married in Canada and moved to England. A few months later, when the marriage was conceded to be unconsummated because Mrs. Orford found attempts at intercourse painful, Mr. Orford went back to Canada. Six years later Mrs. Orford joined him and brought her child with her. When invited to provide an explanation of this event, of which Mr. Orford had no prior warning, she told him and then the court that a neighbor told her that having a baby would cure frigidity and that he also volunteered his services an an AID donor and agreed to adopt the child (on which agreement he later reneged). She claimed that a physician came to her apartment, put her under general anesthesia, and when she awoke the physician and the neighbor told her that she had been artificially inseminated with the neighbor's sperm. Mr. Orford sued her for divorce. The trial judge said, "I find as a fact that she had sexual intercourse in the ordinary way."

Although several earlier cases indicated that an AID child was not the legitimate child of a consenting husband, most invoked some form of estoppel against him that required him to support the child after the couple's subsequent divorce. [40] Finally in 1968 the California Supreme Court held that a consenting husband was the lawful father of an AID child and thus subject to criminal penalties for nonsupport. [41] In 1973 the New York court held that a consenting husband is the legitimate parent of an AID child and that his consent is required for adoption of the child by her second husband. [42]

Although the question of legitimacy would appear to be settled, some legal problems remain in this area that have not been considered by any courts but in all likelihood will eventually become the subject of litigation.

The first of these issues results from the fact that sperm banks can now freeze sperm to be used a considerable time after donation. The first sperm bank in this country was established in Iowa City, Iowa, in 1964. [43] The *New York Times* reported on October 17, 1971, that New York's first commercial human sperm bank had just opened with semen samples from 18 men frozen in a stainless steel tank and that "the phone was already ringing with prospective clients."[44]

A principle of the law of Wills in our legal system, known as the Rule Against Perpetuities, is designed to prevent large estates from being tied up for a century or more. It provides that no legacy or trust may be established that will not have an actual beneficiary or legatee within the life span of an existing individual plus 21 years.

With the era of fertile decedents upon us, obviously a child conceived some years after his father's death may not actually fall within the requirement of a life in being plus 21 years if named as the beneficiary of a trust from the father's parent to "a grandchild". Some years ago W. Barton Leach gave some thought to this problem and wrote the following draft opinion for any court called on to decide the question:

> We hold that a posthumously conceived sperm bank child of the donor's widow is the legitimate child of her and her late husband, at least if she has not remarried at the time of conception. We also hold that the duration of a male "life in being" under the Rule Against Perpetuities should be defined as the period of his reproductive capacity, including any postmortem period during which the sperm remains fertile.

Leach, however, also advocated special accompanying legislation to the effect that any interest in real or personal property that would violate the Rule Against Perpetuities should be reformed to approximate most closely the intention of the creator of the interest.[45]

Vermont enacted a statute in 1959[46] not dissimilar to Leach's suggestion:

> Any interest in real or personal property which would violate the Rule Against Perpetuities shall be reformed, within the limits of that rule, to approximate most closely the intention of the creator of the interest. In determining whether an interest would violate said rule and in reforming an interest, the period of perpetuity should be measured by actual rather than by possible events.

Obviously, statutory regulation and the resolution of such obviously urgent questions are immediately necessary in view of the likelihood that such questions may be raised in the courts at any time. While it may be an exercise in intellectual imagination to speculate on the rights of test tube babies who have not as yet been created, sperm bank problems are already with us, and it is simply luck that such a decision has not already been requested of a court today.[47]

The filing of the first negligence suit against a sperm bank was reported on July 17, 1975.[48] A man in San Francisco stored sperm and then had an elective vasectomy. Some time later he was notified that the frozen sample had been destroyed by equipment failure that allowed thawing to occur. The man brought a class action suit asking for $5 million in damages for emotional and mental anguish. Is this an action for some or all of the following: Breach of a contract of bailment, in which case, was due caution used in storage? Medical malpractice, in which case, who is the "patient," what is the standard of care, and what are the elements of damage? Simple negligence? Breach of a fiduciary relationship? Wrongful death of an unconceived child?

As indicated above, however, in terms of the relationship between the "father" and the AID child, the father does have, in most cases, the same rights to custody and visitation and the same obligation to support the child after a divorce as he would have if the child had been conceived by conventional means. Thus, statutory regulation of the relationship between the husband and child for purposes of determining inheritance rights (particularly with posthumous children) might well be indicated. The same legal issues would probably be presented in the case of an in vitro baby.

Another issue that has generated no legal attention and that has never, as far as can be discovered, been the subject of a legal action, is the physician's malpractice liability in the AID context. Presumably, if the donor selected by the physician transmitted any form of genetic disease or inheritable condition to the child, the physician might well be liable under general principles of malpractice law for failing to use due skill, care, and knowledge to screen the donor prior to use of the sperm. At this time it would be difficult to argue that due care would require examination of the donor by geneticists, but when the supply of skilled genetic diagnosticians is such that this may be reasonably feasible to effect, it is highly likely that a physician who did not refer a prospective AID donor to a geneticist for an examination and who merely relied on the donor's statement that he had no inheritable diseases (which appears to be the standard practice at the present time) would be liable for negligent failure to use due care. Today, as is required by the New York City ordinance, if a physician did not test the donor's blood for Rh compatibility with the woman's, a clear case of negligence would undoubtedly be proved because of the extremely serious effects that might occur to both mother and baby as the result of Rh incompatibility.

Assume that a woman received a donated egg and after birth of the implanted embryo a genetic defect such as sickle cell anemia becomes apparent. Has the physician warranted "fitness for use" in some sort of strict liability context such as is imposed on manufacturers of some dangerous objects? In the absence of any discussion of possible genetic defects and clear proof of informed consent with a concomitant assumption of risk by the recipient woman, courts might hold him liable for negligent failure to make a proper diagnosis of the state of health of the woman who donated the ova.

Second, in the case of a host-mother, it is altogether probable that any medical problems she might have could adversely affect the fetus. Should this occur, the physician would presumably be liable under ordinary principles of malpractice law if due care under the circumstances would have revealed her condition.

Sale or Rental of Organs

Cash payment for donated blood has materially increased the incidence of serum hepatitis in this country because people who are sufficiently impoverished to sell their blood are very often drug addicts. Their unsanitary use of the needles with which they inject their drugs creates subclinical levels of hepatitis in many addicts, and the disease is then transmitted to those who receive the blood in transfusions.[49] Since there are as yet no absolutely reliable tests for detecting hepatitis in donated blood and the effects of serum hepatitis are very serious and frequently fatal, there is increasing pressure by hospitals, medical societies, and other agencies for statutes that forbid the payment of blood donors.[50]

While there are no studies on people who try to sell their organs, desperate poverty and/or addiction might well cause the same sort of subclinical disease problems as are present in paid blood donors.

It is not inconceivable that a desperately poor person might attempt to sell even a vital organ if he thought that the price for his heart or both kidneys would be sufficient to sustain his family after his death. People occasionally do attempt to sell their organs.[51] If the organ is vital, such an act would probably violate state criminal sanctions against suicides.[52] Furthermore, a physician who removed a vital organ from a living donor would presumably be guilty of murder even if the donor requested it. The buyer would also presumably be criminally liable for soliciting another to commit suicide or as an accessory before the fact to murder.[53] At this time the sale of a nonvital organ by a living donor is not specifically prohibited by any state. However, it is possible that a prosecution for criminal assault and battery might result, although consent is generally a good defense in assault and battery actions since the "touching" is not for the benefit of the donor and indeed may cause him serious harm.

Section 2.11 of the American Law Institute's Model Penal Code indicates that the consent of an organ donor for money may be ineffective:

> When conduct is charged to constitute an offense because it causes or threatens bodily harm, consent to such conduct or to the inflic- tion of such harm is a defense if: (a) the bodily harm consented to or threatened by the conduct consented to is not serious. . . .

Obviously, removal of an organ is "serious." Section 210.0 (3) defines "serious bodily injury" as bodily injury that includes "permanent disfigurement, or protracted loss or impairment of the function of any bodily member or organ." This obviously includes the removal of an organ.

The crime of mayhem, where still enforced, may also apply to sale of the organ of a living person, even though the consent of the donor is obtained.[54] Thus, under the law as it exists today, any assumption that a living person has the right to sell a portion of his body, as opposed to voluntary donation of kidneys or other organs, is unfounded, particularly where exploitation of consent might be possible as the result of the gross financial needs of the donor.

Only one decision to date has dealt with a claimed right to donate an organ, with or without economic compensation.

A prisoner under death sentence in Florida wanted to be a kidney donor for a child in Colorado. The warden refused to allow him to go to Colorado because of the expenses that would be incurred in guarding him during the trip and the hospitaliza- tion. The prisoner sued, and both the federal district judge and the court of appeals held that the man had no constitutional right to donate.[55]

The same legal issues would presumably be applicable to a host-mother who rents, although she does not sell, her uterus and to a donor who wanted to sell an ovary. The validity of a consent to rent one's body for a period of nine months to bear another woman's child would seem to be subject to consider- able doubt. At the least, if the host-mother decided to abort because she changed her mind, there would be no ground on which her decision could be challenged.

Abortion

Since *Roe v. Wade*[56] and *Doe v. Bolton*[57] legalized abortions during the first two trimesters of pregnancy, various collateral issues have arisen that are also applicable to the issues inherent in "the new biology."

First, it is quite clear that the law does not recognize as a person a child in utero at least prior to viability. Whatever rights may exist for a fetus, it is hard to imagine that a conceptus has any.

Second, it is now fairly clear that the husband of a married woman or the parent of a minor does not have the authority to stop an elective abortion.[58]

Even prior to the abortion decisions a husband had no right to object to a hysterectomy or therapeutic abortion for the maintenance of his wife's health.[59] Thus, it would appear from the state of the law at this time that if a host-mother agrees to allow incubation of a fetus in her body but changed her mind prior to delivery, the donor of the eggs and her husband who planned to retrieve the child at birth would presumably have no legal interest on which to base an attempt to stop the host-mother from abortion. The abortion laws that apply to normal conception would also apply to fetal implantation. Thus, the physician who realized that the child was defective during the pregnancy would presumably be governed by the same rules as to abortion as those in which conception occurs by natural means.

Since all indications are that couples who agree to implantation experiments are "desperate" for children, it is likely that even if the physician decides that the fetus may be defective and an abortion should be performed, the couple may decide that they would prefer to have a defective child rather than none at all. Even if the physician requires them to sign an agreement consenting to abortion if things should go wrong prior to performance of an implantation, under general principles of self-determination and the right to refuse treatment, it is not likely that the woman could be forced to abort.

Third, in the situation in which the child is being gestated in an "artificial womb," the "mother" (the donor of the egg who would retrieve the child when it was finally pronounced "ready") presumably would not have the same interest in deciding questions of termination as she would if the child was a part of her body. Thus, on that issue a court will eventually have to determine whether the physician who supplies the developing previable child with the food, nourishment, and care that normally gestated infants receive from their mothers, is for purposes of deciding to terminate the experiment the one who has the right to make the decision. Is he given the same right to "abort" as the pregnant woman has? The physician does assume the responsibility for maintenance of the developing life in the same way that a pregnant woman inevitably assumes responsibility for her pregnancy. Thus, the physician might be held to have the same authority, even though there is no question of bodily privacy involved, simply in default of any other logical decision-maker.

Whether he would have the right to terminate an experiment of this nature over the objection of the couple who donate sperm and ova and were to receive the child is a question that probably cannot be resolved on the basis of the common law and the abortion decisions as they exist today. However, when laboratory gestation is undertaken for the first time, any physician is extremely lacking in foresight who does not include in the consent form signed by the "parent" prior any attempt at fertilization or gestation a statement that it is within his sole discretion and the use of his best medical judgment alone to terminate the experiment at any time. Such a consent would constitute a good defense in any later suit by the couple against the physician who terminated the experiment. In the case that has already been filed in New York City, press reports do not indicate whether any such consent was signed by the couple prior to attempts to fertilize the egg.

Malpractice

Any obstetrician owes the same duty of care to an unborn patient as he does to the pregnant woman, and negligent treatment of a fetus that is to be carried to term constitutes actionable malpractice to the same extent as negligence in the treatment of any other patient. In particular, failure to diagnose and treat a pregnant woman's illness with the result that the fetus is deformed is clearly negligent.[60] Obstetrical negligence during delivery that causes injury to the child has resulted in literally hundreds of successful malpractice suits as well. Thus far, however, only one suit can be found in which parents succeeded in recovering damages for preconception, as opposed to prenatal, injuries.

A woman took contraceptive pills for several years before she and her husband decided to have a baby. She had twins, both of whom had Down's syndrome. The parents, both on their own behalf and as guardians of the twins, sued the manufacturer of the medication, charging that the pills had caused chromosome damage to the mother and asking damages for breach of warranty and negligence. The trial court upheld the mother's right to sue for her own damage but dismissed the action for the babies' pain, suffering, and physical damage on the ground that they were nonexistent at the time the cause of action accrued (i.e., the time during which their mother was taking the pills). On appeal, however, the court held that the twins did have the right to sue.[61]

Thus, if a good cause of action exists for preconception damage in that context, it seems quite probable that a cause of action would exist against a physician who negligently damages an ovum during in vitro fertilization or implantation when the child is born with serious defects.

The difficulty will be in determining the standard of care used in an experimental procedure. In any litigation involving the first use of any medical technique, the most serious practical problem faced by the plaintiff is to find an expert witness to testify as to the prevailing standard of care on his or her behalf, since by the nature of the situation the defendant is the only one who has ever done the experiment.[62]

Second, it may be enormously difficult to prove proximate cause, that is, that the manipulation of the ovum deformed it and not some condition during the pregnancy itself. In any malpractice case it is necessary to prove a connection between the negligence and some damage to the patient.

When a sufficient number of in vitro implantations take place so that these two problems of proof can be overcome, however, malpractice litigation would be as routine in this context as in any other. A malpractice suit for negligent performance of the removal of the ova or implantation procedures that damaged the woman would probably present no problems of proof at this time.

Actions for Wrongful Life

A number of recent decisions on the child's right to recover for "wrongful life" indicate that in many states this action exists, and it seems that the number of jurisdictions recognizing the right is increasing.

An illegitimate child sued his father for subjecting him to the damages "inevitably occurring with the condition of illegitimacy." The child asked damages for material harm and mental suffering caused by being born a bastard. Presumably the cause of action was for the father's failure to marry the mother, although in this case he was already married to someone else. The court reasoned that no substantial objection to recognition of the tort could be found, but that the damages were impossible to compute. The court therefore dismissed the action.[63]

Another decision held that an illegitimate child could recover damages against the state of New York for its negligence in caring for and protecting his mother, who was a patient in a state mental institution. Failure to restrain a male patient who had a history of being a rapist resulted in a sexual assault on the mother and the conception of the child. The trial court found the negligence to be the proximate cause of the birth of the child, but the Court of Appeals of New York ordered dismissal on that ground while conceding the right of action.[64]

Malpractice suits for wrongful life began to be filed in large numbers when elective sterilization operations became more frequent.

A woman had a prescription from her gynecologist for contraceptive pills. She took it to the drug store and the druggist negligently dispensed tranquilizers instead. The patient became pregnant and sued the druggist. The court held that she stated a good cause of action for the total costs of raising the child to adulthood and that she had not been obliged to mitigate damages by having an abortion or by surrendering the child for adoption, since either action would be considered "unreasonable."[65]

Two very recent decisions dealt with the situation arising when a physician negligently fails to diagnose pregnancy in time for a legal abortion. In both cases, the women were into the second trimester of pregnancy by the time the physicians realized what was "wrong," although in both cases the women had asked for pregnancy tests early in their pregnancy.

A woman consulted a gynecologist in May 1971 for the purpose of obtaining contraceptive pills. On seven occasions thereafter, from May to December, she consulted him because she thought she was pregnant, and he repeatedly assured her that she was not. On December 21, she was advised by another physician that she was four and one-half months pregnant. The husband and wife brought three separate causes of action against the physician. The wife sought to recover damages for pain and suffering and mental anguish incident to the birth of the unwanted child, for loss of consortium, for the responsibility of the education and medical expenses of the child and, as well, for damages for her inability to work during pregnancy. The husband sought to recover medical expenses, damages for the loss of consortium, and damages arising out of his responsibility for the cost of raising the child. The trial court dismissed the action, but the Appellate Court in New York held that the couple did have a good cause of action. The appellate decision indicated that the action was basically one for malpractice, which it defined as "recovery for damages sustained as the result of the physician's failure to use due care in diagnosis or treatment" and pointed out that in a malpractice action, which is one for personal injury, the person responsible for the injury is responsible for "all damages resulting directly from and occurring as a natural consequence of the wrongful act." Since a legal abortion would have been available to the woman if her condition had been promptly diagnosed, the court held that the physician was responsible for the total cost of raising the child to adulthood.[66]

On the other hand, at about the same time, the Wisconsin Supreme Court held to the contrary in *Rieck v. Medical Protective Co. of Fort Wayne.*

A negligent misdiagnosis was made and the woman was told repeatedly that she was not pregnant. She eventually consulted another obstetrician who diagnosed her as being 17 weeks pregnant. She sued the original obstetrician after the baby was born. The court found that the action was one for damages based on the birth of a normal child, healthy and well and that "public policy may vitiate recovery even when the chain of causation is complete and direct." Thus, it was held that no cause of action existed.[67]

Several cases involving failure of either tubal ligations or vasectomies have resulted in suits for breach of contract and/or negligence, and there is a growing tendency to allow damages for wrongful life in these situations, although this cause of action is still generally considered to be against public policy in most states. Most courts seem to have held that as long as the child born to the plaintiffs is normal, although the mother may recover some damages for the pain and suffering of childbirth and pregnancy, damages will not be awarded for the costs of raising the child.

However, where there is substantial reason to believe that the child is or will be deformed, negligent performance of a vasectomy or tubal ligation has resulted in enormous judgments against physicians for all costs of raising the child.

A man had a vasectomy after he and his wife had two retarded children. The operation was unsuccessful and the couple had a third child, who was also retarded. The court held that the couple had a cause of action against the urologist who performed the vasectomy for all costs of raising the child.[68]

After having eight children, a woman had her tubes ligated. Another child was born. She sued both for negligent performance of the operation and for willful misrepresentation to her as a fact that she was sterile. The appellate court held that she had a cause of action and that she should have a right to prove that the operation had been negligently performed. The court held that if she could prove negligence, she could clearly recover damages for all physical effects and medical expenses. The court also allowed a cause of action for recovery of damages for the change in the family's status if the costs of raising the child could thereafter be measured.[69]

The court in this case was most solicitous about the fact that the mother would have less time and attention to give the new infant. It should be noted that the baby would be the ninth child in this family. It would have been very interesting to discover if the judge would have awarded more damages or less damages for the wrongful life of a second or third child than he did for a ninth, since it may be argued that child care expands to fill the time available whether one is caring for one or a dozen.

A woman had a tubal ligation at the time she delivered a baby, but she thereafter became pregnant and had another child. The court allowed a cause of action for the expenses of raising the second child and held that the jury at the trial level should have been allowed to weigh the economic benefits of parenthood against the economic burden of child raising. The court held that the mother had a cause of action for the costs of the change in the family life style and the economic consequences to her resulting from the birth of a new child.[70]

The Supreme Court of California withdrew without comment the opinion in *Pearson v. Sav-on Drugs* in which the intermediate appellate court allowed recovery of the cost of raising a child to adulthood.

A 40-year-old mother of three children was given a prescription for contraceptive pills by her physician. The pharmacist who handled the prescription negligently gave her phenobarbitol. She became pregnant and gave birth to a normal, healthy baby boy. She and her husband sued the drug store seeking as damages her medical expenses and the cost of raising the child to the age of 21. Several economists testified as expert witnesses for the plaintiff as to the cost of child care, and the jury awarded the plaintiffs $42,000 in damages. On appeal the Court of Appeals held that the jury was more than capable of deciding which benefits of having a child could be written off against the expenses of child raising without an expert witness. The question became one of "net economic loss."[71]

Since these decisions, except *Doerr v. Villate,* involved the birth of healthy children, it would appear that at least some courts would allow parents to bring a wrongful life action for the cost of maintaining and treating a defective child if it could be proven that manipulation of the ovum before or after implantation had created a defect. Presumably, proof that prior to performance of the procedure there was a clear and knowing consent by the parents to the possibility that this might happen would constitute a good defense.

Since many defects engendered by this procedure might not be detected by amniocentesis prior to delivery or, in fact, as in many cases today mild retardation may not even be obvious at the time the child is born, this would apparently insure that a wrongful life action against the physician would enable adequate remedial or custodial care to be given to the child. While some authors take the position that the physician should not be financially liable for defects in the child that occur as the result of these procedures, it would appear that this risk should be assumed by any physician with the temerity to undertake the first of these cases. George A. Hudock, Associate Professor of Zoology at Indiana University, has written a recent article in the *Indiana Law Journal* in which he says the following:

> *In vitro* fertilization and/or embryo transplantation should be performed only by qualified personnel and the rights and responsibilities of all parties involved should be guaranteed before any such action is taken. Specifically if such reproduction is undertaken the potential liabilities of the physician performing the procedure must be predetermined as well as the rights of parents and child. My own view is that such reproductive technology can be justified within the context of basic research. If the technology of *in vitro* fertilization and embryo transplantation is applied, it must be recognized by all involved that it is experimental and mistakes can be made. Accordingly, when this experimental technology is used by a physician at the request of his patient, the physician must be protected and not held liable for damages under any circumstances. Biologically it would be almost impossible to prove that the action of the physician caused any damage. . . . A further issue which is not easily resolved is that of the physician's responsibility for a defective child. Clearly I believe the physician should not be responsible.[72]

On the other hand, the argument can certainly be made that the relevant point is that of questions of foreseeability of risk. Many authors maintain that since Steptoe in England and Shettles in New York City have stated that they do not see the necessity for any primate research prior to in vitro implantation in humans, it would seem that any physician who does not comply with *normally* accepted research practices, including full animal trials before any drug or procedure is tested on a human being where possible, should be held strictly accountable for any errors of judgment, defects, or other difficulties that may ensue.

Another interesting issue is whether a child conceived *in vitro* and either implanted in the uterus of his mother or a host-mother or gestated in a laboratory could maintain an action for wrongful life against his parents if he is defective. It is possible that a child born after ordinary conception and gestation but whose parents knew or should have known after amniocentesis that he would be defective and refused to abort could also file such an action.

At common law an unemancipated child could not sue his parents for a tort committed on his person. The extent of this doctrine is exemplified by two decisions. In 1905 the Supreme Court of Washington held that a daughter could not sue her father for rape,[73] and in 1891 the Supreme Court of Mississippi held that a minor could not sue her mother for maliciously committing her to a mental hospital.[74]

Some states, however, have abrogated the doctrine of immunity in cases where children have been injured in automobile accidents as the result of negligent driving by a parent.[75] Other states allow recovery for willful harm or reckless misconduct causing harm to the child.[76] According to Prosser, a parent's immunity from a tort suit by a child has been abrogated in Wisconsin, Alaska, Arizona, California, Hawaii, Illinois, Kentucky, Louisiana, Minnesota, New Hampshire, New Jersey, New York, and North Dakota.[77] Prosser indicates that the number of states allowing such an action will increase rapidly.

Thus, theoretically a cause of action for negligence would lie. The question remains, however, whether or not allowing pregnancy or in vitro procedures to be carried to term in spite of reasonable or overwhelming likelihood of defect is negligence. If the child alleged that it was, presumably First Amendment religion guarantees would serve as a defense to an assertion that due care required abortion if that was the basis of refusal to abort. If a defective child were allowed to sue his parents, could a child born into abject poverty where lack of necessities such as adequate food precluded his normal development sue them? Could the tenth baby born in a family sue and allege that it was negligent to produce him when he does not receive enough individual attention? Could the first child sue when the sixth (or the second for that matter) is born and allege that negligent procreation has deprived him of adequate parental resources and attention which he had previously enjoyed? It should be noted that in a recent Florida decision the three older siblings of a child born after an unsuccessful vasectomy sued the urologist and asked for damages on precisely that ground. The Florida appellate court threw out the action on the ground that it was "without foundation in the law or logic."[78]

If pregnancy, however unwise, should give rise to suits by children against their parents on the ground that their lives were lived in less than optimum environments (for any reason), a floodgate would be opened. Thus, it would appear that the opening wedge, a suit for wrongful life by a defective test tube baby, should be rejected by a court.

THE LAW TOMORROW: ISSUES AND PROPOSALS

The first question that the law will have to resolve based on the common law as it exists today is responsibility for the defective child born through "the new biology." To whom, in fact, does this child belong, if anyone? An article in the *American Journal of Psychiatry* points out that a child grown to full readiness for "birth" in an artificial placenta may be construed to be either a person or a property.[79] If the child is gestated in an artificial placenta and if by the time he would be considered to be "born" the marriage of the biological parents had broken up or the spouses had embarked on a new life, might the parents refuse to accept the child? Must the child be turned over to an institution, or would the physician who had in effect been the "mother" by providing the child with the means to sustain life in the laboratory suddenly become the legal parent of the child? If a host-mother gestated the child, and at birth the original mother declines to take delivery, whose child is it if the host-mother does not want it?

Statutes will be necessary to indicate who the responsible party is in cases where the parent who arranged to take possession of the child at birth changes his or her mind. Until such statutes are enacted, it appears that the physician, simply because he is the person who performed the procedure without taking the necessary steps to insure that this possibility was thoroughly explored beforehand, should be considered legally responsible for care, nurture, and support of the child. If the presumptive parent refuses to accept delivery, in the absence of signed contractual consents clearly demonstrating that the parent was fully informed of the possibility of defects and made a complete and knowing commitment to accept the child under any circumstances, the physician, instead of the host-mother or the state (in the form of an institution), should probably be responsible for the well-being of the child. This is, after all, a foreseeable risk of the research the physician has chosen to do, and if he does not make his own legal position clear at the outset, he has no one to blame but himself. If such a consent is, however, in existence, the physician could presumably ask a court to declare that the baby has been legally abandoned by its parents. There appear to be no other logical alternatives, although, of course, the physician would have the authority to surrender the child for adoption.

The other basic question, which common law cannot answer at the present state of its development, is very simply, when does a fetus gestated in a laboratory become a child, particularly for purposes of destruction if a defect is discovered during the process? The abortion standard does not apply because laboratory gestation involves viability outside a mother's body. Since this child has never been within a mother's body, no right of privacy, on which the abortion decisions rest, can apply. In terms of deciding when a child who is gestated in an artificial placenta becomes a human person, this will probably be held to be a question of medical not legal judgment, based on the time at which the child's development is such that (like a child of a normal pregnancy) he is capable of surviving outside his life-support system with reasonable care and medical attention. At the point where artificial placentas are used throughout the prenatal period, when the child is able to survive with the ordinary medical care furnished to viable premature babies, it would appear that he should be declared "born" and thus acquire the status of a "person."

NOTES

1. Robert T. Francouer, *Utopian Motherhood,* New York, A. S. Barnes and Co., 1973, pages 57–59.
2. R. G. Edwards and Ruth E. Fowler, "Human Embryos in the Laboratory," 223 *Scientific American* No. 6, page 44, December 1970.
3. Landrum B. Shettles, Letter, 229 *Nature,* page 343, January 29, 1971.
4. Letter, *Lancet,* page 728, September 29, 1973.
5. Report Prepared for the Subcommittee on Science, Research and Development of the Committee on Science and Astronautics, U.S. House of Representatives, 93rd Congress, 2nd Session, by the Science Policy Research Division of the Congressional Research Service, December 1974, U.S.G.P.O., Washington, 1974, page 17.
6. *New York Times,* July 16, 1974, page 8, Col. 3.
7. *New York Times,* July 17, 1974, page 14, Col. 4.
8. *New York Times,* July 19, 1974, page 31, Col. 1.
9. Report, *op. cit. supra* at 5, page 18.
10. David Rorvick, "The Embryo Sweepstakes," *New York Times* (magazine section), September 15, 1974, page 17 et seq.
11. *Ibid.*
12. David Rorvick, "Embryo Transplants," *Good Housekeeping,* page 78, June 1975.
13. Rorvick, *op. cit. supra* at 10; Edward Grossman, "The Obsolescent Mother," 227 *Atlantic* No. 5, page 39, May 1974.
14. *New York Times,* February 27, 1970, page 8, Col. 3.
15. For a lengthy discussion of the technical difficulties involved in creating an artificial womb, see Francouer, *op. cit. supra* at 1, Ch 2.
16. E.g., Hendrix v. Hunter, 110 SE 2d 35, Ga 1959.
17. E.g., A. v. C., 390 SW 2d 116, Ark 1965.

18. E.g., Nev Rev Stats, Section 127.070; Mass Gen Laws Ann, C.210, Section 2; British Adoption Act of 1958. See also C. Foote, R. Levy, and Frank E. A. Sander, *Cases and Materials on Family Law,* 2nd ed., Boston, Little, Brown and Co., 1976, pages 479–485.

19. E.g., Adoption of McKinzie, 275 SW 2d 365, Mo 1955, "Revocation of Parental Consent to Adoption: Legal Doctrine and Social Policy," note, 28 *U Chicago Law Rev,* page 564, 1961.

20. E.g., Adoption of Ashton, 97 A 2d 368, Pa 1953; Foote, Levy, and Sanders, *op. cit. supra* at 18.

21. E.g., Barwin v. Reidy, 307 P 2d 175, NM 1957.

22. E.g., County Department of Public Welfare v. Morningstar, 151 NE 2d 150, Ind 1958.

23. Edwards, *op. cit. supra* at 2, page 53.

24. Leon R. Kass, "Making Babies: The New Biology and the Old Morality," 26 *The Public Interest,* page 31, Winter 1972.

25. *Washington Post,* March 3, 1970.

26. *New York Times,* August 20, 1974, page 39, Col. 6.

27. Rorvick, *op. cit. supra* at 10.

28. Rorvick, *op. cit. supra* at 12.

29. See, for example, Karp v. Cooley, 493 F 2d 408, CCA 5, 1974; Fortner v. Koch, 261 NW 762, Mich 1935; Brown v. Hughes, 30 P 2d 259, Colo 1934; McHugh v. Audet, 72 F Supp 394, DC Pa 1947; "Consent in Clinical Investigation," 203 *JAMA* No. 7, page 281, February 12, 1968.

30. Fiorentino v. Wenger, 227 NE 2d 296, NY 1967.

31. See, for an excellent but very brief discussion of the similarities between AID jurisprudence and in vitro problems, Mary Ann B. Oakley, "Test Tube Babies," 8 *Family Law Quart,* page 385, Winter 1974.

32. Francouer, *op. cit. supra* at 1, page 20.

33. Ga Stats Ann, Sections 74.101.1 and 74-9904.

34. Okla Stats Ann, Title 10, Sections 551–553.

35. People v. Sorensen, 437 P 2d 495, Cal 1968.

36. Cal Evidence Code, Section 621.

37. Kans Stats Ann, Section 23-128–130.

38. New York City Health Code, Art 21. See "The Legal Consequences of Artificial Insemination in New York," note, 19 *Syracuse Law Rev,* page 1009, 1968.

39. Orford v. Orford, 58 DLR 251, 1921.

40. E.g., Strnad v. Strnad, 78 NYS 2d 390, NY 1948; People ex rel Abajian v. Dennett, 184 NYS 2d 178, NY 1958; Gursky v. Gursky, 242 NYS 2d 406, NY 1963.

41. People v. Sorensen, 437 P 2d 495, Cal 1968.

42. In re Adoption of Anonymous, 345 NYS 2d 430, NY 1973.

43. Gerald Leach, *The Biocrats: Ethics and the New Medicine,* Baltimore, Penguin Books, 1972, page 94.

44. *New York Times,* October 17, 1971, page 65.

45. W. Barton Leach, "Perpetuities in the Atomic Age: The Sperm Bank and the Fertile Decedent," 48 *ABAJ,* page 942, 1962.

46. Vt Stats Ann, Title 27, Section 501.

47. Two excellent and extensive law review articles on legal problems in AID are Walter Wadlington, "Artificial Insemination: The Dangers of a Poorly Kept Secret," 64 *Northwestern Law Rev* No. 6, page 777, January 1970; and George P. Smith, "Through a Test-Tube Darkly," 67 *Mich Law Rev,* page 127, 1968.

48. *Charlotte Observer,* July 17, 1975, page 8A.

49. James B. Holder, "Serum Hepatitis," 6 *Lawyers' Med J,* page 79, May 1970.

50. Angela R. Holder, *Medical Malpractice Law,* New York, John Wiley and Sons, pages 140–142; "Liability for Transfusion Hepatitis," 211 *JAMA* No. 8, page 1431, February 23, 1970; "Recent Decisions on Transfusion Hepatitis," 228 *JAMA* No. 6, page 786, May 6, 1974; Hoder v. Sayet, 196 So 2d 205, Fla 1967; Hutchins v. Blood Services of Montana, 506 P 2d 449, Mont 1973; Carl Pitmas, *The Gift Relationship,* New York, Vintage Books, Random House, 1971.

51. See, generally, Jesse Dukenminier, "Supplying Organs for Transplantation," 68 *Mich Law Rev,* page 811, 1970; "The Sale of Human Body Parts," note, 72 *Mich Law Rev,* page 1182, May 1974. For example, the *New York Times,* July 9, 1975, carried an ad in the "personals" column in which a 30-year-old man advertised his kidney for sale.

52. See "Criminal Law: Attempted Suicide," note, 40 *NC Law Rev,* page 323, 1962.

53. E.g., Conn Gen Stats Ann, Section 53(a)–56.

54. See, generally, 53 *Am Jur* 2d, "Mayhem."

55. Campbell v. Wainwright, 416 F 2d 949, CCA 5, 1969.

56. Roe v. Wade, 410 US 113, 1973.

57. Doe v. Bolton, 410 US 179, 1973.

58. E.g., Coe v. Gerstein, 376 F Supp 695, DC Fla 1973, cert den 417 US 279, 1974; Doe v. Doe, 314 NE 2d 128, Mass 1974; Doe v. Rampton, 366 F Supp 189, DC Utah 1973; Jones v. Smith, 278 So 2d 339, Fla 1973; In re Smith, 295 A 2d 238, Md 1972. See, generally, "Abortion: The Father's Rights," note, 42 *U Cinn Law Rev,* page 441, 1973.

59. E.g., O'Beirne v. Sup Ct, Cal, Santa Clara Co, December 7, 1967.

60. E.g., Sylvia v. Gobeille, 220 A 2d 222, RI 1966; "Prenatal Injuries," 214 *JAMA* No. 11, page 2105, December 14, 1970.

61. Jorgensen v. Meade Johnson Laboratories, 483 F 2d 237, CCA 10, 1973.

62. E.g., Karp v. Cooley, 493 F 2d 408, CCA 5, 1974 (experimental use of artificial heart).

63. Zepeda v. Zepeda, 190 NE 2d 849, Ill 1963.

64. Williams v. New York, 223 NE 2d 343, NY 1966.

65. Troppi v. Scarf, 187 NW 2d 511, Mich 1971.

66. Ziemba v. Sternberg, 357 NYS 2d 265, NY 1974.

67. Rieck v. Medical Protective Co. of Fort Wayne, 219 NW 2d 242, Wisc 1974.

68. Doerr v. Villate, 220 NE 2d 767, Ill 1966.

69. Custodio v. Bauer, 59 Cal Rptr 463, Cal 1967.

70. Coleman v. Garrison, 281 A 2d 616, Del 1971.

71. Pearson v. Sav-on Drugs, 108 Cal Rptr 307, 1974.

72. George A. Hudock, "Gene Therapy and Genetic Engineering," 48 *Ind Law J,* page 533, 1973.

73. Roller v. Roller, 79 Pac 788, Wash 1905.

74. Hewellette v. George, 9 So 885, Miss 1891.

75. E.g., Briere v. Briere, 224 A 2d 588, NH 1966.

76. E.g., Meyer v. Ritterbush, 92 NYS 2d 595, NY 1949; Wright v. Wright, 70 SE 2d 152, Ga 1952; Hoffman v. Tracy, 406 P 2d 323, Wash 1965.

77. William L. Prosser, *Torts,* 4th ed., St. Paul, West Publishing Co., 1971, Section 122, pages 866–867.

78. Aronoff v. Snider, 292 So 2d 418, Fla 1974.

79. Leila Schroeder, "New Life: Person or Property?" 131 *Am J Psychiat* No. 5, page 541, May 1974.

CHAPTER II

LEGAL ASPECTS

OF AMNIOCENTESIS,

GENETIC COUNSELING,

AND GENETIC SCREENING

Approximately 250,000 defective babies are born in this country every year, or 5 percent of all live births. Twenty percent of these abnormal births are caused by the effects of environmental factors, such as drugs taken by the pregnant woman, German measles, or exposure to radiation. An additional 50 percent of all birth defects result from a combination of environmental and genetic factors, and approximately 20 percent are attributable to inherited genetic defects alone.[1] The cost in economic and human terms is incredible. Severely afflicted children in institutions maintained by the states are estimated to cost the public approximately $250,000 per child over a lifetime of care, and most of these institutions provide inadequate care.[2] Parents and normal siblings are devastated economically by the cost of treatment for these children, whether they are cared for at home or in an institution. The human suffering for both parents and children is incalculable. It has been suggested in some circles that society has an obligation to insure protection of its resources from further expenditures of this type. It has been argued that elimination of defective children prior to birth, either by prevention of their conception or by their abortion should be a goal of society, although compulsory restrictions on child bearing raise serious constitutional questions.[3]

On the very personal and individual level, however, couples are becoming aware of the fact that in some cases either prior to conception through genetic counseling and screening, or during pregnancy through amniocentesis and prenatal diagnosis, an alternative to bearing a defective child now exists. Although at this time the only type of prenatal therapy that is effective is intrauterine transfusion for fetuses with Rh disease, research is now being done on prenatal treatment of other illnesses. George E. Burch, for example, predicts that within the next ten years prenatal heart surgery and other therapeutic measures may be available to correct cardiac defects in a fetus.[4] At present, however, the major difficulty with prenatal diagnosis is that abortion is the only means by which to "treat" the situation, thus raising moral, ethical, as well as legal issues. This chapter will examine the legal liability of physicians in these areas and suggest answers for future malpractice questions, which, as these procedures become more prevalent, are inevitable. Although there have been numerous articles on the ethical and moral aspects of these procedures, very little if any attention has been paid to simple questions of professional liability.

AMNIOCENTESIS

Description and Indications

The word "amniocentesis" is derived from the Greek "amnion," the membrane around the fetus, and "kentesis," to pierce. The procedure consists of the perforation of the uterus and the subsequent removal of amniotic fluid, which is comprised in part of fetal cells. This fluid is cultured and analyzed to determine certain genetic characteristics of the fetus.[5] Although there was some use of amniotic puncture as a diagnostic technique as early as 1930,[6] the first known use in practical obstetrics was begun by Douglas Bevis in 1952.[7] Since the mid-1950s it has been the only prenatal diagnostic test in wide use in clinical obstetrics, originally because it was discovered that examination of amniotic fluid cells could determine fetal sex, which was extremely important in establishing the possibility of a sex-linked genetic disorder.

Amniotic fluid is aspirated through a needle inserted in the abdominal wall and is then karotyped and subjected to chemical analysis. The procedure is identical to that used to induce saline abortions. The procedure is not usually done prior to the 16th week of pregnancy, since before that time there is too little fluid to aspirate without danger to the fetus. Some experimental use of transvaginal amniocentesis has been tried, but at least in the early stages of pregnancy this approach apparently increases the risk of spontaneous abortion resulting from the procedure as well as causing infections in both mother and fetus.

The diseases that can now be diagnosed by amniocentesis include sex-linked diseases such as hemophilia and chromosome aberrations such as Down's syndrome, Tay-Sach's disease, and many others. A series of three articles in the *New England Journal of Medicine* by a team from the genetics unit of the Children's Service of the Massachusetts General Hospital in 1970 indicated that an enormous number of diseases may be uncovered by this means.[8] Thus, the use of the procedure as a valid diagnostic test is no longer in question.

Furthermore, transfusions by intramniotic needle can be used to treat prenatal Rh disease, its original purpose.

Among reported complications, fetal morbidity appears to be a greater risk than maternal morbidity, at least after 20 weeks of gestation. Fetal deaths may result from a ruptured placenta, amnionitis, and fetal hemorrhage. Puncture of the fetus has been observed in a fair number of cases. Causes of maternal morbidity have included maternal hemorrhage and peritonitis and, less seriously, severe abdominal pain. The authors of the *New England Journal* series strongly urged against transvaginal amniocentesis because of the incidence of infection.[9]

There is a consensus at the present time that the risk of serious fetal or maternal injury during amniocentesis is between 1 and 2 percent without any claims of negligence, and that there must thus exist at least a 2 percent risk that the fetus is genetically affected for amniocentesis to be warranted.[10]

In addition to maternal or fetal injuries, errors in diagnosis are apparently far from unknown. A 1970 study of attempts by amniocentesis to ascertain the gender of fetuses, for example, revealed a 13 percent failure rate.[11] There are cases on record in which the diagnosis was made after amniocentesis that a child would be deformed and after the mother elected not to abort, a normal child was born. In other instances in which there was a failure to diagnose extant abnormalities, defective babies have been born.

Amniocentesis at present is unable to detect the presence of more than one fetus. Therefore, if a woman is pregnant with twins, only one of whom may be affected by a sex-linked disease, which might be very possible with fraternal twins, no information can be obtained about the other fetus. Most errors in diagnosis, however, are attributable to the aspiration of an inadequate specimen of fluid, contamination or delay during shipment to the laboratory in which the tests are to be made, and contamination of the fluid by maternal cells.[12]

Amniocentesis, therefore, is not a procedure to be used without careful consideration of clinical indications. An article in the *New England Journal of Medicine* in 1970 indicates four categories of high-risk pregnancies that are appropriate for amniocentesis:[13]

1. Severe disorders with high genetic risk of autosomal recessive conditions (e.g., Tay-Sach's disease and certain other metabolic disorders), familial chromosome dislocations, and sex-linked conditions.

2. Severe disorders with moderate genetic risk: chromosome disorders in pregnancies of women 40 years of age or over (the incidence of Down's syndrome children born to women over 40 is sufficiently high to lead many obstetricians to feel that amniocentesis should be a routine proce-

dure for all pregnant women at least over 40 and, many now believe, over 35).

3. Severe disorders with low genetic risk: questions of chromosome disorders in pregnancies of women 35 to 39 years of age and questions of recurrence of trisomy 21 after one affected child.

4. Treatable disorders with high genetic risk: questions of autosomal recessive conditions such as galactosemia and sex-linked conditions such as hemophilia.

The editorial points out that in the "severe disorders with high genetic risk" category, it is likely that the appearance of the disorder in a living child will call attention to the family for an estimation of risks of any subsequent pregnancy and that in the "moderate genetic risk" group there seems to be increasing agreement about the wisdom of offering amniocentesis to all older pregnant women. In Massachusetts studies, for example, a pregnant woman 40 years of age has a one-in-80 risk of bearing a Down's child or one with other sex chromosome difficulties, and the total risk in this maternal age group may be about one in 50. The editorial comments that from the purely economic point of view it would actually be sensible for the state of Massachusetts to encourage and pay for amniocentesis in all pregnant women 35 years of age and older. That would, it is argued, be many times more productive than the existing programs of screening for disorders of amino acid metabolism.

Physician Liability

Although to date there has been only one malpractice case against a physician involving amniocentesis, certain foreseeable problems may occur either with the procedure or with a failure to perform it. Thus, some estimation of the risks of future liability can be deduced from analogous principles in other medical professional liability situations.

Failure to perform.   The only amniocentesis case to date, reported at the trial court level, was a suit against an obstetrician who did not refer a patient in her mid-40s for amniocentesis. Her child was born with Down's syndrome. The infant was born in 1970 and the physician claimed, and the jury apparently accepted, that at that time the standard community practice in diagnosis did not require performance of amniocentesis.[14] In this case, the woman testified that she had already had a neurologically handicapped son and, therefore, in view of that fact and her age (42 at the time she became pregnant), due care in diagnosis would have indicated that amniocentesis should have been performed.

At present it is likely that there would be considerable risk of liability in a suit brought by a woman who falls within the four categories discussed above. Scarce resources, however, do enter into failure to order many types of diagnostic tests, and, where laboratories are not readily available to run analyses of fluid, a lack of adequate facilities would probably constitute a good defense for the physician.

Due care in treatment of a patient frequently requires a prudent physician to refer the patient to a specialist for diagnosis and to ask the specialist to consult with him on the subject or to assume responsibility for treatment. Thus, it would appear that if referral to a medical center for amniocentesis and subsequent counseling is economically feasible for the patient, a small-town obstetrician or family doctor who did not at least tell his high-risk patient that the procedure could be performed elsewhere might well encounter a successful liability suit. In innumerable areas of medical practice, if a physician who is not a specialist in the field of the patient's illness (in this case one who does not have adequate resources or knowledge to perform amniocentesis himself) knows or should know that treatment by a specialist is indicated and reasonably available for the patient, he is negligent if he does not advise the patient of that fact.[15] However, before a nonspecialist (in this case an obstetrician who is not trained to perform amniocentesis) can be found liable for failure to refer a patient, the circumstances must be such that the duly careful physician with his educational training should have known that a problem existed that he was not equipped to solve.[16]

A physician who knows that a patient is at risk of harm and who knows exactly what treatment is necessary has an obligation to refer the patient to a hospital or medical center with better facilities, laboratories, or equipment than is locally available. It is therefore highly unlikely that lack of local facilities would be a good defense if it were economically and medically feasible to refer the patient.[17]

One of the most important duties any physician owes his patient—and it certainly would be true in the area of obstetrics, in which knowledge is expanding rapidly—is that under the general concept of due care in treatment the physician is obligated to keep abreast of new developments in medicine. For example, many cases have held that a physician who fails to keep up with drug research and continues to prescribe a drug after there are clear indications in journals that it causes serious side effects may be liable for failure to "keep up."[18]

Failure to utilize appropriate diagnostic tests on which a correct diagnosis can be based is the subject of hundreds of decisions in other fields of medicine. It is highly unlikely that the same principles would not be applied either to failure to perform amniocentesis or to have the patient referred for that purpose if she qualifies as being at risk. In one decision, for example, the court said the following:

> There is a vast difference between an error of judgment and negligence in a collection of factual data essential to arriving at a proper conclusion or judgment. If the physician as an aid to diagnosis does not avail himself of the scientific means and facilities open to him for the collection of the best factual data from which to arrive at his diagnosis the result is not an error of judgment, but negligence in failing to secure an adequate factual basis on which to support his diagnosis.[19]

Although proof of the "community standard of practice" is generally considered to be a good defense in a malpractice case, this concept is no longer immutable. If, in a small town, an obstetrician were sued for having failed to refer the patient for amniocentesis, and argued in defense that in that community none of the other physicians referred a patient at the same degree of risk for the procedure, in most cases until recently he would have provided himself with a conclusive defense. In the one amniocentesis case that has gone to trial to date, that defense was accepted by the jury. It should be noted, however, that in recent years courts have begun to realize that the local custom itself may be negligent, and if it is, the fact that "everybody does it" is no defense if what everybody is doing is negligent practice.[20]

Furthermore, the community standard of care has rarely been applied to specialists within the past decade.[21] Most courts are now willing to rule that physicians who hold themselves out as specialists are obliged to conform to national standards of skill, care, and knowledge in both diagnosis and treatment, although many of the same courts are still applying the community standards of disclosure to the same specialists in the context of an informed consent case. However, although failure to disclose risks while advising a patient to have amniocentesis presents a classical informed consent situation, failure to say anything about amniocentesis would generally be considered negligence in diagnosis, not failure to disclose. In most instances involving suits for failure to perform a diagnostic test or other procedure where the physician never mentions the subject at all, courts proceed on the theory that there was lack of due care in assembling diagnostic data. Only when the physician says something, but not enough, and thus the patient undergoes the test or procedure, do the courts deal with these cases as informed consent questions.

Thus, a woman at risk of having a defective child because of age, family history, or a previous pregnancy that ended in a deformed child should be referred for amniocentesis, and it is highly probable that failure to do so in the current state of accepted practice would constitute actionable negligence if the child is born with a defect that could have been diagnosed by use of the procedure.

Unnecessary amniocentesis. If a physician advocates or performs amniocentesis under circumstances in which it is not reasonably necessary, he also might find himself faced with an award of damages from a successful malpractice case. There are, however, very few successful actions based on unnecessary surgery or performance of diagnostic tests. If the diagnosis itself—that is, that a woman is at high risk for giving birth to a deformed child—has not been negligent, it is highly improbable that she could recover damages on the basis of the fact that her child was born with no deformity. It is evident to both surgeons and judges that a preoperative diagnosis is frequently not confirmed when surgery is performed, and in many cases it has been held that this situation does not indicate negligence on the surgeon's part if he has used standard procedures and tests in arriving at his preoperative diagnosis.[22] As long as the conclusion is reasonable that any diagnostic test is indicated by the history or symptoms presented, the fact that the patient turns out to have no disease is not considered to prove that the test was unnecessary. In a close case a physician runs less risk of being found liable if he orders an unnecessary amniocentesis procedure than if he does not and the child is born with a defect.

Failure to perform amniocentesis with the result that a seriously deformed child is born would undoubtedly lead to a claim for "wrongful life," as discussed in Chapter I. Since courts do seem willing to award all costs of care of a defective child from birth to adulthood against physicians in these cases, prudence would indicate that strictly on an economic basis it would be cheaper to lose a suit for performance of an unnecessary amniocentesis than to lose a suit for negligent failure to perform one.

This raises the question of defensive medical practice, but it is assumed that the indications are genuine that the woman is one who falls into a fairly low-risk category and is not, for example, a perfectly healthy 20-year-old woman with no family history of difficulties and no prior indication that she and her husband are prone to genetic problems who is tested simply because the physician considers it advisable to send all his patients for amniocentesis. In any case in which there are no genuine indications for the procedure and it is performed solely as a matter of routine, a court would probably regard it as unnecessary.

Injuries during amniocentesis. As has been indicated, an irreducible minimum of possible injuries to either the mother or the fetus is present in amniocentesis, as is also true of virtually any surgical procedure.

Some authorities are concerned about the possibility, as yet unproved, that the removal of sufficient amniotic fluid to perform the test may result in an eventual discovery that the children's mental capacities have been limited to some small degree.[23] Even if extraordinary care is used, the possibility of puncture of the fetus's body is also always present. After the procedure has been performed, scars showing damage to the forehead and eyes of the new-born have been particularly noticed.[24]

Failure to disclose risks.   The entire range of questions of informed consent come into play with this procedure. After all, the object of the performance of amniocentesis is to make the woman aware of any existing defect in the fetus, and it is thus highly improbable that any court would hold that failure to disclose to the patient all conceivable risks of harm that might occur to the fetus or the patient herself would be defensible. The procedure is, of course, elective. As is true of other treatment, the duty to disclose seems to increase in inverse proportion to the necessity of the treatment.[25] Since the woman wishes to ascertain damage to her fetus, any attempt to hide from her the fact that further damage might be inflicted on that fetus during the procedure would be extremely indefensible legally as well as morally. Second, therapeutic privilege—the right of a physician to withhold information if in his medical judgment it would be detrimental to the patient's condition to reveal it—by its nature cannot apply in any situation involving elective procedures such as cosmetic plastic surgery.[26] Furthermore, the test is made to determine the condition of the fetus, which is for that purpose the patient. Although it is possible to differ on the ethics of a claim of therapeutic privilege in discussing some information with a patient, it is clear that the law does not recognize any such privilege in dealing with a patient's family since their emotional difficulties cannot interfere with therapy. It is unlikely that any claim of privilege would succeed in this situation since a woman who may be called upon to accept the fact that her unborn child is severely deformed is presumably capable of being told about infection or hemorrhage in the course of a test. Disclosure to the woman of possible injuries to herself is also necessary, since it is quite possible that she would prefer to abort without knowing whether or not her child was defective in preference to assuming any risk of harm to herself from the tests, as there have been a few instances of maternal mortality with amniocentesis.

Thus, whether a court adopts a standard of disclosure determined by the standards of the medical community or whether it accepts the rule that disclosures must be those "which a reasonable patient would find material"—in this particular case, involving an elective diagnostic procedure where there is no present threat to the health of the mother—nondisclosure of any risk such as infection, perforation, or hemorrhage or nondisclosure of the risk that the procedure itself may induce a spontaneous abortion would appear to be action-able if any such results occur.

Errors in reports. Since the primary physician or obstetrician who performs amniocentesis is not usually the same physician who analyzes the amniotic fluid, questions of liability may arise for both if there is an error in a report.

Obviously, an error indicating that a child was deformed which, as a direct result, produced a decision by the parents that the mother would abort would, if negligent, create a cause of action against the medical center or physician who made the diagnosis. If, on the other hand, a mistake in diagnosis is caused by the negligence of a physician or of his employees in interpretation of the chromosome indications in the amniotic fluid and the result is the birth of a defective child who would have otherwise been aborted, the basic elements of a negligence action are also present.

Since failure to use due skill, care, and knowledge in analysis of test data constitutes an actionable breach of a physician's relationship to the patient-parent and it is reasonably foreseeable that such negligence will result in the birth of a genetically defective child, if this occurs an award of substantial damages would be altogether likely. It would, of course, be necessary to prove causation, and although it could not be shown that the condition of the child was the proximate result of the negligence, since the child's defects were not the result of the medical treatment but rather of the genetic condition, it could be easily argued that the pain, suffering, and physical defects the child has at birth are attributable to and are the proximate result of the physician's negligence in analyzing the fluid. It would not be difficult, now that abortion on demand is legal, for parents to prove that they would have aborted if they had known of the genetic defect in the then-unborn child.

Regardless of whether a genetic defect was negligently not discovered or a genetic defect was negligently diagnosed when it did not exist, the liability of the person or persons who performed the test would be the same. In either case, proof of negligent performance of almost any sort of laboratory analysis is sufficient to impose liability.[27]

Although presumably the physician in charge of the actual chemical analysis of the amniotic fluid will probably never see the woman, it is an elementary premise of professional liability law that those physicians who do not come into direct contact with patients, such as radiologists and pathologists, are still assumed to have a physician-patient relationship that is sufficient to impose malpractice liability on them in case of negligence.[28] It is, therefore, very unlikely that a medical center-based biochemist-physician who never sees the woman and in fact may very well have received the amniotic fluid by mail could escape liability for errors of his own or of his employees by claiming the absence of a physician-patient relationship.

An erroneous diagnosis in the laboratory may also under some rare circumstances result in liability for the obstetrician who performs the test and who is continuing to care for the woman. If in any case objective symptoms indicate that there is a possibility of error in laboratory test results, a primary physician who does not investigate the conflict may himself be liable.[29] If, however, the results of the test are reasonably consonant with his understanding of the patient's condition, if an error is made, the hospital or the physician in charge of the laboratory are usually the only parties liable and the treating physician is not. In these cases where there are no overt physical symptoms observable in the pregnant woman to indicate that she is carrying a genetically defective child it would be almost impossible to hold the obstetrician liable after performance of amniocentesis if there is a laboratory error for which he was not personally responsible.

Making a diagnosis after analysis of amniotic fluid is considered to constitute the practice of medicine, as is true of almost all other diagnostic laboratory tests. In many, if not most, cases the persons who perform the analysis are not physicians. They may or may not work under the general supervision of a pathologist or other physician. Where nonphysicians engage in the practice of medicine, courts hold them to the standard of care that would have been expected of a physician undertaking the same procedure. For example, physicians' assistants who negligently provide patient care are normally held to the standard of performance required of a physician, and in most cases if they fail to meet such standards the physician as their employer will be liable. Courts reason that if physicians choose to delegate professional responsibility, they are liable if tasks are performed with less skill, care, and knowledge than would be expected if the physician had performed the procedure himself.[30]

This situation differs markedly from that which, for example, obtains when hospital nurses give routine nursing care without immediate supervision by a physician. There is no true delegation of medical authority, and thus there is no liability for her employer as long as she conforms to the standard of care applicable to the "practice of nursing." However, if she undertakes to diagnose or otherwise "practice medicine," the physician's standard of care prevails and she is negligent if she does not meet it. The general rule in laboratory liability is that routine performance of diagnostic testing procedures is not "practicing medicine" and is thus governed by standards applicable to technicians; but making a diagnosis from the results of those procedures is, and thus the physician's standard of care applies. This is usually a distinction without a difference, however, since if the procedure was performed in a negligent manner the diagnosis is usually incorrect, and whether the report is written by a technician or the pathologist in charge of the laboratory is usually irrelevant.[31]

Thus, the physician in charge of the laboratory in which the amniocentesis analysis is done usually cannot escape liability even if he actually had nothing to do with the test. As long as the technician performed it negligently, either the pathologist, if he is the employer of the technician, the chemist, or the hospital that employed both of them would obviously be liable for any negligent errors.

Since amniocentesis prior to the 16th week of pregnancy is considered dangerous to the fetus because of the lack of an adequate amount of amniotic fluid for testing prior to that date and because the studies of the fluid may require several weeks, a diagnosis that a child is defective means that a decision to abort cannot be made before the close of the second trimester of pregnancy, and any delay in reporting the test results would place the question of abortion squarely into the third trimester, when there is some doubt that abortions are legal except to protect the health of the mother. It is therefore of critical importance that amniocentesis laboratory reports are transmitted not only accurately and properly but as quickly as possible, and it would be clear negligence on the part of the laboratory to fail to transmit the results as promptly as possible to the primary physician. In any situation in which laboratory tests are of importance in arriving at a diagnosis, courts hold that any delays in transmission of the findings that can be shown to have damaged the patient constitute clear negligence.[32] Particularly in this area, where a delay of so much as a week could create serious legal problems for the woman who wishes to have an abortion as well as increasing the risks in the abortion itself, any delay beyond that which is absolutely necessary for proper evaluation of the test results and a diagnosis to be made would presumably be sufficient evidence of proximate cause of damage to the patient to make the laboratory liable.

Failure to disclose test results.   If a woman has amniocentesis to test for one disease and another disease is discovered, is the physician obligated to disclose the existence of the second condition?[33] Assuming that in the physician's judgment the disease is not sufficient to mandate an abortion, it would still seem clear that the woman has the right to know of any defect that her child will have. Since the purpose of amniocentesis is diagnosis, not therapy, there is, as has been indicated above, no argument to justify a claim of therapeutic privilege. In some writing on this subject the duty to disclose is linked with the presence or absence of the duty to tell a dying patient that he is dying.[34] The common element is said to be that a physician may not be obligated to tell a patient tragic or unpleasant news if nothing can be done about it. However, equating the situation of an unborn child with a defect and a dying adult is illogical. The adult patient usually comes to the physician with overt symptoms for which he wants treatment. In other words, his primary motivation in consulting the physician is to get something done about his problems, not to obtain information about them.

It would be extremely unlikely that any court would excuse failure to disclose relevant information about a nonfatal condition to any other medical patient solely on the basis that the patient came to the physician to find out something else. For example, if a patient is being treated for a cardiac problem and chest x-rays reveal tuberculosis, the physician who fails to tell the patient and institute treatment is clearly negligent.[35] In the amniocentesis situation, something can be done about the defective fetus because the woman can have an abortion. Thus, the situation involving tuberculosis would be more analogous to questions involving amniocentesis than is the comparison with the terminally ill patient.

Where the purpose of the physician-patient relationship, as is true with amniocentesis, is to obtain information, it would appear that there are no legal or moral grounds on which to justify withholding any information at all. If the woman did not want to know, she would not have had the procedure in the first place. Therefore, it seems to be a clear duty, since the woman came for information, not treatment, to give it to her even though it was not the information for which she had directly asked.

Abandonment.   A very interesting legal situation is one in which an obstetrician, having agreed with his patient to perform amniocentesis, is advised that the child has a genetic defect that the physician does not think constitutes grounds for an abortion. This could occur if a treatable sex-linked disease is discovered when the original purpose of the test was to discover if the child had Down's syndrome, and if that had been diagnosed the obstetrician would have been willing to abort the mother. The question is, if the mother wants an abortion at that point because she does not choose to have a son who may have hemophilia, is the physician obliged to perform it? A more extreme example, which has been reported, is a situation in which a normal female fetus was diagnosed in a pregnancy at high risk for serious chromosome problems and the woman demanded an abortion because she did not want a daughter.[36] If the physician refuses she may very well sue for abandonment.

Abandonment by definition is the "unilateral severance by the physician of the professional relationship between himself and the patient without reasonable notice at a time when there is still the necessity of continuing medical attention."[37] Even if the physician is willing to continue prenatal care and deliver the baby but refuses to provide the service the mother requests, that is, an abortion, she may contend that she has in fact been abandoned. If the physician in this case argues that the fetal defect is not of a sufficient magnitude to justify an abortion and that his refusal to perform one is simply the exercise of sound medical judgment, he would probably have a good defense. It does appear that a patient cannot compel any physician to perform an abortion solely on the ground that she has a constitutional right to one whether his objection is moral or medical.[38]

In this case it should be remembered that the abortion decisions of the Supreme Court grounded the abortion right in a decision by the patient and her physician to arrive at a *mutually* agreeable medical decision. Thus, refusal to abort a woman as a result of medical judgment in good faith might not make the physician liable for abandonment, but it does raise serious ethical questions about the woman's right of self-determination. It also raises questions of equal importance about the physician's right to adhere to his own professional standards. It is inconceivable that a surgeon would be legally obliged to remove a healthy appendix if a would-be patient came in and said she was going to live in an isolated area of Africa for five years and did not want to risk acute appendicitis while she was there. He certainly would not have been required to agree to a request to amputate a young man's finger to keep the boy out of the Vietnam draft. It is highly unlikely, therefore, that he would be required to perform an abortion, if it did not seem to him advisable, solely on the basis that there is a constitutional right to one. The only difference now between an abortion and an appendectomy is that there have never been criminal sanctions against performance by licensed physicians of appendectomies, and thus the effect of the Supreme Court decisions in terms of the physician-patient relationship was to place the two procedures on the same basis, not to give women a higher right to abortions than to appendectomies. In this case, unless the physician wishes to be the defendant in a test case, the best procedure would be to refer the woman immediately to another physician who would agree to perform the abortion, or to withdraw formally from the case after giving due notice in time to allow her to find another obstetrician before questions of aborting a viable fetus arise.

This issue is bound to arise in a malpractice case sooner or later and has already happened in clinical practice.[39] As a matter of self-preservation for the physician as well as an ethical concern for the patient's rights, it would be advisable for the physician to make clear prior to performance of amniocentesis that he cannot, in conscience, perform an abortion if it is desired for reasons that he does not find justifiable, including such specific conditions that he may reasonably foresee. The woman should at that time be advised that she is therefore free to (1) go to another physician for the amniocentesis, (2) accept the physician's conditions, or (3) proceed with amniocentesis with a prearrangement for an abortion elsewhere if such a condition is discovered, thus eliminating the necessity for searching for an abortionist at the point when even a short delay could result in delivery of a viable fetus. It should always be remembered that the patient, not the physician, has the right to make decisions about her body. Since the courts have held that a woman does have a right to an abortion during the first two trimesters of pregnancy for any reason she chooses, prior to the third trimester the physician would probably be ethically advised to allow her to make the choice, and if as a matter of professional conscience he will not perform the abortion, he has an ethical if not legal obligation to refer her elsewhere.

Informed consent to abortion.   Most physicians will not perform amniocentesis unless the woman agrees in advance to an abortion if the diagnosis is positive for serious genetic defects.[40] This appears to be an extremely unwise and probably legally indefensible example of interference with the woman's right of self-determination. A woman or couple may have a very sensible reason for wanting to know whether or not they will have a deformed child without necessarily wishing to destroy the child for that reason. Just as a dying patient may very much need to know the diagnosis of his fate in order to arrange his household and business affairs and provide adequate care for those he leaves behind, a married couple may wish to make plans if they know that they will have a seriously handicapped child.[41] For one thing, after they know from amniocentesis that their child will be a Down's baby, they may decide they do not wish to keep the child at home but admit him directly from the hospital to an institution. They may need time to raise money. Immediate application to the institution's waiting list may be necessary. They may wish to make immediate preparations for the rearrangement of their life style, such as the case when the mother wants to give notice that she will leave her job to stay at home with her handicapped infant. Since a physician obviously cannot enforce an agreement to abort or perform the abortion without the woman's consent, he knows or should know at the time she agrees to this requirement prior to the test that he is asking her to abide by a bargain she may not realize he cannot enforce except by intimidation. Regardless of her feelings after diagnosis, the agreement itself may pressure her to comply or at least subject her to implicit duress at the hands of her openly disapproving obstetrician. If she has any doubts about abortion after she finds out that her child will be defective, it should be remembered that it is altogether one thing to discuss the merits of abortion on a hypothetical basis, hoping that amniocentesis will make the question moot with a report that the child is normal, and it is quite another to sign a consent form for abortion after the diagnosis is made. There should never be any penalty, psychological or otherwise, or any inducement to a woman to abort a child, and if there is, it is very hard to believe that she would not have an excellent suit against the physician for obtaining her consent by duress after the procedure was over.

The general principles of self-determination to give or refuse consent applicable in all doctor-patient situations should prevent any duress to abort, or for that matter not to abort, regardless of the result of the amniocentesis. Once the patient has been accepted by the physician for obstetrical care, refusal to perform amniocentesis without such a prior agreement to abort where due care would indicate amniocentesis was advisable, would undoubtedly constitute abandonment as well as an invasion of the woman's right to withhold consent. Consent to performance of one necessary medical procedure, that is, amniocentesis, invariably cannot be made contingent on requiring a patient to consent to another procedure. The requirement of an agreement for abortion prior to amniocentesis is clearly duress.[42]

Disclosure of results.   As has been indicated, it is difficult to envision any justification for a claim of therapeutic privilege for refusing to disclose all the facts to the patient about her unborn child, but serious questions may arise concerning disclosure to other persons. Assume hypothetically that a woman is discovered to be pregnant with a male fetus who may be carrying a sex-linked disease such as hemophilia and it is positively established that she is the carrier. She has a sister of child-bearing age with no children. In most instances once the woman finds out about this situation she would presumably tell her sister voluntarily. Suppose, however, this patient refused to do so. Does the physician have either a responsibility or a right to give this information to the woman's relatives who might have a real need to know it?

It is quite clear that in cases of a contagious disease a physician has not only a right but a duty to protect other people who may contract the disease by advising them of the patient's condition, even though the disease is not reportable under the state's public health law.[43] Genetic disease, however, is not "contagious" in the same sense.[44] It should be remembered that a physician's duty is to the patient not to society if there is a conflict, and if, as a practical matter, the physician undertook to notify the patient's sister, he would be obliged to run a genealogical survey and to notify cousins in varying degrees. Therefore, the patient's customary right of privacy in the context of disclosures by her physician would seem to be the same in this case as in any noncontagious disease, and that violation of that right not only makes the physician civilly liable but in some cases may result in criminal charges or revocation of his license.

If a patient refuses to tell her husband that their child is genetically defective, the physician might, however, be in a rather different position. Most courts hold that it is not a violation of confidentiality to discuss a patient's condition with his or her spouse even though they may be separated pending divorce. Several cases have involved actions against physicians for revealing information about wives to their husbands knowing that the information would be used against their patients in a divorce case.[45] The physicians won the cases. However, whereas the physician would probably not be legally liable, it would appear to be an invasion of his ethical duty to the patient, although the husband does have a clear interest in knowing the condition of his child. Because the decision to abort is entirely that of the woman, it would appear that, since the husband cannot force her to have an abortion, he has no legal right to find out the diagnosis after amniocentesis if to do so would violate her right of privacy. He will discover the child's condition at birth in any case.

Actions for wrongful life. With the recognition for an action for wrongful life, which might clearly apply to a physician who made a mistaken diagnosis in amniocentesis or who failed to suggest the test to a woman at risk, the obvious collateral question is whether courts would recognize a wrongful life action brought by a seriously handicapped child against his parents who had either refused amniocentesis or, upon receiving a diagnosis after amniocentesis, elected to continue the pregnancy. As was discussed in Chapter I, it is hoped that to avoid having every child born into any problem environment—including poverty, large families, or physical difficulties—flooding the courts with suits, this cause of action will not be recognized. Parents are legally required to support their children in any case, including the costs of medical treatment, which would cover any costs alleged as actual damages by the child, thus making the only basis for an award that of punitive or punishment damages.

Although it could be argued that refusal to abort a fetus that has been diagnosed as defective was willful, it would appear unconscionable to construe that refusal in the same frame of reference as the other willful behaviors that lead to punitive damage awards in tort suits. Since there is an admitted percentage of error in amniocentesis diagnosis, the parent could claim, first, that she did not believe the report. Second, if the refusal to abort was predicated on religious or moral conviction, to allow such an action against the parent would be a clear violation of the parent's First Amendment right of religious freedom. After all, parenthood, from conception forward, is a series of calculated risks. From the time a pregnant woman hears the announcer on a March of Dimes fund-raising commercial intone, "Ten percent of all babies are born with defects" through preschooler's trips to emergency rooms for sutures, through the adolescent's parent's thought that perhaps the child is about to end up in the penitentiary instead of at Yale, there are no absolute guarantees. One does the best one can and hopes that it works.

VOLUNTARY GENETIC COUNSELING

It is now feasible for couples who have reason to believe that some genetic defect may be inherited by their children to consult genetic counselors prior to conceiving a child and thus be advised of the possibilities. If they are advised that there is a high risk of having a defective child, they may decide not to have any children, to adopt a child, to assume the risk, or, if the father's genetic makeup is responsible for the possible defect, to have a child by artificial insemination by donor.

It should be noted in regard to both amniocentesis and genetic counseling that advances in medicine have resulted in procreation by people who would have died during infancy in early childhood 10, 15, or 20 years ago, but who are now able to survive, lead normal or almost-normal lives, and have children of their own. Thus, the incidence of fairly minor genetic defects in the population is increasing, although severely handicapped persons such as those who have Down's syndrome generally do not have children.[46] A woman with juvenile diabetes can now become pregnant and with proper obstetrical management go to term and deliver a healthy baby who may inherit the same problem. Twenty-five years ago this woman probably would have died before reaching adulthood. Children of such women are more likely to suffer from congenital problems than other women's babies and their numbers are increasing daily.

A large number of voluntary screening programs for various diseases are now available. Under the National Sickle Cell Anemia Control Act the Secretary of Health, Education and Welfare is given authority to make grants to public and nonprofit entities and to enter into contracts for the operation of screening and counseling programs.[47] A substantial number of voluntary programs for sickle cell screening by governmental and nongovernmental agencies have been established with these grants.

The Baltimore-Washington, D.C., Tay-Sach's screening program, one of the most successful, is funded partly by private funds and partly by the Maryland State Department of Health. During its first five months, the program screened approximately eight thousand people who were at risk for the disease.[48] All couples found to be at risk for bearing Tay-Sach's children were informed of the availability of amniocentesis for the purpose of monitoring present or future pregnancies. Of the eight thousand people screened, ten couples were at high genetic risk. None of the ten had a previous history of the disease in their immediate families, and thus presumably would not have known to ask for individual amniocentesis had this program not existed. The ease with which the Tay-Sach's program was implemented, however, may be due to very unusual circumstances.

The screening was limited to persons of Ashkenazi-Jewish origin, which is the high-risk group for the disease. Therefore, the organized Jewish community, particularly the rabbinate, served to educate the population to the existence of the program and to recommend participation. Obviously, a voluntary screening program for other, less discrete, high-risk groups does not have such a well-defined population from which to draw in its attempt to screen. However, in any voluntary program the risk has to be assumed that a certain number of people will not choose to participate or will not find out about the program at all, just as thousands of people do not bother to register to vote. These programs operate for anyone who wishes to be screened and include couples who are contemplating marriage, single people who want to find out if they are carriers of a disease before they make a decision about marriage and child bearing people who have already had one or more children with a genetic affliction, and couples who are currently expecting a child.

Physician and Counselor Liability

Negligence in testing and diagnosis.   The usual procedure in genetic screening programs is to take a blood sample from which the parent's carrier status can be diagnosed. This procedure is far simpler than amniocentesis, and questions of liability in drawing a blood sample are fairly remote. Most writers on the subject dismiss them as so unlikely to occur that they are not worth discussion. While this is no doubt correct, it should be noted that although there are no cases on record of serious suits against physicians for infection or other problems involving drawing blood, there have been a few cases in which people fainted when they saw their blood being drawn, fell, hit their heads, and sustained rather serious injuries. To prevent the likelihood of this occurrence, simple common sense would advise letting the patient sit down while the blood sample is being taken, and if the patient states prior to giving the blood sample that he feels peculiar, it is sensible to let him lie down to prevent any difficulty.[49] This would appear, however, to be the only serious risk of liability in terms of performing the test itself.

Liability for errors in interpretation of the test results would be similar to those discussed in the section on amniocentesis. Failure to use due care in an evaluation would undoubtedly subject the laboratory to liability.

Failure to disclose test results.   The more serious question involving preconception screening is whether or not in this situation there is an obligation to disclose the results of the test.[50] Clearly, the couple or person to be screened has come to the clinic for the sole purpose of acquiring information.

Since the screening process may involve a one-shot relationship without a continuing dialogue between counselor and patient, it has been argued that a counselor, whether or not a physician, is not a treating physician in the sense in which the informed consent doctrine normally applies. By analogy to other legal contexts, this would appear to be incorrect.

If a physician performs a physical examination either in a preemployment situation as a staff member of the employer-company or as a life insurance company examiner for a prospective policyholder, most courts hold that no physician-patient relationship is established in these contexts.[51] A preemployment examination or life insurance examination appears precisely analogous to a genetic screening situation, in contrast to a physical examination given by a physician who intends, if he discovers any illness, to treat the patient. At one time, physicians were excused from liability for failure to use due care in these examinations on the ground that no physician-patient relationship was held to exist. No matter how negligent the physician was in failing to discover tuberculosis or a heart condition, for instance, so that the examinee later could prove damage by reason of his failure to obtain timely treatment, any attempt at a malpractice suit was dismissed for failure to state a cause of action. Because the physicians were under an obligation to report the findings to the prospective employer or insurance carrier, not to the patient, there was no duty to the patient to use care in discovering a condition and therefore there was no duty to report the findings of any difficulties that were known or should have been discovered to the examinee.[52] However, there is a growing tendency for courts to hold that in spite of the fact that no physician-patient relationship exists with an employment applicant, the company physician is still required to use due care in his examination.[53]

It is now clear that there is a duty to use due care to uncover illness and to report to the prospective employee an illness that is discovered at the examination.

A man applied for a position as a test pilot with an aircraft manufacturer and was required to undergo a physical examination. The routine examination included a blood test. The blood test report came back from the laboratory indicating a strong probability of malignancy, but no mention of this was made to the employee, who was hired. Seven months later a terminal-state malignancy was discovered, and it was conceded that if it had been revealed to the patient at the time of the examination, surgery would have saved his life. The court held that the company was liable for its employee-physician's failure to disclose the results of the test.[54]

Since persons who come to genetic counselors come only for the express purpose of availing themselves of information, it would be highly illogical to argue that there is any concept such as therapeutic privilege in this context. By the act of applying for screening, the person indicates that he wishes to know the truth. As Alexander Capron writes:

> My premise is that in genetic counseling the parents have a legal right to be fully informed decisionmakers about whether to have a child; and likewise the genetic counselor has the duty to convey to those he advises a clear and comprehensive picture of the options open to them, the relative risks and benefits, and the foreseeable consequences of each option to the best of his ability.[55]

This is, in my opinion, entirely correct. Capron points out, however, that most genetic counselors at present believe that they have an unqualified right under therapeutic privilege to withhold information from their patients.[56] As he maintains, this should be less logical than it is in the family doctor situation because genetic counselors usually are not well acquainted with their patients and therefore are in a far less justifiable position in terms of deciding to withhold information than might a family doctor who had known his patient for a good many years and had a working knowledge of the family's situation.

The second problem Capron points out is that the pressures operating on counselors interfere with an accurate assessment of their patient's best interests because it is less trouble to be abrupt with patients than to enter into the long and arduous process of genuine counseling. As Capron puts it, "In short, it is more efficient for him [the genetic counselor] to make the choices himself rather than to bring into open discussion facts such as carrier status which is difficult to explain and discuss."[57]

Third, as Capron says, a physician's judgment may also be clouded by his own values, which do not necessarily correspond with his patient's. For example, a physician may believe that a woman ought to have an abortion if there is any serious risk of a genetic defect, whereas the woman may totally reject the concepts of abortion or contraception and merely wish to "know her odds" in order to make plans for the possibility of a defective child.

There is an obvious logical problem as well in any attempt to claim therapeutic privilege in this context. In the normal treatment situation therapeutic privilege clearly exists, but equally clearly a physician cannot tell a patient an outright lie. Courts will tolerate evasion by silence, but any physician who makes a positively false or misleading statement will discover upon being sued that therapeutic privilege is no defense.[58] A physician may not, for example, say that a procedure carries no risks when he knows that it does, even to avoid upsetting a patient.[59] He may, under therapeutic privilege, only justify complete silence on the subject. In a genetic counseling situation it is logically impossible to remain silent. The patient has come with a yes-or-no problem: "Will any children I conceive be at risk of . . .?" The counselor must say yes or no eventually; he cannot logically refuse to answer. If the answer to the question is that the patient is a carrier, which carries certain implications, to respond to the question with no is positively false and thus is not within the scope of therapeutic privilege.

Another logical inconsistency with the argument that therapeutic privilege applies to genetic counseling is that however upset a couple may be to discover that they have a 25 or 50 percent chance of having a child with a severe genetic defect, it is no doubt considerably less upsetting than being given an assurance that all is well and thus deciding to conceive and discovering nine months later that they have a severely handicapped newborn.

Adequate counseling in some situations, however, is a farce. One newspaper reported that 45,000 sickle cell carriers in Chicago were not told of their status.[60]

Liability for failure to disclose an accurate diagnosis has been established in screening programs, which are also separate from any therapeutic relationship, such as the case of employment physical examinations, and it seems to be clear that such failures to disclose which cause demonstrable damage to the patient are actionable torts.

Failure to disclose relevant genetic information followed by the birth of a defective child might very well create wrongful life liability, in keeping with the other decisions on this subject.

Disclosure of results. The third legal issue in voluntary screening is that of a right of disclosure by the counselor to other people. It is clear from several reports that third parties may seek to obtain information about genetic screening or to require as part of preemployment physical examinations or life insurance examinations a screening test for various genetic diseases. It is equally as clear that whether or not a physician-patient relationship exists, morally, if not legally, a physician is obliged to respect the patient's confidence.

It is now established that some employers refuse to hire applicants with the sickle cell trait even though they are entirely free from the disease.[61] There seems to be no justification for revelation of this information to any third party, since authorities agree that the only relevance of the sickle cell anemia trait in terms of function of the person with the trait (as opposed to the disease) is that it can, in some very rare cases, cause problems in the administration of some types of anesthesia used for major surgery, and the only employment that should actually be denied on medical grounds is that of a high altitude airplane pilot.[62]

Those persons who have sickle cell disease are well aware of the fact by the time they are of school age, by which time many of them have died and almost all of them have had at least one attack. Any form of physical disability would have been revealed long before adulthood, applications for employment, or marriage. There is, for example, a recent discovery that at least 39 players in the National Football League are sickle cell anemia carriers, and the trait has caused no impairment of their abilities.[63] It is also clear that because of egregious violations of privacy, stigmatization of sickle cell carriers has occurred both in the contexts of obtaining employment and of being approved for life insurance.[64]

To date there has been no reported instance of a suit for damages on the ground of wrongful disclosure of information by a genetic counseling office, but if there should be, it is likely that the same standard of care in protection of patient privacy would be held to apply as is required of hospitals. As many decisions indicate, unauthorized release of a patient's hospital record is a clear violation of the patient's rights.[65]

COMPULSORY GENETIC SCREENING

The Statutes and the Issues

A number of states have enacted statutes relating to compulsory screening for sickle cell anemia.[66] Some of these statutes make sickle cell testing mandatory for certain classifications of people. Some require the testing of school children, others require sickle cell tests prior to issuance of marriage licenses. New York, for example, makes the sickle cell test mandatory for each marriage license applicant who is not of the "Caucasian, Indian or the Oriental race."[67] A Georgia law requires the Department of Public Health to set up a program for the mandatory sickle cell testing of newborn infants.[68] Maryland has a provision that requires the testing of pregnant women entering hospitals for delivery if blood samples are drawn at that time.[69] Many other states have statutes similar in impact. Some states, however, have repealed their compulsory screening statutes and made all screening voluntary.

These statutes have been enacted under the police power of the state to preserve and protect the health and welfare of all citizens. There is, however, a serious question of the public health aspects of sickle cell anemia. Genetic diseases are not contagious diseases, for which it is quite clear that the state does have the power to require testing, and therefore requirement of sickle cell screening at the time a marriage license is issued is far different from the requirement of a blood test for syphilis. The basic purpose of screening children in school must be to determine if they possess the sickle cell trait, because if they have the disease it has become apparent by the time the child reaches school age, since the symptoms are invariably clinically obvious long before the age of six.

Many constitutional as well as ethical issues arise in the context of compulsory screening for any noncontagious disease, but the primary issue is that of invasion of privacy. Most authorities believe that a number of persons required by law to be screened have suffered serious prejudices and stigmatization as the result of widespread release of test information.[70] The question is whether the legitimate interest on behalf of public health to discourage people at risk of genetic disease from having children might not be adequately served by voluntary screening and extensive dissemination of information as to the availability of voluntary genetic screening.

The definitive study on the problems inherent in screening for genetic disease is the report from the Research Group on Social, Ethical and Legal Issues in Genetic Counseling of the Institute of Society, Ethics and the Life Sciences.[71] This report indicates that basic problems involving compulsory screening and, to a lesser extent, voluntary screening programs are that the traditional applications of ethical guidelines for both confidentiality and individual physician responsibility are uncertain in this context. They suggest the following principles for the design and operation of screening programs:

1. Attainable purpose: The report indicates that screening programs should particularly avoid promising the results of benefits, such as treatment, that do not exist and cannot be delivered.

2. Community participation should be incorporated into the screening program in formulating both design and objectives and in administration of the actual operational program.

3. Equal access: Information about screening and screening facilities should be available to all.

4. Adequate testing procedures: This would appear to be critically important as a legal issue as well as an ethical issue. The report points out that the testing procedure should be accurate, should provide maximum information, and should be subject to minimum misinterpretation.

5. Absence of compulsion: The report advises that no screening program have policies that would in any way impose constraints on child bearing by individuals, and it therefore suggests that all screening programs should be conducted on a voluntary basis.

6. Informed consent: The committee found that "screening should be conducted only with the informed consent of those tested or the parents or legal representatives of minors. We seriously question the rationality of screening preschool minors or pre-adolescents for sickle cell disease or traits since there is a substantial danger of stigmatization and little medical value in detecting the carrier's status at this age."

7. Protection of subjects: Since genetic screening is generally undertaken with relatively untried testing procedures and is vitally concerned with the acquisition of new knowledge, the committee felt that it ought properly to be considered a form of human experimentation and that all rights of experimental subjects be conferred on those who participated.

8. Access to information: A screening program should fully and clearly disclose to the community and all persons being screened its policies for informing those who have been screened about the results of the tests performed on them.

9. Provisions of counseling: Well-trained genetic counselors should be readily available to provide adequate assistance for persons identified as carriers of a disease. As a general rule, counseling should be nondirective with emphasis on informing the client and not making decisions for him.

10. As part of the educational process that precedes the actual testing program, the nature and cost of available therapies for defective offspring combined with an understandable description of the therapeutic benefits and risks should be given to all persons to be screened. Thus, the person being screened who becomes aware that there may be no means of therapy if a defective child is born, has the right to decline to take the test if he would prefer not to know.

11. Protection of the right of privacy: Well-formulated procedures should be set up in advance of actual screening to protect the rights of privacy of individuals and their families. The committee stated: "We note that the majority of states do not have statutes that recognize the confidentiality of public health information."[72]

These requirements would appear to be the minimal level of legal as well as ethical standards.

There is also a serious question raised by compulsory diagnosis of any disease for which there is no cure. To some extent the same questions are raised in voluntary screening. For example, serious issues were raised about the screening project at Harvard to identify newborn males with XYY chromosome aberrations because the parents would be then told that the situation existed but also that there was nothing that they could do about it, with an inevitable impact on the parent-child relationship. As the result of public outcry, this program has been terminated.[73]

Where there is voluntary pretesting on people at risk for Huntington's chorea in particular, but other diseases as well, there is an ethical dilemma raised by telling people that they will inevitably develop a devastating, degenerative disease twenty years later without offering any hope of present treatment.[74] As one author has stated:

> If the condition is chronic, debilitating and slowly progressive like, for example muscular dystrophy or sickle cell disease, and there is no effective therapy available, knowing about the condition prior to its clinical manifestation may merely provoke increased patient or parental anxiety without offering them any positive reassurance."[75]

On the other hand, a young person might have the right to know that his productive years will be much shorter than normal so that he may make plans accordingly. Furthermore, it is conceivable in screening for any genetic disease that nonpaternity of existing children with genetic diseases will become apparent if only one of the married couple is a carrier and the disease occurs only if both parents are, thus creating enormous stress on the family relationship.[76]

This problem arises fairly frequently in situations of unanticipated Rh disease in babies whose mother's husband is also Rh-. The degree of tact in handling these problems presumably varies from pediatrician to pediatrician, but at least in the Rh disease cases it is necessary that something be said in order to obtain consent to treatment of critical illness. That is a far different situation from gratuitously announcing to the noncarrier father of a child with sickle cell disease who has come for counseling about whether to have another child that there is "nothing to worry about."

Howard Pearson of Yale, a pediatric hematologist, feels that if the object of testing is to provide carriers of the sickle cell trait (as opposed to those with the disease) with information applicable to marriage, testing in infancy and early childhood is too early, and he suggests that the teens would seem to be a particularly advantageous age because a junior or senior high-school student is usually receptive to the sickle cell educational program and he is also accessible for testing and counseling.[77] Obviously, counseling six-year-olds about the decisions they must make about child bearing is futile. And, since by the time a marriage license is being issued the decision to marry has been made, it would be extremely cruel to tell people at that stage that they should not have any children.

A recent study by a committee of the National Research Council endorses genetic screening but only on a voluntary basis.[78] The committee endorsed the "often controversial" practice of genetic screening as "valuable to the public health and deserving of nationwide use," but the report concludes that screening should be offered to people as a service, no pressure should be applied to persuade them to cooperate out of a sense of duty, and compulsory screening programs should be absolutely ruled out.

The Right to Reproduce

The ultimate question about any form of compulsory genetic screening is that it may (1) be the precursor of state laws restricting the right of affected individuals to marry and have children or (2) be argued as justification for compulsory sterilization. This is true regardless of the condition for which screening is being done. Some people, for example, have seriously advocated that women over 35 should not be allowed by law to have children because of the high risk of Down's syndrome and the resulting expense to the state of caring for their children. Any attempt to restrict the right of procreation is likely to be held unconstitutional.

Since only 20 percent of all birth defects are of pure genetic origin, if all persons who are known to be genetically at risk for all known diseases were sterilized tomorrow, the number of defective children born every year with physical or mental handicaps would not be appreciably reduced.[79] Most birth defects are caused by environmental factors, unpreventable complications during pregnancy, and even more by lack of health care for the pregnant woman. Senator Ernest F. Hollings of South Carolina, in his book *Hunger in America,* argued that one of the causes of mental retardation in newborns today is a lack of adequate nutrition for the mother prior to and during pregnancy.[80] As an ethical as well as a constitutional matter, if there is serious concern for eliminating mental retardation in this country, it would be more effective to provide adequate diets and medical care for all pregnant women than to sterilize carriers of genetic disease, even though abortion of fetuses that have been diagnosed as genetically afflicted would reduce the numbers to some extent.

Joseph Fletcher and other writers on medical ethics frequently indicate their conviction that no one has the moral right to bring a known defective into the world, and thus they find no ethical problem with restrictions on reproduction where the child is likely to be defective.[81] Even conceding that one has a moral obligation not to bring a defective child into the world knowingly, however, the law is not a proper vehicle for the enforcement of spiritual obligations, and any benefit to society that might be derived from such compulsory legislation would probably be far outweighed by the damage it would do to the country's citizens.

Beginning with *Griswold v. Connecticut,*[82] *Eisenstadt v. Baird,*[83] and the other contraceptive cases, the Supreme Court has held that the decision not to procreate is properly left to the persons involved and clearly indicated that child-bearing decisions fall within the zone of privacy into which no government may intrude. Statutes that prohibited voluntary sterilization were struck down in all states as early as the beginning of the 1960s, and it is now considered a constitutional right to be voluntarily sterilized.[84] Courts have also ruled that public hospitals have no right to prohibit admission of patients for voluntary sterilization operations.[85] Sterilization on demand is thus as much a right as contraception. Abortion, of course, is also a right under the Supreme Court decisions.[86] Furthermore, the Court has also held in *Loving v. Virginia* that state laws prohibiting interracial marriage violated freedom of marital choice and specifically held that the state does not have the right to regulate marital choice except to insure compliance with the contagious disease testing, age, and residence requirements.[87] In that case the Court concluded that "the freedom to marry has long been recognized as one of the vital personal rights essential to the orderly pursuit of happiness by free man. Marriage is one of the basic rights of man, fundamental to our very survival."[88] Under the current jurisprudence the right to marry and have children (or not) as one chooses is a constitutional right.

In 1927 the Supreme Court upheld compulsory eugenic sterilization laws in *Buck v. Bell,*[89] but with the exception of punitive sterilization[90] there has been no consideration of the constitutionality of compulsory sterilization statutes by the Court since that time. Most states that enacted compulsory sterilization laws after *Buck v. Bell* still have them on the books and in some cases are still applying them. As late as 1972, for example, the supreme court of Oregon upheld the compulsory sterilization of a 13-year-old retarded girl.[91] There have, however, been considerable inroads made by state courts on broad powers to enforce these statutes. The rights of due process, counsel, and a fair hearing prior to performance of the operation have been guaranteed for many years.[92]

If a state does not have a compulsory sterilization statute, it has been held that there is no right on the part of either the state or a guardian of a retarded person to request such a procedure. Since the incompetent patient cannot give a valid consent to any medical treatment or sign a contract, several recent decisions have held that sterilization may not be performed even if, within the limits of his or her understanding, the patient wishes to be sterilized.[93] In view of the recent cases on the right of freedom of contraception, abortion, and marriage, the Supreme Court would undoubtedly strike down any compulsory sterilization statute that now came before it. Furthermore, there is a substantial difference between a statute that provides for the compulsory sterilization of a retarded person and any statute that attempts to restrict the right of procreation on grounds of the likelihood of transmission of genetic disease. The main rationale for the former, as Justice Holmes concluded in *Buck v. Bell* when he said that "three generations of imbeciles is enough," is that the public resources cannot be used for generation after generation of the retarded. The theory behind sterilization of the retarded, whether right or wrong, is that not only would their children be likely to be genetically retarded but also that a person of low intelligence cannot properly care for a child or provide the parenting necessary for the child's full development. In that situation it is arguable that the state must expend finite resources to care for these children, either as neglected or as impoverished, and the drain on the public's financial resources is sufficient so that the state has a valid interest in stopping it. This does not apply in a situation involving genetic disease. There is no rational basis on which to conclude that parents of a child with sickle cell anemia or Tay-Sach's disease (or any of the other diseases for which genetic screening is possible at the present time) are incapable in any way of caring for the child as they would a child who has a malignancy or any other serious illness, because the parent's intellectual ability to provide adequate care and nurture is not in question. Thus, even if current statutes providing for compulsory sterilization of the retarded were upheld as constitutional, the "compelling interest" of the state to save money on child care would not appear to be applicable in the case of genetic disease.

Since the conclusion of the abortion and contraception decisions was that a woman has a constitutional right *not* to bear a child she does not want, it would appear that the same rationale will be applied conversely, and it will probably be made clear in any future case challenging involuntary sterilization statutes that these statutes are unconstitutional. If the Supreme Court is willing to say that a woman who wants an abortion has the right to have one, then the woman who might be compulsorily sterilized would appear under the same principle to have an equal right to have as many children as she wants. It should be noted that several recent decisions indicate that states cannot deny fundamental rights merely because the exercise of those rights is an economic burden for the rest of society. For example, recent cases have held that retarded children have a right to education and that the school district may not justify failure to provide special education on the ground of insufficient economic resources.[94] Thus, it may be concluded, since the state cannot show a compelling interest not to educate retarded children, that it also would not be able to show a compelling interest to force abortion or sterilization in cases of possible genetic disease.

Since most states that require compulsory screening make no effort to include adequate counseling in the process, any person who is told that he is a carrier without further explanation would appear to be exposed to extraordinary cruelty. Serious ethical questions and many legal issues are raised by such an approach. Studies indicate that many persons who have been through a screening program have been confused or frightened as the result of receiving insufficient or misleading information.[95] It is obvious that definite standards should be formulated and enforced requiring screening facilities, voluntary or compulsory, to prove adequate care for, and informative genetic counseling to, those persons whose tests indicate genetic deficiency.

Presumably, a person who had been harmed by inadequate counseling in a compulsory screening context would have a cause of action under the same principles that have been applied in the "right to treatment" cases involving involuntarily committed mental patients; that is, that if the state requires a person to submit to medical intervention, the state must provide the care required for proper treatment.[96] Since all states' compulsory screening programs apparently lack adequate counseling, the state might attempt to justify its policies on the theory that if all counseling is inadequate, there is no applicable standard of care. This argument proved to no avail in the "right to treatment" cases since the judges were willing to apply American Psychiatric Association standards for determining the scope of "adequate treatment" of committed persons. Similar standards no doubt exist, or could be created by experts, in the context of genetic screening. It is also obvious that a state cannot decline to provide adequate care to compulsory patients on the ground of inadequate financial resources.[97]

One basic problem with the question of determining standards for mass genetic counseling at the moment is that no one is quite sure who should do it. Some argue that the family doctor, if there is one, is the best person equipped to perform such a function.[98] Others believe that medical specialists should be made available. Other people think that counselors may be trained from the population at large. In any large-scale public health programs mistakes in diagnosis or treatment will inevitably occur. Therefore, it is also clear, as a basic legal principle, that persons who are supposed to be at risk for genetic disease should never be told flatly that they should not consider having a child, because a mistake in diagnosis may have been made.

Physician Liability

Malpractice liability exists in the public health field to the same extent as in the private practice of medicine, although it may be more difficult to particularize the physician-patient relationship if mass screening is done by technicians and the patient never sees the physician in charge. Regardless of that fact, however, several decisions have held that public health departments and/or the physicians in charge of screening programs were liable for negligent care of patients.

This has been true where persons who went through mass tuberculosis screening had x-rays read negligently and either a false diagnosis was made when the disease did not exist or a genuine case of tuberculosis was not recognized.[99] Where mass immunizations against polio have been carried out, there have been a few cases of paralytic polio reported as resulting from live attenuated virus vaccines. In most of these cases the courts have held (1) that the drug manufacturer had a duty to warn the "patient" directly of the possibility of side effects prior to administration of the vaccine, because the manufacturer knew or should have known that no physician-patient relationship would exist, (2) that the health departments or physicians in charge of the vaccination programs were liable, in spite of the fact that no physician-patient relationship had been established between the director of the program and the person who took the vaccine.[100]

It appears likely, then, that there would be a good cause of action for negligent diagnosis in a compulsory screening program in spite of the fact that no actual dialogue takes place between a physician and the "patient" prior to the screening test. If an incorrect diagnosis is given and negligence can be established, it would be unquestionable that a cause of action would result if damages could be proved. One difficulty with the situation, however, is that in most cases courts do not allow malpractice damage to be awarded for mental anguish alone, and therefore the patient would have to prove that some bodily harm had been done.[101] This would not be at all difficult if the result of advice given by a counselor was a sterilization operation. But assuming that an unmarried person was erroneously told that he was a carrier of sickle cell anemia or Tay-Sach's disease but prior to marital plans being made a correct diagnosis was established and thus no action was taken on the basis of the incorrect diagnosis, the possibility of recovery of damages would be extremely remote. Once it can be proved, however, that the diagnosis was acted upon to the bodily detriment of the patient, damages can be awarded as easily as they can in any private practice situation.

The Right of Privacy

It would appear that public health records should be entitled to the same degree of privacy and confidentiality as are private physicians' office files or hospital records of private patients. However, very few states have statutes guaranteeing such privacy and violations are frequent. It should be noted that there is probably legal justification to the same extent as would exist against a private physician for a suit for damages for disclosure of confidential information, but unfortunately most people whose medical problems are cared for by public health departments are sufficiently impoverished not to have access to legal help when it is needed, and thus this may be responsible for the fact that no cases, at least at the appellate level, have ever been brought against health departments for negligent or willful dissemination of information. If such a case arose, however, it is probable that specific information about a specific patient would be protected to the same extent as is information from a private physician. One problem that exists with health departments and not as frequently in private practice is the problem of disclosure in the course of dissemination of statistical information about groups of patients for research or other studies. Where this is done, as is provided under the federal Sickle Cell Act, great care must be taken to remove all identifications of patients from the statistics before they are released, since any patient who can be identified undoubtedly would have a good cause of action.

Suits for defamation of character and/or wrongful disclosure have succeeded against physicians who have performed preemployment physical examinations for the federal government and placed in the medical record unsupported defamatory conclusions about the examinees.[102] Since it was not necessary in these cases to prove the existence of a continuing physician-patient relationship for the right of confidentiality to apply, with the exception of the discovery of some communicable disease, it is likely that the patient in a compulsory screening context has as much right to privacy as he does in private treatment. A physician in a public institution has no higher right to publish articles or discuss the patient's case without the patient's knowledge than he would have if he were in private practice.[103]

The horror of having a child with a serious defect and the expense and suffering of both parents and child make it a very high priority in preventive medicine to improve the ability to make a prenatal diagnosis of such a condition. Hopefully, some day genetic therapy will be available to treat the problems prior to birth,[104] but at the present time, abortion or a decision by high-risk parents not to conceive appear to be the only immediate alternatives.

If the problem is to be solved, the government will necessarily be called on to support much more research on diagnosis and treatment of genetic disorders and to fund new and extensive screening programs in all areas of genetic disease where these are appropriate. Legally, however, it must be concluded that all screening should be done on an entirely voluntary basis. If, for example, a woman is at high risk of having a child with Down's syndrome but believes for religious reasons neither in contraception nor abortion, any interference with her right to produce her baby would infringe on her First Amendment right of religious freedom and on her right to privacy. In concern for human liberty, particularly in an area of life as intimate as the right to decide to have children or not, that right would appear to be the cost that society must bear. Genetic screening and counseling, if properly done, can be of enormous benefit both on an individual and a societal basis. If compulsory, however, these programs can cause abuses of great dimensions. Therefore, it would appear to be of particular importance that the courts take careful notice of preventable errors in these programs, and whatever therapeutic benefit malpractice lawsuits may have in improving the standard of care, errors in this field should certainly not be exempt.

NOTES

1. Jane M. Friedman, "Legal Implications of Amniocentesis," 123 *U Pa Law Rev,* page 93, 1974. This excellent article is the only published discussion of any legal questions involved in amniocentesis, although Friedman's primary concerns involve constitutional questions that would arise with compulsory amniocentesis.
2. John Osmundsen, "We Are All Mutant: Preventive Genetic Medicine," *Medical Dimensions,* page 26, February 1973.
3. E.g., *ibid.*
4. Robert T. Francouer, *Utopian Motherhood,* New York, A. S. Barnes and Co., 1973, page 189. Burch is a noted cardiologist and has recently retired as chairman of the Department of Medicine, Tulane Medical School.
5. For a general discussion of the technique of the procedure, see Theodore Friedmann, "Prenatal Diagnosis of Genetic Disease," 225 *Scientific American,* page 37, November 1971.
6. T. O. Menees, J. D. Miller, and L. E. Holly, "Amniography," 23 *Am J Roentgenol,* page 363, 1930, cited in Friedman, *op. cit. supra* at 1.
7. John Fletcher, "The Brink: The Parent-Child Bond in the Genetic Revolution," 33 *Theological Studies,* page 457, September 1972.
8. Aubrey Milunsky et al., "Prenatal Genetic Diagnosis," 283 *New Engl J Med* No. 25, page 1370, December 17, 1970; No. 26, page 1441, December 24, 1970; No. 27, page 1498,

December 31, 1970. While these articles are incomprehensible to a nonphysician, they are cited generally as the definitive analysis of the subject.

9. All discussion of risks and other medical information on amniocentesis is taken from Part I, *ibid.,* unless otherwise noted.

10. A. B. Gerbie and H. L. Nadler, "Amniocentesis in Genetic Counseling," 109 *Am J Obstet Gynecol,* page 766, 1971.

11. 1 *Brit Med J,* page 523, 1970.

12. R. MacIntyre, "Chromosome Problems and Intrauterine Diagnosis," 7 *Birth Defects* No. 5, page 11, 1971.

13. John W. Littlefield, "The Pregnancy at Risk for a Genetic Disorder," 282 *New Engl J Med* No. 11, page 627, 1970.

14. Park v. Nissen, Cal Sup Ct, Orange Co, Docket 190033, December 13, 1974, reported in 31 *Citation,* OG Counsel, AMA, No. 4, page 38, June 1, 1975.

15. E.g., Logan v. Field, 75 Mo App 594, Mo 1898; Benson v. Dean, 133 NE 125, NY 1921; "Duty to Refer Patient to Medical Specialist," 204 *JAMA* No. 8, page 281, May 20, 1968; "Referral to a Specialist," 211 *JAMA* No. 11, page 1911, March 16, 1970.

16. Manion v. Tweedy, 100 NW 2d 124, Minn 1959.

17. See, generally, "Duty to Refer to Larger Hospital," 224 *JAMA* No. 12, page 1687, June 18, 1973.

18. E.g., Reed v. Church, 8 SE 2d 285, Va 1940. For example, enormous damages were awarded against many physicians who continued to prescribe chloromycetin for minor illnesses after articles indicating that it caused aplastic anemia began to be published. See, among about forty decisions, Sharpe v. Pugh, 155 SE 2d 108, NC 1967; Mulder v. Parke-Davis Co, 181 NW 2d 882, Minn 1970; Incollingo v. Ewing, 282 A 2d 206, Pa 1971; Stottlemire v. Cawood, 213 F Supp 897, DC DC 1963; Love v. Wolfe, 58 Cal Rptr 42, Cal 1967.

19. Clark v. U.S., 402 F 2d 950, CCA 4, 1968.

20. E.g., Lundahl v. Rockford Memorial Hospital Association, 235 NE 2d 671, Ill 1968; Incollingo v. Ewing, *supra* at 18; Morgan v. Sheppard, 188 NE 2d 808, Ohio 1963; Favalora v. Aetna Casualty Co, 144 So 2d 544, La 1962.

21. E.g., Hundley v. Martinez, 158 SE 2d 159, W Va 1967 (ophthalmologist); Brune v. Belinkoff, 235 NE 2d 793, Mass 1968 (anesthesiologist); Christy v. Saliterman, 179 NW 2d 288, Minn 1970 (psychiatrist); Naccarato v. Grob, 180 NW 2d 788, Mich 1970 (pediatrician).

22. E.g., DiMartini v. Alexandria Sanitarium, 13 Cal Rptr 564, Cal 1961; Schwartz v. U.S., 226 F Supp 84, DC DC 1964; Frederic v. U.S., 246 F Supp 368, DC La 1965.

23. Friedman, *op. cit. supra* at 1, page 106.

24. *Ibid.*

25. For example, compare Canterbury v. Spence, 464 F 2d 772, CA DC 1972, in which the patient was quite functional even though in pain, with Dunham v. Wright, 423 F 2d 940, CCA 3, 1970, in which the patient would have died without surgery.

26. E.g., Gluckstein v. Lipsett, 209 P 2d 98, Cal 1949.

27. E.g., Lundberg v. Bay-View Hospital, 191 NE 2d 821, Ohio 1963. See, generally, Angela R. Holder, *Medical Malpractice Law,* New York, John Wiley and Sons, 1975, pages 80-81.

28. E.g., Valdez v. Percy, 217 P 2d 422, Cal 1950, Harvey v. Silber, 2 NW 2d 483, Mich 1942, Tessier v. U.S., 164 F Supp 779, DC Mass 1958.

29. Kern v. Kogan, 226 A 2d 186, NJ 1967; Price v. Neyland, 320 F 2d 674, CA DC 1963.

30. E.g., Thompson v. Brent, 245 So 2d 751, La 1971.

31. E.g., National Homeopathic Hospital v. Phillips, 181 F 2d 293, CA DC 1950; Redding v. U.S., 196 F Supp 871, DC Ark 1961; Callahan v. Longwood Hospital, 208 NE 2d 247, Mass 1965; Davis v. Wilson, 143 SE 2d 107, NC 1965; Mississippi Baptist Hospital v. Holmes, 55 So 2d 142, Miss 1951.

32. Most cases involving successful suits for failure to transmit laboratory reports promptly involve biopsies because delay in instituting treatment for a malignancy may literally kill the patient. See, for example, Capuano v. Jacobs, 305 NYS 2d 837, NY 1969; Jeanes v. Milner, 428 F 2d 598, CCA 8 1970; Welch v. Frisbie Memorial Hospital, 9 A 2d 761 NH 1939.

33. See Robert M. Veatch, "The Unexpected Chromosome," 2 *Hastings Center Report,* No. 1, page 8, February 1972, for a case on these facts which was presented to two ethicists. One concluded that there was no duty to disclose, the other that there was. The legal duty, however, seems clear. Further on this issue, see "Genetic Counseling," editorial, 184 *Science,* page 751, May 17, 1974.

34. For a discussion of disclosure to dying patients, see Jay Katz, *Experimentation with Human Beings,* New York, Russell Sage Foundation, 1972, pages 692–702. For an arguable connection between the dying patient and the defective child, see Willard Gaylin, editorial, 286 *New Engl J Med,* pages 1361–1362, 1972.

35. Maertins v. Kaiser Foundation Hospital, 328 P 2d 494, Cal 1958.

36. Letter, 221 *JAMA* No. 4, page 408, July 24, 1972.

37. For a general discussion of abandonment, see Holder, *op. cit. supra* at 27, Ch 12.

38. See Friedman, *op. cit. supra* at 1, page 148; John Ely, "The Wages of Crying Wolf: A Comment on Roe v. Wade," 82 *Yale Law J,* page 920, 1973.

39. *Op. cit. supra* at 36.

40. Charles J. Epstein, "Legal Implications of Recent Advances in Medical Genetics," 21 *Hastings Law J,* page 35, 1969; John W. Littlefield, "The Pregnancy at Risk for Genetic Disorder," 282 *New Engl J Med* No. 11, pages 627–628, 1970; Paul Ramsey, "Screening: An Ethicist's View," in *Ethical Issues in Human Genetics,* New York, Plenum Publishing Corp., 1973, page 157.

41. See, for example, Fletcher, *op. cit. supra* at 7.

42. For a general discussion of duress in medical treatment, see Holder, *op. cit. supra* at 27, pages 276–277.

43. E.g., Simonsen v. Swenson, 177 NW 831, Neb 1920.

44. See Friedman, *op. cit. supra* at 1, pages 115–117, editorial, 184 *Science,* page 751, May 17, 1974; Marc Lappé, "The Genetic Counselor: Responsible to Whom?" 1 *Hastings Center Report* No. 2, page 6, September 1971.

45. E.g., Pennison v. Provident Life Insurance Co., 154 So 2d 617, La 1963; Curry v. Corn, 277 NYS 2d 470, NY 1966.

46. See, for example, W. French Anderson, "Genetic Therapy," in *The New Genetics and the Future of Man,* Grand Rapids, Mich, Wm. B. Eerdmans Publishing Co., 1972.

47. National Sickle Cell Anemia Control Act, 42 USCA 300b–300b(5).

48. Friedman, *op. cit. supra* at 1, page 112.

49. E.g., Carroll v. Richardson, 110 SE 2d 193, Va 1959.

50. For a definitive discussion of disclosure, decision-making, and genetic counseling, see Alexander M. Capron, "Informed Decisionmaking in Genetic Counseling: A Dissent to the Wrongful Life Debate," 48 *Ind Law J,* page 581, 1973. This article discusses the legal, moral, and ethical aspects of failure to disclose information in the genetic counseling situation, and Capron concludes that the genetic counselor is obligated to make full disclo-

sure. Although I agree with his arguments, I feel that there are far more pragmatic and legally compelling reasons why full disclosure is necessary.

51. E.g., Battistella v. The Society of the New York Hospital, 191 NYS 2d 626, NY 1959; Riste v. General Electric Corp., 289 P 2d 338, Wash 1955; Jines v. General Electric Corp., 313 F 2d 76, CCA 9, 1962; Metropolitan Life Insurance Co. v. Evans, 184 So 426, Miss 1938.

52. E.g., Lotspeich v. Chance-Vought Aircraft Co, 369 SW 2d 705, Tex 1963.

53. E.g., Beadling v. Sirotta, 176 A 2d 546, NJ 1961; Union Carbide and Carbon Co. v. Stapleton, 237 F 2d 229, CCA 6, 1956.

54. Coffee v. McDonnell Douglas Corp., 503 P 2d 1366, Cal 1972.

55. Capron, *op. cit. supra* at 50, page 582.

56. *Ibid.,* page 589.

57. *Ibid.,* page 591.

58. E.g., Funke v. Fieldman, 512 P 2d 539, Kan 1973.

59. E.g., Woods v. Brumlop, 377 P 2d 520, NM 1962; Bowers v. Talmage, 159 So 2d 888, Fla 1963.

60. Jon R. Waltz and Carol R. Thigpen, "Genetic Screening and Counseling, the Legal and Ethical Issues," 68 *Northwestern Law Rev* No. 4, page 702, 1974.

61. See, generally, for accounts of the stigmatizing effects of screening for sickle cell anemia, Tabitha M. Powledge, "The New Ghetto Hustle," *Saturday Review,* page 38, February 1973; Phillip Reilly, "Sickle Cell Anemia Legislation": I. 1 *J Leg Med* No. 4, page 39, 5, September 1973; II. 1 *J Leg Med* No. 5, page 36, October 1973.

62. Charles F. Whitten, "Sickle Cell Programming," 288 *New Engl J Med,* page 318, 1973.

63. Reilly, *op. cit. supra* at 61, II, page 38.

64. See Powledge, *op. cit. supra* at 61; Waltz and Thigpen, *op. cit. supra* at 60, page 702.

65. See E. Hayt and J. Hayt, *Legal Aspects of Medical Records,* Berwin, Ill, Physicians' Record Co., 1964, for numerous decisions; "Legal Implications of Photographing Surgical Operations," 198 *JAMA* No. 13, page 221, December 26, 1966.

66. For an extensive discussion of these statutes and their implications, See Waltz and Thigpen, *op. cit. supra* at 60. See also Tabitha M. Powledge, "New Trends in Genetic Legislation," *Hastings Center Report,* page 6, December 1973.

67. NY Dom Rel Code, Section 13-aa.

68. Ga Code Ann, Section 88-1201.1.

69. Md Code Ann, Art 43, Section 33a(H).

70. See articles cited *supra* at 66.

71. Research Group, Institute of Society, Ethics and the Life Sciences, "Ethical and Social Issues in Screening for Genetic Disease," 286 *New Engl J Med,* pages 1129–1132, May 25, 1972.

72. *Ibid.,* page 1131. See also Marc Lappé, "Mass Genetic Screening Programs," *Medical Dimensions,* February 1973.

73. See 186 *Science,* page 715, November 22, 1974; *New York Times,* June 20, 1975, page 36c.

74. Michael Hemphill, "Pretesting for Huntington's Disease," *Hastings Center Report,* page 12, June 1973.

75. Robert F. Murray, "Problems Behind the Promise: Ethical Issues and Mass Genetic Screening," 2 *Hastings Center Report,* page 10, April 1972.

76. *Ibid.,* page 12.

77. Powledge, *op. cit. supra* at 61; Barbara Culliton, "Sickle Cell Anemia: National Program Raises Problems as Well as Hopes," 178 *Science,* page 283, October 1972.

78. *New York Times,* June 24, 1975.

79. Gerald Leach, *The Biocrats: Ethics and the New Medicine,* Baltimore, Penguin Books, 1972, pages 131–141.

80. Ernest F. Hollings, *Hunger in America,* New York, Cowles Press, 1970.

81. E.g., Joseph Fletcher, *The Ethics of Genetic Control,* New York, Anchor Press, Doubleday and Co., 1974, pages 125–126.

82. Griswold v. Connecticut, 381 US 479, 1965.

83. Eisenstadt v. Baird, 405 US 438, 1972.

84. E.g., Parker v. Rampton, 497 P 2d 848, Utah 1972; Jessin v. County of Shasta, 79 Cal Rptr 359, Cal 1969; "Voluntary Sterilization," 225 *JAMA* No. 13, page 1743, September 24, 1973; Peter Forbes, "Voluntary Sterilization of Woman as a Right," 18 *DePaul Law Rev* No. 2–3, page 560, Summer 1969; "The Right to Sterilization," 226 *JAMA* No. 9, page 1151, November 26, 1973.

85. E.g., Hathaway v. Worcester City Hospital, 475 F 2d 701, CCA 1, 1973.

86. Roe v. Wade, 410 US 113, 1973; Doe v. Bolton, 410 US 179, 1973.

87. Loving v. Virginia, 388 US 1, 1967.

88. *Ibid.,* page 12.

89. Buck v. Bell, 274 US 200, 1927.

90. Skinner v. Oklahoma, 316 US 535, 1942.

91. Cook v. Oregon, 495 P 2d 768, Ore 1972. See also In re Cavitt, 157 NW 2d 171, Neb 1968; "Compulsory Sterilization," 221 *JAMA* No. 2, page 229, July 10, 1972.

92. E.g., State ex Rel Smith v. Schaffer, 270 Pac 604, Kans 1928; In re Hendrickson, 123 P 2d 322, Wash 1942; Brewer v. Valk, 167 SE 638, NC 1933.

93. E.g., Holmes v. Powers, 439 SW 2d 579, Ky 1968; Frazier v. Levi, 440 SW 2d 393, Tex 1969; Wade v. Bethesda Hospital, 337 F Supp 671, DC Ohio 1961.

94. E.g., Mills v. Board of Education, 348 F Supp 866, DC DC 1972; Pennsylvania Association for Retarded Children v. Pennsylvania, 343 F Supp 279, DC Pa 1972.

95. Waltz and Thigpen, *op. cit. supra* at 60, pages 733 et seq.

96. E.g., Wyatt v. Stickney, 325 F Supp 781, DC Ala 1971; "The Right to Treatment," 220 *JAMA* No. 8, page 1165, May 22, 1972.

97. See cases on education of retarded children, *supra* at 94.

98. See, for example, Hymie Gordon, "Genetic Counseling," 217 *JAMA* No. 9, page 1215, August 30, 1971; Lynch et al., "Genetic Counseling," 211 *JAMA* No. 4, page 647, January 26, 1970.

99. See cases cited in "Misdiagnosis of Tuberculosis," 219 *JAMA* No. 4, page 561, January 24, 1972.

100. E.g., Gottsdanker v. Cutter Laboratories, 6 Cal Rptr 320, Cal 1960; Magee v. Wyeth Laboratories, 29 Cal Rptr 322, Cal 1963.

101. See, for example, "Liability for Mental Anguish," 217 *JAMA* No. 6, page 869, August 9, 1971.

102. Smith v. DiCara, 329 F Supp 439, DC NY 1971.

103. See the "Titticut Follies" cases, Cullen v. Grove Press, Inc., 276 F Supp 727, DC NY 1967, Massachusetts v. Wiseman, 249 NE 2d 610, Mass 1969.

104. See, on hopes for genetic therapy, "Genes Are Held Able to Cure Disease," *New York Times,* October 22, 1967, page 67, Col. 1; Theodore Friedmann and Richard Roblin, "Gene Therapy for Human Genetic Disease," 175 *Science,* page 949, March 3, 1972; Walter Eckhart, "Genetic Modification of Cells by Viruses," 21 *Bioscience,* page 171, 1971; Bernard D. David, "Prospects for Genetic Intervention in Man," 170 *Science,* page 1279, December 18, 1970; James F. Danielli, "Industry, Society and Genetic Engineering," *Hastings Center Report,* page 5, December 1972.

CHAPTER III

LEGAL ISSUES

IN FETAL

RESEARCH

If there is a more unspeakable crime than abortion itself, it is using victims of abortion as living human guinea pigs.
John, Cardinal Krol of Philadelphia[1]

The future of any society rests with its children—this truism is the foundation of our nation and deserves the highest priority of attention. Fetal research, which benefits future generations of children, will considerably enhance this objective.
Statement from the American Academy of Pediatrics to the National Commission for the Protection of Human Subjects of Biomedical and Behavioral Research[2]

As the result of the 1973 abortion decisions, an increased number of fetuses, the products of legalized abortions, have been available for research.[3] The issue of whether such research should be prohibited or permitted has rapidly come to the forefront. Prior to the legalization of elective abortions and the resulting increase in the number of fetuses, research was carried on, but most was therapeutic, at least in principle. For example, amniocentesis was largely developed as a diagnostic procedure by attempting to treat pregnant women who were at high risk of Rh disease-afflicted children. With the legalization of elective abortions, however, and the objections to the abortion decisions that exist in many segments of the population, the issues involved in fetal research began to attract public notice.[4] As a result, the act[5] that established the Commission for the Protection of Human Subjects of Biomedical and Behavioral Research mandated that the Commission was to study the issues involved in fetal research and to report to the Secretary of Health, Education and Welfare its conclusions on whether or not such research should be funded and, if so, within what limitations.[6] The enabling act also required the Secretary to impose a moratorium on all subsidies for fetal research before or after induced abortions until such time as the Commission made its report.[7] This chapter will analyze the major legal issues in this area of research and discuss the legal implications of the Commission's recommendations on the subject. It should be noted, however, that religious and ethical questions involving fetal status as a person or a nonperson undoubtedly have more effect on the political and policy contexts in which fetal research is funded by governmental agencies than does the state of the law on the subject. Since consideration of these issues is beyond the scope of this book, the reader is referred particularly to the appendix of the *Report on Fetal Research* of the Commission for the Protection of Human Subjects of Biomedical and Behavioral Research, which includes the papers of the eight ethicists who reported to the Commission on this subject.

THE LEGAL CONTEXT

As will be discussed more particularly in the chapter on abortion, the common law did not recognize abortion as a criminal offense. The first criminal abortion law was enacted in England in 1803.[8] The original statutes were primarily designed to protect the health of the mother, not the life of the infant, in view of the fact that most surgical interventions at that time resulted in fatalities. By the beginning of this century, the primary thrust of the public morality, which approved prohibition of abortion, was that it was considered murder of a human being. The law, however, rarely recognizes a fetus before viability to be a human person. Embryos that are spontaneously miscarried prior to viability are not baptized by any Christian denomination, thus indicating that theologically as well as legally early fetuses are not considered to be "children."[9]

Although the federal statute prohibited only funding of fetal research by the Department of Health, Education and Welfare, pending the conclusion of the studies undertaken by the Commission for the Protection of Human Subjects, at least 16 states have enacted statutes restricting or prohibiting experimentation on human fetuses.[10] Some of these statutes make fetal experimentation a criminal offense, and their legal and constitutional status may therefore be of critical importance for medical researchers.

It thus becomes necessary to examine the law on the subject of the rights of the unborn child prior to the current interest in fetal experimentation in order to determine the constitutionality of restrictions on such research.

Tort Law

The nearest extant analogies to questions raised in the law of fetal research are those in tort law.

At common law, injuries sustained by a fetus were not compensable. The unborn child was considered to be a part of the mother's body and in an action arising from an accident that injured both of them, she was considered the sole plaintiff.[11] In 1946, however, the District of Columbia courts upheld a right of action on behalf of a child who was seriously handicapped as the result of injuries sustained in an automobile accident while his mother was pregnant.[12] Other states followed this precedent in cases involving automobile wrecks, negligent medical care of pregnant women, and other personal injury cases. It is now clear in all jurisdictions that a living child who was injured before birth does have a cause of action against the tortfeasor who maimed him. The usual difficulty in these cases is proof of causation—that is, that the medical malpractice or the automobile accident more probably than not caused the child's handicap—since the usual defense is that the child's condition is the result of a congenital anomaly, not the alleged negligence.[13] Where the injury was inflicted fairly early in pregnancy, medical evidence of causation may be particularly difficult to pinpoint, as is also true in cases where a woman miscarries during the first half of pregnancy and attributes it to trauma caused by an accident.[14]

If, however, the child can present medical evidence to show that he would have been normal if the accident had not occurred, the elements of damage are the same as those in any other personal injury suit: present and future pain and suffering, costs of medical and other care, and loss of present and future income.[15] In the case of any personal injury action brought by a child in which it is possible to show permanent disability, loss of future income is proved by showing what a child with his native ability born to a family of his family's education and socioeconomic status would be likely to achieve in later life. For example, in identical cases brought by two three-year-olds alleging brain damage as the result of being hit by an automobile, a jury is likely to award higher damages to the child of a college professor than to the child of a welfare mother on the theory that the former would have gone on to an adult life as a professional person whereas the latter would not be predicted to do so.

Some states, beginning with a Minnesota Supreme Court decision in 1949,[16] began to interpret their Wrongful Death Statutes in such a way as to allow wrongful death actions to be brought by the families of unborn children who were killed prior to birth but at a time at which they were clearly viable, usually during the last month of pregnancy. At present, the jurisprudence in 21 states is believed by most commentators to indicate recognition of such a cause of action.[17] In some few decisions the court did maintain that a viable fetus was "a human being" but in most the issue was resolved on the question of fundamental fairness—that an automobile driver who runs into a woman who is eight and one-half months pregnant should not be allowed to reduce the judgment awarded against him by causing enough injury to kill her fetus instead of merely inflicting enough damage to cause permanent handicaps in a surviving child.[18] In most cases the decisions have been written without declaring whether or not the fetus had been a "person" at the time of death. The decisions in several of these cases posed the hypothetical question of a woman who is injured while pregnant with twins, one of whom is stillborn and the other of whom lives for five minutes after birth, in which all states would permit a wrongful death action, and concluded that to allow recovery for the death of one twin and not the other would create legal absurdities.

It should also be noted that some of the decisions cited in support of the argument that a wrongful death action is allowed for the death of a viable fetus involve malpractice suits against obstetricians or hospitals for negligence during delivery.[19] These cases usually do not in fact appear as wrongful death actions unless the allegation is made that the child was in fact "born" (i.e., the baby's body had begun to emerge from the mother's) at the time the injury occurred.[20] Most cases arising from death during delivery are actually brought with the mother as the sole plaintiff, and the fact that the child was killed is argued as an element of damage to her and as factual proof of the medical negligence involved.[21] It is obvious that although the majority of states still do not allow a wrongful death action to be brought for the death of a viable fetus, in all jurisdictions and without any determination that the unborn child is a "human being," obstetricians are liable for such lack of due skill, care, and knowledge in their treatment of their primary patient, the pregnant woman, that injury is caused to that part of *her* body known as "fetus." Referring to the wrongful death of a child during delivery in a judicial opinion upholding damages against an obstetrician in an action brought by a woman whom he negligently delivered does not mean at all that the court assumes that it is dealing with a wrongful death action on behalf of a dead child and thus arguably cannot be construed as judicial recognition of the fetus as a human being.

Death of an entirely previable embryo as the result of medical negligence is actionable, but the "damaged patient" is the mother, not the embryo. For example, there are at least 50 appellate decisions within the past 30 or 40 years in which a woman presented herself to a gynecologist with complaints of two or three missed menstrual periods. No pregnancy tests were made, and the diagnosis of fibroid tumors was given with advice to have a hysterectomy. The woman consented, the gynecologist made the incision, discovered that she was pregnant, and terminated surgery. Because of the trauma to the uterus, she miscarried and a malpractice suit resulted. Invariably courts hold that failure to make appropriate pregnancy tests is negligence, and awards of very substantial damages are common. Most of these cases involve first (or very early second) trimester pregnancies and the damages awarded are clearly awarded as compensation to the woman without any recognition of a wrongful death of a child-plaintiff or concomitant recognition of the embryo as a human being.[22]

No state in fact allows action for recovery of damages for the wrongful death of a previable fetus, but negligence that causes an early miscarriage is certainly compensable in all jurisdictions, even those that do not recognize a wrongful death action brought on behalf of a viable fetus. Thus, some legal commentators conclude incorrectly that "person" status is given the fetus in some jurisdictions as the result of decisions involving obstetrical malpractice in which it is clear that the mother was actually the sole plaintiff. On the other hand, it is fair to say that some states, including most of the 21 cited as allowing wrongful death actions specifically for a viable fetus, do consider for pleading and practice purposes that mother and child are separate legal entities, but from that, as indicated above, it may not be correct to conclude that the courts indicate their belief that the fetus is a human being.

Since most states still do not allow wrongful death actions in this context, it should be observed that most of them do not refuse to do so on the grounds that the viable fetus is not a "person." They refuse to do so primarily because the elements of damage in this situation are considered too difficult to prove and too speculative for a jury to make a monetary determination.[23] Since the usual elements of damage in a usual wrongful death case include medical expenses, conscious pain and suffering between the time of the accident and the time of death, and economic loss (i.e., estimated future earnings), it is interesting to note that none of the 21 decisions commonly cited as allowing a wrongful death action on behalf of a viable fetus discussed the courts' concepts of what elements of damage should be considered. In each case the court held that the cause of action existed and remanded the case to the trial court for further determination, thus neatly placing the critical issues back on the shoulders of the trial judges.

Since a normal child who is killed, no matter how young, has in most cases been evaluated as mentally and physically normal before the accident that killed him and since there can even be medical evidence that a neonate who died a few hours or days after birth had normal responses to standard tests, it is possible to argue to a jury quite sensibly about general aspects of the deceased child's probable earning potential. Furthermore, when a child dies at any time after live birth, there are easily demonstrable medical and burial expenses that are clearly attributable to his care and death and not as part of medical services that would have been given in any case to his mother during delivery. For example, even if a child lives only briefly after birth, there is normally a bill from a pediatrician as well as from the obstetrician, and the hospital bill usually reflects his admission to the nursery.

Pain and suffering damages are enormously difficult to ascertain in any newborn patient, whether or not the child survives, because pain and suffering damages in any tort case are linked to "conscious awareness," which is virtually impossible to prove even with a full-term normal newborn. Similarly, in wrongful death cases involving an adult or older child who received head injuries and thus was in a coma from impact until death, or in a cardiac arrest case when the patient was under anesthesia and hence died without regaining consciousness, plaintiffs' attorneys are wont to submit evidence of any noise or motion, however feeble, as proof of "suffering" in the sense of conscious awareness of pain. Without such proof these damages, which customarily are the biggest portion of the award in a personal injury case, are denied.[24]

The only decision that can be located involving determination of the allowability of pain and suffering damages to a normal newborn is a 1972 California decision.

A healthy newborn child contracted a salmonella infection in the hospital nursery and did not make a complete recovery until she was almost one year old. Her parents sued the hospital on her behalf alleging that there had been negligence in the hospital nursery, and in addition to the cost of her treatment for the infection, they asked for damages for her pain and suffering. The trial court refused to allow them to argue the point, and after two appeals the supreme court of the state held that it was a valid claim. However, the decision indicated that the evidence properly submitted to the jury would be the testimony of the baby's mother about the number of times the child obviously had stomach pains and screamed for hours and contorted herself as if she had colic, and this evidence exclusively involved testimony describing the baby's condition from the time she came home from the hospital at about six weeks until she was almost one year old. No evidence at all was submitted about conscious awareness of pain during the first weeks of her life.[25]

As any mother who accidentally sticks a one-month-old child with a diaper pin becomes abundantly aware, babies do feel pain, but since newborn boys are circumcised without anesthesia and apparently are unaware of pain during the procedure, proof of pain and suffering damages on behalf of a child who either dies at birth or is injured but recovers within a week or so is usually impossible. For example, suits on behalf of babies who are dropped onto delivery-room floors but sustain no long-term harm from the experience generally are dismissed.[26]

Thus, it is not at all clear what elements of damage exist in a wrongful death case brought on behalf of a viable fetus killed in utero and, from the parents' point of view, having a cause of action in theory but being unable to establish proof of any damage in practice would seem to be a Pyrrhic victory. It is unlikely that courts would agree that an unborn child is consciously aware of anything, including pain, since they normally do not agree that a newborn is. Since there is no means by which to determine that the child's mental development or reflexes are normal if it is dead on delivery and the Apgar tests cannot be given, it is virtually impossible to counter a defense argument that the child might have been born with congenital mental or neurological problems, and if the child is born dead there are no medical or funeral expenses.

The only decision that can be located involving the elements and measure of damages in a prenatal wrongful death case is *Panagopoulous v. Martin.* [27] That decision, arising from an automobile wreck, involved interpretation of West Virginia's very unusual wrongful death statute, which provides for award of general damages up to $10,000 without proof of any specific pecuniary loss. In holding that the parents of a dead fetus could recover that amount but only that amount, the federal district court said:

> In awarding the initial $10,000, the jury may properly consider as elements of damage the grief and mental distress of a parent on account of the loss of a child or "the sorrow, the mental distress and bereavement of a relative."

However, as to the parents' claim of specific pecuniary loss, the court held that no award could be made because of the "virtual impossibility of knowing or being able to ascertain the child's potential capacity, physical and mental."

Since this discussion indicated that it is the parents' mental pain that is compensated, not the fetus's, it is appropriate to note that if a pregnant woman is injured and miscarries at any stage of pregnancy, an element of her own damages is her mental anguish at the loss of her baby in addition to the physical harm she sustained, so as a very practical matter those courts that are awarding damages in prenatal wrongful death actions are apparently awarding the same damages pregnant women could always recover, albeit affixing a new label. This question could make a decisive difference in a case in which a pregnant woman was injured and remained unconscious until she died, hence never having any mental anguish damages of her own, and the dead fetus's father brought two separate wrongful death actions against the tortfeasor, but in most cases it does not appear that any new cause of action has been created simply because it is now called prenatal wrongful death. Those commentators who claim that recognition of a viable fetus in tort law indicates that the courts have declared fetuses to be human persons and that this may be applied to the fetal research context are not particularly alert to what these decisions actually have said.

The validity of drawing a connection between prenatal rights in tort law and the legal and ethical issues inherent in fetal research thus appears open to serious question.

Wills, Trusts, and Estates

Some legal commentators believe that the inheritance and property rights given to an unborn child indicate that our legal system recognizes the human fetus as a person and that a logical connection can thus be made between that status and issues in fetal research. These writers usually note the following passage from Blackstone's *Commentaries:*

> The right of personal security consists in a person's legal and unin-
> terrupted enjoyment of his life, his limbs, his body, his health, his
> reputation. Life is the immediate Gift of God, a right inherent by
> nature in every individual; and it begins in contemplation of law as
> soon as an infant is able to stir in the mother's womb. . . . An infant
> *en ventre sa mere* is supposed in law to be born for many purposes.
> It is capable of having a legacy or surrender of a copyhold estate
> made to it. It may have a guardian assigned to it and it is enabled
> to have an estate limited to its use and to take afterwards by such
> limitations as if it were actually then born.[28]

Although a child *en ventre sa mere* may, of course, inherit from a testator or become the beneficiary of a trust, it should be noted that because of the peculiar constructions applied to "afterborn" children in Wills and Estates law and in interpretation of trust instruments, this does not necessarily indicate that the law holds a fetus to be a person.

It is, of course, clear that the word "children" as used in a Will may apply to those born after drafting of the will, including both those born before the testator's death and posthumous children. However, it has been also held, for example, that a bequest which read "that in the event of my said wife having any child or children at the time of her death, I devise and bequeath the whole of said estate to such child or children" is not confined to the children of the then present marriage but includes any children the wife may have had by a second marriage after the testator's death.[29] It is clear that under basic princi-ples of inheritance law a child who is not conceived at the time of the testator's death may inherit under a Will. The entire Rule Against Perpetuities discussed in Chapter I, after all, is predicated on the assumption that "the life in being plus 21 years" may involve a vesting of the interest in an inheritance during those 21 years in someone who was not conceived at the time the testator died.[30]

It is extremely common, for example, for Wills that dispose of large estates to provide for bequests to the children of a testator's very young grandchildren as a remainder interest to a life estate vested in his wife, the existing children's grandmother. This approach, if the testator's children are also wealthy and do not need the money for themselves or the existing grandchildren, means that the number of times the estate funds pass through probate proceedings and thus are subject to inheritance tax levies is materially decreased. Thus A, in his 60s at the time he dies, may have a child B, in his 40s, who may be the parent of C, aged 10. A's Will leaving a bequest to his own wife for her life and, upon her death, to C's children, is perfectly valid. Thus, in order to make a logical analysis that probate law which recognizes an unborn child as capable of inheritance provides a context for concluding that a fetus is invested with personhood in the fetal research situation, one must ignore the fact that C's children may not be conceived for 25 years after A's death and that C in fact may never have any children.

Trust law also recognizes the right of an unborn child to be a trust beneficiary but, before assuming that this means that trust law recognizes the unborn fetus as a person, it should be pointed out that a child unconceived at the time the trust was drawn may also have, at birth, a vested interest in the corpus. Scott, in his treatise on *Trusts* discusses at length the rights as beneficiary of a child who is not conceived at the time a trust is created, and points out that "it is not essential that the beneficiaries of a trust should be in existence at the time of the creation of the trust."[31] He notes that it is common in testamentary trusts to provide for children who are not conceived at the time of the death of the testator and indicates that such trusts are undoubtedly valid. If the children are born later they are entitled to enforce that provision of the trust. This is true to the extent that *before* any children are conceived the trust could not be revoked by the settlor at common law even with the consent of the other, existing beneficiaries. Scott also points out that where an unconceived child is the sole beneficiary of a trust, it would seem that as long as there is a possibility that a child may be born the trust cannot be extinguished. Since the child who is not conceived has the same rights in trust and estate law as an existing fetus, it does not seem to be proved that the latter is recognized as a human person in this legal context. Further, it should also be noted that a corporation that has not yet been organized may also be the beneficiary of a trust.[32]

The unborn child's right to inherit is generally considered one of the cornerstones of the arguments of those who claim that such a right indicates legal recognition of the personhood of the fetus, but unless and until a fetus-in-being is distinguished in this context from a nonexistent person who is not yet conceived, it is hard to justify any analogy to or restrictions on fetal research on this basis.

David W. Louisell, who is a member of the Commission for the Protection of Human Subjects, has suggested that in property law the presence of live-born children before the courts in litigation of all property cases originally involving their prenatal interests was merely a "happenstance of litigation" and that judicial observations that the child must be born alive for its property interest to vest appears to him to be "superfluous."[33] Louisell seems to have overlooked the fact that an unconceived child also has inchoate rights in many estates and that the fact that live birth is required for a vested interest to be established is discussed in *Roe v. Wade,* the first of the two Supreme Court abortion decisions.

Welfare Law

The Supreme Court of the United States has recently held that a state does not have to provide AFDC (Aid to Families with Dependent Children) payments to pregnant women for their unborn children, and that the child must be born alive in order to be registered for welfare payments unless the state voluntarily assumes this obligation to unborn children.[34] The opinion states that even though a child might qualify at birth for AFDC benefits these women are not entitled to benefits because the Court found that the statutory term "dependent child" does not include unborn children. The opinion stated:

> Our analysis of the Social Security Act does not support a conclusion that the legislative definition of "dependent child" includes unborn children. Following the axiom that words used in a statute are to be given their ordinary meaning in the absence of persuasive reasons to the contrary and reading the definition of "dependent child" in its statutory context, we conclude that Congress used the word "child" to refer to an individual already born with an existence separate from its mother.

It would thus appear that Congress, as well as the Supreme Court in the abortion decisions, does not intend to offer recognition of personhood to a fetus.

Criminal Law

Whereas most of the criminal laws relating to feticide were swept away by the abortion decisions, two situations may still arise imposing criminal liability for actions toward an unborn child.

On July 14, 1975, a man was convicted of murder in the deaths of twin fetuses.[35] He had shot their mother in the abdomen while burglarizing her house. She was seven months and one week pregnant at the time. When she was taken to the hospital her condition required surgery, and the twins were delivered by emergency Caesarian section before her wounds could be treated. Both babies were born alive and died between 12 and 24 hours later. It should be noted that (1) unlike an abortion, the mother did not consent to the assault on her body and (2) the defendant was tried and convicted under the murder statute, not the feticide statute, since the twins were viable and born alive and were thus as entitled to protection from murder as their mother. It is highly unlikely that the same action directed to a woman who was two or three months pregnant could result in any criminal liability except for the assault on her. In all states, as has been noted, a civil action for wrongful death would also be appropriate in that situation.

Second, nonphysicians who perform abortions are still subject to criminal prosecution.[36] This is not, however, designed to show a state's concern for the personhood of the fetus; it is to protect the woman's health. Practicing medicine without a license is clearly within the state's police power to prohibit as a public health measure. Performing abortions is clearly practicing medicine, and nonphysicians who do it are prosecuted to the same extent and under the same statutes as they would be if they attempted to remove an appendix.

Thus, it appears that to look to the common law for guidance in determining the status of a fetus either indicates that the fetus is not a human person in these contexts or that the other areas of law are totally irrelevant in determining what the law of fetal research should be.

Whether or not a society wishes to provide money for various forms of research is not entirely a legal question, and ethical and theological rationales are also an appropriate basis on which the public may make its decision on financial support of research projects of any kind. Therefore, because the law in different contexts does not recognize a fetus as a person does not mean that in the context of policymaking on publicly supported research there may not be a valid objection to fetal research.

There is certainly no constitutional right to federal funds for a given medical research project, and it should be remembered that what the Commission for the Protection of Human Subjects was mandated to study was whether Department of Health, Education and Welfare funds were to be used for research on fetuses that were to be or had been aborted. Thus, in determination of funding policy, nonlegal considerations such as the opinions of various ethicists are entitled to great weight. On the other hand, as will be seen below, some of the state statutes prohibiting fetal research make the practice a criminal offense and provide jail sentences for violation. In that context, when one man's ethics become another man's prison term, such statutes must necessarily be construed as strictly as possible in favor of the researcher charged with violation, and must be justified purely in the legal context. In the determination of the constitutionality of the criminal statutes enacted by states forbidding fetal research, it does seem relevant to point out the lack of recognition of personhood of fetuses in other areas of the law, because if a fetus is not a person, to forbid research by imposing a criminal penalty would appear to exceed the permitted limits of a state's police power.

The medical community has vigorously argued that fetal research is, in principle, ethical. An editorial in the *American Journal of Diseases of Children,* for example, called on pediatricians to object to any restrictions and cited numerous examples of fetal research that has benefited living children, including those who received liver and thymus transplants with fetuses as the donors of the organs.[37]

The *Journal of the American Medical Association*[38] recently included a commentary stating:

As individuals we see many more reasons to aim our expressions of moral indignation and requests for action at human policies or perhaps the lack of human policies, that have resulted in the births of many infants who will live as cripples, or in an overpopulated environment, partially or wholly destroyed by many types of pollution, infants who will live to die of starvation, neglect, or the calamities of war or other violence, than we see reasons to aim them at responsibly and properly conducted abortus research.

Frequent references to "powerful forces that opposed Galileo" and the Scopes trial can also be found.[39]

The Commission for the Protection of Human Subjects invited eight noted ethicists to report their views on the ethical aspects of fetal research. In each case the issues were joined on the question of the nature of fetal life. Is the fetus a human being or is it not? If one assumes that a fetus—whether viable or nonviable, ex utero or in utero—is a human being, then the further conclusion must inevitably be drawn that fetal research above and beyond that which can be done on a child or on a newborn infant is unethical. On the other hand, if one denies that a fetus, at least prior to viability, is a human being, then it is arguable that experimentation that should be prohibited on newborn infants or older children might be permitted if performed on a fetus. The ethicists involved in the Commission's studies ranged along the entire spectrum of opinion and, in many ways, never agreed on an answer to the basic question. A survey of the positions taken by the ethicists indicates that there were substantial differences of opinion on virtually all aspects of the question.[40]

THE MEDICAL CONTEXT

Prior to making its recommendation, the Commission investigated the nature, extent, and purposes of research on the fetus within the last ten years.[41] Research on the fetus fell into four general categories:

1. Assessment of fetal growth and development in utero, including anatomic studies of the dead fetus, assessment of fetal physiology in utero, and studies of organs and tissues removed from the dead fetus. Studies were also made on the development of fetal behavior, such as fetal breathing, hearing, and vision.
2. Diagnosis of fetal disease or abnormalities including research on amniocentesis, which was first done on pregnant women at risk for Rh disease babies. Current research on prenatal diagnosis involves the chance to extend existing diagnostic capabilities to additional diseases and provide alternatives for amniocentesis and further the development of fetoscopy.

Research has also been directed at the identification of physical defects in the developing fetus and the assessment of fetal longevity.

3. The third area of research was fetal pharmacology and drug therapy, such as the influence of oral contraceptives, analgesics, and other drugs given to the pregnant woman for therapeutic or research reasons. Antibiotics and similar drugs were also tested, as well as live attenuated virus vaccines.

4. The amount of research involving nonviable fetuses ex utero was very small and usually included the nonviable fetus at the extreme end of the spectrum of studies of premature infants in research designed to develop a life-support system for sustaining small babies.

One experiment, the one most frequently cited by opponents to fetal research, involved decapitation of eight fetuses of from 12 to 17 weeks gestation to discover whether or not the brains could metabolize ketone bodies, but it should be remembered that this study was not conducted in the United States. Of the 3,000 projects involving fetal research which the Commission's experts located, the reports of research on the nonviable fetus ex utero numbered less than 20. The researchers concluded that the amount of research conducted on the nonviable fetus has been extremely limited.

Another question that arose was whether or not alternative means for achieving the purposes for which the fetal research had been undertaken could have been established. A second medical study reported to the Commission on fetal research during the development of rubella vaccine, the use of amniocentesis for prenatal diagnosis of genetic defects, the diagnosis, treatment, and prevention of Rh disease, and the management of Respiratory Distress Syndrome. In the case of the development of rubella vaccine, no research on the living human fetus was required for its development, but it was necessary to do fetal research to determine whether or not it was safe to vaccinate a woman who was or might be pregnant. The only alternative to fetal research would have been to wait for the accidental vaccinations of pregnant women and observe the outcome, which, of course, would have taken much longer. Since it was eventually discovered that there was serious damage to the fetus following vaccination, contrary to the results of the earlier primate research, the result of the research is that pregnant women or women who might become pregnant within 60 days of vaccination are no longer given the serum.

Amniocentesis, which is an extremely important diagnostic tool in prenatal diagnosis of genetic disease and treatment of Rh disease, was, of course, first performed on women who planned to abort.

The report indicated that it is very difficult, if not impossible, to develop procedures of this nature on animals because of the physiological and anatomical differences between them and humans. Rh disease research using amniocentesis was done on fetuses after treatment of affected newborns was begun in 1945. By 1963, treatment of severely Rh affected fetuses by intrauterine blood transfusion was initiated, resulting in a 60 percent reduction of the stillbirth rate for Rh affected infants. All significant research on the fetus related to Rh disease was conducted on mothers and fetuses at risk for the disease, thus these studies can be categorized as therapeutic research.

In studying Respiratory Distress Syndrome, the most common cause of death in premature infants, the earliest studies included autopsies of the lungs of babies who had died of the disease. Biochemical studies followed and clinical trials of various therapies were initiated in pregnant women at risk of having infants with the disease.

The study for the Commission arrived at the following conclusions:

1. Animal models were utilized extensively in the early stages of research, but adequate and appropriate models were not always available when needed.

2. Investigators generally proceeded to clinical trials characterized by very high ratios of benefit to risk.

3. A total ban on all fetal research would probably have significantly delayed or halted indefinitely the progress in three of four areas that were analyzed, and only development of the rubella vaccine could have progressed unimpeded.

Thus, whether one thinks fetal research is ethical, there is no question that it has been enormously useful in lowering the death rates of premature infants and preventing severe deformity or death in children with many diseases.

THE STATE LAW CONTEXT

Research Involving the Fetus After Death

The Uniform Anatomical Gift Act has been adopted in all 50 states and the District of Columbia. Research on a dead fetus would presumably be covered by this act, since a "decedent" under the act is defined to include a stillborn infant or fetus.[42] The statute requires consent by either parent to anatomical research on a fetus or child but further specifies that a person may not make an anatomical gift if she or he "has actual notice of opposition by the member of the same or similar or prior class, nor shall a donee accept a gift under these circumstances."[43] Thus, the other parent has a clear right to veto the donation.

It should be noted that this section of the statute has been interpreted only in regard to a donation of the body of an adult decedent, Grace Metalious, who wrote *Peyton Place*.

Mrs. Metalious left instructions in her Will that she did not want any form of funeral service and that she wanted her body donated to either Dartmouth or Harvard Medical School. Her widower and children sought to have those portions of the Will invalidated, and both medical schools voluntarily declined to accept her body in view of the objections. Further litigation involved a suit by the widower against the Executor to force him to have a funeral. The court held that the instructions in the Will should have been carried out in preference to the opposing wishes of the survivors but by the time the decision was made, the body had been buried for a year.[44]

Where consent to donation of the fetus's body has been given by one parent, although the other is clearly empowered to stop the donation, there does not appear to be an obligation to make positive inquiries of the other parent if no objection is heard, since the statute presumes that a gift is valid in the absence of actual notice to the contrary.[45] It is clear, however, that the parent, not the abortionist, is the person to give permission for the study of a dead fetus. Several comments on fetal research indicate that it is not the customary practice to ask women for permission for anatomical studies on their dead fetuses, but it does seem to be a clear legal duty.

Several states, in the wake of increasing political hostility to fetal experimentation, passed statutes specifically involving fetal remains, fetal tissue, and dead fetuses:

1. Indiana: The Indiana statutes prohibit experiments except "pathological examinations" on any aborted fetus and further prohibit "exploitation of or experimentation with" aborted tissue. Further, shipment of fetal remains out of state for experimentation is prohibited.[46]
2. Illinois: The Illinois statute requires pathological examination of all aborted tissue and prohibits "exploitation of or experimentation with" such tissue.[47] This statute would appear to prohibit experimentation on dead fetuses but not living fetuses.
3. Massachusetts: The Massachusetts statute permits experimentation on a dead fetus with the mother's consent but waives consent for "routine pathological study."[48] This would appear to abrogate the father's right to object under the Uniform Anatomical Gift Act consent provisions.
4. Ohio: The Ohio statute bans fetal experimentation ex utero without regard to whether the fetus is alive or dead but does permit authorized autopsies.[49]
5. South Dakota: The South Dakota statute requires maternal consent but apparently does not prohibit any form of experimentation as long as

consent is given by the mother.[50] This, like the Massachusetts statute, appears to abrogate the father's consent rights under the Uniform Anatomical Gift Act.

6.   California and Minnesota: These statutes specifically exempt experimentation on fetal remains in their fetal research statutes.[51,52]

There appear to be serious constitutional questions of equal protection of the laws under the Fourteenth Amendment involved in any statute that gives to the body or tissue of a dead fetus a sanctity that does not apply to the body of a dead adult. Thus, if a woman wished to consent to experimentation on her dead fetus and was prohibited by state law from doing so, if she could validly consent to such experimentation on the body of her dead husband, it would appear that a good case could be made for the allegation that she has been denied a right.

Most of these statutes clearly and explicitly apply only to fetuses that are the products of induced abortions and have nothing to do with the products of spontaneous miscarriages. This would also appear to be unconstitutional since it discriminates among fetuses of the same class—that is, the same gestational age—on the basis of the method by which the fetus was extracted from the mother. Since abortion is legal, any attempt to interfere with the woman's right to privacy in any areas of the abortion context would seem to be subject to the requirement of a showing by the state of compelling interest in regulation of such matters. It is impossible to envision any rational basis on which a state could claim that under its powers to protect public health it has a compelling interest in prohibiting experimentation on the bodies of some dead fetuses but not others. A mother who wished to allow research on the body of her dead fetus could thus conceivably have grounds for a valid constitutional attack on a statute that prohibited it. The likelihood of such an attack, however, is remote because it is unlikely that any woman who has decided to have an abortion would delay the procedure while she obtains a court order holding a fetal research statute unconstitutional.

"Grave robbing" statutes in some states may also make performance of an unauthorized autopsy a criminal offense. In Boston a grand jury has indicted four physicians from Boston City Hospital for allegedly violating an 1814 Massachusetts statute when they studied fetal remains after the mothers had taken an antibiotic in anticipation of their abortions.[53] The mothers had consented to the experiments, but the indictment charged that they had not consented to postmortem examination of the fetuses.

It would appear that normal rules of civil liability that apply to autopsies would also prohibit unauthorized examination of fetal remains without the consent of the parents. Under normal principles of common law, unless there is some statutory justification such as suspicion of foul play, a cause of action exists against both the coroner who orders and the physician who performs an autopsy without the consent of the next of kin of the deceased.[54] The next of kin both under our law and under the early common law of England has a right of possession of any corpse in order to "afford it decent burial,"[55] and thus any interference with the right of possession of a corpse is also an interference with the rights of the next of kin.[56] Many decisions have held that parents must consent to an autopsy on their child.

Thus, the normal common-law rules, in addition to the provisions of the Uniform Anatomical Gift Act, indicate that maternal permission should always be obtained before an examination (much less experimentation) is undertaken of the body of a dead fetus in order to prevent suits against the physicians involved as well as charges of violations of criminal statutes. As far as can be determined, no civil action has ever been filed against physicians who experimented on or examined bodies of dead fetuses, even though the mothers did not consent prior to performance of the abortion. Presumably, if a woman were interested enough to inquire as to the disposition of the fetal remains and discovered that such examinations had been made without her consent, the physician would be liable if she brought an action against him.

Research Involving the Living Fetus

Since the abortion decisions of the Supreme Court, at least 16 states have enacted laws that restrict experimentation on live fetuses:

1. California: California statutes prohibit experimentation on "any aborted product of human conception" but exempts experimentation to protect or preserve the life of the fetus.[57]

2. Illinois: The Illinois statute prohibits research on dead fetuses but apparently not on living ones.[58]

3. Kentucky: The sale or transfer of any "live or viable aborted child" for purposes of experimentation is prohibited, and whoever consents for such a "child" to be used (presumably the mother) is equally guilty of a criminal offense with the person who performs the experiment.[59] There is no exception for therapeutic research. Research in utero is not mentioned.

4. Louisiana: The Louisiana statute forbids *any* human experimentation without the consent of the subject, and nontherapeutic research in utero is also prohibited.[60] The penalties for violation range from a minimum of five years to a maximum of twenty at hard labor. Due to the extraordinary wording of this statute, this penalty could apparently be enforced in any experimental situation.

5. Maine: The Maine statute forbids experimentation ex utero or in utero on "any live born product of conception" (which would, of course, include adults) and does not provide for consent of the subject.[61] Thus, if the statute is read literally, any medical research—therapeutic as well as nontherapeutic—is now illegal in Maine.

6. Massachusetts: The Massachusetts statute provides that live fetuses in utero and ex utero may not be used for experimentation with the exception of "procedures incident to the study" of the fetus in utero if (a) such study will not jeopardize the health of the fetus and (b) it is not the subject of a planned abortion. Procedures therapeutic for either mother or fetus are specifically allowed.[62] Obviously, consent to experimentation can be obtained and "then" the woman can "suddenly" decide to have an abortion, and the statute will technically not be violated.

7. Minnesota: The Minnesota statute permits "harmless" experimentation on a human conceptus, defined as a human organism from fertilization through 265 days thereafter, whether conceived inside or outside the body.[63] Experimentation that is not "harmless" is not prohibited if it is to protect the life or health of the conceptus. This statute is the only one, federal or state, that would appear to apply to in vitro experimentation.

8. Missouri: The Missouri statute forbids in utero or ex utero experimentation on aborted fetuses except experiments to preserve the life of a premature infant.[64]

9. Montana: The Montana statute does not mention research in utero but prohibits nontherapeutic research on "premature infants born alive."[65]

10. Nebraska: The sale or transfer of a live or viable "aborted child" for purposes of experimentation is prohibited, and anyone who consents to such a transfer is guilty of a criminal offense.[66] The experimentation itself is not prohibited and thus would presumably be legal if the mother did *not* consent.

11. New York: There is no experimentation statute in New York, but the public health law states that a "viable child" which results from an abortion is accorded immediate legal protection.[67] This would appear to be superfluous legislation since any viable newborn is a "person" under the common law.

12. Ohio: The Ohio statute forbids any "experimentation on or sale of an aborted product of human conception."[68] In utero experimentation is not regulated.

13. Pennsylvania: The Pennsylvania statute does not mention in utero research but prohibits nontherapeutic research on "premature infants born alive."[69]

14. South Dakota: The South Dakota statute permits any experimentation as long as written consent is obtained from the mother.[70]

15. Utah: The Utah statute appears to prohibit in utero research, and in abortions of viable fetuses, the procedure least detrimental to the welfare of the fetus must be used.[71]

16. Indiana: The Indiana statutes prohibit any experimentation in connection with aborted fetuses except "pathological examination."[72]

The statutes that contain restrictions on experimentation with fetuses resulting from induced abortions, but that do not prohibit the same research on the products of spontaneous abortion would presumably be subject to the same constitutional objections as would apparently be raised by the statutes involving disposition of fetal remains.

As is demonstrated by *Brown v. Board of Education,* although a state may, under the Fourteenth Amendment, classify citizens into groups for some reasonable purposes (e.g., child labor laws), discrimination among members of the *same* class of the population is subject to "strict scrutiny" tests and therefore highly unlikely to be upheld by any court.[73] For example, it is unconstitutional to discriminate in distribution of educational resources on the basis of mental ability.[74] Any laws that divide children into groups and enact special statutes for each group of children are in most cases subject to a finding of unconstitutionality.

Assuming that those charged with arguing that one of these statutes should be upheld as constitutional are prepared to argue that fetuses are in fact "children" (and if they are not, there is no reason for the statute), it is unlikely that a statute which prohibits a physician from performing an experiment on an aborted fetus but which does not involve any restriction on experimentation that may be carried out on the product of a spontaneous abortion would be upheld as constitutional. Since the Supreme Court decisions have made the abortions themselves legal, it would appear that there is no legal justification that would withstand an "equal protection" argument in an attempt to attach criminal penalties to subsequent research done on a fetus simply because it is the product of a legal abortion and not a spontaneous miscarriage.

Second, in seven states the statute explicitly permits research that is intended to "preserve the life or health" of the fetus,[75] which would be basic, good medical practice if the fetus is at a stage where there is some purpose in attempting to preserve its life and health, since a *viable* fetus that is the result of an abortion is subject to the same legal protections as those that would apply to a premature infant. In fact, serious questions involving manslaughter would be raised by failure to treat a viable fetus, even in the absence of such a statute.

A literal reading of five other statutes indicates that they *prohibit* livesaving research on a viable fetus and would therefore presumably be subject to attack on the ground that they require commission of manslaughter by omission, thus conflicting with child abuse laws.[76]

Another objection to these statutes is the First Amendment right of religious freedom. Since the differentiation is made in most statutes between a fetus that is the result of a spontaneous abortion and a fetus that is the result of an induced abortion, the state would find it difficult to argue that moral or religious objections to abortions were not the fundamental rationale behind the legislation. That being the case, to impose restrictions on a woman's right to consent to fetal research or on a physician's right to perform experiments, if neither one in good conscience finds it repugnant to their religious beliefs, might be the subject of serious constitutional attack on the grounds of "establishment of religion." All four school prayer cases that prohibited sectarian religious advocacy in public schools indicated that a parent had a right of privacy in determining matters of religion, conscience and morality in his relationship to his child, and that even if he disagreed with the majority religious position in his community, he still had the right to freedom of religious conscience and the freedom of untrammeled privacy in the moral education of his children.[77]

Assume the following hypothetical situation: A woman, after careful consideration of alternatives, decides that an abortion is a less detrimental alternative than giving birth to a child she is carrying. Assume further that her decision is made because she has had amniocentesis and knows that her child suffers from Down's syndrome. She decides that the most moral act that she can perform is to abort the child. She does not, however, wish to destroy in vain her child, whom she believes to be a living human person. Therefore, because of her religious and moral beliefs, she seeks to have the abortion performed at an institution where the fetus can be used for research purposes in order that some other woman's mongoloid child might have a better chance for normal life. Assume that at this point she is told that under the state's law, research on an aborted fetus is prohibited. If she brought a suit to have the statute declared unconstitutional as in being in violation of her religious beliefs, she might have an excellent case. A suit of this nature is actually not improbable at some point since there are a great many women who do have abortions on this ground after careful consideration and consultation with their physicians and ministers. Such an infringement on the woman's beliefs would appear to place the burden of proof that the restrictions are proper on the state. Since these statutes differentiate not on the basis of fetal age or other universal criteria but on the basis of the nature of the process by which the fetus was expelled from the mother, it would appear that they might be open to attack on First Amendment grounds.

Amendment of these statutes to provide for a total ban on fetal research without regard to the nature of the process by which the fetus was "born" would eliminate equal protection problems as well as First Amendment problems, since presumably the state would argue that it was necessary in order to protect the health of its citizens, the fetuses. At that point, a pregnant woman who had a history of spontaneous miscarriages and who wished to have in utero research performed to determine why she could not have children would presumably have good reason to argue that such a comprehensive statute would deprive her of her rights to privacy within the physician-patient relationship and be an unconstitutional ban on the legitimate practice of medicine.

Thus, there are serious constitutional objections to state statutes that discriminate between aborted fetuses and nonaborted fetuses or even in instances in which they might apply to all fetuses where there are therapeutic indications for performance of the research. It does, however, appear that a statute banning all nontherapeutic fetal research might be upheld as constitutional.

THE POLITICAL CONTEXT

Prior to the Supreme Court's abortion decisions, which opened the floodgates for public concern and proposals for restriction on fetal research in this country, the issue arose in Great Britain. In May 1972 a committee chaired by Sir John Peel, a Fellow of the Royal College of Obstetrics and Gynecology, presented to the government recommendations on "the use of fetuses and fetal material for research." The Peel report stated that a fetus of a gestational age of over 20 weeks would be regarded as viable for purposes of research policies, and that research on such a fetus was prohibited unless "consistent with treatment necessary to promote life." Experimentation on an intact, previable fetus was permitted only if it weighed less than 300 grams, and the report defined a previable fetus as one that shows "some, but not all, signs of life." The Peel report also stated that in the view of that committee, it was unethical for a medical practitioner to administer drugs or to carry out any procedures on a pregnant woman with the deliberate intent of ascertaining the harm that this might do to the fetus, even if arrangements might have been made to terminate the pregnancy. This report appears to be the guideline applicable in Great Britain today.[78]

Early in 1973, shortly after the Supreme Court's abortion decisions were handed down, the *OBGYN News* published a report on fetal research that created a public uproar. By April 1973, newspapers reported that the National Institutes of Health was preparing guidelines for fetal research. Protests from Washington area Roman Catholic school students resulted.

On June 7, 1973, the *New England Journal of Medicine* published an article reporting the findings derived from fetal research at Boston City Hospital on the passage of antibiotics across the placental barrier. As the result of the investigations by the Boston district attorney after reading the article, Kenneth Edelin was arrested for manslaughter and four other physicians were charged with violations of the "grave-robbing" statute, thus escalating hostilities between the medical community and the antiresearch groups.[79]

Soon after the episode in Boston, the National Institutes of Health proposed guidelines on fetal research that were published in the *Federal Register,* causing further objections. As a result, Senator Edward Kennedy began holding hearings on fetal research.

When the controversy was debated in Congress, Representative Angelo Roncallo of New York cosponsored a constitutional amendment proposal that would make abortion illegal. He also introduced a bill that would make it a crime to do research in federally supported facilities on fetuses ex utero whose hearts are still beating. He succeeded in attaching a rider to that effect to the National Science Foundation funding Bill, which was approved by the House.[80]

In September 1973, however, Senator Kennedy had the Roncallo amendment rewritten to eliminate the total ban on fetal research and to call for study by a national commission. Senator James Buckley of New York moved to restore the ban as a permanent one and broaden its prohibitions to cover experimentation "on a living human fetus or infant whether before or after induced abortion unless for the purposes of insuring the survivability of that fetus or infant." Senator Kennedy, however, gathered 53 votes (to 35) to make the ban effective only until the proposed commission would report. The Kennedy rider was then approved 88 to 0.[81]

Public Law 93-348 was signed by President Nixon on July 12, 1974. In addition to establishing the National Commission for the Protection of Human Subjects of Biomedical and Behavioral Research, the Commission was directed as follows:

> The Commission shall conduct an investigation and study of the nature and extent of research involving living fetuses, the purposes for which such research has been undertaken and alternative means for achieving such purposes. The Commission shall, not later than the expiration of the four month period beginning on the 1st day of the 1st month that follows the date on which all the members of the Commission have taken office, recommend to the Secretary policies defining the circumstances (if any) under which such research may be conducted or supported.[82]

The same act provides:

> Until the Commission has made its recommendations to the Secretary pursuant to Section 202(b) the Secretary may not conduct or support research in the United States or abroad on a living human fetus before or after the induced abortion of such fetus unless such research is done for the purposes of assuring the survival of such fetus.[83]

The stage was set for the report of May 1975.

AN ANALYSIS OF THE REPORT OF THE NATIONAL COMMISSION FOR THE PROTECTION OF HUMAN SUBJECTS OF BIOMEDICAL AND BEHAVIORAL RESEARCH

It should be noted that the definition of a "fetus" accepted by the Commission is "the human from the time of implantation until a determination is made following delivery that it is viable or possibly viable." Thus, experimental procedures such as embryo implantation, in vitro fertilizations, gestation in an artificial placenta, and all the procedures discussed in Chapter I are *not* within the purview of these recommendations since they all occur at a time prior to implantation of the blastocyst.

The Commission's recommendations, with comments, are given below.[84]

> 1. Therapeutic research directed toward the fetus may be conducted or supported, and should be encouraged, by the Secretary, DHEW, provided such research (a) conforms to appropriate medical standards, (b) has received the informed consent of the mother, the father not dissenting, and (c) has been approved by existing review procedures with adequate provision for the monitoring of the consent process. Adopted unanimously.

This recommendation apparently is directed toward a fetus that will be carried to term, since a fetus intended to be aborted hardly constitutes a "patient" for purposes of therapy. Therefore, the following observations would seem to be in order: (1) Any treatment of a therapeutic nature must "conform to appropriate medical standards" as a matter of existing law or the physician involved in administration of the treatment would be liable for malpractice. (2) Consent of the mother would appear to be required in any case if the fetus is still in utero, since she cannot be treated in most cases against her will, although, of course, there have been a few Jehovah's Witness blood transfusion cases that hold that a pregnant woman can be given a transfusion over her objections.[85]

This recommendation appears to allow the father standing to consent and therefore, logically, the right of veto. Assuming that abortion is not intended in this situation, it would appear that the father should have no right, whether the fetus is in utero or ex utero, to object to reasonable therapeutic treatment for the fetus and that the mother has no such right after the point of delivery. The right of a parent to refuse treatment for a newborn baby with serious defects will be discussed in a subsequent chapter, but if a fetus ex utero can benefit from therapy at all, such a fetus, by definition, is viable. At that point the fetus qualifies as a premature newborn and, as will be discussed in the next chapter, probably has all the rights to life of any other human being in this country.

If treatment of a fetus in utero is to be therapeutic and there is a desire to carry the fetus to term, it is very difficult to see on what legal basis the father of the child has a right to dissent to medical treatment as long as the fetus is within the mother's body. Since the father has no right to require the mother to abort, it is improbable that any court would hold that a woman's husband (or even less likely the father of her illegitimate child) would have the right to force her to deliver a deformed or injured child by objecting to prenatal therapy.

If, however, standard therapy is developed for prenatal treatment of disease, then the father would presumably have the right to a voice in determining whether an experimental or nonexperimental alternative is selected in the particular therapeutic situation. Since all prenatal therapy except for the treatment of Rh disease is now highly experimental and clearly labeled as such, at the present time, however, a fetus receives "experimental therapy" or none at all. Thus, the father's right to object under present circumstances appears to be questionable.

> 2. Therapeutic research directed toward the pregnant woman may be conducted or supported, and should be encouraged by the Secretary, DHEW, provided such research (a) has been evaluated for possible impact on the fetus, (b) will place the fetus at risk to the minimum extent consistent with meeting the health needs of the pregnant woman, (c) has been approved by existing review procedures with adequate provision for the monitoring of the consent process, and (d) the pregnant woman has given her informed consent. Adopted unanimously.

This recommendation requires no comment since it would seem to fall within the normal standard of medical practice and allowable research on pregnant women. Even prior to the abortion decisions a woman had the right to therapy even if it damaged her fetus.[86]

> 3. Non-therapeutic research directed toward the pregnant woman may be conducted or supported by the Secretary, DHEW, provided such research (a) has been evaluated for possible impact on the fetus, (b) will impose minimal or no risk to the well-being of the fetus, (c) has been approved by existing review procedures with adequate provision for the monitoring of the consent process, (d) special care has been taken to insure that the woman has been fully informed regarding possible impact on the fetus, and (e) the woman has given informed consent. Adopted unanimously.

> It is further provided that non-therapeutic research directed at the pregnant woman may be conducted or supported (f) only if the father has not objected, both where abortion is not at issue (adopted by a vote of 8 to 1) and where an abortion is anticipated. Adopted by a vote of 5 to 4.

This section raises several very interesting questions involved with the right of the father of the fetus to object. It is clear from several cases that have been decided since the Supreme Court abortion decisions that a fetus's father, whether or not he is married to the mother, has no right to veto her decision for abortion.[87]

Courts have held without exception that a woman's body is her own and that her decisions about medical procedures to be performed upon it, therapeutic or otherwise, are not subject to veto by her husband. It appears to interject a new concept into the law to say that a woman does not have the right to consent to nontherapeutic research on her own person if the father of her unborn child objects. If her husband has no right to stop the abortion under the law, it is inconsistent to argue that he should be able to stop the research on her body to which she has consented. This would presumably not be the case only if the effects on the fetus that will be carried to term might reasonably be expected to increase the father's paternal obligations, such as the increased costs of caring for an injured child.

It should be remembered that as long as a patient is mentally competent, the consent of the spouse to medical treatment is never required.[88] The only situation in which this principle may be tested at some point is that of elective sexual sterilization, either by vasectomy or tubal ligation, or of impregnation by artificial insemination by donor. Neither sterilization nor impregnation is relevant to any situation involving an already pregnant woman.

> 4. Non-therapeutic research directed toward the fetus *in utero* (other than research in anticipation of, or during, abortion) may be

conducted or supported by the Secretary, DHEW, provided (a) the purpose of such research is the development of important biomedical knowledge that cannot be obtained by alternative means, (b) investigation on pertinent animal models and non-pregnant humans has preceded such research, (c) minimal or no risk to the well-being of the fetus will be imposed by the research, (d) the research has been approved by existing review procedures with adequate provision for the monitoring of the consent process, (e) the informed consent of the mother has been obtained, and (f) the father has not objected to the research. Adopted unanimously.

The same objections to allowing the father to object to other research in utero applies to this situation as well.

> 5. Non-therapeutic research directed toward the fetus in anticipation of abortion may be conducted or supported by the Secretary, DHEW, provided such research is carried out within the guidelines for all other non-therapeutic research directed toward the fetus *in utero*. Such research presenting special problems related to the interpretation or application of these guidelines may be conducted or supported by the Secretary, DHEW, provided such research has been approved by a national ethical review body. Adopted by a vote of 8 to 1.

This recommendation permits fetal research in anticipation of abortion with the informed consent of the mother and in the absence of objection by the father. It is again arguable that since the father cannot impinge on the mother's decision to abort, he has no right to object to in utero research connected with the procedure. The increase in his responsibilities that might occur if the fetus is to be carried to term clearly does not apply in this case.

This recommendation indicates that the consent to abortion research is properly that of the parent(s) and not of some entity such as a court or review board.

The moral and legal right of a woman who has decided to abort to give valid proxy consent to research on her fetus has been contested by numerous ethicists, including several who were consultants to the Commission.

In his report to the Commission, for example, Leroy Walters wrote, "In the case of a fetus which will be aborted . . . the mother has decided, perhaps for good reason, that the life of the fetus should be terminated. Because she will not be obliged to consider the interests of the child on a long-term basis, she cannot give proxy consent in the same sense as the mother or both parents of an already born or a fetus-to-be-born."[89] Seymour Siegal wrote, "The consent of the parents is made questionable by the fact that they have decided to terminate their relationship to the fetus by consenting to an abortion."[90] Richard McCormick wrote, "The consent requirement is premised on the fact that the parents are the ones who have the best interests of the child (here the fetus) at heart. But does such a premise obtain when an abortion is being planned? Does a mother planning an abortion in the circumstances described have the best interests of the fetus at heart? I think not."[91]

Paul Ramsey's book *The Ethics of Fetal Research* states the following: "It would be odd if we do not rescue from the deputyship of parents abortuses who have been abandoned by them as we would children abandoned in institutions. . . . The question is whether a woman by her abortion decision has not waived any claim to consent on behalf of, or render any supplementary judgments, in behalf of, the abortus. . . . A strong case can be made that a woman—at least in many instances of abortion—has no standing to claim social endorsement of her moral authority to decide in cases of fetus or abortus research."[92]

In his testimony before the Commission, Monsignor James T. McHugh of the United States Catholic Conference said, "Consent by the mother is a mockery, since the mother has presumably already decided to extinguish the life of the fetus.[93] . . . The consent of the mother, who has already decided to end the life of her yet unborn offspring, cannot be accepted as a fair, just decision on behalf of the unborn."[94] Marc Lappe's paper to the commission repeats the same theory that the mother who decides to abort forfeits the right to consent to fetal research.[95]

Although motivations for abortion vary with the individual, a conclusive presumption of unconcern appears to be unwarranted. Alexander Capron stated in his study on the legal issues in fetal research that a ban on maternal consent would probably be unconstitutional.[96] No parent is completely impartial, as he points out, in making a choice for a child. Second, he also points out that since the Supreme Court has declared that women have a constitutional right to abortion, basing the maternal disqualification on the exercise of that right—that is, saying that a woman who spontaneously aborts may consent to experimentation and a woman whose abortion is induced cannot—raises serious constitutional issues and imposes a constitutional penalty on abortion. Capron continues:

> It would appear likely that automatic revocation of parental decisionmaking authority could chill the exercise of the abortion option because it would face women with the prospect of an infant to whom they are psychologically attached and whom they have an obligation to support without the concommitant power of decision which usually accompanies such obligations. It must be assumed that the abortion itself was legal and hence did not deprive the fetus of any rights which the parents were obliged to protect. . . . The rule of

disqualification seems to be based on a misperception of the significance of the parental choice. Even when a woman has opted for an
abortion on the grounds of her own interests and not because she
believes this to be best for her fetus, she has not necessarily cast
herself as being irrevocably opposed to the fetus' interest.[97]

It would appear, therefore, that the law must presume that a woman has
an abortion for a sensible reason, and any conclusive presumption that she is
unconcerned about the fetus would be indefensible, morally as well as legally.
Parents, after all, abandon their living children every year, fathers as well as
mothers, and a large number of fathers fail to provide child support payments
under court orders. Just because *some* parents do not live up to their obligations would be no justification for a legal presumption that *all* parents do not
care about their children with concomitant abolition of all parental rights in
our society, and the same principle would apply to a pregnant woman, whether
or not she decides for an abortion.

> 6. Non-therapeutic research directed toward the fetus during the
> abortion procedure and non-therapeutic research directed toward
> the non-viable fetus *ex utero* may be conducted or supported by the
> Secretary, DHEW, provided (a) the purpose of such research is the
> development of important biomedical knowledge that cannot be
> obtained by alternative means, (b) investigation on pertinent animal
> models and non-pregnant humans (when appropriate) has preceded
> such research, (c) the research has been approved by existing review
> procedures with adequate provision for the monitoring of the con-
> sent process, (d) the informed consent of the mother has been
> obtained and (e) the father has not objected to the research; and
> provided further that (f) the fetus is less than 20 weeks gestational
> age, (g) no significant procedural changes are introduced in the
> abortion procedure in the interest of research alone, and (h) no
> intrusion into the fetus is made which alters the duration of life.
> Such research presenting special problems related to the interpreta-
> tion or application of these guidelines may be conducted or sup-
> ported by the Secretary, DHEW, provided such research has been
> approved by a national ethical review body. Adopted by a vote of
> 8 to 1.

At the point where the fetus, viable or nonviable, leaves the mother's body,
paternal rights would appear to vest. Thus, at the point where research ex
utero can be performed, under normal principles of parental consent, the
father's objections should be considered valid.

As Commissioner Karen Lebacqz pointed out in her addendum to the
Commission's recommendations, this recommendation would appear to pro-

hibit research on the development of an artificial placenta, but since such research is actually therapeutic in principle, if not for the particular fetus, it may be permissible.

It should be noted that if research on the prolongation of fetal life becomes successful, parents may be presented with a "saved" fetus they attempted to abort. Thus, it would seem that both parents, even if unmarried (since the father of an illegitimate child is legally obliged to support it) should be required to consent to life-prolonging research. During consent negotiations it should be emphasized to them that they have the right to surrender the child for adoption. Several states' fetal research statutes include a specific provision for surrender of parental rights to the state in this situation.[98]

> 7. Non-therapeutic research directed toward the possibly viable infant may be conducted or supported by the Secretary, DHEW, provided (a) the purpose of such research is the development of important biomedical knowledge that cannot be obtained by alternative means, (b) investigation on pertinent animal models and non-pregnant humans (when appropriate) has preceded such research, (c) no additional risk to the well-being of the infant will be imposed by the research, (d) the research has been approved by existing review procedures with adequate provision for the monitoring of the consent process, and (e) informed consent of either parent has been given and neither parent has objected. Adopted unanimously.

If the "possibly viable" fetus is actually a viable child, it would appear that the parental relationship is identical to that which exists with any newborn.

> 8. Review Procedures. Until the Commission makes its recommendations regarding review and consent procedures, the review procedures mentioned above are to be those presently required by the Department of Health, Education and Welfare. In addition, provision for monitoring the consent process shall be required in order to insure adequacy of the consent process and to prevent unfair discrimination in the selection of research subjects, for all categories of research mentioned above. A national ethical review, as required in Recommendations 5 and 6, shall be carried out by an appropriate body designated by the Secretary, DHEW, until the establishment of the National Advisory Council for the Protection of Subjects of Biomedical and Behavioral Research. In order to facilitate public understanding and the presentation of public attitudes toward special problems reviewed by the national review body, appropriate provision should be made for public attendance and public participation in the national review process. Adopted unanimously, one abstention.

No comment is necessary on this recommendation.

> 9. Research on the Dead Fetus and Fetal Tissue. The Commission recommends that use of the dead fetus, fetal tissue and fetal material for research purposes be permitted, consistent with local law, the Uniform Anatomical Gift Act and commonly held convictions about respect for the dead. Adopted unanimously, one abstention.

As indicated above, this recommendation appears to be in keeping with the current jurisprudence on the subject.

> 10. The design and conduct of a non-therapeutic research protocol should not determine recommendations by a physician regarding the advisability, timing or method of abortion. Adopted by a vote of 6 to 2.

Although the welfare of the pregnant patient is, of course, the first consideration, this recommendation would appear to restrict a woman's right to participate in abortion research if she wishes to do so and thus might be open to attack on that ground under the principles, if not the direct precedent, of the abortion decisions.

> 11. Decisions made by a personal physician concerning the health care of a pregnant woman or fetus should not be compromised for research purposes, and when a physician of record is involved in a prospective research protocol, independent medical judgment on these issues is required. In such cases, review panels should assure that procedures for such independent medical judgment are adequate, and all conflict of interest or appearance thereof between appropriate health care and research objectives should be avoided. Adopted unanimously.

It should be noted that any physician who compromises the welfare of any patient (pregnant or not) for research purposes can be, and in many cases has been, successfully sued for malpractice.[99]

> 12. The Commission recommends that research on abortion techniques continue as permitted by law and government regulation. Adopted by a vote of 6 to 2.

No comment is necessary since this recommendation does not change existing law.

13. The Commission recommends that attention be drawn to Section 214(d) of the National Research Act (P.L. 93-348) which provides that: "No individual shall be required to perform or assist in the performance of any part of a health service program or research activity funded in whole or in part by the Secretary of Health, Education and Welfare if his performance or assistance in the performance of such part of such program or activity would be contrary to his religious beliefs or moral convictions." Adopted unanimously.

This clause might, in the exercise of First Amendment rights, allow fetal research connected with abortion in some cases where states have attempted to prohibit it. The "conscience clause" was written to protect physicians, nurses, or other personnel who are employees or staff members of hospitals from disciplinary action for refusal to participate in abortions or sterilization operations for reason of moral or religious conviction. It would seem logical that medical personnel who do find fetal research permissible on the same basis should be allowed the same right to exercise their beliefs.

14. No inducements, monetary or otherwise, should be offered to procure an abortion for research purposes. Adopted unanimously.

No comment is necessary.

15. Research which is supported by the Secretary, DHEW, to be conducted outside the United States should at the minimum comply in full with the standards and procedures recommended herein. Adopted unanimously.

The research that most provoked antiresearch outcries was conducted with federal support but performed outside the country.

16. The moratorium which is currently in effect should be lifted immediately, allowing research to proceed under current regulations but with the application of the Commission's Recommendations to the review process. All the foregoing Recommendations of the Commission should be implemented as soon as the Secretary, DHEW, is able to promulgate regulations based upon these Recommendations and the public response to them. Adopted by a vote of 9 to 1.

No comment is necessary.

The one legal issue that the Commission did not mention in any of its conclusions or recommendations is that of the right of a pregnant minor to consent to fetal research. The right of an unmarried minor to consent to an abortion without parental concurrence will be discussed in a later chapter, but it does seem that such a right exists, at least with girls of 14 and over or where specifically permitted by the minor-treatment statute in the state where the abortion is to be performed.[100] Married minors, it is clear, do have such a right.

Assuming that the consent to abort is valid, it logically follows that the girl would have the right to consent to fetal research. Where the research is performed in utero, if she is competent to give knowledgeable consent to the abortion, it would be hard to argue that she cannot give equally knowledgeable consent to other procedures performed on her body. In determining her right to consent to research on a fetus ex utero, it should be remembered that all states allow a minor mother to consent to the surrender of her baby for adoption without requiring the consent of her parent or guardian.[101] Since the state's jurisprudence clearly assumes that a minor mother is legally competent to protect the best interest of her child in a knowledgeable way in the adoption context, it would be illogical to argue that the same girl should not be considered competent to consent in the research context.

THE RESPONSE OF THE SECRETARY OF
HEALTH, EDUCATION AND WELFARE

On July 29, 1975, the Secretary of Health, Education and Welfare lifted the ban on funding of projects involving fetal research that comply with regulations issued by him on that date.[102] After provision for review of applications for funding of fetal research projects by ethical advisory boards, the regulations delimit the specific boundaries of permissible research as follows:

§ 46.206 General limitations.

(a) No activity to which this subpart is applicable may be undertaken unless: (1) Appropriate studies on animals and nonpregnant individuals have been completed; (2) except where the purpose of the activity is to meet the health needs of the particular fetus, the risk to the fetus is minimal and, in all cases, is the least possible risk for achieving the objectives of the activity; (3) individuals engaged in the activity will have no part in: (i) Any decisions as to the timing, method and procedures used to terminate the pregnancy, and (ii) determining the viability of the fetus at the termination of the pregnancy; and (4) no procedural changes which may cause greater than minimal risk to the fetus or the pregnant woman will be introduced into the procedure for terminating the pregnancy solely in the interest of the activity.

(b) No inducements, monetary or otherwise, may be offered to terminate pregnancy for purposes of the activity.

§ 46.207 Activities directed toward pregnant women as subjects.

(a) No pregnant woman may be involved as a subject in an activity covered by this subpart unless: (1) The purpose of the activity is to meet the health needs of the mother and the fetus will be placed at risk only to the minimum extent necessary to meet such needs, or (2) the risk to the fetus is minimal.

(b) An activity permitted under paragraph (a) of this section may be conducted only if the mother and father are legally competent and have given their informed consent after having been fully informed regarding possible impact on the fetus, except that the father's informed consent need not be secured if: (1) The purpose of the activity is to meet the health needs of the mother, (2) his identity or whereabouts cannot reasonably be ascertained, (3) he is not reasonably available, or (4) the pregnancy resulted from rape.

§ 46.208 Activities directed toward fetuses *in utero* as subjects.

(a) No fetus *in utero* may be involved as a subject in any activity covered by this subpart unless: (1) The purpose of the activity is to meet the health needs of the particular fetus and the fetus will be placed at risk only to the minimum extent necessary to meet such needs, or (2) the risk to the fetus imposed by the research is minimal and the purpose of the activity is the development of important biomedical knowledge which cannot be obtained by other means.

(b) An activity permitted under paragraph (a) of this section may be conducted only if the mother and father are legally competent and have given their informed consent, except that the father's consent need not be secured if: (1) His identity or whereabouts cannot reasonably be ascertained, (2) he is not reasonably available, or (3) the pregnancy resulted from rape.

§ 46.209 Activities directed toward fetuses *ex utero,* including nonviable fetuses, as subjects.

(a) No fetus *ex utero* may be involved as a subject in an activity covered by this subpart until it has been ascertained whether the particular fetus is viable, unless: (1) There will be no added risk to the fetus resulting from the activity, and (2) the purpose of the activity is the development of important biomedical knowledge which cannot be obtained by other means.

(b) No nonviable fetus may be involved as a subject in an activity covered by this subpart unless: (1) Vital functions of the fetus will not be artificially maintained except where the purpose of the activity is to develop new methods for enabling fetuses to survive to the point of viability, (2) experimental activities which of themselves would terminate the heartbeat or respiration of the fetus will not be employed, and (3) the purpose of the activity is the development of important biomedical knowledge which cannot be obtained by other means.

(c) In the event the fetus *ex utero* is found to be viable, it may be included as a subject in the activity only to the extent permitted by and in accordance with the requirements of other subparts of this part.

(d) An activity permitted under paragraph (a) or (b) of this section may be conducted only if the mother and father are legally competent and have given their informed consent, except that the father's informed consent need not be secured if: (1) His identity or whereabouts cannot reasonably be ascertained, (2) he is not reasonably available, or (3) the pregnancy resulted from rape.

§ 46.210 Activities involving the dead fetus, fetal material, or the placenta.

Activities involving the dead fetus, macerated fetal material, or cells, tissue, or organs excised from a dead fetus shall be conducted only in accordance with any applicable State or local laws regarding such activities.

§ 46.211 Modification or waiver of specific requirements.

Upon the request of an applicant or offeror (with the approval of its Institutional Review Board), the Secretary may modify or waive specific requirements of this subpart, with the approval of the Ethical Advisory Board after such opportunity for public comment as the Ethical Advisory Board considers appropriate in the particular instance. In making such decisions, the Secretary will consider whether the risks to the subject are so outweighed by the sum of the benefit to the subject and the importance of the knowledge to be gained as to warrant such modification or waiver and that such benefits cannot be gained except through a modification of waiver. Any such modifications or waivers will be published as notices in the Federal Register.

For the most part, the Secretary adopted the recommendations of the Commission. The Department of Health, Education and Welfare regulations, however, require paternal consent for nontherapeutic research on the pregnant woman or on the fetus in utero. These requirements apply unless the father's identity or whereabouts cannot reasonably be ascertained, he is not reasonably available, or the pregnancy resulted from rape.

The physician who is called on to determine the legal definition of "reasonably available" may presumably wonder if the father is to be considered unavailable if he is out of the room when consent is requested or if the man must be proved to be on a submarine cruise or lost in Tibet.

Furthermore, with regard to research on the fetus in utero, consent may be given only if the mother and father are "legally competent," without any definition of the term. This requirement may mean that only fetuses of adult women of sound mind may be used in research; it may include fetuses of minors emancipated in fact; it may include only fetuses of legally emancipated (i.e., married) minors and adults; or it might be argued that it would apply to any fetus of any pregnant woman who had not been declared mentally incompetent.

The precise meaning of "the pregnancy resulted from rape" is also not clear. Does this require prior to vitiation of paternal consent requirements that a medical diagnosis of probable rape has been made? Does it require that the woman has filed a complaint with the police or that a man has been convicted of the offense? On the other hand, is a woman's unsupported statement to the research physician that the pregnancy resulted from rape sufficient? If a married woman is raped, how is the physician to determine whether the pregnancy resulted from marital intercourse one day or a clear case of rape the next, since the fact of pregnancy cannot be established for several weeks?

It appears that the regulations are replete with definitional obscurities in addition to the substantive objections noted in the comments to the commission's recommendations.

NOTES

1. *Washington Post,* April 13, 1973, page A1.
2. Transcript of Public Hearings of the National Commission for the Protection of Human Subjects of Biomedical and Behavioral Research, February 14, 1975, page 130c.
3. Roe v. Wade, 410 US 113, 1973; Doe v. Bolton, 410 US 179, 1973.
4. See, for one example, the account of a demonstration of 200 Roman Catholic high-school students, led by Sargent Shriver's daughter, at the NIH protesting the drafting of guidelines for fetal research in the *Washington Post,* April 13, 1973, page A1.
5. PL 93-348, 93rd Congress, July 12, 1974.
6. PL 93-348, Section 202(3) (b).
7. *Ibid.*
8. "The U.S. Supreme Court and Abortions": I. 225 *JAMA* No. 2, page 215, July 9, 1973; II. 225 *JAMA* No. 3, page 343, July 16, 1973; III. 225 *JAMA* No. 4, page 447, July 23, 1973; M. S. Guttmacher, "The Legal Status of Therapeutic Abortions," in Harold Rosen, ed., *Abortion in America,* Boston, Beacon Press, 1967.
9. Joseph Fletcher, *The Ethics of Genetic Control,* New York, Anchor Press, Doubleday and Co., 1974, page 140.

10. For a general discussion of state statutes on fetal research, see Gary E. Reback, "Fetal Experimentation: Moral, Legal and Medical Implications," 26 *Stanford Law Rev,* page 1191, 1974.

11. E.g., Dietrich v. Northhampton, 138 Mass 14, 1884.

12. See, for a brief general discussion of the evolution of the principle that a child may sue for his prenatal injuries, with citations of some of the landmark decisions, "Prenatal Injuries," 214 *JAMA* No. 11, page 2105, December 14, 1970. The first case on the subject was Bonbrest v. Kotz, 65 F Supp 138, DC DC 1946.

13. See, for example, Dinner v. Thorp, 338 P 2d 137, Wash 1959. This case was a medical malpractice action for the death of a baby born to a diabetic. The parents claimed that the negligence killed the child; the defense argued that the mother's condition was the cause. The obstetrician lost.

14. E.g., Valence v. Louisiana Power and Light Co., 50 So 2d 847, La 1951.

15. E.g., Sylvia v. Gobeille, 220 A 2d 22, RI 1966; Scott v. McPheeters, 92 P 2d 678, Cal 1939; Korman v. Hagen, 206 NW 650, Minn 1925; Brooks v. Serrano, 209 So 2d 279, Fla 1968 (all malpractice suits against obstetricians).

16. Verkennes v. Corniea, 38 NW 2d 838, Minn 1949.

17. Eich v. Town of Gulf Shores, 300 So 2d 354, Ala 1974; Hatala v. Markiewicz, 224 A 2d 406, Conn 1966; Worgan v. Greggo and Ferrara, Inc., 128 A 2d 557, Del 1956; Simmons v. Howard University, 323 F Supp 529, DC DC 1971; Porter v. Lassiter, 87 SE 2d 100, Ga 1955; Chrisafogeorgis v. Brandenburg, 304 NE 2d 88, Ill 1974; Britt v. Sears, 277 NE 2d 20, Ind 1971; Hale v. Manion, 368 P 2d 1, Kans 1962; Mitchell v. Couch, 285 SW 2d 901, Ky 1955; Valence v. Louisiana Power and Light Co., *Supra* at 14; State ex Rel Odham v. Sherman, 198 A 2d 71, Md 1964; O'Neill v. Morse, 188 NW 2d 785, Mich 1971; Verkennes v. Corniea, *supra* at 16; Rainey v. Horn, 72 So 2d 434, Miss 1954; White v. Yup, 458 P 2d 617, Nev 1969; Poliquin v. MacDonald, 135 A 2d 249, NH 1957; Stidam v. Ashmore, 167 NE 2d 106, Ohio 1959; Libbee v. Permanente Clinic, 518 P 2d 636, Ore 1974; Fowler v. Woodward, 138 SE 2d 42, SC 1964; Baldwin v. Butcher, 184 SE 2d 428, W Va, 1971; Kwaterski v. State Farm Mutual Automobile Insurance Co., 148 NW 2d 107, Wisc 1967. See also "Damages for the Wrongful Death of a Fetus," note, 51 *Chicago Kent Law Rev,* page 227, 1974.

18. E.g., Baldwin v. Butcher, 184 SE 2d 428, W Va 1971; Fowler v. Woodward, 138 SE 2d 42, SC 1964.

19. E.g., Libbee v. Permanente Clinic, 518 P 2d 636, Ore 1974.

20. E.g., Dinner v. Thorp, *supra* at 13.

21. See, for example, "Liability for Obstetrical Injuries," 217 *JAMA* No. 7, page 1015, August 16, 1971; "Birth Injuries," 219 *JAMA* No. 1, page 129, January 3, 1972.

22. See, among many examples, Smith v. Wright, 305 P 2d 810, Kans 1957; Pugh v. Swiontek, 253 NE 2d 3, Ill 1969; Jarboe v. Harting, 397 SW 2d 775, Ky 1965.

23. E.g., Endresz v. Friedberg, 248 NE 2d 901, NY 1969; Keyes v. Construction Service, 165 NE 2d 912, Mass 1960.

24. See, for an example of an article on trial techniques in wrongful death cases including proof of moans and groans, "Trials of Wrongful Death Actions," 20 *Am Jur Trials,* as well as many articles on trial techniques written by Melvin Belli.

25. Capelouto v. Kaiser Foundation Hospital, 500 P 2d 880, Cal 1972.

26. See, for example, Larrabee v. U.S. 254 F Supp 613, DC Cal 1966. In this case, however, the baby did sustain permanent damage although the opinion does cite other cases where

recovery was denied. Incidentally, new mothers who are awake and see their babies dropped on the delivery room floor frequently recover damages for their own distress.

27. Panagopoulous v. Martin, 295 F Supp 220, DC W Va 1969, page 227.

28. Blackstone, *Commentaries,* Book I, cited in Porter v. Lassiter, 87 SE 2d 100, Ga 1955.

29. Schapiro v. Howard 78 A+1 58, Md 1910.

30. See, for lengthy discussions *Page on Wills,* Cincinnati, The W. H. Anderson Co., 1960, Section 17.4, and Simes and Smith, *Future Interests,* St. Paul, West Publishing Co., 1956, Section 227 et seq.

31. *Scott on Trusts,* 3rd ed., Section 112.1, "Unborn Children," Boston, Little, Brown and Co. 1967.

32. *Ibid.,* Section 112.2.

33. David Louisell, "Abortion, the Practice of Medicine and the Due Process of Law," 16 *UCLA Law Rev,* page 233, 1969.

34. Burns v. Alcala, 43 L Ed 2d 469, page 475, 420 US 575, 1975.

35. *Charlotte Observer,* July 15, 1975.

36. E.g., New Jersey v. Haren, 307 A 2d 644, NJ 1973; Michigan v. Bricker, 208 NW 2d 172, Mich 1973; Spears v. Mississippi, 278 So 2d 443, Miss 1973.

37. Editorial, 128 *Am J Diseases Children,* page 295, September 1974.

38. "Regulations and Legislation Concerning Abortus Research," commentary, 229 *JAMA* No. 10, page 1303, September 2, 1974.

39. E.g., *ibid.* See also Alan G. Fantel and Thomas J. Shepard, "Legislative Threats to Research on Human Congenital Defects," 38 *Conn Med,* No. 10, page 535, October 1974.

40. Stephen Toulmin, "Exploring the Moderate Consensus," 5 *Hastings Report* No. 3, page 31, June 1975.

41. All the information in this section is taken from the appendix to the Report on Fetal Research of the Commission for the Protection of Human Subjects of Biomedical and Behavioral Research.

42. Model Uniform Anatomical Gift Act, Section 1B.

43. Ibid., Section 2B.

44. Holland v. Metalious, 198 A 2d 654, NH 1964.

45. Report of Professor Alexander M. Capron to the Commission for the Protection of Human Subjects. This and another legal study are printed in the appendix to the Report on Fetal Research.

46. Ind Code, Section 10–112.

47. Ill Crim Code, Title 38, Section 81 (26).

48. Mass Gen Laws, Ch 112, Section 12J as Amended by Ch 421, Mass Ann Laws, 1974, 257.

49. Ohio Rev Code Ann, Section 2919.14.

50. SD Compiled Laws Ann, Section 34-23A-17.

51. Cal Health and Safety Code, Section 25956.

52. Minn Public Health Laws, Section 145.38.

53. Barbara Culliton, "Grave Robbing: Charges Against Four from Boston City Hospital," 186 *Science,* page 420, 1974.

54. See, generally, "Authorization for Autopsies," 203 *JAMA* No. 5, page 199, January 29, 1968; "Unauthorized Autopsies," 214 *JAMA* No. 5, page 967, November 2, 1970.

55. See, generally, Leo Gelfand, "Modern Concepts of Property in a Dead Body," in C. H. Wecht, ed., *Legal Medicine Annual,* New York, Appleton-Century-Crofts, 1971.

56. Larson v. Chase, 50 NW 238, Minn 1891; Jackson v. Rupp, 228 So 2d 916, Fla 1969.

57. Cal Health and Safety Code, Section 25960.

58. Ill Crim Code, Title 38, Section 81 (18).

59. Ky Crim Code, Section 436.026.

60. La Rev Stats Ann, Section 14:87.2.

61. Me Rev Stats Ann, Title 22, Section 1574–1576.

62. Mass Gen Laws, Ch 112, Section 12J.

63. Minn Stats Ann, Section 145.422 (3).

64. Mo Gen Laws, Section 188.035.

65. Mont Crim Code, Section 94-5-617.

66. Neb Rev Stats, Section 28-4, 161.

67. NY Pub Health Code, Section 4164.

68. Ohio Rev Code Ann, Section 2919.14.

69. Pa Stats Ann, Title 35, Section 6605.

70. SD Compiled Laws Ann, Section 34-23A-17.

71. Utah Code Ann, Section 76-7-312.

72. Ind Crim Code, Section 10–112.

73. Brown v. Board of Education, 347 US 483, 1954.

74. E.g., Mills v. Board of Education, 348 F Supp 866, DC DC 1972; see also Leopold Lippman and I. L. Goldberg, *Right to Education,* New York, Teachers College Press, 1973.

75. California, Louisiana, Massachusetts, Minnesota, Missouri, Montana, and Pennsylvania.

76. Kentucky, Maine, Nebraska, Ohio, and Utah.

77. See, generally, Angela R. Holder, "The School Prayer Cases and the Right of Privacy," 12 *J Church State* No. 2, page 289, Spring 1970; McCollum v. Board of Education, 333 US 703, 1948; Zorach v. Clauson, 343 US 306, 1952; Abington Township v. Schempp, 374 US 203, 1963; Engel v. Vitale, 370 US 421, 1962.

78. The status of fetal research in England is discussed from several points of view in "Research Investigations and the Fetus," symposium, *Brit Med J,* pages 464–468, May 26, 1973. A summary of the Peel Report may be found in 38 *Conn Med* No. 10, page 539, October 1974.

79. For a detailed account of the public and political history of the bill that established the Commission, see Paul Ramsey, *The Ethics of Fetal Research,* New Haven, Conn, Yale University Press, 1975, Ch 1.

80. "Live Abortus Research Raises Hackles of Some, Hopes of Others," *Medical World News,* October 5, 1973, pages 32–36.

81. *Ibid.*

82. PL 93–348, Section 202 (b).

83. *Ibid.,* Section 213.

84. In addition to the copies of the conclusions and recommendations provided by the commission, the recommendations are published in full in 5 *Hastings Center Report* No. 3, pages 45–46, June 1975.

85. E.g., Raleigh-Fitkin Memorial Hospital v. Anderson, 201 A 2d 537, NJ 1964.

86. E.g., Guttmacher, *op. cit. supra* at 8. This article was written 19 years before the abortion decisions.

87. Coe v. Gerstein, 376 F Supp 695, DC Fla 1973, cert den 417 US 279, 1974; Doe v. Doe, 314 NE 2d 128, Mass· 1974.

88. E.g., Nishi v. Hartwell, 473 P 2d 116, Hawaii 1970; Karp v. Cooley, 493 F 2d 408, CCA 5, 1974.

89. Leroy Walters, 5 *Hastings Center Report* No. 3, page 15, June 1975.

90. Seymour Seigel, 5 *Hastings Center Report* No. 3, page 25, June 1975.

91. Richard McCormick, 5 *Hastings Center Report* No. 3, pages 28–29, June 1975.

92. Ramsey, *op. cit. supra* at 79, page 93.

93. Transcript, *supra* at 2, page 203.

94. *Ibid.,* page 210.

95. Commission Report, page 45.

96. Capron, *op. cit. supra* at 45, page 42.

97. *Ibid.,* pages 42–43.

98. See, for example, La Rev Stats Ann, Section 13:1569–70; Mo Gen Laws, Section 188.040; Mont Rev Stats Ann, Section 94-5-617 (2) (b). See also Capron, *op. cit. supra* at 45, pages 44–46.

99. E.g., Fiorentino v. Wenger, 227 NE 2d 296, NY 1967; "Critical Areas in Clinical Investigation," 203 *JAMA* No. 8, page 241, February 19, 1968.

100. E.g., In re Boe, 322 F Supp 872, DC DC 1971; Ballard v. Anderson, 484 P 2d 1345, Cal 1971.

101. E.g., Re Adoption of Anderson, 50 NW 2d 278, Minn 1951; Austin v. Collins, 200 SW 2d 666, Tex 1947.

102. 40 *Fed Reg,* pages 33526–33552, August 8, 1975.

CHAPTER IV

THE CHILD

AND

DEATH

Pediatricians are frequently called on to make decisions involving ethical and legal aspects of treatment, with or without consultation with parents, in cases where children are critically or terminally ill. Three different areas that involve specific and discrete legal problems appear with distressing frequency in the normal course of a pediatric practice. Little, if anything, has been written on these subjects from the legal point of view, and physicians generally do not seem to be aware of the legal liabilities inherent in these issues. This chapter will attempt to indicate possible legal liability, criminal as well as civil, and discuss other relevant considerations that arise in these three circumstances:

1. Is a pediatrician obliged to treat a severely defective neonate who is born with either (a) a severe mental handicap such as Down's syndrome in addition to an unrelated physical defect such as an intestinal obstruction or (b) birth defects such as spina bifida and concomitant brain difficulties that will result in the child's death if he is not treated?

2. What obligation do physicians and parents have to treat an older child who has led a normal life and becomes ill with a terminal disease where treatment for that disease will result in a prolongation of life but leave the child with serious residual handicaps?

3. What is the physician's legal responsibility toward the child who requires long-term treatment to keep him alive but who refuses treatment, with or without the concurrence of his parents?

The issues involved in all three of these cases are legally diverse, and in most of these situations the law has no direct answers, but analogies to principles from other contexts of the physician-patient relationship may help resolve the liability question. Prosecutions in these cases are virtually nonexistent but, with the increasing attention paid to the problem, it is quite likely that some district attorney may undertake to prosecute some physician at some time. Parents also could be prosecuted for their role in a decision not to treat a child and charged either with manslaughter or child abuse. Therefore, the physician should understand that he does assume some risk of prosecution if he allows a child to die.

THE DEFORMED NEWBORN

Medical Aspects

Newborn babies unfortunately are not always perfect human beings. Many of them have serious defects, as has been noted in prior chapters. One in 600 has Down's disease.[1] Down's babies do not die of being mongoloid, and the question of allowing such a child to die arises because these children also have a very high rate of physical anomalies such as heart problems or intestinal obstructions. Other newborns, however, have serious conditions that may cause mental retardation and/or serious physical handicaps that will usually result in their death without surgical intervention. In this category fall, for example, infants with myelomeningocele. Until recently children in both groups rarely survived the first few days of life. As neonatal surgery has improved, however, these children can be kept alive after surgery to grow up with serious handicaps.

Nineteen percent of the children in one study who were born with myelomeningocele but who were not treated survived for a year; thus, they were likely to remain alive indefinitely. Where active treatment is given, including several operations shortly after birth, most survive, but of that number virtually all are totally paralyzed from the waist down and incontinent with no present hope for improvement. As a result of the accompanying hydrocephalus, at best 40 percent of these children will be intellectually normal. Of the other 60 percent, the degree of retardation may vary from moderate to so severe that the child is in effect properly termed "a vegetable." In typical cases by the time a child of normal intelligence with myelomeningocele reaches his ninth birthday, he will have had 18 major operations to maintain his life, not to allow him to walk.[2]

As one pediatric surgeon writes:

> All pediatric surgeons, including myself, have "triumphs"—infants who, if they had been born 25 or even five years ago, would not have been salvageable. Now with our team approaches we can wind up with "viable" children three and four years old, well below the 3rd percentile in height and weight, propped up on a pillow, marginally tolerating an oral diet of sugar and amino acids and looking forward to another operation.[3]

The increasing efficiency of pediatric surgery has created the dilemma in which a pediatrician finds himself, because prior to the early 1960s the question was irrelevant, since there was nothing that could be done for the children even if treatment was desired.

Some persons argue that a child should not be declared to be a "person" at all for some stated time after birth. For example, one writer has argued, in determining what to do about a defective child, "It may be that two or three days or weeks of probationary life should be accepted as a period during which doctors could check for defects and parents could decide whether or not they wanted to keep and rear a damaged baby."[4]

We must first look to the law for a determination of when a "person" becomes a person. Legally, a human being is entitled to all the rights and statuses possessed by all other human beings from the time he is born. Prior to that moment, as has been indicated in the earlier chapters in this book, it is at least highly debatable that our legal system recognizes the fetus as a human person in terms of protection of his rights. Once his first breath is drawn, however, and he signifies that he is alive, even if such a period of viability is a very short one and he dies in a few minutes, that baby in the eyes of the law has joined the human race and is entitled to the protection of our legal system.

A legal system of any type, including ours, is obliged to deal with status questions on a mass basis. Individual variances normally cannot be accommodated because in many status situations it is more important that the law be certain and easily ascertainable than that it be correct. Thus, an unusually mature 12-year-old has no claim to a variance in order to obtain a driver's license, which, by statute, is restricted to those 16 and over. Whether one is married *de facto* may be subject to a discussion of human covenants and/or ethical obligations; *de jure* one is either married or one is not. Whether one is "alive" for legal purposes is also not amenable to individual variances because of the enormous implications of the status. Therefore, the legal system quite sensibly has chosen the moment of birth as the moment of being alive. It is an easily ascertainable moment, understood by all, and it can be universally applied to the population. Thus, for administrative convenience, if for no better reason, legally one cannot be a little bit alive. The question of nontreatment thus arises quite clearly in the legal context that to fail to treat a deformed baby and allow him to die is indisputably allowing a living person to die.

The argument that no treatment should be given to a severely deformed newborn is predicated on the theory that the long-term physical suffering and mental anguish of the child, his parents, and perhaps his other siblings, their economic losses, their future prospects, and their other human interests, make it more merciful for both child and parents if the child dies within the first few hours or days of life.

One noted pediatric neurosurgeon has written of babies with myelomeningocele:

> There are large numbers who are so severely handicapped at birth
> that those who survive are bound to suffer from a combination of
> major physical defects. In addition, many will be retarded in spite
> of everything that can be done for them. It is not necessary to
> enumerate all that this means to the patient, the family and the
> community in terms of suffering, deprivation, anxiety, frustration,
> family stress and financial cost. The large majority surviving at
> present have yet to reach the most difficult period of adolescence
> and young adult life and the problems of love, marriage and employ-
> ment. . . . It is unlikely that many would wish to save a life which
> will consist of a long succession of operations, hospital admissions
> and other deprivations, or if the end result will be a combination of
> gross physical defects with retarded intellectual development.[5]

Others who argue that medical ethics allows or perhaps requires nontreatment maintain that the harm done to the baby's family by his life outweigh
the benefits of allowing that life to continue. In their view the minimal benefit
of treatment of a person incapable of full development does not justify the
burden that care of the defective infant imposes on parents, siblings, and
others.[6] Caring for such a child is far more difficult and the costs are greater
than for any normal child. The rewards common with parenthood of a normal
preschooler do not exist. It is not at all uncommon for parents of a handicapped child to get a divorce when economic and emotional resources are
exhausted to the breaking point and either the husband or the wife just runs
away.

It is not seriously questioned that pediatricians everywhere are willing to
allow these children to die. There is simply no open admission of the practice.

Raymond Duff and A. G. M. Campbell of Yale Medical School published
an article in 1973 in the *New England Journal of Medicine* in which they
discussed the fact that 43 newborn babies died from deliberate withholding of
treatment in the Yale-New Haven Hospital after consultation between parents
and physicians.[7] All of these children would have been seriously defective.
Their report raised the issue that no one else had been willing to discuss openly.
Their thesis was that the parent has the right to decide whether or not the child
should be treated if the handicap is sufficiently serious so that physicians
conclude that treatment cannot give the child a normal life. It is generally
conceded, as the authors wrote, that there are limits on vigorous applications
of treatment to extend life for deformed newborns, but the limits largely
depend on the ethical views of the physician in charge.

As has been demonstrated in many studies, initial parental response to the knowledge that a newborn child is seriously defective is usually one of rejection of the child.[8] John Fletcher writes:

> Despite a readiness in modern consciousness to accept a scientific explanation of congenital defects, both literature about and experience with parents of defective newborns in the United States and Great Britain shows almost a universally negative initial reaction to the child and a personal assumption of guilt on the part of the parents. Grief and anger are almost universal responses.

Unfortunately, at the very moment when the parents are overwhelmed with feelings of rejection of the child, they are called on to consent or to withhold consent to lifesaving treatment. The mother has just been through labor and delivery and is usually exhausted, since most of these decisions have to be made within the first few hours after birth. A normal and common response in the first moments or hours of being presented with this situation is anger at the baby for putting the parent in this position, a purely irrational response but one that is perfectly understandable. Fletcher points out:

> The parental response to the newborn defective usually represents an initial rejection based upon disappointed hope and the rejection may be conditioned by two factors. One, the nature of the defect and two, the social status of the parents. They feel disgusted, grieved, helpless, full of rage and it is very common in handicapped children who obviously will not die for parents to wish first to get rid of the child and this feeling is followed by intense guilt, blame and intense anxiety.[9]

Where the decision for or against surgery has to be made at a time before the parents have worked through their wish to "get rid of" the child, they may make a decision not to treat, which could very easily fill them with guilt and horror later, thus raising serious problems in the physician-parent relationship.

Because of the peculiar vulnerability of the parents at this moment, the physician, whether he wants to or not, plays an extremely important role in helping them make a determination of what to do, but he does so as an ethicist, not as a treating physician. An editorial in the same issue of the *New England Journal* as Duff and Campbell's article entitled "Bedside Ethics for the Hopeless Case" indicates that the physician is and should be the one to decide to live with that decision. The author states:

> So when Duff and Campbell ask "who decides for the child" the answer is you: you, the child's doctor, for who else is in a similarly pivotal position to make sure that the proper medical consultation

has been obtained in ascertaining the hopeless condition of the patient, that the parents receive sympathetic and thorough explanation, that they are exposed to broadly based advice? Who else can lead all those involved to a decision and who else is more responsible for consoling after the decision has been reached? Social ethics, institutional attitudes and committees can provide the broad guidelines but the onus of decision-making ultimately falls on the doctor in whose care the child has been put.[10]

This may be a much more honest view than any writers' attempts in this context to argue for the possibility of meaningful parental consent. If the physician raises the issue of nontreatment with the parents at all, it may be assumed that by so doing he is indicating the parents do have a choice. Presumably he would not make such a choice available if he thought there were any indications that the child could be given a near-normal life. Duff clearly stated that any physician would get a court order for surgery on a defective newborn if the child's condition was not one in which the physician thought a failure to treat was medically justifiable.[11] Where, for example, the defect was cosmetic, such as a club foot, the author indicated that he would not hesitate to get a court order consenting to surgery and in fact has done so. Thus, the medical context within which the decision to treat or not to treat is made is that the physician offers the parents the option only if he thinks the child should not be treated. If parents initiate discussion of allowing the child to die under circumstances in which the physician thinks treatment is indicated, he is not bound by their desires. It is obvious that the parents are doing what the physician thinks best, no matter how conscientiously the physician attempts to make them aware that the right of decision is theirs and not his.

It may be hypocritical not to say so. Some pediatricians, unlike Duff and Campbell, simply make a unilateral decision not to treat the child, do not discuss it with the parents, and announce either at the time of delivery or shortly thereafter that the child was born dead. This may lead to a malpractice suit, but in many ways, unless one believes that there is a duty to apply vigorous treatment in all cases, this seems to be more honest than maintaining that the parents made the choice. On any rational basis the choice should be the parents', but it may be logically impossible that the choice can ever genuinely be the parents'. As one neurosurgeon writes:

> Parents should obviously be part of such a decision, but their decision can hardly be an informed one. Despite the best efforts of the physician to educate parents, such education and full understanding of the consequences cannot take place in the short time before a decision should be made.[12]

Under the circumstances, when the parents are in shock and feeling enraged by the child and wish to reject him, they cannot make the same type of rational decision they would make in calmer contexts, and the physician obviously has assumed more influence over what that decision will be than he does in most other treatment situations by his presentation of a choice at all. In this context the ethics of a physician-patient relationship are quite different from the one in which a physician sits in his office and discusses the merits and demerits of surgery for a rational, adult patient. Even if he must tell a patient that a life-threatening condition exists and radical surgery is necessary, the patient rarely must decide to have treatment or to forego it within the few minutes within which the decision to treat a newborn frequently must be made.

In terms of the aspects of this situation, the physician should realize that he is probably making the decision. If a physician can console himself with the idea that it was really the parents' choice and that he himself did not decide not to treat a child, he could become less sensitive to the medical needs of his patients. As an editorial in the *Journal of Pediatrics* has pointed out, "It is not the patient or the problem that goes away—it is the physician who goes away from the problem, leaving the family and the patient to suffer."[13]

None of the commentators who have written on this subject doubts that the primary motivation for refusing to treat a defective newborn is unwillingness to struggle with the problems of life as the parent of a retarded child, and the retardation is the primary factor in the decision not to treat in most cases.[14]

Several years ago there was a great deal of comment about a case at Johns Hopkins Hospital where parents refused permission to operate on a mongoloid baby who took 15 days to starve to death.[15] Nearly everyone who has commented on this case has disagreed with the decision, and most objection has centered on the fact that the child took so long to die.

Only one trial court decision exists on this subject.

Baby Houle was born on February 9, 1974, in the Maine Medical Center. His entire left side was malformed, he had no left eye, he was practically without a left ear, he had a deformed left hand and some of his vertebra were not fused. He also had a tracheal fistula and could not be fed by mouth. Surgery for repair of the fistula, the only immediate threat to his survival, could have been performed easily, but the parents refused to consent. Several physicians at the medical center, including the pediatric surgeon who was to operate, felt differently and took a neglect case to the Superior Court. The trial judge ordered the surgery to be performed and stated in his Order: "At the moment of live birth there does exist a human being entitled to the fullest protection of the law. The most basic right enjoyed by every human being is the right to life itself." The child died the day after the surgery was performed.[16]

At the time Baby Houle was born, there was no suspicion of brain damage, but as a result of either heart or lung abnormalities his blood transmitted

insufficient oxygen and his brain was quickly damaged. His reflexes deteriorated, and prior to the last day of his life he had ceased to kick when his knee
and ankle were touched. One physician said that the six-day delay between his
birth and the surgery ordered by the court had caused a gradual deterioration
and that if he had been operated on at once he could have been saved.

Apparently the defects were primarily cosmetic and yet the parents elected
not to treat. From all reports of this case, the child was not paralyzed and, with
extensive treatment, could have enjoyed all the activities that anyone with one
eye can lead.

Peter Rickham, a pediatric surgeon in England, has written an article[17] in
which he divides infants into five categories: (1) infants who are likely to be
completely cured by surgery, (2) infants who after treatment will be handicapped to some extent but still may be able to lead a relatively normal life, (3)
infants who after treatment will have a severe physical handicap and will have
to lead a more or less sheltered life, (4) infants in classes 1–3 who in addition
are of subnormal intelligence but who can be trained to some extent, (5) infants
in classes 1–3 who in addition are idiots, leading a vegetable existence. Rickham points out that these classes denote different degrees of "living as human
beings" and continues, "One might ask whether the class five can be regarded
as being humanly alive in the sense in which we usually understand those
words" and would allow nontreatment only for that group.

My own ethical views differ markedly from those of any ethicists who have
written on this question. It seems to be legally mandatory for treatment to be
instituted if it can cure the condition for which it is performed. If a Down's
baby has an intestinal obstruction or, as in Baby Houle's case, an infant has
a fistula, either one of which can be cured by relatively simple surgical procedures *and if* those procedures would clearly be performed by court order if
necessary on an otherwise normal newborn, then it is arguable that treatment
is legally required.

On the other hand, neurosurgery for a paralyzed newborn is by no means
"ordinary care," since normal babies do not require it. Second, the condition
for which surgery might be performed is not curable, and thus the operation
may be regarded as both futile and one that would subject the baby to more
pain than he would have felt if left alone. Third, if the child survives he may
well have sufficient self-awareness to suffer the agonies of knowing his limitations and to be tormented by them. Thus, it may be possible to justify as good
medical practice a determination that a child whose condition is incurable
should not be subjected to surgery for that condition solely to keep him alive.

Legal Aspects

Criminal law and the parent.   In all other circumstances a parent's failure to
provide adequate medical treatment for his child is a criminal offense under
child abuse statutes. All jurisdictions that have considered the matter have

held that a child whose parents refuse to permit blood transfusions for religious reasons is "abused," even though their refusal is grounded in religious convictions protected by the First Amendment. Courts are always willing to declare a child neglected and issue an order to administer blood transfusions when they are necessary to save a child's life.[18] Parents may also not refuse on religious or other grounds to comply with state laws requiring inoculations of children prior to entering public school and may be prosecuted under truancy statutes if the unvaccinated child is refused admission.[19]

In many but not all cases, refusal to permit medical treatment where it is "highly desirable" even if it is not absolutely necessary to save the child's life is also considered child neglect for purposes of prosecution of the parents.

One decision involved four children whose custody had been voluntarily surrendered by their parents to the county department of child welfare. Prior to placement in foster homes all four were given physical examinations, and serious infections of tonsils and adenoids were found. The father had religious objections to surgery of any kind and attempted to enjoin removal of the tonsils, even though there was clear medical evidence that the children's hearing was already impaired by the enlarged adenoids and permanent deafness would follow if they were not removed. The court invoked the "best interest" rule since the surgery was "minor" and ordered the operations performed. It is not, however, at all certain from this opinion that if the parents had not already permanently surrendered custody to the welfare department that the result would have been the same, since the primary issue in the case was whether the father had any legal standing to object to any action, medical or otherwise, taken by the welfare department and the court held that parental rights had been terminated.[20]

A 15-year-old boy had a massive facial deformity. He was so grotesque that he had been exempted from compulsory school attendance and was illiterate, although he was unquestionably mentally alert and of normal intelligence. Plastic surgery would have made his appearance nearly normal. His mother, a widow, did not object to surgery *per se;* she was a Jehovah's Witness and objected to the blood transfusions that were a necessary part of the procedure. Surgeons testified that any attempt to perform the operation without transfusions, to which the mother was willing to consent, would have been to subject the child to a high risk of death, although with transfusions the operation was not likely to result in impairment. The surgeons refused to operate within the limitation imposed by the mother. The court ordered the procedure on the ground that the child was "neglected" because he was being unreasonably deprived of all opportunities for a normal education and social life.[21]

The courts are, however, willing to concede that a parent has a right to refuse radical or dangerous surgery for a child where the condition is not life-threatening and the parent simply refuses to submit the child to the operative risks. Thus, in many cases child abuse petitions accompanied by requests for an order to perform nonemergency surgery have been dismissed on grounds that the decision not to operate is within the permissible scope of parental authority.

A girl in elementary school had a monstrously enlarged arm. Her condition made it impossible for her to participate in any normal physical activities although she did attend school. At the request of her teacher, the local welfare department had her examined by a surgeon who advocated amputation since no other treatment would be successful. Citing her social adjustment problems and limitations on her activities caused by the condition, the welfare department attempted to obtain a court order allowing the amputation when her mother, a widow, refused to consent to surgery. The mother defended on the ground that the risk of death from surgery was far greater than the risk of death from infection if the arm was left untreated. The court held that the choice of risks was properly one for the child's mother to make and dismissed the petition.[22]

A 15-year-old boy had a harelip and a cleft palate. His parents' religious convictions forbade any medical treatment. Both parents and the child refused consent to surgery when school authorities alerted welfare officials to his problem, and a petition requesting a declaration of criminal neglect and an order to operate was filed. The court refused to order the surgery unless the boy wished to have it, in which case the judge indicated that he would override the parental veto. As long as the boy agreed with them, the trial judge held that they had the right to make the decision and that the welfare department and the court had no right to interfere since his life was not in danger.[23]

A 1911 Pennsylvania trial court decision involved a seven-year-old with rickets. His parents refused to consent to an orthopedic procedure to prevent permanent crippling on the ground that it was at that time a major operation that might cause his death. The court noted that the couple had lost seven of their ten children already and that their fears of the results of medical intervention appeared amply justified. Since the surgeon who would have performed the operation testified at the hearing that he would not absolutely guarantee that the child would survive it, the court refused to order the operation.[24]

Thus, in a high-risk procedure where the condition itself will not immediately threaten the child's life, courts are inclined to abide by the concept that establishment of "priorities of risk" is a legitimate parental function even though child-protection authorities would have chosen the other alternative.

Simple failure to obtain any medical care for a child when it is obviously necessary will, if the child dies, sustain a manslaughter conviction against the parents. If the child has died, it is totally irrelevant in law to argue that the reason the child was denied medical care was that the parents' refusal to provide it was rooted in religious conviction.[25]

In cases involving defective children there have been a few manslaughter or murder prosecutions of parents who took active steps to terminate the children's lives. Since most of these convictions were never appealed, written decisions are not available, but accounts of the facts in many are related in

Glanville Williams's book *The Sanctity of Life and the Criminal Law,*[26] arguing for legal recognition of euthanasia, and in Yale Kamisar's response.[27]

It should be noted from a survey of these cases that juries are reluctant to convict a parent in a clear mercy killing case, but that if the manner of the death was inhumane, first-degree murder verdicts are likely.

In one case a lawyer killed his six-month-old mongoloid son by wrapping an uninsulated electrical cord around his wet diaper and putting the baby on a silver platter to insure good contact before plugging the cord into the wall. At the trial he claimed that the child's death was an accident, and he was convicted of first-degree murder and sentenced to electrocution himself, although the sentence was later commuted to life.[28]

In a case where the sole surviving parent of an imbecile was herself faced with cancer surgery and killed her child with aspirin, she was convicted but the jury recommended an immediate pardon, which was granted.[29]

In *United States v. Repouille,* one of the few appellate decisions available, for example, a man had been convicted of manslaughter for killing his hopelessly defective 13-year-old child with chloroform. He received a suspended sentence. He later applied for citizenship and the court held that his act was sufficient to deny his petition on the ground of "moral turpitude."[30]

It is not seriously questioned that a parent has a legal duty to provide necessary medical assistance for his minor child and can be prosecuted for failure to do so. The question becomes one of defining "necessary assistance."

Whereas it is commonly assumed that a parent who does not provide necessary medical care is guilty of child neglect or abuse and, if the child dies, of murder or manslaughter, there is substantial difference between the cases on which that assumption is based and the situation of a deformed neonate.

As indicated above, all decisions have held that a Jehovah's Witness whose child's condition required blood transfusions has no right to forbid the giving of blood on the grounds of religious conviction. Religious conviction, as Justice Holmes said, may permit a parent to make a martyr of himself but "he is not free to make a martyr of his child."[31] The other cases involving religious objections to surgery or other medical treatment have also uniformly held that religion cannot be used as a defense and that the best interests of the child prevail, even to the extent of preemption of parental rights to First Amendment freedoms. A search of all the decisions, blood transfusion or otherwise, however, indicates that in each one the prognosis for the child if the treatment was given was for a normal or a near-normal life thereafter.

At least until decisions to the contrary are on the books, it may be assumed that a prosecutor will take the position, based on prior jurisprudence, that a failure to treat creates the same sort of liability as that applied in manslaughter convictions of parents who refused to give a diabetic child insulin. In a test case, however, it would be entirely appropriate to argue as a defense that radical surgery which cannot alleviate the condition should not be regarded in the same legal context as compulsory treatment given a child who will be able to live a normal life if a blood transfusion is given under court order.

If that differentiation is made, it would clearly distinguish between a situation involving a mongoloid with an intestinal obstruction and one presented by a child with spina bifida who will live, if at all, as a paraplegic. In the former case, the obstruction, totally unrelated to the defect by reason of which the parents wish the child to die, can be entirely corrected by nonheroic surgical procedures. This baby, it would appear logically, is in the same position medically as is a Jehovah's Witness child who has been in an automobile accident: reasonable medical care can restore normal function to the part of the child's body for which treatment is indicated. The fact that the child is also retarded is medically irrelevant to the difficulty for which surgery is permitted or denied.

Apparently there would be no difficulty in a manslaughter trial in proving that failure of ordinary care in not performing ordinary surgery, such as a routine repair of an intestinal obstruction, was the proximate cause of the baby's death, since it can be demonstrated from the medical literature that those normal children who have had the same operation usually recover without difficulties.

On the other hand, there is an old legal maxim that the law does not require performance of impossible conditions: *lex neminem cogit ad vana seu inutilia* —the law will not force anyone to do something that will be vain and fruitless. In those situations in which a child cannot be cured by surgery and in fact the first operation immediately after birth is the precurser of 15 or 20 to follow, merely to maintain the child's life but never to enable that life to be normal, it can be argued that refusal to begin a long and painful course of treatment with no hope of success cannot constitute neglect, and that sparing the child the pain of further surgery throughout childhood is a reasonable exercise of parental discretion.

In *Wisconsin v. Yoder* the Supreme Court allowed Amish parents to "protect" their children from a hostile environment by withdrawing them from public schools.[32] Only Justice Douglas's opinion reflected any concern for the rights of an adolescent who wanted a high-school education, and the rest of the justices assumed this to be a proper area in which parental decision-making was absolute and protected by First Amendment rights. It seems logical to apply the same principle to the medical setting. If the parent, if capable of making a sound and reasoned judgment with the speed required in these situations, honestly believes for religious or other reasons that it is a more loving act to allow a child to die of the same condition that will prevent him from leading a normal life with the best medicine can offer, than to treat the child and expose him to the "hostile environment" of pain and fear of semiannual major surgery and the taunts of his thoughtless peers as he gets older, it does not appear that a manslaughter charge could succeed as a matter of law.

There was no evidence, for example, presented in the press reports of Baby Houle's condition that at some point a plastic surgeon could not have helped correct his facial deformities or that he would have been retarded if immediate surgery had been performed. Baby Houle, therefore, would not fall under the second category, the "hopeless" case mentioned above. If a series of operations could have allowed him to function reasonably normally, then he would seem to belong to the same category as the Down's baby, in that the life-threatening malformation was curable and that it was unrelated to the reason for parental rejection. Thus the *Houle* case does not serve as precedent, nor do any other cases, for a determination that noncurative surgery is required under child abuse or manslaughter laws.

Criminal law and the physician.   Presumably the physician would also be liable under the same manslaughter or child abuse laws under which parents can be prosecuted. There is no doubt in this country that one is not legally obligated to be a Good Samaritan. A physician is fully entitled legally to drive by an automobile accident in which people have been injured, but once he does assume responsibility for the care of any patient he is civilly liable if he refuses to use due care in the treatment of the patient, and the standard is not "due care in treatment of the patient's family."

Furthermore, he may be criminally liable for willful refusal to provide care, thereby causing the death of the person to whom the duty, once assumed, is owed.[33] Prosecutions of physicians for the death of a patient are virtually unknown within the past 50 years, however, even where the patient died of gross stupidity on the part of the physician or treatment was given while the physician was drunk or drugged.[34] When proposed surgery is "ordinary" and the probability of a successful outcome assured, failure to perform it for reasons extraneous to the correctable medical condition appear to be sufficient to sustain a prosecution on the basis of willful refusal.

The only decisions, however, that can be located involving criminal proceedings charging willful refusal to obtain medical care for infants other than the prosecutions of parents have involved nonmedical personnel who were acting as foster parents of the babies as the result of contractual arrangements with the babies' mothers.[35]

It would seem that the possibility of prosecution of a physician for manslaughter or abuse if he fails to treat a defective newborn's correctable deformities and the child dies is less likely as a practical matter than prosecution of the parents who consented to his action. Such a charge cannot be entirely ruled out, however, particularly if a prosecutor wants to generate some favorable publicity for himself as a savior of innocent babies, and especially if the child has died of slow dehydration.

By contrast, in a case involving a child with spina bifida or other physical deformities in which a failure to treat will result in the child's death from that same condition and in which extraordinarily delicate neurosurgery or other radical treatment is necessary to keep the child alive, a different question is presented. In this case, it seems that "necessary medical care" has been provided if the child's routine needs were met, he was fed, he was not allowed to starve to death, and death resulted from an incurable condition. Since a very high percentage of children who have surgery for myelomeningocele die anyway,[36] either immediately or within a few weeks of birth, a physician's statement that in his judgment the child would probably have died if treatment had been given would appear to constitute a valid defense. Since neurosurgery on a neonate carries a high degree of risk a physician's argument that good medical judgment on a "cost-benefit analysis" basis—that is, that the risk of death from the surgery, plus certain knowledge that the procedure would not have *cured* the child's condition, justified nontreatment—would appear to constitute a complete defense to a criminal charge of either manslaughter or child abuse. This would appear particularly true since some children with myelomeningocele do survive if left untreated, and in fact the percentage is roughly the same as the number who die during or immediately after surgery.[37] Where the risk of surgical death is approximately the same as the rate of survival without treatment, the long-term benefits of surgery (which are nonexistent), in keeping with the existing judicial decisions holding that a parent, not a welfare department official, has the right to "weigh the odds," would seem to be the paramount legitimate factor in any conclusive determination of alternatives. To postulate a similar situation, it is unthinkable that a surgeon could be prosecuted for manslaughter for having refused to operate on an adult patient with a terminal malignancy because his professional judgment indicated that the pain of surgery or of operative complications would be more likely to harm the patient than surgery would be likely to prolong normal life for an appreciable period of time.

This appears to be an entirely different legal context from that of the mongoloid baby with an intestinal blockage. There is no legal requirement under criminal statutes to provide "extraordinary care," and only ordinary care for the maintenance of life, which it appears should include being adequately nourished, is required. The child with myelomeningocele is dying as the result of his condition and that condition is intractable. The mongoloid with an intestinal blockage could have been cured of that condition, and in any other child with the same problem the surgery would have been performed. If a child is suffering from unmanageable pain, it could also be argued that the best interest of the child requires prevention of pain by whatever method is necessary, including the withholding of surgical trauma in an admittedly hopeless case.[38]

In the legal decisions to be made in the future about treatment of the newborn child, it would appear that the ethical and moral standard that courts could very easily convert into an acceptable, reasonable legal standard is that if the treatment is more painful to the child than is a failure to treat, either on a short-term or a long-term basis, there is no criminal liability if treatment is omitted. If the child will grow up aware of a totally disabling physical handicap, then his emotional pain is also a legitimate legal concern. If, on the other hand, the child is so retarded that he will be virtually unaware of his handicap, it is not.

If definite standards on this subject have previously been established by the medical profession in the community in which a deformed child is allowed to die, they also would serve as a defense if a physician is prosecuted, since he would be able to demonstrate that he was acting within the boundaries of accepted medical opinion. If a staff committee at the hospital in which the baby was born has already provided that "in cases 1–6 treatment will be given even if parents refuse consent and, if necessary a court order will be obtained, but under the following circumstances treatment is not required if parents do not consent. . . ." at least the physician would not be required to justify his individual and unilateral medical judgment to a jury. If he could show that the diagnosis was such that the child fell within the category in which by staff by-law lack of treatment was permitted, either he would have a good defense or the prosecutor would be obliged to indict the entire staff committee at that hospital for conspiracy to commit manslaughter, a most unlikely possibility.

Established standards may also be advisable if a hospital committee is allowed to make other life-and-death decisions such as, "which is the more valuable life?" when only one person of several who need it can have hemodialysis or other treatment. If established standards indicate criteria for which treatment may be denied but provide that any other child, no matter how unwanted, whose condition does not meet those criteria must be treated, a great many problems might be solved. If the parent does not want a normal baby, he obviously cannot demand that the child be starved to death in the hospital nursery. There is no particular reason why it should be assumed that some parents would not like to do precisely that, since they quite frequently starve these children after they get them home. Murder of normal children by child abuse is not unusual. Many surgeons seem to agree that a retarded baby has no right to life. Thus, predetermined standards would, it seems, clarify the issues. If a child came within those provisions the pediatrician or obstetrician might in conscience suggest to the parents that they have a right to decide if treatment is to be withheld. If the child does not, treatment must be given. This, it would seem, would eliminate the unanswered question of the fate of a cosmetically deformed child who was otherwise healthy but whose parents do not want him.

The ultimate legal and ethical question is whether or not the family faced with financial and psychological hardships as well as serious effects on their marriage, their other children, and their personal aspirations for their child, may conclude that a life capable of only minimal mental development is a genuine "life." In connection with fetal research all the statements presented to the Commission for the Protection of Human Subjects by medical groups indicated that the standard practice, if a viable child is born after an abortion, is to treat the child as a normal, premature newborn and to provide appropriate medical care. Thus, it appears that an aborted viable child who is clearly unwanted by his mother currently has a greater legal rights than a full-term baby born with a handicap.

Thus, for determining questions of criminal liability for parents or physicians, the usual legal concept of the difference between ordinary versus extraordinary care should be used. Although this distinction has not been expressly recognized by any court in this context, a cogent argument can be made for such a distinction, as John A. Robertson has pointed out.[39]

At least one pediatric neurosurgeon has advocated differentiation of the treatment required by good medical practice on this basis and defined "ordinary care" as treatment which in that particular location is standard treatment, is likely to be carried out with a *reasonable degree of success* in the case at hand, and for which there is a possibility, either actual or potential, of satisfactory after-care.[40]

It is highly unlikely that with a critically ill adult patient any physician could be prosecuted for homicide or manslaughter for refusing to place the patient on hemodialysis or on a heart/lung machine or a respirator as long as he provides intravenous infusions to keep the patient from starving to death. Although it may be quite difficult in some cases to determine the difference between ordinary and extraordinary care in the neonatal situation, complex neurosurgery would surely be considered "extraordinary," whereas allowing a child to die by starvation would appear to be a criminal denial of "ordinary" care. Another aspect in determination of the difference in care is the degree of pain caused by the procedure itself to the child.

It should be observed that the legal system in general would be extremely unwise to get itself involved in a "quality of life" argument. Although it is unlikely that many prosecutors will wish to inject themselves into tragic situations of this nature, it is extremely difficult to justify establishment of a precedent that our legal system values some babies' lives over others. Once this is done, the "slippery slope" argument applies for future differentiation between other kinds of lives. It is therefore very improbable that any trial judge would do anything other than the judge did in the case of Baby Houle and order the operation to be performed since the "quality of life" was the only argument the parents made.

Determining degrees of humanness as a matter of law seems to be an extremely futile endeavor in the first place and an extremely dangerous one for any legal system in the second. Although many people believe that the deformed child's suffering and diminished quality of capacity to interact with others do not justify the social and economic cost of treatment, we do not normally measure the legal value of a life in this country on the basis of dollars and cents.

One pediatric psychiatrist who specializes in the problems of retarded children wrote in the *New York Times,* after making a comparison between the rights of Jehovah's Witnesses' children and noting that all courts order them to be transfused but that deformed newborns are allowed to die, "Can a just society tolerate two classes of infants and children, one of whose right to life is at the mercy of parents and physicians and another whose right to life is assured through judicial intervention and the full protection of the law?"[41]

Richard McCormick wrote in the *Journal of the American Medical Association,* "Concretely if there are certain infants that we agree ought to be saved in spite of the illness or deformity and if there are certain infants that we should agree should be allowed to die, then there is a line to be drawn and if there is a line to be drawn there ought to be some criteria even if very general."[42] McCormick believes that the cut-off point should be between ordinary and extraordinary care. His definition of ordinary care is "those means whose use does not entail grave hardship (i.e., pain) to the patient."[43] He would also argue that a valid guideline would be the potential for human relationships associated with the infant's condition. Many mongoloids, for example, are loving, happy children. Thus, McCormick does not think that it should be said that a mongoloid cannot "have the potential for relationship," but he admits that other categories of deformed children clearly cannot. The child who is normally intelligent but paralyzed may in fact have less capacity for "meaningful relationships" on his own level. The clearest guideline should be that no child should be faced with pain in dying, which would totally eliminate, legally and ethically, ever allowing a child to starve to death. Conversely, if the pain connected with surgery is intractable and the life cannot be made whole, surely there is a moral obligation not to cause a newborn excruciating pain. Therefore, the primary legal principle of criminal liability may be clarified. There is a legal duty to provide ordinary medical treatment for newborns or for any other child. If that treatment is not provided and the child dies, the physician or the parents are open to charges of child abuse or manslaughter. Extraordinary treatment, particularly when futile, does not appear to be a legal duty.

Civil liability and the physician: misdiagnosis.   It is perfectly obvious under normal principles of medical professional liability law that a careless diagnosis of the condition of any newborn baby is actionable negligence. Failure to recognize that a baby has phenylketonuria[44] or Rh disease[45] within the first hours of life has been the subject of several cases, and since expert testimony was presented by the plaintiffs that a duly careful physician would have diagnosed the problem in each case, the physicians were liable. Since failure to institute treatment for a newborn can cause lifelong handicaps, the damages awarded in these cases are usually enormous.

Any error in diagnosis, including an estimate of the probability of death, with or without treatment, in the case of a deformed newborn would, if negligent, subject the physician to a successful action by the parents, and any jury would probably be most sympathetic in computation of the award. If the child is suspected of having Down's syndrome, due care in the current state of medical practice would probably, although there are no cases on the subject, require that the child be kept alive while an examination of the baby's chromosomes is made by a geneticist.[46] Only after the original diagnosis has been clearly confirmed by the best laboratory analysis available should the possibility of nontreatment be explored. If the physician who examines the child erroneously concludes that the child is a mongoloid, the child is allowed to die, and the mistake is discovered on autopsy, the only defense to a wrongful death action and one for ordinary malpractice that could be argued is that failure to make an accurate diagnosis was an "unavoidable error," and with precise laboratory techniques available this defense is not likely to succeed.

Conversely, if Down's syndrome or another condition is not discovered and a correctable defect is treated, insuring survival of a defective infant, the parents at least hypothetically might succeed in a wrongful life suit. Juries, however, would probably be disinclined to award very substantial damages to any couple who appeared before them claiming that if they had known what was wrong with their baby they would have "gotten rid of it" and asking an award of damages against the physician who saved the baby's life, even if his action was undertaken by mistake.

In any case in which laboratory tests cannot conclusively determine the existence of a suspected defect and there is even a remote possibility of error, common sense and minimal self-protection demand that a prudent physician should obtain a consultation with, and confirmation of his diagnosis from at least one other specialist, and if possible, two specialists, with whom he is not associated in practice. If all three concur that the defect exists, the chance of error is remote. If, however, an error has been made, such consultations will serve in any subsequent suit to prove that the standard of diagnostic care expected has been met.[47]

Even if there is no question that a defect exists, determination of the degree of permanent disability is of critical importance in making the decision of whether the child should be treated.[48] Some babies with myelomeningocele are able, with proper care, to lead normal lives. Some babies who are mongoloid are only slightly retarded. Thus, prior to raising the issue of nontreatment with the parents, due care in treatment would certainly mandate a very high degree of precision in estimation of deformity, and a negligent error that affected the decision to allow a child to die would be clearly actionable. In this case perhaps even more than in diagnosis of the condition itself, consultation is clearly indicated, both to eliminate error as completely as possible, and, if one occurs, to provide proof of due care.

Civil liability and the physician: informed consent. Although as an ethical matter it may be impossible for parents of a defective newborn to make a genuinely informed decision to treat or not to treat their child, as a matter of law it is mandatory to provide them with as much information as possible so that distrait or not they may at least attempt to make a valid judgment.

Particularly in the case of a baby with myelomeningocele, it would be absolutely necessary to tell them that an untreated baby may survive and that if he does, his handicaps will be demonstrably worse than if immediate surgery had been performed. Failure to do so would be clearly actionable.

In cases where mongoloid or other children may die as the result of untreated digestive or respiratory problems, the parents should, it seems, be clearly advised that the condition can be corrected and would be if the child were an otherwise normal baby. Furthermore, if the child's death is going to be protracted and the child will suffer, this must be made absolutely clear to them. A parent might very well be convinced that a choice for death is an act of love if the child will die painlessly within the next 15 minutes, but absolutely refuse to allow the child to dehydrate for a period of 15 days, as happened in the Johns Hopkins case.

Failure to warn them that the death will be slow and painful would appear to be a total denial of their right to give a genuine informed consent. Therapeutic privilege would seem totally inapplicable since their developing horror as they see the child cling to life day after day would appear far more likely to upset them than a verbal explanation by the physician at the outset.

Furthermore, a parent who thinks that a baby's death will be swift and painless and who is left to discover that the baby is dying slowly and painfully may very well change his or her mind and demand that the child be treated.[49] If, as in the case of Baby Houle, the delay weakens the child and adversely affects the results of the treatment once it is given, thus presenting the parents with a viable child in worse condition than would have been true if treatment had been immediate, it would seem clear that they would have an action on behalf of the child for negligent treatment and one on their own behalf for failure to obtain their informed consent.

Civil liability and the physician: abandonment. Failure to treat a patient when treatment is reasonably required is, by definition, abandonment for which damages are frequently awarded.[50] In some situations parents might have an abandonment action against a physician who did not treat their deformed newborn.

First, however ethically commendable it might be for a physician to realize that he is the real decision-maker in this context and that the real responsibility is his, if he therefore concludes that he has no duty to discuss the situation with the parents and unilaterally decides not to treat the baby, abandonment has clearly occurred. For example, if a premature child has probable brain damage from Respiratory Distress Syndrome and the pediatrician decides to put him into an ordinary nursery bassinet and ignore him instead of placing him in a pediatric intensive care unit, abandonment has occurred. If parents are not told that surgery can cure a mongoloid's intestinal obstruction, either or both abandonment of the baby and abuse of parental rights to consent have occurred.

Second, an action for abandonment might very well be successful if, as indicated above, parents were not told that the child's death would be protracted instead of, as they assumed, immediate, even if they consented to nontreatment. A parent may consent to the death of a child without in any way intending to consent to the infliction of pain or allowing the baby to "wither and dehydrate," and if that in fact occurs, it is at least arguable that they can contend that the child was abandoned.

The claim of abandonment might also arise in a third situation: an action brought against the physician by grandparents or other family members for nontreatment even if the parents consented with full knowledge of the consequences. This claim, however, is unlikely to be successful since the grandparents have no legal right to be consulted as long as the parents are competent adults.

If the mother is an unmarried minor, consent of her parents not to treat probably should be obtained, if they are reasonably available, in the exercise of prudent practice. If a conflict between a minor mother and her parents erupts, a reasonably sensible physician will ask for a court order directing him to treat the child, as a less detrimental alternative to himself than a later suit for abandonment.

The same response might be made if one parent wants the child treated and the other does not. In that circumstance, if there is no wish to have a court resolve the conflict, the only prudent course of action is "when in doubt, treat."[51]

THE DUTY TO PROLONG LIFE

A related legal issue may arise when a normal child develops a terminal illness in which treatment to prolong life is available but would leave the child severely handicapped for his remaining life, as the following example illustrates: A school-age child who has developed normally and who is of normal or above-normal intelligence (i.e., is unquestionably consciously aware of his situation) becomes ill and a brain tumor is diagnosed. There is no possibility that the child can be cured, but surgery is available that will prolong life for some considerable time, perhaps a year or more, during which it is conceivable that new procedures to save the child's life will be developed. The surgery will leave the child's intelligence, perceptions, and awareness unimpaired, but will utterly destroy his sight. Suppose that the parents decide that since the child will die rather quickly without surgery but will be able to lead a more normal life until almost the very end without being blind, they will refuse to consent to surgery. Are either the surgeon or the parents guilty of any criminal offense? It would appear that in this case they are not.

As was pointed out in the context of the deformed newborn, in the Jehovah's Witness's cases, and in all other cases in which surgery was ordered, the child, given proper treatment would have made a full recovery. That is not true in this case. Again it would appear that a refusal to permit treatment that would allow the child to swallow, digest food, and breathe and when in its absence the child is condemned to die an agonized and painful death would constitute clear abuse, but as long as the effects of the surgery would be devastating to the child and cause him physical and mental pain, it is highly improbable that any court would hold that such an operation was necessary medical care. Thus, it would seem that a child in this situation, given such ordinary therapy as is reasonably available without undue discomfort to him and who thus dies months or perhaps a year before he would have with surgery has received treatment that has met the requirements of the law.

In this situation reasonable parental decisions, it would seem, should control. Unlike the case of a defective newborn, where the mother has not yet recovered from the effects of childbirth and where the diagnosis is a tremendous shock in addition to her physical exhaustion, the diagnosis of an older child as having a malignancy or some other disease does not present a situation in which a decision must be made within a few minutes or hours by at least one exhausted parent. Thus, the ethical dilemma of obtaining a genuinely informed consent is not presented.

It is clear that a mentally competent adult patient has the right to refuse on his own behalf life-saving treatment that will prolong a miserable and painful existence.[52] No ethicist, theologically inclined or otherwise, has argued that a terminally ill patient has any moral or ethical obligation to God, his family, or himself to consent to heroic measures that will only prolong his suffering or in fact increase it without offering any hope of recovery. In fact, the entire concept of "death with dignity," on which many books and articles have recently been written by eminent ethicists, reflects a growing concern with the refusal of many members of the medical profession to desist from extraordinary treatment when it is arguably inhumane to pursue it.[53]

It would seem, in this case, that a parent should be able to make the same decision for death with dignity for his child. As long as ordinary care is provided, it would appear that the parents have a legal right to refuse extraordinary care.

Quite a different situation, however, would be presented by disagreeable but nonmaiming treatment. For example, children with leukemia are given drugs with severe side effects, including hair loss and nausea. They also must spend long periods of time in hospitals. If a parent refused to allow treatment on the ground that the child would suffer anguish from baldness or would get homesick in the hospital, it is presumable that any judge would rule that such chemotherapy is now "ordinary treatment" and that failure to provide it would constitute neglect. Furthermore, as research continues, the child in remission with leukemia and living a normal life may well eventually survive the disease. Where recovery even with a handicap is probable, there is probably an arguable ethical duty to treat a child, but whether a court would order brain surgery that would blind or paralyze a child but which could completely remove a tumor would undoubtedly depend less on strict adherence to common law than on the judge's personal philosophy. A decision either way could be based on the existing jurisprudence.

One pediatric hematologist has written about prolonged treatment of children with leukemia: "Personally, I will fight for every day if I have even the slightest chance of doing something more than just gaining one more day. . . . I do not believe in throwing the towel in if there is any chance of even a small and temporary victory, but when defeat is completely certain with the medical armamentarium we have presently available, then we are entitled to use supportive care only and not overdo it."[54] This would appear not only to constitute good medical practice but also to comply with any requirements the legal system, civil or criminal, may demand.

THE CHILD'S RIGHT TO DIE

Only one article can be located discussing a case of an adolescent who decided to refuse life-saving treatment.

A 16-year-old girl with acute kidney problems received a transplanted kidney from her father. The transplant, however, failed and the girl was placed on hemodialysis.

She tolerated this poorly, vomited constantly, and about 8 months after she began dialysis she announced following a lengthy period of acute illness that she no longer wanted to be maintained on hemodialysis. The parents concurred. Treatment was stopped and she died quickly.[55]

This child was evaluated by several psychiatrists, none of whom found any evidence of psychosis and all of whom were convinced that the girl had carefully thought out her decision and grasped its implications. The issue is whether the legal system should accept such a decision by a minor or whether the physician should ask the court to order treatment.

Most literature on the subject of the dying child indicates that prior to 14 or 15 years of age most children do not understand the real implications of death.[56] In numerous discussions of proper medical management of the emotional needs of a terminally ill child, most of which have involved children with acute leukemia, it becomes clear that even a very young child is aware of some terminal "events" which happen to other children in the hospital, at least that they disappear permanently, but it also seems clear that prior to adolescence it is extremely unlikely that a child has a serious concept of the meaning of death.[57]

The report of the girl with kidney disease indicated that it is rare that children who have not reached adolescence decide to die, but the statistics on children's suicides (probably before they fully comprehend the finality of their act) would appear to argue against that conclusion. It might be reasonable to argue the principle that prior to adolescence a child's rejection of life-saving treatment should not be considered as being an informed consent and that the child prior to that time is incapable of comprehending the meaning of what he has decided.

If a 12-year-old child with bone cancer declined to consent to amputation of his leg because he would sincerely rather die than live with one leg (which many boys at that age might very well believe), it is unlikely that a wise physician would accede to the child's request even if the parents agreed to be bound by the child's decision. The handicap would not be an overwhelming one. By contrast, if a younger child wished to discontinue hemodialysis, it would seem that a refusal by the parents to continue the treatment, even if instigated by the child's request, would probably be a valid and legal determination since there is no hope of normal life.

Assume, however, that a competent adolescent, aged 16 or 17, wishes to refuse treatment and the parents do *not* concur. The parents wish the child to be treated as completely as possible with life prolonged as long as possible. It would appear in this case that the physician is legally bound to abide by the judgment of the parents who are responsible for the child legally, morally, and economically.

It should be remembered that adolescents are generally consulted about a petition for court-ordered treatment if their parents refuse permission.

In one case parents refused for religious reasons to allow surgery for a harelip and a cleft palate and the child was very vehement in his agreement with their views. The court held that ordering major surgery over the objection of the patient would diminish its success, since his full cooperation in postoperative therapy would be essential. The petition of the welfare department was therefore denied.[58]

A 17-year-old boy's parents refused for religious reasons to permit orthopedic surgery for a severe curvature of the spine if blood transfusions were to be used. Medical testimony indicated that the transfusions were vital. The appellate court remanded the case for the trial judge's determination of the boy's wishes and implied that those wishes would control and an order would issue if he wanted surgery.[59]

It is perfectly sound logic and law to conclude that if a terminally ill child wants treatment and his parents do not, a physician is entitled to abide by a wish to preserve life and, if necessary, do so by court petition. The same principle should apply if one or both parents want to have the treatment given and the child does not.

Only two decisions can be located that have held that an adolescent has a right to refuse treatment if his parents wish him or her to have it, and in neither situation was the child in danger of death.

A 16-year-old pregnant girl wanted to marry her boyfriend and raise their child. Her mother wanted her to have an abortion, and the gynecologist asked the court to decide the issue. The trial court held, and the Maryland supreme court agreed, that the child could not be aborted against her will.[60]

The Supreme Court of Connecticut held that a teenage boy had the right to be released from a mental hospital over his parents' objections since an adult would have had the right to leave at will and no claim was made that the boy was dangerous to himself or others.[61]

In neither case would the issue appear at all analogous to that of an adolescent with a serious, intractable disease who wishes to refuse treatment, since neither child was in any serious danger of death.

In most cases involving conflicts between parents and children the legal system automatically assumes that the parent is correct. While this assumption may be seriously questioned in cases involving commitments of children by parents to mental hospitals or juvenile institutions as unmanageable and in some other contexts, it does seem that where the child life is at stake, a conflict between the parents and the child should be resolved in favor of preservation of the child's life, even if treatment is given over the child's objection. Only when all three agree or the one parent who is available concurs with the child and it is also clear the child understands the meaning of a decision to die, should life-prolonging treatment that cannot restore the child to health be terminated.

If an emancipated child, either *de facto* (such as a runaway) or *de jure,* should refuse treatment for a condition that could be terminal without the full consent of the parent, who may not be available, it would appear to be extremely unwise as a matter of law for a physician to accede to an unmarried adolescent's "right to die" in the absence of clear and convincing proof that (1) reasonably normal function cannot be restored in any case and (2) the parents cannot possibly be located. Unless the parents are notified, come to the scene if they wish, and fully concur in the child's right to die, it would seem to be extremely unwise to allow an adolescent to make that decision on his own. A married minor whose spouse is an adult presumably should be requested and probably required to give consent before treatment is terminated. If both are minors, prudence would dictate parental consultation where a life is at stake.

NOTES

1. Anthony Shaw, "Doctor, Do We Have a Choice?" *New York Times* (Sunday Magazine), January 30, 1972, page 50.

2. John M. Freeman, "To Treat or Not to Treat, Ethical Dilemmas of Treating the Infant with a Myelomeningocele," 20 *Clin Neurol,* page 135. For a lengthy survey of the eventual outcome of 524 cases all of whom received vigorous treatment at birth, see J. Lorber, "Results of Treatment of Myelomeningocele," 13 *Develop Med Child Neurol,* page 279, 1971. Lorber had at one time opposed denial of any available treatment, but after surveying long-term results of these cases he changed his position and now selects newborns for surgery with extreme care.

3. Anthony Shaw, "Informed Consent in Children," 289 *New Engl J Med,* page 889, 1973.

4. Gerald Leach, *The Biocrats: Ethics and the New Medicine,* Baltimore, Penguin Books 1972, pages 207–208.

5. Lorber, *op. cit. supra* at 2, pages 286 and 300.

6. See, for example, John A. Robertson, "Involuntary Euthanasia of Defective Newborns: A Legal Analysis," 27 *Stanford Law Rev,* pages 255–259, 1975; David H. Smith, "On Letting Some Babies Die," 2 *Hastings Center Studies* No. 2, pages 40–42, May 1974.

7. Raymond Duff and A. G. M. Campbell, "Moral and Ethical Dilemmas in the Special-Care Nursery," 289 *New Engl J Med,* page 890, October 1973.

8. E.g., John Fletcher, "Attitudes Toward Defective Newborns," 2 *Hastings Center Studies* No. 1, page 21, January 1974; "The Birth of an Abnormal Child: Telling the Parents," editorial, *Lancet,* page 1075, November 13, 1971; G. H. Zuk, "The Religious Factor and the Role of Guilt in Parental Acceptance of the Retarded Child," 64 *Am J Mental Deficiency,* page 139; Philip Pinkerton, "Parental Acceptance of the Handicapped Child," 12

Develop Med Child Neurol, page 207, 1970; Pauline Cohen, "Impact of the Handicapped Child on the Family," 43 *Social Casework,* page 137, 1962; Arnon Bentovin, "Emotional Disturbances of Handicapped Preschool Children," 3 *Brit Med J,* page 579, 1972.

9. Fletcher, *op. cit. supra* at 8, page 25.

10. "Bedside Ethics for the Hopeless Case," 289 *New Engl J Med,* page 914, October 1973.

11. Raymond Duff, "Interview," *Hastings Center Report,* page 7, April 1975.

12. Freeman, *op. cit. supra* at 2, page 141.

13. "Is There a Right to Die—Quickly?" editorial, 80 *J Pediat,* page 904, 1972.

14. E.g., James M. Gustafson, "Mongolism, Parental Desires and the Right to Life," *Perspectives Biol Med,* page 529, Summer 1973.

15. See, among other comments on the Johns Hopkins case, Gustafson, *op. cit. supra* at 14; Richard A. McCormick, "To Save or Let Die: The Dilemma of Modern Medicine," 229 *JAMA* No. 2, page 172, July 8, 1974.

16. *Washington Post,* February 25, 1974, page A1.

17. Peter Rickham, "The Ethics of Surgery in Newborn Infants," 8 *Clin Pediat,* page 251, 1969.

18. E.g., Hoerner v. Bertinato, 171 A 2d 140, NJ 1961; People ex rel Wallace v. Labrenz, 104 NE 2d 769, Ill 1952; State v. Perricone, 181 A 2d 751, NJ 1962; In re Clark, 185 NE 2nd 128, Ohio 1962.

19. E.g., McCartney v. Austin, 298 NYS 2d 26, NY 1969.

20. In re Karwath, 199 NW 2d 147, Iowa 1972.

21. In re Sampson, 328 NYS 2d 686, NY 1972.

22. In re Hudson, 126 P 2d 765, Wash 1942.

23. In re Seiferth, 127 NE 2d 820, NY 1955.

24. In re Tuttendario, 21 Pa Dist 561, Pa 1912.

25. E.g., Craig v. State, 155 A 3d 684, Md 1959; People v. Pierson, 68 NE 243, NY 1903; State v. Clark, 261 A 2d 294, Conn 1969; Eaglen v. State, 231 NE 2d 147, Ind 1967; People v. Edwards, 249 NYS 2d 325, NY 1964.

26. Glanville Williams, *The Sanctity of Life and the Criminal Law,* New York, Alfred A. Knopf, 1957, pages 20–32.

27. Yale Kamisar, "Some Non-religious Views Against Proposed Mercy-Killing Legislation," 42 *Minn Law Rev* No. 6, page 969, May 1958.

28. *Ibid.,* page 1022.

29. *Ibid.,* page 1021.

30. United States v. Repouille, 165 F 2d 152, CCA 2, 1947.

31. Prince v. Massachusetts, 321 US 158, 1944.

32. Wisconsin v. Yoder, 406 US 205, 1972.

33. Robertson, *op. cit. supra* at 6, page 225.

34. "Criminal Prosecution for Patient's Death," 222 *JAMA* No. 10, page 1341, December 4, 1972.

35. E.g., Jones v. United States, 308 F 2d 307, CA DC 1962; People v. Montecino, 152 P 2d 5, Cal 1944; State v. Lowe, 68 NW 1094, Minn 1896.

36. Lorber, *op. cit. supra* at 2, page 280.

37. *Ibid.*

38. See, for an ethicist's approval of this point, McCormick, *op. cit. supra* at 15.

39. Robertson, *op. cit. supra* at 6, page 235.

40. Rickham, *op. cit. supra* at 17.

41. Frederick Grunberg, "Who Lives and Dies?" *New York Times,* April 22, 1974, page 35, Col 2.

42. McCormick, *op. cit. supra* at 15.

43. *Ibid.*

44. E.g., Naccarato v. Grob, 180 NW 2d 788, Mich 1970.

45. Price v. Neyland, 320 F 2d 674, CA DC 1963.

46. This is apparently the current practice at least at the University of Virginia Hospital. See Shaw, *op. cit supra* at 3, page 886.

47. See, generally, "Duty to Consult," 226 *JAMA* No. 1, page 111, October 1, 1973.

48. For a lengthy discussion of the physician's duty to discuss probable prognosis with parents, see Freeman, *op. cit. supra* at 2, pages 141–143.

49. See, for an example of such a situation, "Case Studies in Bioethics: On the Birth of a Severely Handicapped Infant," *Hastings Center Report,* pages 10–12, September 1973.

50. See Angela R. Holder, *Medical Malpractice Law,* New York, John Wiley and Sons, 1975, Ch 12.

51. See, for a similar case of parental conflict involving cardiac surgery on an older child, Durfee v. Durfee, 87 NYS 2d 275, NY 1949.

52. E.g., In re Maida Yetter, 62 Pa D & C 2d 619, 1973; Palm Springs General Hospital v. Martinez, Fla Cir Ct, Dade Co, 1971; In re Petition of Nemser, 273 NYS 2d 624, NY 1966.

53. E.g., Paul Ramsey, *The Patient as Person,* New Haven, Conn, Yale University Press, 1970; "Facing Death," symposium, 2 *Hastings Center Studies* No. 2, May 1974; Jay Katz, *Experimentation with Human Beings,* New York, Russell Sage Foundation, 1972, pages 692–718.

54. Rudolph Toch, "Management of the Child with a Fatal Disease," 3 *Clin Pediat* No. 7, pages 423–424.

55. John Schowalter, Julian Ferholt, and Nancy Mann, "The Adolescent Patient's Decision to Die," 51 *Pediatrics* No. 1, page 97, January 1973.

56. E.g., Albert J. Solnit and Morris Green, "Pediatric Management of the Dying Child: Part II, The Child's Reaction to the Fear of Dying," in *Modern Perspectives in Child Development,* New York, International Universities Press, 1963; Toch, *op. cit. supra* at 54; Joel Vernick and Myron Karon, "Who's Afraid of Death on a Leukemia Ward?" 109 *Am J Diseases Children,* page 393, May 1965.

57. Schowalter, Ferholt, and Mann, *op. cit. supra* at 55, page 79.

58. In re Seiferth, 127 NE 2d 820, NY 1955.

59. In re Green, 292 A 2d 387, Pa 1972.

60. In re Smith, 295 A 2d 238, Md 1972.

61. Melville v. Sabbatino, 313 A 2d 886, Conn 1973.

CHAPTER V

THE MINOR'S

CONSENT TO

TREATMENT

An increasing problem in the practice of pediatrics and particularly of adolescent medicine is the determination of whether a minor has the right to consent to medical treatment over the objection or without the knowledge of his or her parents. Questions involving the minor's right to abortion and contraception as well as of involving a minor in therapeutic research are sufficiently complex so that they will be discussed in later chapters; but standard treatment that the minor's condition requires may or may not in any given case lead to a finding of liability on the physician's part if the parent is not consulted before the treatment is given. With the increasing number of runaways, some of whom may be quite young, and other situations in which a large number of adolescents are not living with their parents, the number of these young people requesting treatment appears to be increasing remarkably. Concomitant with this development is an increasing appreciation in the legal system generally for the rights of children when these rights conflict with parental desires or demands imposed by the public school system or the society. Thus, the question of what to do with the young person of 13, 14, 15, or 16 years of age who requests treatment is becoming an acute problem for physicians. Five different family situations may be presented, and the probable legal consequences of each to the physician may be different:

1. The parent or parents are known and available for discussion of the problem and the minor has no objection to notification of the parent.
2. The parent or parents are known and available but the minor refuses to allow the physician to discuss the problem with them.
3. The parent or parents are known but not available and cannot be located prior to institution of treatment that should be begun immediately.
4. The minor refuses to tell the physician who his parents are and how they can be located.
5. The parent or parents are located and notified and refuse consent to treatment that the minor wishes to have.

Moreover, in any one of these situations, the minor may be:

1. living at home.
2. living away from his parents with their consent but supported by them, such as a student in boarding school or college.
3. living away from his parents with their consent and self-supporting.
4. living away from his parents without their consent, such as a minor who has run away.

The question of the child's constitutional right to medical care, if any, might well be raised if he were denied treatment at a publicly supported facility such as an emergency room or tax-supported clinic solely on the ground that he refused to reveal the identity of his family for purposes of obtaining their consent.

The Supreme Court held in 1974 that an indigent had a constitutional right to necessary medical care at a public hospital and that failure to admit him was a denial of one of the basic necessities of existence.[1] Numerous decisions of the Supreme Court, particularly in the field of the rights of juvenile offenders, have held that a child may be treated differently from an adult by a governmental entity only if the difference accrues to the child's benefit and not to his detriment.[2] Where the difference in the medical treatment of a minor and an adult with the same illness is that the minor is sent away and the adult is treated, substantial questions of equal protection of the laws under the Fourteenth Amendment would appear to be raised if the minor is in fact, if not in law, capable of giving a knowing consent to treatment.

The same issue could conceivably be raised in a situation in which an adolescent's parents refused consent to necessary treatment to which the minor himself could give knowing consent and which he desired as long as he was able to pay his own bills. This issue will be discussed in more detail in the chapter on abortion, since virtually all decisions involving parent-child conflict in which the issue is parental refusal to consent involve that procedure.

The common-law rule was and is that treatment of a minor even without negligence and where the treatment led to a satisfactory result but for which the parents did not consent gave rise to an action for assault and battery brought by the parents.[3] The child at common law was considered to be virtually a chattel of his parents, and thus the parent had an almost absolute right to make decisions affecting his welfare. Therefore, any interference with the parent's control of the child even if intended as beneficial treatment gave the parent, not the child, a cause of action against the physician.

This is undoubtedly still the case in nonemergency situations where very young children are concerned. In dealing with children under the age of puberty, it is clear that parental consent should be obtained. Thus, for example, a pediatrician who prescribes drugs for a seven-year-old at the behest of the child's teacher, who has decided that the child is hyperkinetic, without consulting the child's parents is clearly acting at his own peril.

CONSENT OF ONE PARENT

Where parental consent must be obtained and the parents are separated or divorced, the parent with legal or actual custody has a clear right to consent to medical treatment without approval of the other parent. Under English common law the father's right of custody was paramount to the mother's, and she could direct a child's life only after the father's death.[4] By this century, however, and certainly today each parent stands as an equal partner in matters concerning the children while they are living together. In case of the dissolution of a marriage, the custodial parent has the right to make the usual decisions about the child's life, including any matters concerning the child's medical treatment. If separation has occurred, the parent with custody in fact may not know where the other parent is. In informal separations as far as third parties such as physicians are concerned, the parent who has possession of the child is in the same legal position as if custody had been awarded by a court. There are also, of course, circumstances under which the marriage is not dissolved but one parent is absent for some reason, such as a father who is overseas in military service. In all cases the custodial parent's right to consent to treatment is indisputable.[5]

Any surgeon, for example, who would refuse to perform necessary surgery on a child whose father was overseas and whose mother gave consent would be altogether overcautious. There are no recent reported cases in which a father has sued for failure to consult him before treating a child when a mother with custody consented. In only a few situations has this subject ever been litigated.

A 15-year-old girl was in the legal custody of her mother following a divorce. Surgery had been arranged by her mother for a condition that was not discussed in the opinion but which was apparently quite serious. Her father vehemently objected on the grounds that the procedure would be extremely dangerous and that it was highly experimental. Inferences made in the court's opinion indicated that the father also considered the surgery to be unnecessary. The trial judge resolved the problem by pointing out to both parents that the child's health was further deteriorating as a result of the protracted difficulties between the parents. To attempt to resolve the conflict, the trial judge required the father to suggest names of surgeons of whom he approved and directed the mother to take the child to at least one of them for consultation hopefully to arrive at a solution satisfactory to all. The court held, however, that since the mother had legal custody of the child, her decision would prevail if no compromise could be effected.[6]

In most states a father is liable for his child's "necessary expenses" even in the absence of any court order of child support. This may be true even though he had not been consulted before the expense was incurred and may be opposed to it.[7] It is perfectly clear and has been for many years that medical care is included among "necessary expenditures". However, where the mother arranges for the medical treatment of the child when she is divorced or separated, she assumes the primary responsibility for the bill, and the physician and hospital are justified in expecting her to pay it. She may then proceed against the father for reimbursement if she wishes. Alternatively, a physician may proceed directly against the father for payment, but any legal action against the father, particularly if he lives in a different state, might well prove to be more time-consuming and troublesome than it is worth.

If the father is available when medical treatment becomes necessary, the physician will normally request his signature on consent forms. In his absence, however, neither the hospital nor physician should be concerned that they might suffer an adverse judgment if the father sues on the ground that the child has been treated without consultation with him if the mother has assumed responsibility for the child's care.

EMERGENCY CARE

In a genuine medical emergency, a child may be treated without parental consent and the parents may not recover damages for proper treatment without their consent from the physician who administered it.[8] If the treatment given in an emergency is negligent, of course, the child may by his guardian, usually the parent, sue the physician just as he would if parental consent had been given. Other than in emergency cases, however, parents do have a right to sue a physician for administering nonnegligent care to a young child without parental consent. Although it is unlikely, as will be discussed below, that courts would be disposed to take a narrow view of the definition of "emergency," it should always be presumed that purely elective treatment of a young child should never be undertaken without parental consent. For example, if a ten-year-old who wears glasses and thus is receiving adequate attention to any abnormality of his eyes requests an ophthalmologist to prescribe and fit contact lenses so that he can participate in contact sports with greater ease, parental consent should certainly be obtained. Young children are not as likely as adolescents to seek medical help on their own initiative, but they may well be brought to the physician by a teacher or relative who concludes that the parents are at fault for not submitting the child to various forms of elective treatment and thus, sometimes quite officiously, undertake to arrange the treatment themselves. A teacher may conclude that a child is hyperkinetic and should be given drugs; a grandmother may be outraged that parents have not initiated treatment from a plastic surgeon for a child with a cosmetic defect. In these cases the parents may have a well-reasoned objection to the treatment, but even if they are genuinely unconcerned about the problem, they are likely to resent such intermeddling. In these cases the physician should refuse to treat the child without the explicit consent of the parents given directly and clearly to him.

Under no circumstances should a child be subjected to any nontherapeutic procedure without parental consent.

A 15-year-old boy who lived with his mother was persuaded by his aunt to donate skin for grafts for the aunt's child who had been badly burned. The child went to the hospital alone and was admitted. Hospital personnel knew that he lived with his mother, but she was not told of the procedure or asked for consent. Complications arose and the boy was hospitalized for more than two months. In addition to the action brought on behalf of the child for improper treatment, the court held that the mother had a cause of action in her own right because the procedure was performed without her knowledge and consent.[9]

EMANCIPATED MINORS

An emancipated minor has been recognized as "one who is not subject to parental control or regulation" in a wide variety of legal contexts for many years. The precise definition of emancipation varies among jurisdictions, but an emancipated minor is one who usually is not living at home and is self-supporting, is responsible for himself economically and otherwise, and whose parents (voluntarily or involuntarily) have surrendered their parental duties and rights. Married minors, for example, are considered emancipated and, without any question at all, may consent to medical treatment for themselves or their own minor child.[10] If the marriage is dissolved, the minor remains emancipated unless the basis of the dissolution is an annulment action brought by the parents on the ground of the minor's incapacity to consent. Minors in military service are considered to be entirely emancipated, and no parental permission is ever required in dealing with them.[11]

College Students

A college student who is living away from home, even if he is financially dependent on his parents, is usually considered in most medical contexts to be an emancipated minor, and medical treatment may be administered without parental consent. It is probably wise to attempt to notify the parent of a college student who requires a major surgical procedure or medical intervention that carries a high degree of risk but, if the physician proceeds to treat him without doing so and certainly if the college student has objected to notification of the parent, it is highly unlikely that a successful suit could be maintained by his parents.

Boarding School Students

A child in boarding school below the college level should, in general, be dealt with as if he were living at home. If the treatment involves minimal risk and could be given without notification to parents if the child were at home, then notification would be unnecessary. If, on the other hand, treatment would not be given without notification, it should not be assumed that the fact that the child is in boarding school obviates consent by the parents. Most schools require parental signature on a form allowing school authorities to consent to necessary or emergency treatment if the parent is not immediately available by telephone. If notification is necessary, the child should be allowed to decide if the parent or the school should be asked to consent. If a child has a medical problem arising from a situation such as drug abuse that would result in disciplinary action by the school, he may infinitely prefer that his parent, not the headmaster, be informed. On the other hand, in the same situation he may prefer to have the information withheld from his family. In the latter case, however, the school authorities, to protect themselves, will usually feel compelled to notify the parents even if the physician does not, and therefore the physician should make clear to the child that his parents will probably hear about the problem in any event.

Runaways

A runaway presents a very difficult situation. A runaway child, unlike a resident student the same age, is not away from home with the consent of the parent. Therefore, the parents cannot be presumed to have consented to at least some decision-making by the child alone. As a practical matter, however, any court would undoubtedly hold that a runaway in need of treatment who refuses to identify his parents or tell a physician how to locate them so that they may be contacted for their consent may be presumed to be emancipated for purposes of consent. This would be true even if the treatment is necessary but cannot be classified as an emergency. The physician should, however, maintain careful records of the fact that the child refused to allow notification, including a statement to that effect signed by the minor. Courts are not unmindful of the practical realities of this situation. Confronted with a child with pneumonia or appendicitis who refuses to reveal how his parents may be reached, the physician must treat the child or send him away, and no court would expect him to do the latter.

MINOR TREATMENT STATUTES

As a result of the increasing number of problems in this area, most states have now enacted what are known as "Minor treatment statutes."[12] Any physician who treats children or teenagers should be aware of the minor treatment statute, if any, which exists in the state in which he practices. The age of majority in all states is now 18, with statutes to that effect enacted after ratification of the constitutional amendment that allowed 18-year-olds to vote. Minor treatment statutes vary widely in both age limits and substantive provisions but generally provide an age that may range from 14 in Alabama through 18 in many states at which the minor may consent to "ordinary medical treatment." Many statutes provide specifically that a married or emancipated minor, usually defined as one who is living away from home and self-supporting, may consent to medical treatment, but these provisions are largely unnecessary since emancipation as interpreted by courts has long meant that these young people may consent to medical care. Many statutes also provide that a minor who is a parent may consent to medical treatment of his own child without the consent of his parents, but this right also should be assumed to exist in all states, with or without a special statute. Some statutes allow a pregnant minor to consent to medical treatment for any condition, including those unrelated to the pregnancy, apparently on the theory that pregnancy constitutes emancipation in fact. Many statutes allow a minor of any age to consent to treatment for venereal disease without parental knowledge.

Venereal Disease Treatment

The epidemic of venereal disease in teenagers was the precipitating cause in the enactment of many of these statutes. Children obviously did not want their parents to know that they had gonorrhea or syphilis and would refuse to allow the physician to treat them if such treatment required notification of their families. In order to prevent further spread of these diseases, it became obvious to both physicians and legislators that a minor with a venereal disease had to be treated even though the parents could not be notified.[13] The following statement appeared in the *AMA News* in April 1967:

> The inability to obtain parental consent to treat a minor for venereal disease should not cause a physician to withhold treatment if in his professional judgment treatment is immediately required.

This applies even though action might appear to make the physician liable to a technical charge of assault and battery.

It is, of course, better if the physician can persuade the minor to inform his parents and thereby provide the necessary consent, but where this is impossible and it appears that without the physician's promise of confidentiality the youth will probably delay seeking treatment, the youth's health is paramount to any other consideration.[14]

This approach to the problem has been codified in many states, including Alabama, Alaska, Arizona, Arkansas, California, Colorado, Connecticut, Delaware, Florida, Georgia, Hawaii, Iowa, Kansas, Kentucky, Louisiana, Maine, Maryland, Michigan, Minnesota, Mississippi, Missouri, Montana, Nebraska, Nevada, New Jersey, New Mexico, New York, North Carolina, North Dakota, Ohio, Oklahoma, Oregon, Pennsylvania, South Dakota, Tennessee, Texas, Utah, Vermont, Virginia, Washington, and West Virginia. In these states, treatment may be given under a special statute allowing treatment for venereal disease even though treatment for all other conditions may require parental consent under state law. Even in those states where there is no statute, it is extremely improbable that any parent could bring a successful suit against a physician solely because the child is treated for venereal disease as long as the child's treatment is not negligent. In the first place, it is highly speculative that any parent would go to court and ask for damages, since to do so would advertize the fact that his child had been treated for venereal disease. In the second place, the condition clearly constitutes a medical emergency. Thus, assuming that a suit was brought, it is very unlikely that any court would hold that the physician violated any legal duty to the parent if he did not refuse to treat, thereby allowing the young person to remain untreated and spread the condition when the minor refused to let him call his parents. The consequences of untreated contagious diseases in general and venereal diseases in particular are so enormous both to the child himself and to society in general that common sense would require a physician to take the view that something has to be done and to do it. It is, of course, preferable that parents be informed, but if this is not possible any physician should be willing to treat a minor with venereal disease.

Drug Abuse Treatment

The same problem may arise in regard to treatment for drug abuse. Although there are fewer statutes allowing treatment for drug problems without parental consent than there are venereal disease statutes, many do exist. Even in the absence of a statute, however, a child with a drug problem who flatly refuses to tell his parents that he needs treatment or to permit the physician to do so undoubtedly would be held competent by a court to give consent to such treatment, since the societal and personal consequences to the child of the addiction are so profound. Furthermore, continuing to make illegal purchases of drugs will subject the child to serious risks of arrest and punishment. It is at least arguable that a physician, confronted with a minor who refuses to submit to treatment unless the physician agrees not to reveal the drug problem to his parents, who knows that the child will engage in future criminal activities to procure the drugs, and who refuses to treat the minor without parental consent is himself guilty of contributing to the delinquency of his patient.

Blood Donations

Most states that have minor treatment statutes have set the age at which a minor can donate blood at 18, although in Delaware it is permitted at 17. Since blood donations are not for the benefit of the donor, in the absence of statutory authority it is highly unlikely that a minor can consent to become a blood donor prior to the age of majority unless he is clearly emancipated. College physicians who are involved in blood donation drives should be extremely careful that students under 18 years of age obtain parental consent before they donate. Married minors and those in the military may, however, be accepted as blood donors without fear of parental action.

General Consent to Treatment

Many minor treatment statutes allow the minor to consent to treatment for any communicable disease at any age, and any communicable disease undoubtedly should be considered an emergency even in the absence of a statute. Some statutes include prohibitions against certain procedures, such as abortion or donation of an organ, without parental consent prior to a certain age. In these situations, the statutory prohibition must be observed. Minor treatment statutes relating to abortions and contraception in particular will be discussed in a later chapter, but any provision as to any condition that is specifically exempted from consent by a minor under a state statute would be held binding on the physician. Ignorance of the law is rarely if ever an excuse, and, if there is a statute in a state prohibiting treatment of a minor for a specific condition without parental consent, the physician cannot defend an action brought by the parents on the ground that he knew nothing of the statute. A local attorney should always be asked what the statutes in the state provide on the subject prior to any necessity for immediate interpretation in the physician's office or at the hospital.

The Committee on Youth of the American Academy of Pediatrics has written as Model Act to allow for consent of minors to health services.[15] This act was to be submitted to the legislatures of all states but has thus far not yet been adopted in any. Under the act, a minor who has been separated from his parents, parent, or legal guardian for whatever reason and is supporting himself by whatever means is considered capable of consenting to treatment. Further, a general right to consent to medical treatment under the act would be permitted to those at the age of majority as defined by the state or 18, whichever is lower. The Model Act suggests that any minor who is found to be pregnant, afflicted with any reportable communicable disease, including venereal disease, or drug or substance abuse has the right to consent to preventive treatment, diagnostic treatment, and treatment of those conditions specified, although the act specifically precludes self-consent of minors to sterilization or abortion. The act provides that any minor who has physical or emotional problems and is capable of making rational decisions and whose relationship with his parents or legal guardians is in such a state that by informing them the minor will fail to seek initial or future help may consent to treatment. The same section of the Model Act indicates that the professional may thereafter inform the parents or legal guardian unless such action will jeopardize the life of the patient or the favorable result of the treatment.

The act provides that if major surgery, general anesthesia, or a life-threatening procedure has to be undertaken on a minor without parental consent, the physician should obtain approval from another physician for management of the case except in an emergency in a community where it is impossible for the surgeon to contact any other physician within a reasonable time for the purpose of concurrence.

Further, the act provides that any health professional may render nonemergency services to minors for conditions that will endanger the health or life of the minor if services would be delayed by obtaining consent from a spouse, parent, parents, or legal guardian. This would appear to be a very comprehensive act protecting the rights of (1) the minor who needs treatment to obtain it, (2) the parents who are in control of the minor, and (3) the physician who wishes to provide necessary treatment without running substantial risks of being sued.

The Pediatric Bill of Rights, adopted by the board of trustees of the National Association of Children's Hospitals in 1974 as a proposed legislative model, provides even more sweeping guidelines for consent by minors.[16] The bill provides that every person, regardless of age, should have the right to seek and consent to treatment involving contraception, venereal disease, pregnancy including consent to abortion, psychiatric problems, and drug or alcohol abuse and that confidentiality between physician and patient precludes notification of parents without the patient's consent. This confidentiality provision is much broader than the Model Act of the American Academy of Pediatrics.

In addition to the provisions allowing consent to specific types of care, canon 8 of the bill specifies that:

> Any person, regardless of age, who is of sufficient intelligence to appreciate the nature and consequences of the proposed medical care and if such medical care is for his own benefit, may effectively consent to such medical care in doctor-patient confidentiality.

Presumably this section would, if adopted by a legislature, entirely preclude an action by parents who were not consulted before treatment, elective or otherwise, was begun unless they contend that the child was incapable of comprehension. The Pediatric Bill of Rights does not, however, deal in any way with a child's right to refuse treatment, which must logically be granted to the same degree that he is allowed the autonomy to consent, and therefore the proposal does not indicate whether the physician would be obliged to maintain confidentiality in a case where he considered the treatment to be necessary but the minor refused it. Any general statute that omits reference to a right to refuse treatment might well create more problems than it solves.

THE MATURE MINOR RULE

No decision can be located within the past 20 years in which a parent recovered damages, even in the absence of a minor treatment statute, for treatment of a child over the age of 15 without parental consent.[17] This is known as the "mature minor rule." Parents were unsuccessful in the few cases in which the issue has been raised.

A 17-year-old girl went to visit her mother who was in a hospital recovering from surgery. As she was leaving the building she broke her finger in the front door. She was taken to the emergency room and minor surgery was performed. The girl gave her own consent. She was not in shock and was in good physical condition. There was no allegation that the surgery had been improperly performed, but the mother sued on the ground that her daughter had not asked for her permission. The court held that the girl was perfectly able to consent for herself and no cause of action would lie against the surgeon.[18]

An 18-year-old girl arranged for cosmetic surgery on her nose. Her father brought an action after the surgery for assault and battery. The court held that a minor of 18 had the right to consent to what the jury might have determined was only a "simple operation." Therefore, the father did not recover damages.[19]

Although there are very few decisions on the subject, there has been considerable discussion of the issue in legal journals. One authority concludes that parental consent for medical treatment may be omitted if (1) the patient is of the age of discretion, by which is meant 15 or older, and he would appear able to understand the procedure and its risks sufficiently to give a genuinely informed consent; (2) the medical measures are taken for the patient's own benefit, meaning that a minor certainly could not be used as a transplant donor without parental permission (this would be true even if the minor is clearly emancipated, unless the minor is married); (3) the measures can be justified as necessary by conservative medical opinion; and (4) there is some good reason, including simple refusal by the minor to request it, why parental consent cannot be obtained.[20]

Another authority has analyzed the existing cases and arrived at a very similar conclusion.[21] He concludes that from the decisions available, inferences may be drawn about the types of situations in which courts that recognize the mature minor rule would be likely to apply it and dispense with the requirement of parental consent. The cases in which the rule has been applied generally have had the following factors in common:

1. The treatment was undertaken for the benefit of a minor rather than a third party.
2. The particular minor was near majority (or at least in the range of 15 years of age upward) and was considered to have sufficient mental capacity to understand fully the nature and importance of the medical steps proposed.
3. The medical procedures could be characterized by the court as something less than "major" or "serious" in nature.

The mature minor exception to requirements of parental consent would, along with the clear right to treat a child in an emergency, appear to constitute a sensible rule. Apparently, a medical emergency for these purposes does not have to be categorized as a life-threatening situation, but rather includes acute illness of any type. A runaway with an acute appendix or fractured leg probably would not die before the parents could be located, but most courts would have no hesitation in concluding that treatment should be given, even if the child refuses to tell the physician how to locate his parents. All of the early cases also involved acute illness. In the example above involving cosmetic surgery, the court held that parental permission was not required, but it should be remembered that the girl was 18. Totally elective treatment of this nature on a patient under 18 would appear to fall within a different category from that of "necessary medical care." There may be, therefore, some serious doubt about performance of such elective therapy unless the child has been emancipated with the consent of his parents and is able to prove it.

The American Law Institute's *Restatement of the Law of Torts* seems to give substantial support to the mature minor rule. Section 59a provides:

> If a child ... is capable of appreciating the nature, extent and consequences of the invasion (of his body) his assent prevents the invasion from creating liability, though the assent of the parent, guardian, or other person is not obtained or is expressly refused.

Financial Liability of Parents

It should be noted that parents are liable for necessary expenses for their children. Medical bills are clearly the responsibility of the parents under normal circumstances. Except in an emergency, however, if no effort is made to contact the parents and inform them that the child requests treatment, particularly if the procedure is entirely elective, it is likely that a court would hold that the parent is not liable for payment of the bill. Several decisions in recent years have held that a parent is not liable for the hospital expenses of emancipated minors.

A minor girl whose parents were divorced and who had previously lived with her mother moved in with her father after her high school graduation. She obtained a job in a department store and supported herself. When a dispute arose over her life style shortly thereafter, she moved out of the house with her father's knowledge. She moved into a mobile home with another girl the same age until she was hospitalized for treatment of diabetes. The father refused to pay her bill. The hospital sued the father to recover for the care given his daughter during her minority. The trial judge found that the girl was emancipated because she supported herself and "led an adult existence" and was not subject to parental control. At no time had her father consented to her treatment in the hospital, and he had not at any time agreed to pay any of her expenses. The appellate court upheld the trial judge's judgment that complete emancipation had occurred and that the emancipation relieved the father of any liability to the hospital without his prior consent or approval.[22]

An 18-year-old girl was a minor under applicable state law. She left home permanently after a dispute with her parents and became completely self-supporting. Her father paid none of her bills and provided no money except for reasonable social amenities that might be provided for a child who was independent. She came to the home for meals and visited on other occasions. A month after she left the household, she entered the hospital as an emergency patient, and her father refused to sign a financial responsibility document. He did sign a consent to surgery because hospital personnel assured him that they could not provide treatment without it. The hospital sued the father to recover the amount of the hospital bill, arguing that the father was liable for the debt as a "necessity of life" provided for his daughter. The trial court ruled in favor of the hospital and the father appealed. The appellate court found that the facts revealed that the daughter was emancipated at the time she entered the hospital and therefore her father was not liable for medical treatment.[23]

Financial Liability of the Minor

It is clear, however, that the minor himself is liable for his medical bills if he has the funds to pay for them. Thus the minor himself can be sued. If he has no money, however, such an action is usually not worth the time and trouble required.

A 19-year-old girl ordered contact lenses. She told the physician she wanted them as soon as possible and agreed to the cost of $225. She gave the physician a check for $100. He examined her eyes and ordered the lenses from a laboratory, incurring an indebtedness of $110. He received the lenses the following day, a Saturday, and the next Monday the girl called and broke her contract at the insistence of her father. She also stopped payment on her check. The physician sued the girl and her father to recover damages for the girl's breach of contract. He proved at the trial that the lenses could not be used by anyone but the girl and had no market value, thus resulting in an absolute loss of $110. However, since the lenses were ordered by a minor, the court held that she was not liable for a sum in excess of their "fair value," even though she had agreed to pay more, and awarded the physician $150. The girl in this case was living at home with her parents, but working and paying them for room and board. The court found that no judgment could be granted against her father since she was emancipated and therefore dismissed the suit against him.[24]

It thus appears that if consent is not obtained from the parents prior to performance of medical services, if the child is emancipated or claims to be, the parent is not liable for the physician's or hospital's bills. The minor, however, is. Of course, in the treatment of a young child or a child who is clearly not emancipated the parents are liable for the costs of all necessary treatment.

INFORMED CONSENT

Assuming that the minor is one who, under a treatment statute or otherwise, is considered to be capable of consenting to treatment without the notification of his parents, the same standards of informed consent would apply as to an adult patient. The primary reason in fact for requiring parental consent is that children are considered to be fundamentally incapable of giving a truly informed consent. Thus, in the last analysis the child's capacity to understand the risks and benefits of the proposed treatment is the criterion for obtaining his consent to that treatment.

Consent to Treatment

The physician-patient relationship is a fiduciary relationship whether the patient is an adult or a minor.[25] A fiduciary relationship in the professional context is one in which one party is considered to be an expert in a field such as law or medicine and the other, the patient or client, is not aware of the intricacies of the field. In a fiduciary relationship, the fiduciary has a positive obligation to disclose fully all relevant facts in an affirmative way, unlike a relationship between presumed equals, such as a car salesman and a customer in which the salesman does not have to reveal negative information about the product unless the prospective purchaser asks him specific questions. Second, under our legal system, a person of sound mind has the right of self-determination and the right to make his own decisions about what becomes of his body.[26]

In any case involving either an adult patient or a minor patient, the doctrine of informed consent may be defined as "the duty to warn a patient of the hazards and possible complications and expected and unexpected results of the treatment."[27] The patient must also be clearly told what alternatives, if any, exist for the proposed treatment. As the probability or severity of risk to the patient increases, so does the duty to inform him of it. There seems to be a common assumption by the courts that where elective treatment is considered, the duty to warn the patient of all risks is virtually absolute. If the patient, adult or minor, does not understand all material facts, any consent that he does give will be held to be legally invalid. If an untoward result occurs of which the patient was not warned and he should have been, he has a cause of action against the physician for failure to obtain a valid consent even though no negligence is shown. The basis of the complaint is not that the procedure has been performed negligently but rather that it has been performed at all.[28]

Although in some cases with an adult patient, the physician does not have to disclose information about risks if he thinks in the use of reasonable medical judgment that the patient will be upset by it and that this distress would interfere with the patient's recovery, this concept of therapeutic privilege presumably does not apply to a minor patient. No physician who is treating a minor without parental knowledge should fail to disclose any risks to the child. If the child's condition is such that therapeutic privilege would be considered justified, the parents should clearly be notified, because under these circumstances the physician is assuming that the child cannot handle the situation sufficiently well to give an informed consent.

In most states, whether or not a disclosure of risks is sufficient is established by the standard of the "reasonably careful medical practitioner in the same or

similar community in the same or similar circumstances." Whether the physician has the duty to disclose the facts and if so what facts he is obliged to reveal
depends on the normal medical practice in his community. The physician is
not usually required to inform his patient of risks that other physicians in his
community would not think necessary to disclose.[29]

In an increasing number of states, however, courts have held that the scope
of disclosure that the physician must make to a patient is not to be determined
by what the reasonable physician would disclose under similar circumstances
but by the patient's understanding of what he needs to know.

A 19-year-old young man was paralyzed after a laminectomy. His mother had been
contacted by the surgeon and had given permission for the operation but no risk of
paralysis was discussed with her or with her son. When the boy was paralyzed, he
sued. The court rejected the defendant's claim that there was no practice to disclose
the risk of paralysis in that community and upheld the plaintiff's cause of action. The
court stated that the patient's right of self-determination shapes the boundaries of the
physician's duty to disclose all material risks, all serious inherent and potential hazards, alternative methods of treatment, and the likely results of nontreatment.[30]

This rule—that the patient's need, not the standard of medical practice, determines what the patient has the right to know—has been adopted in New
York,[31] California,[32] and the District of Columbia,[33] and there is every reason
to believe that this standard of disclosure will soon become the majority if not
the universal rule in this country. Therefore, in dealing with minors it is
particularly necessary that they be fully informed.

If the child's capacity for understanding risks, benefits, and alternative
methods of treatment is subject to any question, treatment without parental
consent should not be attempted except in cases of acute emergency. Furthermore, if the minor's capacity to understand is not questioned, the physician
should be extremely careful to disclose all material risks. If the physician
thinks that he should not for any reason tell a minor something that he would
normally tell an adult patient or the parent of a minor about the proposed
procedure, he should immediately conclude as a matter of logic that parental
consent or a court order is necessary. The nature of the situation is such that
any court would be likely to construe any withholding of information from a
minor as failure of due care in treatment, although there are no cases on this
subject to date.

It should be noted that in the case described above, *Canterbury v. Spence,*
which first established the patient's right to receive all information that a
reasonable patient would be deemed to need, the patient was 19, was entirely
self-supporting, worked as a clerk for the Federal Bureau of Investigation, and
lived in a different area of the country from his mother. At the trial of that
case, apparently no argument was made that he was not capable of giving an

informed consent to the treatment. The only allegation was that the physician had not offered him the information, as would be true of any adult patient. His mother brought no action for treating him without informing her of the risks, but this might be expected to occur at some time in the near future as the number of minors receiving treatment without parental consent increases. Therefore, full disclosure would appear to be mandatory.

In any situation where a minor has no objection to his parents' knowledge of his condition, the parents should be asked to consent. It is preferable, both in terms of the physician's potential liability and in terms of the family relationships to attempt to involve the parents. Where the minor objects to notification of his family, reasonable efforts to convince him that they are likely to be more understanding and supportive than he expects should be attempted. If the minor remains adamant, however, and appears to be capable of consenting to the proposed treatment, careful documentation of genuine understanding should be made.

If the proposed procedure is one that carries any appreciable degree of risk, including all surgical procedures, in addition to a carefully worded consent form which should include a detailed statement of potential risks, the minor should sign a statement that he has refused to permit notification of his parents. The concept of a two-part consent form should then be employed. A series of written questions based on the information given the minor about the procedure should be answered in the minor's own handwriting. This questionnaire will serve as an immediate indication to the physician of the degree to which the minor has genuine understanding of what he was told and, should any legal problems arise from the parents later, would serve as the best possible evidence that the minor gave a truly informed consent. If the minor is illiterate, he should probably be presumed incapable of consent to a procedure carrying any substantial risk, and if an emergency is presented the physician has no recourse but to obtain a court order if the child refuses to tell him where his parents may be contacted.

It thus appears that if consent is not obtained from the parents prior to performance of medical services, if the child is emancipated or claims to be, the parent is not liable for the physician's or hospital's bills. The minor, however, is. This, of course, does not apply to treatment of a young child or a child who is clearly not emancipated. In that case the parents are liable for the costs of all necessary treatment.

Refusal of Treatment

If a minor has the right to consent to treatment, it is probable that he also has the right to refuse treatment. Should the parents wish to have a minor of 14 or over given medical treatment, the child's consent should also be obtained.

o decisions can be located in which a minor on reaching the age
_ought an action against a physician for assault and battery for
treating him over his objections but with the consent of his parents. Such a
case, however, is not at all unlikely at some future date particularly if the
treatment is one that causes permanent effects or disfigurement to the child.
In a situation where the parents wish to have the child treated but the child
refuses, the prudent physician should obtain a court order as he would do if
a parent refused to allow a blood transfusion for a dangerously injured child.
It is extremely risky as a matter of law to treat a teenager under any circumstance that violates the child's right of self-determination, as was indicated in
two cases.

A 16-year-old girl could not be forced to have an abortion over her objection at the
request of her mother.[34]

A teenage boy who had been committed by his parents as a "voluntary patient" to
a mental institution was entitled to leave the hospital when he wished to do so. The
court held that since a statute in that state allowed the child to seek treatment for
mental disorders at the age of 16, the child would be held to have the right to refuse
that to which he was statutorily entitled to consent.[35]

Therefore, in any case where a child can be treated at his own request and
without the consent of his parent, under a minor treatment statute or otherwise, it is quite probable that the same child has the right to refuse treatment
at least if the condition is not life-threatening. The two concepts appear to be
interlocked: a child who has the right to consent has an equal right to refuse
to consent. Thus, it would appear to be extremely unwise to treat any such
minor over his objection.

A younger child, however, probably does not have this right. A 7-year-old
who needs surgery may take very definite exception to the idea of the operation. Until such time as a court holds that a child does not have the right to
refuse treatment which his parents wish him to have, it should be presumed
as a matter of practice that the right to consent is equated with the right to
refuse, at least where the minor's life is not at stake. A 7-year-old obviously
cannot consent to treatment himself; therefore, equally, he cannot refuse it. A
17-year-old is quite able to do both. In any event, however, for practical
purposes of deciding what to do about a sick or injured child who refuses to
notify his parents or who refuses to consent to their request that he be treated,
the physician should remember that in case of doubt a court will probably
uphold the validity of any reasonable medical judgment designed to benefit the
child who is the patient. Thus, in case of doubt a sick child should not be
turned away because he will not tell his parents of his needs.

As is suggested by the Model Act of the American Academy of Pediatrics,[36] if a minor is to be treated without parental consent and the procedure involves "major surgery, general anesthesia, or a life-threatening procedure," consultation with another physician is advisable. Consultation probably should be requested where there is any material risk of harm, both to obtain corroboration as to the accuracy of the diagnosis to avoid a later charge of unnecessary surgery or treatment and to provide another opinion on the ability of the patient to understand the potential risks.

CONFIDENTIALITY

Assuming that the child is properly accepted for treatment without the knowledge of the parent, the issue of confidentiality in the physician-patient relationship then arises. There have been no cases and very few articles in the literature on the subject of confidentiality between a minor and a physician where the person to whom the information would be disclosed is apparent. Most physician-patient confidentiality cases involve disclosures to third parties such as schools, insurance companies, or employers.

Until recently, it was clear that a physician is not liable for disclosing information to a spouse, although there is some reason to believe that courts are beginning to revise their judgments in these situations. Even if a couple is separated and the information conveyed by the physician to the other spouse will, to the physician's knowledge, be used against his patient in a divorce case, until recently courts held that there was no violation of confidentiality.[37] However, in one recent decision a psychiatrist was held liable for making disclosures about his patient, the mother of several children, to her estranged husband's lawyer in the course of a child custody case.

A woman got custody of her three small children at the time she was divorced from her husband. After she obtained custody, by agreement between the parties, she allowed the children to live with their father for a period of several months. At the end of that period, when the wife wished to have the children returned to her home, the husband refused to allow them to do so. She filed suit to obtain physical possession of the children. At the time she filed the action, she was seeing a private psychiatrist. She had been in a mental hospital as a voluntary patient for a few weeks at some time during her marriage and had been in psychotherapy most of the time for several years prior to the divorce. The husband's attorney contacted her psychiatrist and the psychiatrist voluntarily and without the knowledge of his patient gave the attorney an eight-page affidavit declaring that in his opinion the mother was unfit to have custody. The affidavit also included factual information to the discredit of the patient of which the husband had been previously unaware. As the result of the affidavit's admission into evidence in the custody case, the husband was allowed to keep the children. The wife sued the psychiatrist for malpractice. The trial judge gave judgment for the defendant psychiatrist on the ground that confidentiality did not apply in custody cases because the best interests of the children prevailed over any parental right. The appellate court, however, reversed. It held that in some circumstances psychiatrists can be subpoenaed to testify in a custody case as to the mental condition of one of the litigants but that there is absolute privilege in the absence of a subpoena. In this case the court noted that the psychiatrist had in fact volunteered the information, and therefore the former patient did have a cause of action against him for so doing.[38]

There have been no decisions in which a minor sued a physician for revealing information to his parents. However, it would seem that if the physician does not feel the need to obtain consent of the parents to treat the child, he is by that decision assuring the child that the normal physician-patient relationship that would obtain if he were an adult has begun to apply. If confidentiality is to be breached, the child, it would seem, must be warned of this fact prior to institution of treatment. By accepting the child as a responsible patient who has the right to consent to treatment, the physician has implicitly accorded that child the normal rights of a patient within the physician-patient relationship. If the physician does not think that confidentiality should be maintained as to the treatment, he should obtain parental consent to treat the child first.

The Model Act of the American Academy of Pediatrics apparently does not regard confidentiality as to parents as a right of a minor patient. Section 3(4) of the act provides:[39]

> Any minor who has physical or emotional problems and is capable of making rational decisions, and whose relationship with his parents or legal guardian is in such a state that by informing them the minor will fail to seek initial or future help may give consent to health professionals for health services.

The section, however, continues:

> After the professional establishes his rapport with the minor, then he may inform the patient's parents or legal guardian unless such action will jeopardize the life of the patient or the favorable result of the treatment.

It seems clear that this section approves acceptance of a minor for treatment without parental consent when the patient specifically does not want them to be informed and then, later, breaching that acceptance and the implicit terms of the relationship. In addition to the clear deceit involved, if the circumstances are such that the parents' consent is legally necessary at all, it is necessary for the institution of treatment, not at a later time or after treatment is concluded.

Any physician who fully intends to tell a minor's parent about the circumstances of treatment but accepts the child as a patient without making that fact clear at the outset of the treatment relationship has in a very real way violated any reasonable definition of the fiduciary relationship.

The Pediatric Bill of Rights[40] of the National Association of Children's Hospitals makes clear that the child's treatment is to be conducted according to normal rules of physician-patient confidentiality if consent from the parent is not required at the time the relationship commences. This approach would appear to be by far the more ethical and responsible.

There are, of course, exceptions to principles of physician-patient confidentiality even if the patient is an adult. One of these exceptions is a situation in which a patient has a contagious disease. It is a perfectly clear law that where a patient has a contagious disease, a physician is entitled to reveal that fact to those members of the household or other parties to which the patient may be reasonably expected to come into close contact and who are thus in some material danger of contracting the disease.[41] Therefore, if the child does have a contagious disease, particularly venereal disease, and is living with his parents, since the family of an adult patient with such a disease would be notified it is clear that the physician is also entitled if necessary to notify the minor's parents. If the minor is not living with his family, however, it is also obvious that they are not in any particular danger of contracting the disease. In that case, the physician would have no more authority to reveal the facts to the parents than he would have to tell a sibling of an adult patient with whom the patient has very little contact.

Another exception to confidentiality might be if the physician was convinced that the child's life or health were in imminent danger. If he believes that the child is on the verge of suicide, parents presumably should be notified in order to take reasonable and proper precautions to protect the child's safety. This would also be permitted in the case of an adult patient, and in fact it has been held in several cases that the parents of an adult patient who is in residence at their home have a right to know that the patient is likely to be suicidal in order to protect him from the consequences of his own actions. In at least one case a psychiatrist was found liable for failing to warn the parents of a returned Vietnam veteran that his depression was so serious that suicide was likely. The young man killed himself. No precautions had been taken. The parents sued the psychiatrist and their cause of action was upheld.[42]

Thus, the normal exceptions to confidentiality, contagious disease, and danger to life that would apply to an adult patient would seem to apply equally to a minor patient. On the other hand, it would be extremely difficult to argue that confidentiality does not exist in the case of a minor patient who has been accepted for treatment without parental consent to the same extent as would be allowed to an adult patient.

In resolving the issues of treatment of minors without consent of their parents, both in cases in which the minor will not divulge their identities and in cases in which they refuse consent, the physician can always ask a juvenile judge for authority to proceed. This process is usually reserved for treatment that is indisputably necessary for the minor's well-being or for emergency care, but in all situations of this nature in which the physician needs an answer urgently, the juvenile judge in the community is the primary resource as well as judicial authority.

NOTES

1. Memorial Hospital v. Maricopa County, 415 US 250, 1974.
2. E.g., In re Gault, 387 US 1, 1967.
3. E.g., Zaman v. Schultz, 19 Pa D & C 309, 1933.
4. "Mother's Right to Consent," 213 *JAMA* No. 8, page 1393, August 24, 1970.
5. Burge v. City and County of San Francisco, 262 P 2d 6, Cal 1953; Campbell v. Campbell, 441 SW 2d 658, Tex 1969; Leithold v. Plass, 413 SW 2d 698, Tex 1967.
6. Durfee v. Durfee, 87 NYS 2d 275, NY 1949.
7. Yarborough v. Yarborough, 290 US 202, 1933.
8. Luka v. Lowrie, 136 NW 1106, Mich 1912; Sullivan v. Montgomery, 279 NYS 575, NY 1935.
9. Bonner v. Moran, 126 F 2d 121, CA DC 1941.
10. E.g., Bach v. Long Island Jewish Hospital, 267 NYS 2d 289, NY 1966.
11. E.g., Swenson v. Swenson, 227 SW 2d 103, Mo 1950.
12. Full tables of all minor-treatment statutes as of the dates of publication may be found in Health Law Center, *Hospital Law Manual;* Harriet S. Pilpel, "Minors' Rights to Medical Care," 36 *Albany Law Rev,* pages 472–487, 1972; Lawrence P. Wilkins, "Children's Rights: Removing the Parental Consent Barrier," 1975 *Ariz State Law Rev* No. 1, page 31.
13. "Treating a Minor for Venereal Disease," 214 *JAMA* No. 10, page 1949, December 7, 1970.
14. AMA *News,* April 17, 1967, page 4.
15. Model Act, 51 *Pediatrics* No. 2, page 293, February 1973.
16. Although the Pediatric Bill of Rights has apparently not been published, all of its provisions are quoted as footnotes and exhaustively discussed in G. Emmett Rait, Jr., "The Minor's Right to Consent to Medical Treatment," 48 *So Cal Law Rev,* page 1417, 1975.
17. Pilpel, *op. cit. supra* at 12, page 466.
18. Younts v. St. Frances Hospital and School of Nursing, 469 P 2d 330, Kans 1970.
19. Lacey v. Laird, 139 NE 2d 25, Ohio 1956.
20. Burke Shartel and Marcus Plant, *The Law of Medical Practice,* Springfield, Ill, Charles C Thomas Publisher, 1959, page 26.
21. Walter Wadlington, "Minors and Health Care: The Age of Consent," 11 *Osgoode Hall Law J* No. 1, page 115, 1973.
22. Poudre Valley Hospital District v. Heckart, 491 P 2d 984, Colo 1971.
23. Ison v. Florida Sanitarium and Benevolent Association, 302 So 2d 200, Fla 1974.

24. Cidis v. White, 336 NYS 2d 362, NY 1972.
25. E. g., Hinkle v. Hargens 81 NW 2d 888, SD 1957, David W. Louisell and Harold Williams, *Medical Malpractice,* New York, Matthew Bender and Co., 1960, and annual Supplements Section 8.11.
26. E.g., Pratt v. Davis, 79 NE 562, Ill 1906; Schloendorff v. Society of New York Hospital, 105 NE 92, NY 1914.
27. Mitchell v. Robinson, 334 SW 2d 11, Mo 1960; Natanson v. Kline, 350 P 2d 1093, 354 P 2d 670, Kans 1960.
28. Darrah v. Kite, 301 NYS 2d 286, NY 1969.
29. Dietze v. King, 184 F Supp 944, DC Va 1960; Williams v. Menehan, 379 P 2d 292, Kans 1963; Di Filippo v. Preston, 173 A 2d 333, Del 1961.
30. Canterbury v. Spence, 464 F 2d 772, CA DC 1972.
31. Zeleznik v. Jewish Chronic Disease Hospital, 366 NYS 2d 163, NY 1975.
32. Cobbs v. Grant, 502 P 2d 1, Cal 1972.
33. Canterbury v. Spence, *supra* at 30.
34. In re Smith, 295 A 2d 238, Md 1972.
35. Melville v. Sabbatino, 313 A 2d 886, Conn 1973.
36. Model Act, *supra* at 15, Section 5.
37. Curry v. Corn, 277 NYS 2d 470, NY 1966; Pennison v. Provident Life Insurance Co., 154 So 2d 617, La 1963.
38. Schaffer v. Spicer, 215 NW 2d 134, SD 1974.
39. Model Act, *supra* at 15.
40. Raitt, *op. cit. supra* at 16.
41. Simonsen v. Swenson, 177 NW 831, Neb 1920; Golia v. Greater New York Health Plan, 166 NYS 2d 889, NY 1957; Hofmann v. Blackmon, 241 So 2d 752, Fla 1970.
42. Hall v. United States, 381 F Supp 224, DC SC 1974.

CHAPTER VI

THE MINOR

AS RESEARCH

SUBJECT

OR TRANSPLANT

DONOR

THE MINOR AS RESEARCH SUBJECT

The use of children as subjects in medical or behavioral research is a very controversial subject on which lawyers, ethicists, and physicians display a variety of views. There is little litigation in the field to provide a basis for clear inferences that may be drawn about the outcome of any malpractice case that a minor, on reaching majority, might bring against a physician for injuries sustained in the course of an experiment; but by analogy to the legal principles applicable to medical practice, certain policy guidelines may be established.

Therapeutic Research

Therapeutic research is defined as those activities undertaken for the systematic collection of data, in accordance with a designed protocol, that are intended to improve the health of the subject by diagnostic or treatment methods that depart from standard practice. Therapeutic research on a child is clearly permissible. A parent may consent to innovative treatment for his child in the same way that he is allowed to consent to standard treatment. However, the parent must be advised explicitly that the treatment proposed is in fact experimental.

A teenage boy had an operation for curvature of the spine. The procedure had been invented by the surgeon who performed it. The mother of the child consented to the operation after a reasonable explanation of the risks. She was not, however, advised that only 30 cases had ever been attempted, that only this surgeon performed the operation, and that all the other patient-subjects had been adults. Two weeks after the operation the boy died of a massive hemorrhage. The mother sued the surgeon, and the court held that, because she did not know that the procedure was experimental, the surgeon was liable without proof of negligence in the performance of the procedure.[1]

It is also clear that the parent must precisely understand the purpose of the experiment, since he may not agree with that purpose. The possibility of a disagreement on the purpose of the study, even though the child would obtain a direct benefit, might well arise in some form of psychological, social, or behavioral research. For example, research on children who have reading disabilities could conceivably benefit the particular child-subject, but the data could later be used to "prove" that the social or ethnic group of which the child is a member is inferior to other groups in reading aptitude, not achievement. Recent press reports, for example, indicate that research comparing aptitude levels in mathematics of boys and girls "proved" that boys were clearly superior, and numerous objections from women's groups followed. Thus, particularly in any comparative study based on hypotheses that some group may be superior or inferior to another in some respect, it is absolutely necessary that the overall purpose of the study be explained to the parent when consent is requested. That aspect of the investigation might well be of equal or greater interest to the parent than the immediate benefit which he hopes will accrue to his child.

In experiments designed to test innovative medical interventions, it is obviously necessary that the parent also understand what alternative treatments, if any, are available.[2] In a non-life-threatening illness, for example, standard treatment may be less effective than a new drug seems to be, but the parent who knows that his child will recover eventually in any case may not be willing to subject the child to any degree of unknown risk.

Innovative drug therapy. The possibility of an adverse reaction to a drug given as innovative therapy is the most probable source of malpractice suits against a physician in the pediatric research context. In addition to the restrictions on drug testing since 1962 imposed by the Kefauver-Harris Act,[3] there is general agreement that new drugs should not be tested on children in Phase One drug trials. Therefore, a great many drugs, some of which may be quite helpful in the treatment of children, are labeled "Not for pediatric use" or "This drug has not been tested and approved for use on children and infants." Therefore, a pediatrician confronted by a sick child in a course of ordinary clinical practice is in effect conducting Phase Three drug trials if he prescribes such a drug, whether he considers himself a researcher or not.

Liability for drug reactions is not determined solely by the restrictions on package inserts. It is clear that in adult patients a physician may exceed recommended dosages of any drug if, in his medical judgment, no alternative therapy would be as effective and the recommended dosage has been ineffective in treatment of the particular patient. If the patient has an adverse reaction and sues for negligence, citing deviation from the package insert as *prima facie* evidence of negligence, the physician is not automatically liable. In most cases, however, the burden of proof shifts to the physician to show that good medical judgment required departure from the manufacturer's recommendations.[4] Several decisions, however, indicate that if he can do so, the departure will not be considered evidence of negligence in treatment.

A physician prescribed Chloromycetin for treatment of an adult patient's serious ear infection after information was generally available and included in the package insert that the drug could cause aplastic anemia. The patient died of aplastic anemia, and her estate sued the physician and the manufacturer.

The court held that in this particular case use of the drug was not justified but said:

> Where a drug manufacturer recommends to the medical profession (1) the conditions under which its drug should be prescribed; (2) the disorders it is designed to relieve; (3) the precautionary measures which should be observed; and (4) warns of the dangers which are inherent in its use, a doctor's deviation from such recommendations is prima facie evidence of negligence if there is competent medical testimony that his patient's injury or death resulted from the doctor's failure to adhere to the recommendations. Under such circumstances, it is incumbent on the doctor to disclose his reasons for departing from the procedures recommended by the manufacturer. Although it will ordinarily be a jury question whether the doctor has justified or excused his deviation, there may be situations where as a matter of law the explanation exonerates him unless rebutted by other competent medical testimony.[5]

It is probable that when a pediatrician prescribes a drug that has only been tested on adults the same rule will apply if there is no other effective medication for the child's complaint and the parents are fully informed of known risks and advised that there may be some unknown risk. The burden of proof that a reasonably prudent physician would have used the drug in the dosage given will clearly be on the pediatrician.

A pediatrician prescribed *adult* doses of a drug clearly marked on the label in red letters "Not for pediatric use," for a nine-month-old infant who had severe bronchitis.

The child became permanently deaf from the effects of the medication. The physician was found liable for violation of such clear instructions and admitted that he had not read the manufacturer's package insert or the label.[6]

The opinion did not deal with any differentiation as to liability for use of a drug that is untested on children and is prescribed in reasonable doses. It may be assumed that substantial inadvertent overdoses of any drug, tested or untested, will be held to be negligent. This case clearly indicates the principle that although proper dosage of any medication is a matter of medical judgment and there may be ample and justified reasons why a patient's condition necessitates administration of a dosage in excess of that commonly prescribed or suggested by the manufacturer, the physician is presumed as a matter of law by the courts to know what the suggested and correct dosage is and to use extreme caution when exceeding it.[7] If he exceeds it as a matter of ignorance and not deliberate choice, he will assuredly be liable for the resulting damage to the patient. It does appear, however, that as long as the reasonably prudent pediatrician would, on the basis of a careful examination of the child, prescribe a drug that has not been tested and approved for children, he is not liable if the child has a reaction that could not have been foreseen on the basis of reports of the tests performed on adult patients.

The American Academy of Pediatrics has suggested that in drug trials, Phase One testing should be carried out only on adults, but if a therapeutic effect has been confirmed in adults with reasonable evidence of safety, the investigator may proceed with treatment of a sick child combining Phase One and Two trials and that such treatment of the sick child can be approved; "in fact, it may be demanded if equivalent alternative therapy is lacking." Their recommendation points out that since concern regarding drug effects is greatest for the infant, cautious investigation might require successive trials at different age levels, beginning with older school-age children and then progressing to younger children and finally to infants. The committee's report concluded:

> The sometimes unpredictable effects of drugs on children require that drug testing in this age group be conducted, but tests should be conducted with caution. While "social benefit" may not constitute justification for drug testing of healthy children (who could not, in any case, "volunteer" on an informed basis) the great need for information regarding effects of drugs, especially on very young children, can be met by carefully conducted tests of new drugs on ill children who may be expected to benefit from the administration of the drug. The design, recording and reporting of such studies is in the interest of the profession, the drug industry and most important, the children.[8]

It is difficult to argue with such conclusions when the alternatives are no treatment at all for the "therapeutic orphan"[9] or widespread distribution without proper clinical testing of drugs to children by physicians in private practice under uncontrolled conditions. If a hospitalized child has an acute drug reaction, treatment is far more readily available than is the case if the child is taking the drug at home without immediate medical supervision, and this should be borne in mind when drugs are prescribed under the current system.

Dangerous therapeutic research. If a parent consents to clearly dangerous research—even with therapeutic intent—where an effective and demonstrably safer therapy exists, it is altogether probable that the parent and the physician are arguably in violation of the child abuse laws. In the "Willowbrook Experiments," in which institutionalized retarded children were used as experimental subjects to test the effectiveness of a vaccine for hepatitis, the response to the publication of these research findings was a feeling by many that the physicians involved had violated ethical standards.[10] The experiments were justified on the basis of therapeutic intent since the children at Willowbrook, a state institution for the retarded, would presumably have caught hepatitis in any event since it was epidemic in the institution, and the inoculations might have served to protect them from the disease.[11] Parental consent was given in most cases in these experiments. If a child who had been exposed to the virus as an experimental subject had died, which was certainly not impossible, it is conceivable that the parents as well as the research physicians could have been tried under ordinary child abuse laws. Therefore, even though there is therapeutic justification to some extent for a particular research project using children as subjects, it is not in the least unlikely that courts would hold that a parent cannot validly consent to dangerous research on a child where standard and customary therapy for treatment of the child's complaint could be provided. For example, in the Willowbrook situation, standard sanitation procedures and isolation of those children who had hepatitis could have prevented the widespread occurrence of the disease. It should also be noted that the adults who worked at Willowbrook and who were equally exposed to the disease were never used as experimental subjects.[12] In this case, if any criminal proceedings had resulted because of the death or serious injury of any of the children, the researchers and parents would doubtless have been required to justify experimentation on children under circumstances where adults were readily available to use as subjects.

Coercion. Courts would also presumably take a very cautious view of the validity of a parent's consent to research on his child if there were any element of coercion involved in that consent. Admission to Willowbrook, for example, was at one point restricted to children whose parents consented to their participation in the hepatitis research projects. Considering the enormous burdens on the family that a severely retarded child creates and the urgent necessity to place some of these children in institutions, no court confronted with the situation would have upheld parental consent under these conditions as "free and voluntary."[13]

Even in cases of therapeutic research where admission to facilities for treatment is restricted to children whose parents agree to their participation in research and the child would otherwise be denied existing standard and approved treatment for his condition for economic or other reasons, serious questions of the validity of parental consent are raised. This dilemma does not occur in those rare situations in which the child suffers from a condition for which there is no known treatment and the sole potential therapy for his problem is experimental. In that case, the circumstances are such that a parent who consents to his child's admission to a hospital for research studies is not presumably "coerced" in the normal sense of the word.

Another potentially coercive element in a research design is payment to the parents for allowing their child to participate as a research subject. Whereas several authors have discussed the effects of payment on questions involving nontherapeutic pediatric research,[14] the same principle appears to be involved to some extent in therapeutic experimentation. In the absence of an inherently coercive element, such as extreme poverty, payment of adult volunteers for their inconvenience, discomfort, and risk appears to be ethically acceptable and is clearly legally permissible. Where children are involved, however, payment to the parent, not the child, to submit a minor who cannot give a valid consent or refusal of consent to inconvenience, discomfort, or risk would appear to be seriously questionable at law. It would be impossible for the researcher to insist that the fee paid would accrue to the benefit of the child unless all such funds were administered as guardianship accounts by a judge, an administratively difficult situation. It should be noted, however, that income from a child's trusts for a child's benefit may not be expended by a parent for his own use.[15] The effects of payment on the validity of parental consent to research on a child has never been the subject of litigation, but in view of the number of press reports on those persons arrested for selling their children for adoption and the clear illegality of such action, it is doubtful that a court would assume that research on a child that generated income for the parent was performed with proper regard for the subject's best interests.

Consent probably is required from the minor himself even though his capacity to understand what will be done to his body may be limited. Proposed regulations from the Department of Health, Education and Welfare would require the consent of any child over the age of six who is the subject of any research sponsored by that department.[16]

One study indicates that many children who are hospitalized in a research unit do not understand that they are being regarded as research subjects. In this study, 36 children aged 4 to 17 years were hospitalized as research subjects to determine the efficacy of drugs that were being given as therapy for their growth problems. The hospitalization required was fairly protracted, and psychiatrists and other personnel made surveys of the children after their admission to the research unit. They concluded that none of the children under 11 were in the least aware of the fact that they were research subjects, in spite of the fact that there was clearly documented evidence that the children had been present at several discussions with their parents about the hospital admissions for research purposes. Nineteen of the children were over 11 years old. Of those 19 only 6 were aware of the research purposes of their stay in the unit. The only two, both teenagers, who understood that they were hospitalized for research purposes signed themselves out of the hospital a few days after admission.[17]

It may be unlikely that any child prior to adolescence can genuinely understand the fact that he is being used as a subject in therapeutic research. Notwithstanding that limitation on capacity to understand, however, children should be made aware insofar as possible that their hospitalization or treatment is not entirely restricted to those activities that are designed for their benefit alone.

Of course, research, therapeutic or otherwise, that is conducted in a negligent manner or poorly designed so that a preventable accident occurs and damages a subject will support an ordinary malpractice action. Although no decisions can be located involving children as subjects, there are several involving adult patients. In those in which the patients had terminal cancer[18] or heart disease,[19] actions were brought against physicians who used innovative treatments instead of standard therapy. Since the patients could not show that their chances for survival would have been any better if other methods had been chosen, the physicians were not negligent in their choice of treatment. Given a situation in which standard treatment is available, however, and a child can show that he was more likely to be harmed or his recovery delayed by an innovation in therapy to which his parents had consented, it is quite likely that he could recover damages on reaching majority and filing an action in his own right.

PARENTAL CONSENT TO NONTHERAPEUTIC RESEARCH

Nontherapeutic research provokes even greater difficulty in terms of the legal issues involved. Some authorities, both legal and ethical, have taken the position that a parent cannot give a valid consent for any medical procedure on a minor that is not for the direct benefit of the child. Paul Ramsey denies the validity of such consent even for a procedure that carries no risk of harm but merely constitutes "offensive touching." Ramsey concludes that non-therapeutic experimentation on a child reduces the child to the status of "an object" and is therefore unethical.[20]

In 1963 the Medical Research Council of Great Britain issued a report that stated, "In the strict view of the law parents and guardians of minors cannot give consent on their behalf to any procedures which are of no particular benefit to them and which may carry some risk of harm."[21] The Assistant General Counsel of the Department of Health, Education and Welfare in a letter to the *Journal of the American Medical Association* in 1970 upheld this view and said:

> I would reject without qualification the legal efficacy of the consent by parents as to procedures involving a risk of harm with no benefit to the particular child-subject. I share the views of Sir Harvey Druitt, KCB, legal advisor to the British Medical Research Council, which bear repeating in part here for emphasis.
>
> But I am confident that the parent has no legal authority to consent to medical procedures being carried out on his child for the advancement of scientific knowledge or for the benefit to humanity, if these procedures "are of no particular benefit to" the child and "may carry some risk of harm."[22]

The view that parents may consent to nonbeneficial research if the minor is exposed to no discernible risk was presented as early as 1969 in an article in the *Journal of the American Medical Association* by William J. Curran and Henry K. Beecher.[23] Curran and Beecher concluded that children under 14 years of age may be involved in nontherapeutic research with parental consent if: (1) there is a strong reason in professional judgment for using children (as opposed to adults) in the research, and the research has firm medical support and justification and promises important new knowledge of benefit to science; and (2) there is no discernible risk to the child-subject. Curran and Beecher would allow more hazardous research on minors over 14 who are capable of understanding the nature and purposes of the experiment and its risks, as long as both minor and parent consent.

This view, at least that parental consent to nontherapeutic research which carries no discernible risk of harm is valid, has apparently been adopted by the American Medical Association in its *Principles of Medical Ethics,* as long as "consent in writing is given by a legally authorized representative of the subject under circumstances in which an informed and prudent adult would reasonably be expected to volunteer himself or his child as a subject."[24]

If the issue of nontherapeutic research is viewed from the legal standpoint alone, however, it is difficult to argue that a parent's capacity to consent to research that carries no discernible risk should be invalidated. Some research authorities, however, have taken the position that this is precisely what the law demands. For example, Donald T. Chalkley, current Director of the Office of Protection from Research Risks of the Department of Health, Education and Welfare, said in 1973, "A parent has no legal right to give consent for the involvement of his child in an activity not for the benefit of that child. No legal guardian, no person standing *in loco parentis* has that right."[25]

A reasonable consideration of the risks of daily living for any normal child would indicate that large segments of his time are spent in activities that are by no means "beneficial" and which may in fact carry substantial risks of serious physical harm.[26] Outside the context of medical research, no one questions the right of a parent to consent to his child's participation in such activities. In fact, as many child custody cases indicate, a parent who is so neurotic as to forbid a child's participation in normal activities in order to protect the child from injury or germs is quite likely to lose custody on the ground that such overprotection is harmful to the child.[27] A ten-year-old who climbs a tree and sits on a branch is probably not, by any reasonable definition, engaged in "beneficial" activity, and the material risk of his falling out and fracturing his leg is fairly high. If he does fall out, it would be unthinkable that his orthopedist would refer the matter to a juvenile court as a child neglect case on the ground that the child's mother had no authority to allow him to engage in "nonbeneficial" activity. If a parent can consent to a child's participation in Little League football, where statistics show that a variety of serious injuries or even death can occur, it seems unlikely that any court would rule that the same parent has no authority to allow the same child to have a blood sample drawn by a licensed physician because the blood will be used in research of no direct benefit to the child.

It would seem logical that a prudent parent should be able to consent to nontherapeutic research as long as the risk of harm to the child is less than that to which a child at that age is reasonably likely to be exposed in his normal daily life. Observational research, such as weighing the child, would clearly be allowed. If, to return to the football analogy, participation is encouraged because the child learns sportsmanship and other values, it is equally arguable that a child who is encouraged to donate a small sample of blood for the benefit of other children may be learning something about altruism and empathy.

Where the risk of harm is minimal—and no one seriously argues that a child should ever be subjected to unnecessary substantial risk in the course of any research—it is most difficult to imagine on what ground the child could later bring a legal action. If a child is a subject in a blood sample study at age 10, it is most unlikely that at age 18 an action for pain and suffering from the prick of a needle would succeed. Where damage to the extent that would justify a legal action is remotely possible and therapeutic benefits to the particular subject are nonexistent, clearly the research should not be performed in the first place.

A parent who subjects a child to unnecessary and serious danger of any sort is at least technically guilty of child abuse. Therefore, ethical considerations aside, any physician who accepted a parental consent to dangerous non-therapeutic research on a child would, if challenged in the courts, undoubtedly be held to have obtained an invalid consent. In addition to the ethical consideration, any material harm to a child resulting from an intervention that is not designed in any way for the child's own benefit is undoubtedly a tort against that child regardless of parental consent or the lack of it. Clearly, a child's best interest is never served by exposing him to unnecessary dangers, and the more serious the risk, the less likely any court would be to hold that the parent had the right to give consent to a harmful procedure. Since there is no cost-benefit analysis in nontherapeutic research on children, as a matter of law it probably would not be allowed if there is any material possibility, not probability, of harm.

There are thousands of harmless procedures that provide valuable and necessary information when performed on normal children as controls for therapeutic research. Courts have long held that a parent's right of privacy in raising his children permits him to allow or provide non-physically harmful activities for a child of which other parents might well disapprove on moral or other grounds.[28] For example, there are many parents in this country who would consider enrolling a child in a segregated private school to be an immoral act. There is no thought that a court would hold that a parent does not have the right to do so if he wishes, even though the societal attitudes that the child acquires in the segregated environment are contrary to those espoused by the government and a majority of persons in this country.

In the case of Amish children whose parents wish to remove them from school after the eighth grade, the Supreme Court of the United States held that the parents had the right to decide that the children had received a sufficient academic education at that level for purposes of living successfully within their religious community.[29] It may be seriously questioned that the children who were thus deprived of opportunities for advancement which would have allowed them to leave the Amish community had received a decision based on their best interests, but the Supreme Court held that parental rights included the right to raise one's child according to one's own convictions in the absence of physical danger.

By analogy it would seem that if a parent has the constitutional right to deprive a child of a high-school education, the same parent would have the right to consent to the child's participation in nondangerous medical research that has no direct benefit to that child. Such research might include noninvasive medical practices, such as psychological or intelligence tests, physical examinations, regulation of diet (as long as the child was not deprived of necessary nutrition), or studies of urine or blood samples. Even minimal-risk invasive practices would presumably be allowed. For example, it is hard to argue that a parent has violated the child's right to autonomy if he allows a pediatrician to stick the child's finger to remove a small sample of blood for research purposes. Venipuncture under properly controlled circumstances would also probably not be held to constitute a material risk of harm to the child as long as the child was not unduly frightened by the procedure. It should be noted, furthermore, that "material risks" of harm particularly with a child subject should certainly include any procedure that, although non-physically harmful, may frighten or upset the child. Psychological tests that involve misleading or deceiving a child might well be held to constitute "serious risk" in some children and ethically deplorable for all.

Any genuine pain, as opposed to momentarily minor discomfort, to a child is clearly "harm." Although the Supreme Court has upheld a teacher's right to spank a misbehaving child, that decision also held that the discomfort must be preceded by guarantees of due process and fundamental fairness, such as the right of the child to be heard in his own defense before the spanking is administered.[30] It is not illogical to adopt the same principle in the research context. Any child who is to be subjected to any discomfort at all in a nontherapeutic context would thus have, based on that decision, a clear right to object and to present his reasons for refusing to participate in the experiment. "I don't want to be stuck with a needle" would be amply sufficient. If the child consents to a minor discomfort once it has been explained to him, if he is not afraid, and if his parents have consented, it is probable that such an intervention is legally permissible. Since an adult has the right to refuse to participate as a subject for any reason he likes, and since a child deserves the same respect for his autonomy that the researcher is prepared to accord an adult, in these cases the child's withholding of consent should also be sufficient to eliminate his participation as a research subject in invasive procedures. Where the child is too young to communicate, the parent alone may do so.

There is only one case on the subject of the legality of parental consent to the participation of children in nontherapeutic research.[31] The suit sought to enjoin a research proposal for a prospective study of development of allergic disease in infants born in families with histories of allergy. The protocol included a number of invasive techniques as well as the administration of drugs to normal children at regular intervals from infancy to five years of age. Families participating in the program were paid approximately three hundred dollars a year. The injunction had been requested by a lawyer who was a member of the institutional review board of the university in which the research was proposed and sought to enjoin the use of children as research subjects. The plaintiff had requested a ruling that the parent of a normal minor child does not have the legal right to subject his child to experimental procedures not intended for the child's benefit and a further ruling that such a child may at any time up to his majority void such parental consent and institute a legal action against the principal investigator and the university. The suit did not specify what potential harm a child subject might incur in this experiment that could have formed the basis of a legal action for damages.

The trial judge denied the injunction. His denial was apparently based on his view that the California legislature, in enacting the child abuse law that formed the basis of the action, had in mind cases of deliberate torture of children, not low-risk, controlled medical research. The outcome of this case will be of utmost importance as a precedent in subsequent decisions on the use of children as subjects in nontherapeutic experimentation.

To expose a child to unnecessary or unjustified genuine harm or pain in any context, medical or otherwise, constitutes child abuse. Where no physical, emotional, medical, or social harm can result, it appears that a parent does have the right to consent to such interventions on behalf of his child.

The usual quotation cited by those who object to the use of minors as subjects in nontherapeutic research is from a Supreme Court opinion: "Parents may be free to become martyrs themselves but it does not follow that they are free in identical circumstances to make martyrs of their children before they have reached the age of full and legal discretion when they can make the choices for themselves."[32] Although this case involved a guardian's First Amendment right of religious freedom in permitting her ward to sell religious literature on the street, it is hard to imagine that a court would hold that a child whose finger was pricked for a few drops of blood has thus been made "a martyr" in any sense of legal damage.

Thus, it seems both legally and ethically, that therapeutic research may validly be the subject of consent by a parent of an ill child as being in the best interest of the child and is considered well within the scope of parental decision-making. On the other hand, nonharmful, nontherapeutic research may also be conducted on a child without drawing a conclusion that the child is being abused.

It is, however, quite clear that if nonnegligent damage results from a nontherapeutic experiment, the child would have a good cause of action against the investigator. There are numerous precedents for the conclusion that a parent cannot waive a child's rights under the law. For example, a parent cannot sign an enforceable agreement at the time of a divorce waiving a minor child's right to future support from the other parent.[33] The child himself may bring an action to override any such agreement. The same principle would undoubtedly apply in the research context. If a parent consented to a nontherapeutic experiment on a child and real damage occurs, in addition to potential criminal liability for child abuse on the part of both the investigator and the parent, it is quite clear that the child would not be bound by the consent signed by the parent.

Even in the absence of such obvious harm as would support a criminal indictment, any permanent damage to the child, even in the absence of negligence, would probably be compensable even if the parent had consented to the risk. The difficulty, however, is that the parent is the usual guardian *ad litem* appointed by a court to bring a suit on behalf of a minor plaintiff. If the parent was the consenting party to the child's participation in the research, he may be estopped by his own action, and thus another guardian must be appointed or the child must wait until majority to bring the action on his own behalf. In the latter case, the damages awarded to cover costs of remedial medical care are not available until years after the injury is sustained, and the child could be deprived of treatment. In an effort to overcome this problem in the case of a minor kidney donor, one judge ordered the hospital to procure insurance for the child before the operation was performed. The order was vacated, however, because no American company would issue such a policy, the donee's condition deteriorated dangerously, and the transplant had to be performed before negotiations with Lloyd's of London could be concluded.[34]

Since, as was noted in Chapter I, intrafamily tort actions are now allowed in most states against parents by their children, usually for automobile accidents in which the child was hurt while a parent was driving, it is not unlikely that if a parent negligently consented to nontherapeutic experimentation that injured his minor child, the child would have a cause of action against the parent for his injuries as well as against the investigator.

Department of Health, Education and Welfare Regulations

The Department of Health, Education and Welfare has very strict regulations for research involving children as subjects in any research that is funded by that department. Regulations proposed on November 13, 1973, would provide that all research that places children at risk must comply with the following exclusions:

> § 46.27. Certain children excluded from participation in DHEW activities.
>
> A child may not be included as a subject in DHEW activities to which this subpart is applicable if:
> (a) The child has no known living parent who is available and capable of participating in the consent process: Provided That this exclusion shall be inapplicable if the child is seriously ill, and the

proposed research is designed to substantially alleviate his condition; or

(b) The child has only one known living parent who is available and capable of participating in the consent process, or only one such parent, and that parent has not given consent to the child's participation in the activity; or

(c) Both the child's parents are available and capable of participating in the consent process, but both have not given such consent;

(d) The child is involuntarily confined in an institutional setting pursuant to a court order, whether or not the parents and child have consented to the child's participation in the activity; or

(e) The child has not given consent to his or her participation in the research: Provided That this exclusion shall be inapplicable if the child is 6 years of age or less or if explicitly waived by the DHEW; or

(f) The Protection Committee established under § 46.26 of this subpart has not reviewed and approved the child's participation in the activity.[35]

If it is adopted, this regulation would appear to be more stringent in several respects than is the existing jurisprudence. As was discussed in the chapter on consent to treatment, a divorced or separated parent with custody has the right to consent to medical treatment of a child without the knowledge, or over the objection, of the other parent. This regulation would apparently preclude therapeutic research on a child under those circumstances unless the noncustodial parent consents.

The regulation forbids research, therapeutic or not, on a child who is in an institution under court order even if parental consent is obtained. It does not, however, regulate research on children who are placed in institutions by their parents. There is an increasing agreement that none of these children should be used as subjects because their representatives are in no position to exercise unfettered choices,[36] and, in some cases, parental concern for the child may diminish after institutionalization.[37]

Proximate Cause and Recovery of Damages

The absence of demonstrable harm arising from any medical procedure, research, or therapy, would preclude a successful action by a minor who has participated in research activities. It is quite possible that clearly unethical research would not be compensable at law, although it could result in suspension or loss of the researcher's license.

In the *Jewish Chronic Disease Hospital*[38] case, live cancer cells were injected into elderly patients who were not informed of the nature of the experiment. The only legal action that arose out of the research project was a suit brought by a member of the hospital's board of trustees to obtain the records of the patients involved in the experiment. The Board of Regents of the state of New York, however, suspended the investigators' licenses for six months but allowed them to practice on probation.[39]

The legal system is not and does not pretend to be a system for the enforcement of moral and ethical obligations, and the only harm that can be compensated in law is that which flows from physical injury. Furthermore, in order to support a cause of action, the injury must be fairly substantial. It is unlikely for example, that a minor who suffers acute pain for a minute or two but no further effects could prove sufficient damage to sustain a suit against the researcher upon reaching his majority. The most liberal interpreter of the ethical aspects of pediatric research would not, however, condone that experiment merely because it did not constitute a provable legal wrong to the child.

Where the parent alleges lack of informed consent, however, and brings an action in which he claims that the risks to his child were not explained at the time he consented, all effects of the procedure, including momentary pain, whether or not they resulted from negligence, are clearly compensable at law. This is true of claims arising from lack of consent in both the research and practice contexts.[40]

Thus, as a practical matter, if all risks are carefully explained to the parent and the minor before consent to participate as a research subject is requested, the parent cannot bring a successful legal action on behalf of the minor unless he can submit evidence of negligence—failure to use care—in the performance of the experiment. Since there is serious question of the validity of parental consent to a risk of serious harm, the minor may be able upon reaching majority to sustain an action for provable physical injuries and the mental anguish flowing from them even in the absence of negligence, but this point has not yet been the subject of litigation. It is highly improbable that a minor on reaching majority could bring a successful action against a researcher for dignitary harm or damage to his autonomy for recruiting him as a subject with parental consent if no substantial injury occurred during the experiment.

Until quite recently the legal and ethical issues involved in pediatric research were not even recognized as worthy of discussion. For example, in 1968 the World Health Organization published a study on the types of pediatric research that its experts felt should be sponsored by the organization, but this study made no mention of any legal or ethical questions raised by their proposals.[41]

Courts will undoubtedly be faced with actions involving pediatric research within the next few years as the public becomes more sensitive to the issues. Until some precedent is established, however, faced with sharp conflicts within the community of ethicists, a researcher today is left largely to rely on his own common sense and the judgment of his institution's review board. While no firm guidelines can be established, the following principles would appear to be basic to decision-making:

1. No minor should be a research subject if adults, volunteers or patients could be subjects. Under no circumstances should a minor ever be used as a research subject because no adults will agree to participate.

2. If the participation of minors is essential, the rule of selection should be that the older children should be first selected and infants and young children enrolled as subjects only after the experiment has proved harmless or if the nature of the experiment is such that only an infant or young child is an appropriate subject, such as research on respiratory problems in neonates. Particularly in drug trials where the drug has been found safe in adults, the older child, who is more physiologically similar to the adult, should be given the drug before it is used on infants or young children. In addition to the safety factors inherent in selecting older children first, the adolescent's consent is likely to be informed and more rational in fact, even if it is not binding in law.

3. Payment for participation of a minor in research should be restricted to those situations in which the minor is old enough to receive the compensation himself or in which there is a guarantee that the compensation will be set aside for his use and is not available for the parent to spend at will.

4. The risk-benefit ratio should be applied only in terms of the individual child, and a serious risk to a child should never be justified solely on the basis of a substantial benefit to humanity.

5. Research that carries any element of genuine harm, even if designed as therapeutic research, should not be permitted on children confined to residential institutions, even with parental consent, without an order from an appropriate court. These children should never be selected as research subjects unless the purpose of the research is related to treatment of a serious medical problem from which the child is currently suffering or to the condition for which they are confined and thus the research cannot be performed elsewhere. If, for example, a researcher proposes to study some aspect of Down's syndrome, he should select a population of Down's children who are living at home with their parents before considering research on those who have been placed in institutions, and only if the institutionalization is relevant to the study should a court permit it.

Within these limitations, the potential for litigation arising from pediatric research is likely to be quite limited.

THE MINOR AS TRANSPLANT DONOR

Transplantation of kidneys began as an experimental procedure in the mid 1950s but now is an accepted method of treatment of patients in renal failure. While the donors of kidneys are not technically considered the subjects of nontherapeutic research, particularly with minor donors, the legal issues are quite similar.

In Boston in 1957 the first minor was used as a transplant donor for his twin who was suffering from chronic glomerulonephritis. The twins were 19 years old.[42] That same year two other kidney transplants were performed with other sets of twins, both 14.[43] In all three cases, since counsel for the hospital was unsure of the validity of parental consent to an operation that provided no physical benefit to the minor donor, court orders were requested and granted. Since that time judges in Massachusetts have allowed kidney or bone marrow transplants from minor donors in 22 cases and refused permission in none.[44]

Similar requests for court approval have been granted at least in Connecticut,[45] Georgia, Illinois, Maryland, and Virginia.[46] Minor bone marrow donors have been as young as three or four years of age, with one recipient less than one year old.[47] Concomitant with the increasing number of children considered as donors, the Supreme Court of Kentucky in 1969 allowed an incompetent adult to be a kidney donor for his brother.

A severely retarded adult who was a resident of a state institution was allowed by court order to donate a kidney to his brother after a petition by his mother. There was psychiatric testimony to the effect that the link between the brothers was so strong that the death of one would impair the welfare of the other. The court invoked the rule of "substituted judgment," which had previously been used to permit guardians to make decisions about disposition of the property of incompetents and minors, and ratified the mother's consent.[48]

Most legal commentators felt that the number of courts granting approval for these procedures was reaching the point where it could be assumed that permission would be forthcoming in virtually any case, but in 1973 the Supreme Court of Louisiana refused to permit a retarded adolescent to donate a kidney to his adult sister,[49] and in 1975 the Supreme Court of Wisconsin refused to allow an adult who was mentally ill to be a donor.[50]

One major difficulty in evaluating the impact of the decisions in these cases or even arriving at a clear understanding of how many there have been is that all but a very few have been resolved at the trial court level, hence few decisions in these cases have been published. Appeals, by the nature of the situation, are only taken if permission for the donation is refused, and therefore there are currently only two published opinions allowing donations and two refusing such permission. Thus, the sources of information on all other judicial rulings must be obtained from secondary sources, such as articles published by those who have access to the original court records. Since these sources rarely reprint excerpts from the trial judges' opinions, the reasoning behind the decisions is extremely difficult to interpret for use in future cases.

The Massachusetts courts have been the source of almost all the opinions on this subject, with 22 cases to only 1 or 2 in other states. Most jurisdictions have not yet considered this subject, but it is likely that these issues will be raised more frequently and in more areas of the country as kidney and bone marrow donations become more commonplace.

The basic legal problem involving minors of any age as donors is one of obtaining effective consent to protect the minor's rights and to protect his parents, the surgeons, and the hospital from a suit for assault and battery when the minor donor comes of age. Because of his minority the would-be donor cannot give a legally effective consent, and the capacity to give factually effective consent decreases the younger the donor. In the early days of kidney transplants the technology was such that children under 10 could not be accepted as donors for medical, not legal, reasons.[51] This is no longer the case, so the original precedent established by a 19-year-old is being applied to children as young as 3 or 4. Furthermore, as indicated in the preceding section, it is highly questionable whether a parent can give consent to any medical procedure on a minor that carries a serious risk for the benefit of another and in which the donor child receives no medical benefit. Thus, physicians in all states where the problem has arisen have been advised by their own counsel or hospital counsel to seek a court order granting permission to use the minor or the adult incompetent as a donor.[52] The earliest case on the subject of a minor as a donor was *Bonner v. Moran.*

A 15-year-old boy was persuaded by his aunt to go to the hospital and volunteer as a skin graft donor for the aunt's child who had been badly burned. The boy went to the hospital where all personnel who talked with him knew that he lived with his mother. No attempt was made to obtain the mother's permission for the operation. The skin graft was performed, complications ensued, and the donor was hospitalized for several months. The mother brought an action on his behalf for negligent treatment and on her own behalf for performance of the operation without her permission. The court held that she had a cause of action in her own right since the child's consent alone was legally ineffective.[53]

This case, however, does *not* answer the question of whether or not the mother would have had the capacity to consent to a nontherapeutic surgical procedure on behalf of her child for the benefit of a collateral relative if she had been asked.

Scope of Court Orders

All the kidney donation cases in which permission has been granted have resulted in decrees insulating the hospital and the surgeons from liability for assault and battery only. These decrees do not insulate anyone from liability for negligent performance of the transplant operation. If the donor is injured during the surgery, negligence liability exposure remains unaffected. Since reports of all the decisions indicate that surgeons testified that the risk to the donor was minimal except for the risks inherent in any administration of general anesthesia, if an untoward surgical result had occurred, it is clear that informed consent issues could also be raised by the donor's parents in their own right.[54] These decrees simply preclude an action by the minor upon reaching majority against either the surgeons or the hospital and, quite possibly, his parents, based on the nonnegligent removal of his kidney without his legally effective consent. The same issues are raised where the prospective donor is an adult who for some reason is incompetent, since the legal status of incompetents is similar to that of minors.

Allowing a teenager to be a donor is quite a different matter legally from allowing a very young child to do so. A normal teenager, although unable to give a legally effective consent, can clearly comprehend the nature and consequences of the donation, whereas few, if any, preschool children are able to understand the nature of the request if they are asked to give a kidney or bone marrow to a sibling. The minor's inability to understand the gravity of what he was asked to do was the primary reason that the Supreme Court of Louisiana refused permission for a transplant donation in one case.

A 17-year-old retarded boy was the sole medically acceptable donor of a kidney for his adult sister. The retardation was sufficiently severe so that the boy had no reasonable understanding of what was being asked of him. The procedural device used in the case was that his mother refused to consent to his donation, and his father brought an action against her, asking the court to order her to consent or to allow the procedure over her objection. The Supreme Court of Louisiana refused to allow the boy to be used as a donor on the ground that it was against the best interest of the minor incompetent to be asked to donate a kidney and that they would not measure the interests of the child against the interests of an adult. The opinion appears to indicate that the result would have been the same even if both parents had been willing to consent on the record.[55]

The Supreme Court of Wisconsin used much the same reasoning in refusing to allow an adult incompetent to be used as a donor.

The prospective donor was an adult catatonic schizophrenic who had been committed to a mental institution for almost 20 years. Psychiatrists testified that his effective capacity to comprehend the meaning of the donation was that of a 12-year-old. His married sister, who had small children, lost both kidneys, and her husband and several other siblings asked the court for permission to allow the incompetent to be a donor. This case is somewhat unusual in that there were adult, competent siblings in the family who refused to be tested for their histocompatibility as possible donors. The court held that the mental illness of the prospective donor totally precluded consent and pointed out that it was entirely undisputed that the prospective donor did not understand anything about the procedure. The court held that his interests would in no way be served, since the alternative, the death of his sister, would cause him no substantial mental anguish. The decision specifically rejected the concept of "substituted judgment" of either a court or other family members and held that there was no power in a court to permit such a donation, since no advantage should be taken of an incompetent.[56]

These two cases apparently limit the extent to which courts will, under any circumstances, allow a minor or an incompetent to be a donor, and it should be noted that they had certain unusual elements. In the first case there was disagreement between the parents as to the desirability of the donation. It is highly improbable, as a matter of practice, that any court would permit a child to be a donor unless both parents are willing to consent if both are available. None of the cases to date discussed in any of the articles on this subject has involved a single-parent household. The adversarial attributes of most of the trial court cases appear to be minimal, and those persons appointed as guardians for the prospective donors have not raised serious objections to the procedure.[57] Faced with a genuine dispute over the merits of a donation by a minor, most judges will doubtless adopt the position of "when in doubt, don't."

Second, in all cases a court will presumably be most unwilling to permit a minor or an incompetent to be used as a transplant donor unless all competent adults who are available in the family have been medically eliminated as acceptable donors.[58] In the second case cited, there could not be a determination that no competent donor was available, since at least one brother refused to be tested. He testified to the trial judge that he thought his responsibilities to his own young children precluded him from taking the risks inherent in the donation.

In no case is an adult ever ordered to surrender a kidney, bone marrow, or any other part of his body for donation to his child, to another relative, or to anyone else. Judges are therefore very aware that a minor donor is being required, by their orders giving permission for the transplant, to do what an adult cannot be required to do. At the very least a court will insist on being presented with solid medical evidence that no competent adult can donate instead of the minor and that those adults in control of the child are in accord on the desirability of the procedure.

Handicapped Minors

In one recent trial court case, a 15-year-old boy suffered from aplastic anemia. There were three other children in the family—a retarded and almost psychotic 13-year-old boy, a normal girl of 11, and the youngest, a normal boy whose age was not given. The parents told the physicians that only the retarded child could be a bone marrow donor and they would never consent to a donation by either of their normal children. A Guardian *ad Litem,* who was a physician, was appointed to represent the interests of the retarded child. He spent a great deal of time with the prospective donor and had him examined by several psychiatrists. There was no dispute that the child was totally unable to understand anything about the procedure or to answer any questions about the information provided him by any of the physicians involved. The guardian's report to the court refused to grant permission for the donation but also refused to "deny the boy the right to help his dying brother" and thus left the decision to the judge. It was then discovered that the retarded child was the only one of the three who was histocompatible. The trial judge allowed the procedure.[59]

Given the same facts in a situation where a normal child and a retarded child are both histocompatible donors, it seems unlikely, as long as the normal child is old enough to understand the nature of the procedure and to give a meaningful consent, that any court would allow the choice of the retarded child as the donor if the parents have refused to consent to donation by the normal child. It would seem that the minimal fairness and basic distributive justice a handicapped child should be able to expect from his parents and a court in this situation is that if he were the prospective donee, his normal sibling would be asked for the same degree of sacrifice for him. Where this is not the case, a judge may be put on notice that the family's attitude that the handicapped child alone is "expendable" may be creating severe problems for him altogether aside from the transplant issue. A decision to tax the wisdom of a modern-day Solomon would be a situation in which the only two histocompatible siblings are a retarded teenager and a normal child of four or five who is too young to understand the meaning of the donation.

In all cases dealing with minors where there is more than one sibling, all judges are very likely to hold that the one nearest majority and with the greatest capacity for comprehension should be the first choice as donor as among histocompatible equals, and most would view with great suspicion any attempt by parents to enlist a retarded child for this purpose when another child is available.

There are no reported decisions in which parents have attempted to consent to donation by a minor of any age where the donee is a nonsibling. Although it is highly improbable that the courts would allow a minor to be a donor for a nonrelative or a related nonsibling such as a cousin, it is not unlikely that a minor donor would be acceptable as a donor when one of his parents is the patient. In most of these cases, the courts have allowed the donation on the basis that there is a psychological benefit to the minor donor resulting from the preservation of the life of a member of the family. The judges have held that the death of the donee sibling would adversely affect the donor child to such an extent that the best interests of the donor will be served by the procedure. It would be hard to argue that any child would not be more seriously traumatized by the death of a parent than by the death of a sibling, but as far as can be determined this issue has not been raised in any court.

Reasoning of the Courts

Beginning with the Massachusetts cases in 1957, courts have adopted several rationales for granting permission to allow a minor to serve as a donor. In the early cases involving teenagers, quite reasonably on the basis of psychiatric testimony as to the effect that the death of a twin would have on the emotional development of the would-be donor, the courts found that it was within "the best interests of the donor" to be allowed to provide the kidney.[60] This approach, that to donate a kidney to a sibling whose life will be saved is a greater benefit to the prospective donor's development than is retention of both kidneys, is a logical conclusion to draw where older minors are involved. With younger children, however, the psychological benefit of a sibling relationship may be far less important to long-term development, since the younger the child the less able he is to feel a severe loss as the result of the sibling's death. Some young children may in fact be quite jealous of a sibling and dislike him intensely, particularly if the child feels that the ill child has received undue attention from their parents and he himself has been shoved aside. This might well occur if one or both of the parents stayed at the hospital with the sick child for long periods of time and the other child was left to the care of others. The sense of loss in these cases may be quite minimal.

A seven-year-old girl had both kidneys removed and was maintained on an artificial kidney machine pending a transplant. Neither parent was an acceptable donor, but her identical twin was determined to be compatible. The girl's parents were willing to consent to the transplant, but the physicians refused to proceed without a judicial determination that parental consent was effective and brought an action in which the court was asked to decide if the parents could give a valid consent. The court in this case allowed the parents to consent, but the decision was not entirely based on the rationale that the best interests of the donor would be served by the operation. The parents were allowed to consent to the operation on the basis of a familial cost-benefit analysis: the court found that they had the right to decide that the importance to the donee substantially outweighs the risks to the donor.[61]

In a situation in which a parent or parents must make the choice of a serious operation involving loss of a kidney or bone marrow for one child in order to save the life of their other child, serious questions are obviously raised about the freedom of choice of the parents or of their ability to make a genuine commitment to the interests of the donor child. The only reasonable solution would seem to be that their decision be reviewed by other, nonrelated persons who can be more objective about the situation. In the case above, the court specifically held that since the parents were incompatible donors, the donor child's psychological interests would be better served by living in a happy family than one in which a child had died, and emphasized that the judge had talked to the donor child, who, within the capabilities of her age, desired to donate. That being the case, the court held, "The parents can consent after a close, independent and objective investigation of their motivation and reasoning where there are negligible risks to both children." Allowing the parents to decide on the basis of all the relevant interests, subject to objective review by a court, would appear to be, at least in any situation where the donor child is quite young, a much more rational basis on which to conclude that a donation should be allowed than attempting to show great benefit to a donor.[62]

However, it may not be assumed that all courts in a situation involving young children will agree with that analysis. In view of the pressures of the parents, other courts may hold that they are incapable of making a rational judgment in this situation. One writer has suggested the following:

> In a bone marrow or kidney transplant case involving sibling donor recipient, the parents necessarily are confronted with a painful dilemma. Although they have a desperately ill child who may die if no transplant is performed, and although they wish to do whatever may save his life, presumably they do not want to injure their healthy child, the prospective donor. Generally, the only possible resolution of this conflict for the parents will be to attempt to save the life of the sick child by consenting to the minor donor's participation because of the comparatively minimal risk to the healthy child.[63]

Consent of the Minor

An unresolved question at present is a determination of what role, if any, the prospective donor's consent or refusal to consent should play. This question is fairly easy to resolve where the prospective donor is a teenager. The age of majority is now 18 years for all practical purposes, and therefore the consent of a donor who is almost that age should be considered effective in fact if not in law.[64] Equally, his refusal to participate should be respected to the same degree that it would be respected if he were an adult.[65]

Even though a minor who is of a sufficient age to understand the meaning of a donation and who would be allowed to consent to treatment for his own illness cannot give a legally binding consent to a procedure of this nature, most commentators feel that judges view the expression of willingness as evidence that the procedure will be in his best interests. The validity of that evidence, as would be true of a situation involving an incompetent adult, is in proportion to the extent to which he is capable of making rational decisions with lifetime consequences. The younger the child or the more incompetent the adult, the more compelling should be other independent evidence that the prospective donor will be in some way benefited by the procedure.[66]

Recent studies have focused on the psychological adjustment of adolescent kidney donors and their abilities to make and live with an enduring decision to donate a kidney without subsequent emotional trauma.[67] A study of 26 minors from 16 to 21 years of age who had agreed to donate a kidney revealed that the primary motive was rescue of the terminally ill sibling. Another frequent motivation was that these adolescents had great desires to prove to themselves and to their families that they were "grown up," that they were able to make mature decisions and to perform adult acts of significance. The authors of the study discovered that 89 percent of the teenagers appeared to be under no family pressure to donate, and in most cases, in fact, the parents tended to protect them from the process as long as possible. There were, however, some instances of pressure by the parents on the child to consent. Pressure on the parents to risk the health of one child to save the life of the other and the obvious pressure this could create on a child who may be in effect forced to donate a kidney is the primary reason that some writers feel that donations by minors should not be allowed.[68] If courts simply refused to permit any minor to be a donor, parental guilt at refusing to consent or pressure on a child to agree once the parents have consented would be eliminated. When the ill child dies, the entire family could attribute the death to the judge's actions, not their own.

Given the financial, emotional, and legal dependence of teenagers on their parents, even if a teenager is presumed to understand the significance of an agreement to donate, courts should investigate with particularity the obvious potential for parental pressure or coercion on the child, no matter how much he may appear to wish to do it. Guilt-induction in this situation would be almost impossible to withstand.

Questions have been raised in recent commentaries about whether a very young child should be allowed to refuse to donate. As one author asks, "What if a three- or four-year-old potential donor refused to undergo the procedure because he did not like needles? Should his sibling forego transplantation because of the express refusal of the younger child? One might prophesy that when this very young donor reaches adolescence he would be disturbed that an older sibling was allowed to die without a transplant of his bone marrow."[69]

It would appear that any judge might be legitimately inclined to refuse to allow a donation by a three-year-old donor particularly because a child of that age was frightened and did not like needles. The possibility that a parent might, as the author suggests, blame the child a decade later for allowing the older sibling to die would appear to be the most important reason a judge might have to forbid the donation. If a three-year-old's alternatives are terror or guilt, a wise judge will shoulder the burden.

The right to refuse to donate should be as carefully preserved for a minor as for an adult. In addition to the ethical questions raised by compulsory donations from children, if the minor is old enough to understand what is being done to him against his will and the court records reflect his objections, it is not impossible to envision a successful action for assault and battery at the time he reaches majority in spite of the original court order.

In the few decisions in which opinions are available, however, it is obvious that trial judges made sincere efforts to elicit the donor's views on the subject and included the stated willingness of the donor child among their reasons for allowing the transplant. The implication is that they would have respected a refusal as conclusive. It is hoped that these discussions are held in the absence of the parents so that the potential for coercion or fear of parental retribution is minimized.

As has been indicated, although courts are not reluctant to order treatment for life-threatening medical problems over the objections, religious or otherwise, of a parent, it is improbable that any court would order that an ill child should be treated where that treatment requires surgical intervention on another child in the absence of parental concurrence. Although one author states with apparent disapproval that there is now no mechanism by which transplants can be ordered over parental objection,[70] the alternative would totally denigrate parental power of decision-making within the family unit. A parent might legitimately decline to take any risk with a healthy child in view of the fact that a kidney transplant may not save the life of the donee. In the first three transplant cases involving minors, for example, two donees died following surgery.[71]

Michigan has recently enacted a statute that attempts to clarify the issues in kidney donations by minors and eliminate the necessity for protracted hearings.[72] The statute provides that a person of 14 years of age or more may give one of his two kidneys to a father, mother, son, daughter, brother, or sister for transplantation when authorized by an order of the probate court that has jurisdiction of his person. The statute provides that the petition for such an order may be made by the person himself or his guardian, parents, spouse, child, or any other next of kin except the intended donee. The statute further provides that the probate judge shall hold a hearing and that the prospective donor shall be present at the hearing. If the court determines that the prospective donor is "sufficiently sound of mind to understand the needs and probable consequences of a gift to both the donor and donee and agrees to the gift, the court may enter an order authorizing the making of the gift."

This statute would apparently provide that with the assent of a probate judge a minor over 14 may consent to donate a kidney without the necessity of obtaining parental consent or of appointment of a guardian. It is, however, unlikely that any judge would, in fact, issue such an order without parental consent. This statute, of course, also appears to require a competent adult donor to appear at a hearing prior to agreeing to be a kidney donor, since it applies to persons old enough to have "sons and daughters" who are the recipients of the transplants under the terms of the statute and since the subject is "persons of 14 years of age or more." It is unclear whether this statute is designed to preclude donations by persons under 14 entirely.

It therefore appears that before an incompetent adult or a minor of any age is legally acceptable as a donor, a surgeon or hospital should request a court order and be prepared to present the consent of the would-be donor and both parents and to justify the position that it is in the best interests of the donor that such a procedure should be allowed. It would be almost impossible to convince a court that a donor would benefit by providing an organ to a recipient who is not a sibling or perhaps a parent. It is also obvious that any court would require a showing on sound medical evidence that there is no competent adult or older minor donor available who is suitable for the purpose and that the proposed operation is absolutely necessary to preserve the life of the recipient.[73] While adults occasionally attempt to sell a kidney or other nonvital organs, it is unthinkable that any court would permit a minor's parents to negotiate a sale of a child's bone marrow, kidney, blood, or any other portion of the child's body.

In no case should it ever be contemplated that any donation from a minor may be accepted without a court order, even in the case where the recipient of the organ is the minor's own child. To do so would risk an assault and battery suit against the surgeon and perhaps the parents as well when the minor donor reaches majority. It must also never be assumed that any given judge will in fact issue such an order, at least for children who are too young to give a comprehending consent.

As was discussed in detail in the chapter on fetal research, the Uniform Anatomical Gift Act, now adopted in all 50 states and the District of Columbia, permits a parent to consent to the use of a deceased minor's organs for transplantation. The consent of either parent is sufficient in the absence of a stated objection by the other.[74] If the minor was married, the surviving spouse should be asked for consent. Few if any legal problems can be seen in the area of donations from cadavers as long as the parent gives an informed consent.

NOTES

1. Fiorentino v. Wenger, 272 NYS 2d 557, NY 1966, rev'd on other grounds, 227 NE 2d 296, NY 1967.
2. See, for example, Canterbury v. Spence, 464 F 2d 772, CA DC 1972; Cobbs v. Grant, 502 P 2d 1, Cal 1972.

3. Kefauver-Harris Act, 21 USC, Section 355.

4. E.g., Mueller v. Mueller, 221 NW 2d 39, SD 1974.

5. Mulder v. Parke Davis and Co. 181 NW 2d 882, Minn 1970.

6. Koury v. Follo, 158 SE 2d 548, NC 1968.

7. "Package Inserts as Evidence," 208 *JAMA* No. 3, page 589, April 21, 1969.

8. "Drug Testing in Children: FDA Regulations," 43 *Pediatrics* No. 3, page 463, March 1969.

9. Harry Shirkey, "Therapeutic Orphans," 72 *J Pediat* No. 1, page 119, January 1968. See also Jean D. Lockhart, "The Information Gap in Pediatric Drug Therapy," *Mod Med,* page 56, November 16, 1970.

10. Stephen Goldby, "Experiments in the Willowbrook State School," 1 *Lancet,* page 749, 1971.

11. S. Krugman, J. P. Giles, and J. Hammond, "Viral Hepatitis, Type B (MS-2 Strain): Studies on Active Immunization," 217 *JAMA,* pages 41–45, 1971.

12. Paul Ramsey, *The Patient as Person,* New Haven, Conn, Yale University Press, 1974, page 48.

13. *Ibid.,* page 54; "Studies with Children Backed on Medical, Ethical Grounds," 8 *Medical Tribune,* February 20, 1967, page 23.

14. E.g., Alexander Capron, "Legal Considerations Affecting Clinical Pharmacological Studies in Children," *Clin Res,* page 146, February 1973; C. U. Lowe, D. Alexander, and B. Mishkin, "Nontherapeutic Research on Children: An Ethical Dilemma," 84 *Pediatrics* No. 4, page 472, April 1974.

15. E.g., McKinnon v. First National Bank of Pensacola, 82 So 748, Fla 1919.

16. 33 *Fed Reg* No. 221, page 31747, November 16, 1973.

17. A. Herbert Schwartz, "Children's Concepts of Research Hospitalization," 287 *New Engl J Med* No. 12, page 589, September 1972.

18. E.g., Baldor v. Rogers, 81 So 2d 658, Fla 1955.

19. E.g., Karp v. Cooley, 493 F 2d 408, CCA 5, 1974.

20. Paul Ramsey, *The Patient as Person,* New Haven, Conn, Yale Univeristy Press, 1974, page 17. An excellent summary of the different viewpoints on the subject of parental consent to nontherapeutic research on minors, including views of both ethicists and legal scholars, may be found in Richard A. McCormick, "Proxy Consent in the Experimental Situation," 18 *Perspectives Biol Med* No. 1, page 2, Autumn 1974.

21. The statement of the Medical Research Council is quoted and discussed in the following: McCormick, *op. cit. supra* at 20, page 4; Letter, *supra* at 20; Curran and Beecher, *infra* at 21, Capron, *op. cit. supra* at 14, page 143; A. G. M. Campbell, "Infants, Children and Informed Consent," 3 *Brit Med J,* page 335, 1974.

22. Letter from Edward J. Rourke, Assistant General Counsel, DHEW, 211 *JAMA* No. 2, page 301, January 12, 1970.

23. William J. Curran and Henry K. Beecher, "Experimentation in Children," 210 *JAMA* No. 1, page 77, October 6, 1969.

24. See McCormick, *op. cit. supra* at 20, page 4.

25. Donald T. Chalkley, *Medical World News,* June 8, 1973, page 41, quoted in McCormick, *ibid.,* page 2.

26. For an application of the "daily living" concept of allowable research risks, see Ross G. Mitchell, "The Child and Experimental Medicine," 1 *Brit Med J,* page 721, 1964.

27. "Mental Illness and Parental Rights," 216 *JAMA* No. 3, page 575, April 19, 1971.

28. For example, one court has held that a mother who advocated contraception, not absti-

nence, to a sexually active teenage daughter could not be guilty of contributing to delinquency. Ohio v. McLaughlin, 212 NE 2d 635, Ohio, 1965.

29. Wisconsin v. Yoder, 406 US 205, 1972.

30. Baker v. Owen, 000 US 000, 1975.

31. Neilson v. Regents of the University of California, 665-047, Sup Ct of Cal, County of San Francisco, 1973, discussed in Lowe, Alexander, and Mishkin, *op. cit. supra* at 14. The decision is reported in *OPRR* (NIH, PHS, DHEW) *Reports,* February 1976, pages 2 and 3.

32. Prince v. Massachusetts, 321 US 158 at 170, 1944.

33. E.g., Burke v. Burke, 75 A 2d 42, Conn 1950; Buchanan v. Buchanan, 197 SE 426, Va 1938.

34. For a discussion of attempts to obtain insurance in this case, see C. H. Baron, M. Botsford, and G. Cole, "Live Organ and Tissue Transplants from Minor Donors in Massachusetts," 55 *Boston U Law Rev,* pages 189–192, 1975.

35. See 33 *Fed Reg* No. 221, page 31747, November 16, 1973.

36. Capron, *op. cit. supra* at 14, pages 145–146.

37. McCormick, *op. cit. supra* at 20, pages 17–18.

38. Hyman v. Jewish Chronic Disease Hospital, 206 NE 2d 338, NY 1965.

39. 151 *Science,* pages 663–666, 1963.

40. E.g., Darrah v. Kite, 301 NYS 2d 286, NY 1969; Salgo v. Leland Stanford Board of Trustees, 317 P 2d 170, Cal 1957.

41. Report of WHO Scientific Group, *Paediatric Research,* WHO Tech. Rep. Series, No. 400, Geneva, 1968.

42. The unpublished opinion in the first minor transplant case, Masden v. Harrison, is reprinted in its entirety in C. E. Wasmuth, and C. E. Wasmuth, Jr., *Law and the Surgical Team,* Baltimore, The Williams and Wilkins Co., 1969, Ch 8, pages 342–344.

43. William T. Curran, "A Problem of Consent: Kidney Transplantation in Minors," 34 *NYU Law Rev,* page 891, May 1959.

44. C. H. Baron, M. Botsford, and G. F. Cole, "Live Organ and Tissue Transplants from Minor Donors in Massachusetts," 55 *Boston U Law Rev,* page 169, 1975.

45. Hart v. Brown, 289 A 2d 386, Conn 1972.

46. Baron, Botsford, and Cole, *op. cit. supra* at 44, page 162, n 16.

47. See, for example, *ibid.,* page 171, n 63; and M. D. Levine, B. M. Camitta, D. Nathan, and W. J. Curran, "The Medical Ethics of Bone Marrow Transplantation in Childhood," 86 *J Pediat* No. 1, page 145, January 1975.

48. Strunk v. Strunk, 445 SW 2d 145, KY 1969.

49. In re Richardson, 284 So 2d 185, La 1973.

50. In re Pescinski, 226 NW 2d 180, Wisc 1975.

51. Curran, *op. cit. supra* at 43, page 895.

52. "Transplant Problems," 223 *JAMA* No. 11, page 1315, March 12, 1973.

53. Bonner v. Moran, 126 F 2d 121, CA DC 1941.

54. E.g., Hart v. Brown, 289 A 2d 386, Conn 1972.

55. In re Richardson, 284 So 2d 185, La 1973.

56. In re Pescinski, 226 NW 2d 180, Wisc 1975.

57. Baron, Botsford, and Cole, *op. cit. supra* at 44, pages 181–188.

58. See, for example, Strunk v. Strunk, *supra* at 48; and Hart v. Brown, *supra* at 54.

59. This unreported case is discussed in detail in Levine et al., *op. cit. supra* at 47, pages 147–148.

60. E.g., Curran, *op. cit. supra* at 43.

61. Hart v. Brown, *op. cit. supra* at 54.

62. See discussions of Hart v. Brown in note, 4 *Tex Tech Law Rev,* page 244, 1972; and William J. Curran, "Kidney Transplantation in Identical Twin Minors: Justice Is Done in Connecticut," 287 *New Engl J Med,* page 26, 1972.

63. Baron, Botsford, and Cole, *op. cit. supra* at 44, page 167. See also Levine et al., *op. cit. supra* at 47, page 147.

64. See, for example, Curran, *op. cit. supra* at 43, pages 895–897; and Baron, Botsford, and Cole, *op. cit. supra* at 44, pages 176–178.

65. See Levine et al., *op. cit. supra* at 47, page 149.

66. Baron, Botsford, and Cole, *op. cit. supra* at 44, pages 180–181.

67. D. M. Bernstein and R. G. Simmons, "The Adolescent Kidney Donor: The Right to Give," 131 *Am J Psychiat* No. 12, page 1338, December 1974.

68. E.g., David Daube, "Transplantation Acceptability of Procedures and the Required Legal Sanctions," in *Ethics in Medical Progress,* Boston, Little, Brown and Co., 1966, pages 198–199; "The Sale of Human Body Parts," note, 72 *Mich Law Rev,* May 1974, pages 1196–1197.

69. Levine et al., *op. cit. supra* at 47, page 148.

70. *Ibid.,* page 149.

71. Curran, *op. cit. supra* at 42, page 898.

72. Mich Stats, Section 701.19(b), "Kidney Transplant: Donor's Qualifications; Procedure."

73. "Organ Donation by Incompetent," 213 *JAMA* No. 3, page 513, July 20, 1970.

74. Uniform Anatomical Gift Act, Section 2(b).

CHAPTER VII

THE PEDIATRICIAN

AND

THE SCHOOLS

Very frequently pediatricians are called on to deal with their patients' school problems. Additionally, the school may approach the pediatrician for help with a particular child who may or may not be a regular patient, or the school may attempt to obtain information about a patient from the pediatrician. Few discussions by courts or in legal journals can be located on a variety of common situations involving interaction between a pediatrician and a teacher or school administrator. This chapter examines four of these problems in terms of their legal implications: (1) the pediatrician's role in the placement of children in special education, (2) the pediatrician's role as a team physician, (3) the pediatrician and the child who is suspected of being hyperkinetic, and (4) questions of confidentiality that may arise in school situations.

SPECIAL EDUCATION

Placement of a child in classes for the handicapped or the educable mentally retarded carries enormous significance for that child's future. Improper placement of a child in a special education class clearly violates his right to an adequate educational opportunity and would presumably, although there are no cases on the subject, impose liability for that injury on the pediatrician if the placement had been the result of medical negligence.

The Right to Proper Education

Determining placement in an educational system solely on the basis of scores on IQ tests has been demonstrated to be extremely unsatisfactory. As many courts and educational experts have discussed, children who are culturally deprived, speak English as a second language, or have other social handicaps commonly do not score well on these tests, which reflect middle-class biases. For this reason placement solely on this basis may infringe basic civil rights.[1]

189

There is a clear constitutional right to an education in the public schools for all children, handicapped or not. Many recent decisions have held that a handicapped child cannot be excluded from an education suitable for his needs on the ground of school administration claims that it cannot afford the special classes.

Seven school-aged children sued the school board of the District of Columbia, which provided no classes for their special needs. Some of these children were mentally retarded, others were emotionally disturbed or physically handicapped. Some were hyperactive or had other behavioral problems. The estimate presented to the trial court was that there were 22,000 children in the District with special problems for whom there were no special classes. The court held that the Constitution of the United States required provision of publicly supported education for these exceptional children. The failure to fulfill this clear duty to include and retain these children in the public school system could not be excused by the school board's claim that there were insufficient funds. The court held that if sufficient funds are not available to finance all of the services and programs that were needed or would be desirable in the system, then the available funds must be apportioned equitably in such a manner that "no child is entirely excluded from a publicly supported education consistent with his needs and ability to benefit therefrom."[2]

The judgment in a suit against the state of Pennsylvania on behalf of numerous retarded children required Pennsylvania to provide:

> ... a free public program of education and training appropriate to the child's capacity within the context of a presumption that, among the alternative programs of education and training required by statute to be available, placement in a regular public school class is preferable to the placement in a special school class (a class for handicapped children) and placement in a special school class is preferable to placement in any other type of program of education and training.[3]

Once is it understood that these children have the right to an education, the question of placement becomes the critical issue. It is undeniable that placement in a class of educable mentally retarded children carries with it extraordinary stigma for a child. His self-image may be adversely affected as the result of peer group judgments or teacher attitude. Children have been shown in many studies to be "self-fulfilling prophesies": if a child is told that he is retarded he will begin to behave as if he were.[4] Furthermore, inclusion by mistake in a special education class for any appreciable length of time is likely to handicap the child in terms of acquisition of skills to the extent that if the mistake is rectified and he is returned to the regular classroom he may be too far behind to catch up with the rest of the group.[5] For this reason, although there are some seriously handicapped children who obviously cannot function well in the ordinary public school classroom, in any borderline case serious legal questions may arise from improper placement.

An 11-year-old boy had been tested by the San Francisco School District and found to have an IQ of 75. A suit was brought on his behalf to eliminate IQ tests scores as a criteria for placement in classes for the educable mentally retarded. An individual test given by a psychologist using the Wechsler Intelligence Scale resulted in a finding that his full-scale IQ was actually 100. The psychologist suggested that the child was not retarded, but as the result of improper placement for a protracted period he required remedial instruction. This suit resulted in a finding by the trial judge that to use IQ tests as the sole or primary determinant of placement in special education classes results in serious disadvantage to minority-group children such as the plaintiff. The court held that the IQ tests were not rationally related to the determination of ability to learn, at least insofar as those tests had been applied to black children, and ruled that the children who had been so tested and placed had been deprived of their rights to equal protection of the law as guaranteed by the Fourteenth Amendment to the Constitution. The court order held that the school system was restrained from "placing blacks or other minorities in classes for the educable mentally retarded on the basis of criteria which places primary reliance on results of IQ tests as currently administered if the consequences of such criteria is a racial imbalance in the classes."[6]

The "tracking" system of the District of Columbia schools was declared unconstitutional on the same basis. In that case the court held:

> The evidence shows that the method by which track assignments are made depends essentially on standardized aptitude tests, which although given on a systemwide basis, are completely inappropriate for use with a large segment of the student body. Because these tests are standardized primarily on and are relevant to a white middle class group of students, they produce inaccurate and misleading tests scores when given to lower class and Negro students. As a result, rather than being classified according to ability to learn, these students are in reality being classified according to their socio-economic or racial status or more precisely, according to environmental or psychological factors which have nothing to do with innate ability.[7]

It is clear that many children have been misclassified on the basis of criteria that have nothing to do with ability. The longer the misclassification obtains, the further behind the child is likely to become in terms of keeping up with the children in ordinary classes.

Diagnosis of Retardation

The pediatrician who is called in by a parent or who is asked to examine a child for evaluation of his abilities at the request of a school official is presumably subject to the same standard of care in diagnosis as he would be if he were making a diagnosis of any other condition. As was indicated in an earlier chapter, it is extremely unlikely that a court would hold justifiable any examination of such a child without the knowledge or consent of his parent. It is not inconceivable that a suit for assault brought by the parent whose preadolescent child was examined without his consent in these circumstances might succeed.

Once the parent has consented, however, the usual standard of care required in diagnosis applies. To make a determination that a child is "probably retarded," even for referral to a psychologist who administers IQ tests, imposes serious responsibility on the pediatrician. The standard of care required in making a diagnosis of this or any other condition is the use of the same degree of skill, care, and knowledge as would be used by the average prudent physician with the same training.[8] Pediatricians are normally held to a national standard of care as opposed to the "community standard," in which a general practitioner is adjudged negligent only in reference to the standard that prevails in his community.[9]

Obviously, in this case the pediatrician must have an adequate history of the child's behavior. If the child or parent is capable of relating an adequate social and medical history and the physician does not ask for it, he may be negligent. In particular, a child who is being seen for diagnosis and evaluation of "intelligence problems" may well be suffering from serious physical complaints, particularly deafness or impaired vision. Failure to elicit a sufficient history of the child's physical condition to permit further investigation of any health problems would be negligence.[10]

The examination of the child should conform to standards that a prudent physician would consider to apply to ordinarily careful and thorough examination such as the circumstances permit. For example, failure to test the child's hearing and vision or to refer the child for these examinations would indicate to any jury that the examination was incomplete. The most usual cause of litigation arising from any form of misdiagnosis is the allegation that the physician did not make a careful examination. If this is proved and the patient has been damaged, as would certainly be true in this case, the physician is usually held to be liable.[11]

These examinations are certainly not emergencies, and thus a court would find it very hard to believe that a thorough, careful, and considered examination was made if the diagnosis is later invalidated by a more careful investigation.

Any diagnosis of retardation without utilization of appropriate psychological tests would be negligence. In any situation where misdiagnosis of a physical ailment has occurred, failure to utilize the appropriate tests on which a correct diagnosis could be based has been held to be negligence.[12] In most if not all cases the pediatrician will refer the child to a psychologist, pediatric neurologist, or psychiatrist for testing. If that individual is then negligent, the pediatrician, as referring physician, will not be negligent unless he has failed to use due care in selection of the specialist. Therefore, referral to a psychologist or psychiatrist whose credentials are subject to question, if any qualified person is available for the purpose, might well impose liability on the pediatrician for any errors in administration of the tests. Unless the pediatrician is sure that a particular psychologist who does not have a Ph.D. is otherwise qualified, both in experience in the administration of these tests and in working with mentally retarded children, it is highly unlikely that a court would absolve him from liability if the psychologist made a mistake. There are, however, no cases that can be located to support this view as clear precedent, although in analogous medical situations in which patients have been referred to unqualified specialists liability has been imposed on the referring physician.[13] If the referral is made, and the person who performs the psychological test is qualified, and there is no reason to suspect that he would administer his examination in a negligent way, the pediatrician's involvement with the matter terminates at that time. Any negligence by the specialist responsible for carrying out the tests would not be imputed to the pediatrician and he is not liable for it.[14]

Although there are relatively few malpractice suits against psychologists, in those that have been litigated it is clear that the courts expect that psychologists will make a properly careful examination. In determining the adequacy of the professional care, courts consider time spent by the psychologist with the patient, the nature of the examination, the evaluation of the results, and the length of his report.[15]

If a pediatrician undertakes to administer psychological tests himself without the customary qualifications in the field, he would be held to the standard of care expected of a qualified person since he is practicing outside the scope of his expertise. His ignorance would be no excuse if he made an error, since the standard of care applied is the standard of care normally expected of a trained and reasonably prudent specialist.[16]

If a physician attempts to make a diagnosis of retardation on his own, he should also be aware that failure to refer a patient to a specialist where the reasonably prudent physician would do so would clearly constitute malpractice. If a physician who is not trained in the administration of such tests as are likely to reveal the existence of mental retardation, knows, or should know, that a referral for this purpose is reasonably available and would aid in the diagnosis of the patient's condition, he is negligent if he does not advise the parent, the patient, or, if appropriate, the school to that effect.[17] However, before a physician can be found liable for failure to refer a patient for testing, the circumstances must be such that the duly careful practitioner should have known that a problem existed that he was not equipped to solve.[18] In this case, however, since most pediatricians do not consider themselves experts in the field of evaluation of mental capacity, it would be most difficult to argue that the duly careful practitioner would not have made the referral.

Thus, any determination that a child is retarded can subject the pediatrician to serious liability exposure on constitutional as well as negligence grounds. Such obvious causes of inability to function in school as malnutrition, physical illness, family difficulties, or extreme poverty and such obvious situational problems as the fact that the child who has no place to study in an overcrowded apartment rarely can do his homework, should be quite carefully ruled out before any such diagnosis is made. Moreover, if the pediatrician is acting on behalf of the school in making an examination of a child and a physical condition is discovered, the pediatrician has a clear duty to disclose this fact to the parent, endeavor to help the parent obtain adequate medical care for the child, or at least refer the matter back to the school or appropriate agency for assistance.

Under the Buckley Amendment[19] a parent has the right to see his child's records in any public school. Any unsupported statement that a child is deficient or any stigmatizing remark that appears on the school record may be seen by the parents. Ill-considered and inaccurate entries in school records (which followed the child for years) made by both teachers and consultants were in fact the primary reason that Congress chose to enact this law. The effects on a child of any improper, incorrect, and damaging statements, medical or otherwise, made by pediatricians that appear in his school records cannot be calculated. Teachers tend to evaluate children in the light of all information, correct or otherwise, available in their records, and errors may seriously affect the way the teachers interacts with their students. Any evidence of psychological, as opposed to intellectual, difficulties must in particular be backed up with hard diagnoses and not speculation based on a brief interview with the child in an examining room.

As the court said in one case: "For example, teachers acting under false assumptions because of low test grades will treat the disadvantaged student in such a way as to make him conform to their low expectation; this acting out process—the self-fulfilling prophecy—makes it appear that the false assumptions were correct and the student's real talent is wasted."[20] Therefore, the importance of careful evaluation of these children and the magnitude of the damage caused by error, far more than can be compensated by any law suit, should be realized by all concerned in the field.

THE SCHOOL TEAM PHYSICIAN

Surprisingly enough there is only one reported decision involving a physician who has acted as a team doctor for sports events involving children or young people below the college age. With the current climate of litigation, however, it is quite possible that an increase in the number of malpractice suits in general will bring an increase of actions in this circumstance.[21]

Failure to Discover Medical Problems

There are two situations in which an allegation of malpractice could arise in this context. In the first, a physician who either receives pay from a school district or volunteers his time examines children prior to their participation in an athletic program either in school or such non-school-sponsored activities as Little League and fails to discover a medical condition that causes the child serious damage in the normal course of athletic participation. Second, a team physician who is present at a game in which a student is injured may be sued for negligent care at the scene and, if he continued to treat the child thereafter, negligent treatment.

In most cases physicians in this capacity are not considered employees of the school district, even though they may receive a nominal fee for their services. In most instances the "fee" is two season tickets to the high school football games, and most physicians in this situation have acted from a sense of community involvement. However, if the physician receives a full-time salary from the school system, the school district may be subject to suit as his "employer" and thus may incur liability for the physician's negligence.

It is clear that ordinary employees of a school district, such as coaches and teachers, may subject a school district to liability for negligence if a child is hurt either by inadequate supervision during a potentially dangerous activity or by failing to obtain medical care as soon as possible for an injured child.[22] If the physician is paid a salary by the school district for part-time work but also maintains a private practice, it is unlikely that his negligence will be imputed to the school board.[23] In most if not all of these situations, courts would probably hold that the physician was an independent contractor.

It would appear that the standard of care in diagnosis of conditions, congenital or otherwise, that should keep a child from participation in active sports is determined by the same standard of care as would be applied in any other diagnostic situation. If the reasonably prudent physician would have been aware, under the circumstances, that the child had a condition of any sort that would preclude him from safely participating in sports, then the physician is unlikely to escape liability.

The only decision on this subject that can be located involved a high school boy with a known heart condition who was allowed to participate in cross-country track and died during a run. A physician who was a salaried employee of the school system had known of the condition and asked the student's family physician if the boy should participate. The family physician said yes, so the school physician certified the boy for membership on the team. After his death, his parents sued the school board for the physician's negligence. That claim was settled and the school board sued both physicians for indemnification. The court held that since a state statute expressly forbade governmental agencies from receiving indemnification from its own negligent employees, no action could be brought against the school physician. The school board was, however, held to have a cause of action against the student's family physician.[24]

In one case against a college contract physician, a student had been released from the hospital after an infection only a few days before he engaged in varsity football. He was severely injured in the game and sued the university, not the physician, for negligence in failing to realize that his weakened condition would increase his risk of injury. The circuit court held that the alleged negligence of the physician, who was not a party defendant in the case, was not attributable to the university because he was a contract physician. The question of the inadequacy of the diagnosis in this case was not considered by the court, since the doctor was not sued in his individual capacity. However, the assumption throughout the opinion was that evidence relevant to show negligence in that diagnosis would have been the same as is required to prove negligent diagnosis in any other situation.[25]

Clearly, a child who has a serious heart condition, has lost substantial hearing, or has visual problems, any one of which would be detected in an ordinary physical examination and would be relevant to his ability to participate in sports, would have a cause of action against the physician who failed to discover it.

The analogy to the physician-patient relationship, if the child is not a regular patient of the examining physician, would appear to be that of a physician employed by an employer or insurance company to screen candidates for jobs or insurance policies. While early cases held that no physician-patient relationship existed,[26] more recent cases indicate that for purposes of diagnosis and disclosure to the examinee in order to insure treatment by the applicant's own physician, the employee-physician does have a duty to disclose all relevant information about the existence of any serious condition that he discovers in the course of the examination.[27] Thus, it seems that in addition to discovering that the child should not be permitted to participate in the athletic program as a result of a physical defect or illness, the parents of the child should be notified and, if a high school student, the child himself as well, so that adequate treatment of the condition may be obtained. It would be very difficult for a pediatrician to claim that he had no obligation to tell a parent that his child had a serious problem simply because he was not the child's regular physician.

Treatment of Injuries

The quality of emergency care at the scene of an athletic accident may be the critical factor in determining if the player will recover, particularly if, as sometimes occurs in football injuries, he has a broken neck or back. If the physician is present on the field in his capacity as team physician, he would appear to be subject to the same standard of care required of any other physician who acted in an emergency. Normal due care under the circumstances should be provided, but the standard in an emergency situation is less stringent than that which would be expected in a hospital emergency room with facilities and assistance at hand.[28]

A physician who is not asked to participate as team physician may still be present as a spectator in the stands at the time a player is injured. It would appear likely that a Good Samaritan statute would apply in this case unless the statute in the state in which the injury occurred is one of the few that specifically cover only automobile accidents. In states where such a statute has been enacted, no action can be brought against a physician who does not receive payment for his services and who stops at the scene of an accident to render assistance as long as any negligence in treatment is not at the level of "gross and willful" negligence. Thus, in the more usual context of an automobile accident, if a physician stopped at a wreck while he himself was under the influence of alcohol and as a result of his inebriation the patient was injured, Good Samaritan statute or not, the physician might be liable. On the other hand, research conducted by the Legal Department of the American Medical Association has never been able to discover the existence of a single malpractice suit against a physician who stopped at an accident.[29]

In an emergency situation, which an athletic injury surely is, the standard of care required of a physician is to act in the same manner as a prudent physician with equal training would have acted under similar circumstances.[30] In any case of this nature in which it was alleged, for example, that injuries to a student were aggravated by the manner in which he was removed from the football field after being hurt, negligence would have to be proved by presentation of expert medical testimony probably by orthopedists or other specialists on behalf of the patient.

A school system was held liable for the coach's lack of foresight in hurriedly moving a player with a broken back who became a paraplegic as the result of the way he was handled. A physician who was present did not examine the boy until after he had been taken to the sidelines, but if the physician had participated in moving the student, he too would have been found negligent if it had been done improperly.[31]

While a pediatrician may routinely suture minor cuts for his patients, although many do not, his ability to treat a broken bone or deal with other such serious injuries would probably not be assumed by a court to equal the skill that an orthopedist would have shown if he had been present at the scene of a football injury. On the other hand, all physicians regardless of specialty are held to a certain level of performance in treatment of emergency cases and are obliged to know at least how to perform those activities that would constitute "necessary medical care" at the scene of an accident prior to transporting the player to a hospital. The physician would at least be expected to know how to splint a leg, how to keep a player warm to prevent shock, how to move a player with a broken neck so as to minimize further damage, and other basic first aid procedures. If the player's condition is such that a life-threatening emergency exists, the pediatrician who is at a football game or other type of athletic contest, either as a spectator or a team physician, is probably obliged to accompany the child to the hospital. Once he is there, however, and specialists in the field involved in the injury are present, the pediatrician's responsibility would cease.

In any situation in which a minor is to participate in athletic activities, such as varsity football, Little League baseball, or similar activities, parental consent to that participation should be obtained in writing. The form should also include parental consent to emergency treatment by the team physician. It should be noted, however, that such a consent is not a defense to proof at a trial that the treatment was negligent. The doctrine of informed consent applies only to the inherent material risks of treatment and not to any negligence that may occur.[32]

THE HYPERKINETIC CHILD

The hyperkinetic child has, without serious question, a severe medical and psychological problem. A great deal of medical and educational research has been devoted to the difficulties involved in both the diagnosis and treatment of these children.[33] The pediatrician who confronts a child who has been referred by a parent, a teacher, or both, however, must understand that a hasty or ill-considered diagnosis of this problem can have lasting stigmatizing effects on the child, may prevent treatment of a genuine problem, behavioral or medical, and may cause serious legal complications for the physician.

As a result of considerable media exposure of what was regarded as drugging children into submission,[34] the Department of Health, Education and Welfare, Office of Child Development, sponsored a conference in 1971 to discuss the use of stimulant medication in the treatment of these children.[35] This report noted the following:

> In diagnosing hyperkinetic behavioral disturbance, it is important to note that similar behavioral symptoms may be due to other illnesses or to relatively simple causes. Essentially healthy children may have difficulty maintaining attention and motor control because of a period of stress in school or at home. It is important to

recognize the child whose inattention and restlessness may be caused by hunger, poor teaching, overcrowded classrooms, or lack of understanding by teachers or parents. Frustrated adults reacting to a child who does not meet their standards can exaggerate the significance of occasional inattention or restlessness. Above all, the normal ebullience of childhood should not be confused with the very special problems of the child with hyperkinetic behavioral disorders.

The diagnosis is clearly best made by a skilled observer. There unfortunately is no single diagnostic test. Accordingly, the specialist must comprehensively evaluate the child and assess the significance of a variety of symptoms. He considers causal and contributory factors—both permanent and temporary—such as environmental stress. He distinguishes special dysfunctions such as certain epilepsies, schizophrenia, depression or anxiety, mental retardation or perceptual deficiencies. The less severe and dramatic forms of hyperkinetic disorders also require careful evaluation. Adequate diagnosis may require the use of not only medical but special psychological, educational and social resources.[36]

Diagnosis

In viewing this condition as a legal, not a medical, issue the first problem is that of the referral by a school administrator, guidance counselor, or teacher. As was discussed in the chapter on consent, it is absolutely unjustifiable for a physician to examine or treat a child of this age, since most of these children range from ages of five to twelve,[37] without the knowledge or the consent of the parent. It is quite probable that if the question of liability was raised, a school person who referred a child to a physician without the knowledge of the parents would be liable to the same extent as the physician for failing to obtain parental consent. Teachers and school principals are not physicians, cannot make medical diagnoses, and certainly cannot require medical interventions, except in emergencies for one of their students. In this context, they have no more authority than does an officious neighbor.

If, however, a child is brought by a parent for evaluation at the request of a teacher, the physician then has the authority to evaluate the child. It is extremely unlikely that such a diagnosis can be made in one visit, and it is also clear that the prudent standard of practice requires exclusion of other causes (such as failure to eat breakfast) prior to giving drugs to any child for this condition. The estimation made by educators is that as many as 20 percent of the children in public schools need treatment for hyperactivity or have some problems in this line.[38] Medical opinion, however, places the proportion at approximately 3 percent.[39] Therefore, statistically, 17 percent of the children in the public schools stand at least some risk of being sent unnecessarily to a physician to have "something done" to make them behave. Any physician who attempts to medicate a child because the child's teacher is exasperated with his energy should not undertake to do so without clear-cut diagnostic criteria. As is very clear from a series of studies on these children, this diagnosis is very difficult to make.[40]

Serious legal questions would arise if a school attempted to require a child to take drugs of any sort for any reason as a condition for continuing in the educational process. It has been reported that at the present time between 150,000 and 300,000 children in the country are being given psychoactive drugs for hyperkinetic behavior.[41]

The Right to Refuse Medication

The courts have assumed, at least since *Brown v. Board of Education*[42] struck down segregated school systems, that education is a fundamental right. In that decision the court said, "Today education is probably the most important function of state and local governments," and subsequent decisions have emphasized that a child who is denied the right to an education suffers a severe handicap. The only condition under which a child may be expelled from school is that the school is able to show that the protection of other children, either physically or in their abilities to learn, requires exclusion of the child.[43]

If a public school requires drug therapy as a condition for admission to the school or retention of the pupil, it would be hard-pressed to defend in court the proposition that such a requirement is necessary to maintain order.[44] The child with a behavior problem is clearly being subject to a discriminatory standard unless the school can successfully argue that the child is different from all other children, which would be quite difficult since some educators maintain that 20 percent of the children in the classroom are hyperkinetic. It would thus seem highly improbable that school authorities could justify singling out one child or a very small number of pupils for special treatment, particularly without any definitive diagnosis made after an extraordinarily careful medical evaluation.

If the parents do not wish for any reason (adherence to the Christian Science faith, for example) to have their child take drugs, it is probable that the school could not require it even if there was a definitive diagnosis of hyperkinesia.[45] The point for the pediatrician to remember, however, is that if a parent comes to him and says, "If you don't do something about giving Johnny drugs, they will not let Johnny back in school," he should reassure the parent that the use of drugs with these children is a matter of medical judgment. If any such condition is placed by the school on retention of a child in a situation in which a physician felt that the medication was unwarranted, it would assuredly result in a legal victory for the parent who decided to bring a suit against the school. It is highly improbable that in a situation where the pediatrician did not feel that it was good medical practice to give a child a drug, a school's order expelling him for failure to take that drug, no matter how difficult the child might be, would be upheld by any juvenile judge in the country. Thus, if the parent wishes support in a stand against the teacher or if the parent feels frightened or threatened by the teacher's demands that the child be given a drug but does not himself see the child as having a specific problem, the pediatrician should support the parent.

Many of the commentaries, medical and otherwise, on the hyperkinesia problem indicate that these children may have no particular problems other than in the classroom. If that is reasonably the case and particularly if the parent has no complaints about the child's behavior at home, it is unlikely that the child has a serious case of hyperkinesia. If disturbing behavior appears only in the classroom and in no other sphere of the child's life, the pediatrician might assume for purposes of making a diagnosis that the teacher and not the child has problems or that nonmedical factors, such as an inadequate diet, overcrowded classroom, or an impatient teacher, are far more likely to be the cause of the child's problem than minimal brain dysfunction. The parent should be able to rely on the pediatrician to support the child's best interests in case of doubt. Merely because school authorities think that the child has a problem, the pediatrician should beware of buying "peace at any price" for the school system at the expense of the parent's desires, explicit or implicit.

Failure to Discover Another Condition

Another very serious problem in situations where a definitive diagnosis cannot be made is that a serious medical problem may be overlooked by making the assumption that the child is hyperkinetic. No reported cases can be located in which a pediatrician has been sued for failing to discover a serious medical problem because he had thought that a child was hyperkinetic and prescribed accordingly, but it certainly is not beyond the realm of possibility that such a case may occur eventually. For example, an early sign of a brain tumor in a child may be a change in behavior. Clearly, the standard of care required in making any diagnosis applies in this situation. The standard of care required in diagnosis is the use of the same degree of skill, care, and knowledge as would be used by the average prudent physician with the same training.

As one decision states, "Malpractice may consist of lack of skill and care in diagnosis as well as treatment. A patient is entitled to a thorough and careful examination such as his condition and attending circumstances permit with such diligence and methods as are usually approved in practice by physicians of the same school of medicine, judgment, skill and under similar circumstances."[46]

In order to make a careful diagnosis of any illness and particularly with all the variables present in this situation, a pediatrician must obtain a very careful history, although he usually has the right to assume that a patient or the parent is telling the truth.[47] Questions designed to elicit all necessary and relevant information must be asked, and the physician may not make any diagnosis by relying solely on information the patient volunteers without asking more probing questions. Where the issue is whether a child is hyperkinetic, the medical and behavioral history is of critical importance. The circumstances under which the behavior disorder, if any, occurs, how long the situation has lasted, any particular stress in the child's life at the time the consultation is requested, and basic information about that life, including such things as the adequacy of the child's diet, are absolutely relevant to the specific diagnosis.[48] A sudden onset of bizarre behavioral symptoms, for example, should indicate to a pediatrician that something other than hyperkinesia is present, and an appropriate neurological examination could well reveal the presence of a serious medical problem.

Once the history has been obtained the child is entitled to a careful and thorough examination not only by the physician but presumably in referral for appropriate psychological or psychiatric tests and any other procedures that would assist in diagnosing the case. It is malpractice to misdiagnose a case because the examination itself was careless. If this is proved and the patient has been damaged by such a failure, the physician is clearly liable.[49] If a child is incorrectly diagnosed as hyperkinetic and in fact has a serious medical problem that thereby goes untreated, damage would not be difficult to prove and certainly no more difficult than proof of failure to diagnose any other conditions. A child who brought a suit for malpractice in this context, however, could probably show that the fact that school personnel knew he had been diagnosed as hyperkinetic, even though he had no other actual medical problems, caused him damage in the same way that the child who is incorrectly diagnosed as being retarded has a cause of action. The effects on the education the child receives, on teacher expectations, and on placement are seriously affected by a physician's determination of *any* special problem the child has, and the stigmatization alone would probably support a recovery of substantial damages on behalf of such a child.

Drug Reactions

The next area that could precipitate a malpractice action on behalf of a child is the possibility of an adverse drug reaction, even if the child is actually hyperkinetic. No reported cases could be found in which a child on methylphenidate or some other psychoactive drug for the treatment of hyperkinesia had a serious adverse reaction and sued either the manufacturer or the prescribing physician. However, it is not impossible that the physician could be liable if such a reaction occurred.

A physician's liability for a patient's reaction to a drug he has administered or prescribed is largely determined by general standards of due care. If he has used the degree of skill, care, and knowledge that prevails in his specialty in prescribing the drug, as well as in managing any reaction symptoms that do occur, he is not liable.[50]

There are, however, certain basic principles that would apply regardless of the particular drug in use. A physician is deemed to understand the properties of any drug that he prescribes or administers and is supposed to be aware of any dangers of side effects or after effects.[51] If the manufacturer issues warnings about the drug, the physician must be aware of them in order to avoid liability.[52] The physician may, of course, be using the highest standard of medical practice in prescribing a very dangerous drug if the patient's condition is such that the calculated risk is justified. Ignorance of the possibility of the drug reaction is, however, clear evidence of negligence.[53]

Another question that may arise in any drug case is the propriety of having used the drug in treatment of the particular disease from which the patient suffers.[54] In the case of a hyperkinetic child, there is no clear indication of which drugs should be used. The issue raised in such a drug reaction case probably would be an allegation that the child was not hyperkinetic rather than questioning the propriety of using the drug. In any case in which a drug is given that is not a suitable remedy for the disease in the first place, liability on the part of the physician for a drug reaction is virtually certain.[55]

The physician may also be liable if he does not warn a patient, or in this case, the patient's parents, of any side effects that might occur while the patient is taking the drug.[56] Under the same general principle applied to informed consent requirements in any other situation, the physician is also required to discuss with the parents the possibility of long-term or permanent effects of drug treatment on the child. Although some studies have shown that long-term use of these drugs with hyperkinetic children have not produced any serious adverse reactions, this point is by no means entirely established.[57] It may be some years before definitive results on the effects of long-term use are available, but as long as a physician is sure that the child has hyperkinesia, that the drug he is using for the relief of the problem is proper from the therapeutic standpoint, is a standard and effective treatment of the disease, and as long as the possibility of reaction is outweighed by the necessity to take the risk, the use of the drug can be defended even if the child should develop an adverse reaction.

One problem raised by the nature of pediatric practice is that of "the state of the art." If a standard and approved practice is later discovered to entail major damage to the patient, the standard of care is determined by the medical thinking at the time the treatment is given, not a decade or two later when the child reaches majority and files a suit. The best examples of this principle are the recent decisions in retrolental fibroplasia cases. In all the cases that have been appealed, the courts have held that in cases that occurred before it began to be known and reported in journals that excessive oxygen could cause blindness in premature babies physicians could not be held liable. After such reports were published, pediatricians were, of course, responsible for knowing about them and revising standard practice accordingly.[58] In cases involving drug reactions after long-term use, presumably the same concept would apply. If use of a drug with a child who has been correctly diagnosed as hyperkinetic is proper by current standards, discovery in another 15 years that some problems may arise with long-term use of that drug will not subject the physician to liability for having given it today.

CONFIDENTIALITY

It is not, apparently, unusual for a school principal or a teacher to attempt to obtain information about a student from the child's physician. Disclosure of confidential information to unauthorized persons about any patient without his or her consent generally gives rise to a successful action for damages.[59] Because of the extreme importance of the confidential relationship between a physician and his patient, there are statutes in some states that provide that a physician may even lose his license for unjustified dissemination of confidential information, and it is a criminal offense in at least one state.[60]

Disclosures to School Personnel

In the absence of a statute requiring disclosure of such conditions as a contagious disease, a pediatrician or a physician for an adult patient does not have the right to disclose information without the consent of the patient or, in the case of a child, of his parent. Even a college student has the right of confidentiality when he sees a school physician as any other patient has with a physician unless he is a danger to himself or others.[61]

Medical reports written in good faith to agencies that have a legitimate interest in dealing with the patient do not violate confidentiality requirements.[62] It is extremely likely, however, that unless a child has been referred to a pediatrician by the school authorities with the explicit knowledge by the parent that the diagnosis will be reported to school personnel, there is no right to disclose the information without the child's consent or that of his parents.

If such a disclosure is made, the parents might have a cause of action, although no cases on this point could be located.[63]

Defamation of Character

Even if the parent asks the physician to disclose information to the school, if the information is untrue the physician may be liable for defamation of character. Defamation of character is a communication by one person (the pediatrician) about a second person (the child) to a third person (school authority) in such terms as to diminish unjustifiably the reputation of the person discussed. Suits against physicians for defamation of character are closely intertwined with those charging invasion of the patient's right of privacy or disclosure of confidential information, but in general have involved those cases where the disclosure was untrue either by design or accident.[64]

A 13-year-old girl developed a foot infection. She was taken to her family physician for treatment, and he advised her parents that she should stay at home in bed for a protracted period. He suggested that they ask the school superintendent to send a visiting teacher. The form signed by the physician which was sent to the superintendent incorrectly stated that the girl was pregnant. Her parents tried repeatedly to obtain the report or to have it corrected, and he first told them he had checked his files and found nothing that would indicate that he had made such a report. He also told the parents that if they would get the form from the school superintendent and bring it to his office, he would do what he could to correct the error if he had made one, but the school would not release the report. The parents called the physician several times, and finally his office nurse told the parents to "stop bothering him." The father brought a libel action on behalf of his daughter and was awarded $7,000 in damages. The opinion on appeal indicated that if the error had been made in good faith, which it undoubtedly was, but had been retracted immediately the physician would not have been liable. His persistent refusal to correct or retract the false report was sufficient to induce the jury to return substantial damages.[65]

If a physician has been consulted for the express purpose of evaluating a child for a report to a school, however, as long as the parent knew and consented to disclosure at the time the consultation was made, the reported information is considered privileged and thus not subject to an action for defamation even if it is untrue.[66]

The Parents' Right to Inspect Records

It should be noted that under the Buckley Amendment a parent has the right to inspect all school records pertaining to his minor child if he wishes to do so. Even without the provisions of this act in some states parents have had a long-standing right to obtain school records.

A father was advised by his son's teacher that his child was in need of psychological treatment. He took the child to a private psychiatrist who wrote to the school psychologist, with the written authorization of the child's father, requesting an abstract of psychological findings from interviews that had already been made at school. The school psychologist forwarded to the psychiatrist a copy of his report, which had been given to the school personnel in connection with the student. The father, however, made a formal demand upon the school board that it direct the superintendent of the school to allow him access to all his son's school records, which the superintendent refused to do. The court said, "We are therefore constrained to hold as a matter of law that the parent is entitled to inspect the records. This is in accord with the common law right of the patient to inspect his own hospital records; of a client to be given open and frank information by his attorney as to the state of his business and to be given his attorney's file upon posting proper security for the retaining lien; of a stockholder to inspect the records of his corporation; and indeed, of a member of a board of education to inspect records compiled by the superintendent of his own school district." The court further pointed out that the adoption of compulsory education would seem to deprive a parent of some of his natural rights in the vital area of the education of his child. Therefore, the parent has the right to exercise his rights to supervise such education and to discharge this duty by keeping abreast of the child's development and advancement. The court found that the father's right stems from his relationship with school authorities as a parent who, under compulsory education, had delegated to them the educational authority over his child.[67]

Thus, any records furnished to the school by the pediatrician must first be forwarded with the full knowledge and consent of the parent. If the parent has been required by the school to ask for transfer of the records or evaluation of the child, the parent should be advised that he undoubtedly has a right to refuse to submit these records without exposing the child to disciplinary action. Second, the records must be accurate, since if they are not, as the result of misdiagnosis or mistake, the parent may well have a right to bring an action for libel or defamation of character. Third, once the records have been sent to the school, either after the child has been examined by a private pediatrician or where the physician is employed by the school to examine the child, the parent clearly has access to the original records and not merely to abstracts of them. Only where a child's condition involves a contagious disease or where there might be some reasonable apprehension that the child is dangerous to others should any information be disclosed to the school without parental consent.

CONCLUSION

This chapter has discussed some of the more obvious problems that may confront a pediatrician who is dealing with school-age children in terms of their relationship with their teachers and other school personnel. Whereas the ideal situation is one of a good working relationship among the school, the parent, and the pediatrician, this ideal may be difficult to achieve in many cases. Thus, in case of doubt, the pediatrician should remember that his responsibility and the physician-patient relationship run in favor of the child's interests, and that at no time should the physician be willing to take action that will adversely affect the child simply because it is requested by a school system. A school employee has no more business making medical diagnoses, advocating treatment, or interfering with the privacy of a child patient than does anyone else, including a neighbor of that child. The school teacher may be a trusted ally in the development of the child, but in some cases he or she may not have the child's interests at heart. Therefore, pediatricians should be extremely cautious about attempting to resolve educational impasses in a misguided effort to help the child by dealing directly with school personnel without the knowledge of the child or his parents.

NOTES

1. See, for example, M. S. Sorgen, P. S. Duffy, W. A. Kaplin and E. Margolin, *State, School and Family,* New York, Matthew Bender and Co., 1973, Ch 11; David L. Kirp and Mark G. Yudof, *Educational Policy and the Law,* Berkeley, Cal, McCutchan Publishing Corp., 1974, Ch 7 and pages 636–644; David L. Kirp, "Schools as Sorters," 121 *U Pa Law Rev,* page 705, 1973; Lau v. Nichols, 412 US 938, 1973.

2. Mills v. Board of Education, 348 F Supp 866, DC DC 1972.

3. Pennsylvania Association for Retarded Children v. Commonwealth, 343 F Supp 279, DC Pa 1972.

4. E.g., Kirp and Yudof, *op. cit. supra* at 1: Walter E. Shafer, Carol Olexa and Kenneth Polk, "Programmed for Social Class: Tracking in High School," *Transaction,* page 39, October 1970; M. L. Goldberg, A. Harry Passow, and Joseph Justman, *The Effects of Ability Grouping,* New York, Teachers College Press, 1966.

5. E.g., Hobson v. Hansen, 408 F 2d 175, CA DC 1969; Patricia C. Sexton, *Education and Income,* New York, The Viking Press, 1961.

6. Larry P. v. Riles, 343 F Supp 1306, DC Cal 1972.

7. Hobson v. Hansen, *supra* at 5.

8. E.g., Alden v. Providence Hospital, 382 F 2d 163, DC CA 1967; Pearce v. United States, 236 F Supp 431, DC Okla 1964; Booth v. United States, 155 F Supp 235 (Ct Cl), 1957; Wheatley v. Heideman, 102 NW 2d 343, Iowa 1960.

9. E.g., Naccarato v. Grob, 180 NW 2d 788, Mich 1970.

10. E.g., Johnson v. St. Paul Mercury Insurance Co., 219 So 2d 524, La 1969; Rewis v. United States, 369 F 2d 595, CCA 5, 1966. Both of these cases involve a failure to ask if a small child had eaten aspirin, and the misdiagnoses which followed the failures led to the children's deaths from aspirin poisoning.

11. E.g., Domina v. Pratt, 13 A 2d 198, Vt 1940.

12. "Failure to Make Diagnostic Tests," 210 *JAMA* No. 1, page 213, October 6, 1969; Smith v. Yohe, 194 A 2d 167, Pa 1963; Clark v. United States, 402 F 2d 950, CCA 4, 1968.

13. "Liability of Referring Physician," 204 *JAMA* No. 3, page 273, April 15, 1968.

14. E.g., Ross v. Sher, 483 SW 2d 297, Tex 1972; Harwick v. Harris, 166 So 2d 912, Fla 1964.

15. Hendry v. United States, 280 F Supp 27, DC NY 1968.

16. Toth v. Community Hospital at Glen Cove, 239 NE 2d 368, NY 1968; Crovella v. Cochrane, 102 So 2d 307, Fla 1958; Price v. Neyland, 320 F 2d 674, CA DC 1963.

17. Duty to Refer Patient to a Medical Specialist," 204 *JAMA* No. 8, page 281, May 20, 1968; "Referral to a Specialist," 211 *JAMA* No. 11, page 1911, March 16, 1970; Logan v. Field, 75 Mo App 594, Mo 1898; Benson v. Dean, 133 NE 125, NY 1921.

18. Manion v. Tweedy, 100 NW 2d 124, Minn 1959; Wohlert v. Seibert, 23 Pa Sup Ct 213, 1903.

19. Buckley Amendment, 20 USCA, Section 1232g.

20. Hobson v. Hanson, 269 F Supp 401, DC Cir 1967. See Merriken v. Cressman, 364 F Supp 913, DC Pa 1973, in which a court enjoined the use of school-administered "personality tests" for this reason.

21. Crawford Morris, "Doctors and the Sporting Life," 39 *Ins Counsel J,* page 283, July 1972.

22. E.g., Keesee v. Board of Education, 235 NYS 2d 300, NY 1962; Cirillo v. Milwaukee, 150 NW 2d 460, Wisc 1967; Bellman v. San Francisco High School District, 81 P 2d 894, Cal 1938; Gardner v. State, 22 NE 2d 344, NY 1939; Clark v. Board of Education, 107 NYS 2d 582, NY 1951.

23. See, generally, on the difference between an "employee physician" and an "independent contractor physician" in terms of hospital liability, an analogous situation, Angela R. Holder, *Medical Malpractice Law,* New York, John Wiley and Sons, 1975, Ch 7, "Vicarious Liability."

24. Board of Education v. Homer, 362 NYS 2d 798, NY 1974.

25. Cramer v. Hoffman, 390 F2d 19, CCA 2, 1968.

26. Battistella v. Society of the New York Hospital, 191 NYS 2d 626, NY 1959, Riste v. General Electric Corporation, 289 P 2d 338, Wash 1955; Jines v. General Electric Corp., 313 F 2d 76, CCA 9, 1962; Metropolitan Life Insurance Co. v. Evans, 184 So 426, Miss 1938.

27. Beadling v. Sirotta, 176 A 2d 546, NJ 1961; Union Carbide and Carbon Corp. v. Stapleton, 237 F 2d 229, CCA 6, 1956; Coffee v. McDonnell-Douglas Corp., 503 P 2d 1366, Cal 1972.

28. For an excellent discussion of all facets of a physician's liability in dealing with emergency cases, see Neil L. Chayet, *Legal Implications of Emergency Care,* New York, Appleton-Century-Crofts, 1969.

29. *Ibid.,* pages 24–25.

30. Rockhill v. Pollard, 485 P 2d 28, Ore 1971.

31. Welch v. Dunsmuir High School, 326 P 2d 633, Cal 1958.

32. Mull v. Emory University, 150 SE 2d 276, Ga 1966; Block v. McVay 126 NW 2d 808, SD 1964.

33. Most of the articles in medical or educational journals involving the diagnosis and treatment of hyperkinetic children are listed as references in Lester Grinspoon and Susan B. Singer, "Amphetamines in the Treatment of Hyperkinetic Children," 43 *Harvard Educational Rev* No. 4, page 515, November 1973.

34. E.g., Edward T. Ladd, "Pills for Classroom Peace?" 53 *Saturday Review* No. 47, page 66,

November 21, 1970; Charles Witler, "Drugging and Schooling," *Trans-Action,* page 31, July/August 1971.

35. The report of the conference is reprinted in full in 9 *Inequality in Education,* page 14, 1971.

36. *Ibid.,* page 15.

37. *Ibid.,* page 15.

38. Ladd, *op. cit. supra* at 34; Grinspoon, *op. cit. supra* at 33; William W. Wells, "Drug Control of School Children: The Child's Right to Choose," 46 *So Cal Law Rev,* page 585, 1973.

39. Report, *supra,* at 35, page 15.

40. E.g., J. Gordon Millichap, "Drugs in Management of Hyperkinetic and Perceptually Handicapped Children," 206 *JAMA* No. 7, page 1527, November 11, 1968; Leon Eisenberg, "Role of Drugs in Treating Disturbed Children," 2 *Children* No. 5, page 167, September-/October, 1964; Stephen I. Sulzbacher, "The Learning-Disabled or Hyperactive Child," 234 *JAMA* No. 9, page 938, December 1, 1975.

41. Wells, *op. cit. supra* at 38, page 585.

42. *Brown v. Board of Education,* 347 US 483, 1954.

43. See, for example, for a case involving a child expelled from school when he had narcotics in his possession, People v. Jackson, 319 NYS 2d 331, NY 1971.

44. For lengthy discussions of the legal and constitutional issues involved in requiring a hyperkinetic child to take drugs as a condition for retention in school, see Wells, *op. cit. supra* at 38; Roderick L. Ireland and Paul R. Dimond, "Drugs and Hyperactivity: Process is Due," 9 *Inequality in Education,* page 19, 1971.

45. See Winters v. Travia 495 F 2d 839, CCA 2, 1974, for a discussion of an adult Christian Scientist's right to refuse medication while involuntarily hospitalized.

46. Wheatley v. Heideman, 102 NW 2d 343, Iowa 1960.

47. "Misdiagnosis Without Fault:" I. 219 *JAMA* No. 7, page 967, February 14, 1972; II. 219 *JAMA* No. 8, page 1127, February 21, 1972.

48. "Failure to Take Medical History," 226 *JAMA* No. 4, page 509, October 22, 1973.

49. E.g., Domina v. Pratt, 13 A 2d 198, Vt 1940.

50. "Physician's Liability for Drug Reactions," 213 *JAMA* No. 12, page 2143, September 21, 1970.

51. E.g., Reed v. Church, 8 SE 2d 285, Va 1940.

52. "Package Inserts as Evidence," 208 *JAMA* No. 3, page 589, April 21, 1969; F. J. Barnett, "Liability for Adverse Drug Reactions," 1 *J Leg Med* No. 2, page 47, May/June 1973.

53. Marchese v. Monaco, 145 A 2d 809, NJ 1958; Henderson v. National Drug Co., 23 A 2d 743, Pa 1942; Agnew v. Larson, 185 P 2d 851, Cal 1947.

54. See, for example, Millichap, *op. cit. supra* at 40; Barbara Fish, "Drug Use in Psychiatric Disorders of Children," 124 *Am J Psychiat* No. 8, page 31, February 1968; C. K. Conners, L. Eisenberg, and A. Barcai, "Effects of Dextroamphetamine on Children," 17 *Arch Gen Psychiat,* page 478, October 1967.

55. E.g., Rotan v. Greenbaum, 273 F 2d 830, CA DC 1959; Johnston v. Brother, 12 Cal Rptr 23, Cal 1963.

56. E.g., Whitfield v. Daniel Construction Co., 83 SE 2d 460, SC 1954; Kaiser v. Suburban Transportation System, 398 P 2d 14, Wash 1965.

57. E.g., M. Menkes, J. Rowe, and J. Menkes, "A Twenty-five Year Follow-up Study on the Hyperkinetic Child with Minimal Brain Dysfunction," 39 *Pediatrics* No. 3, page 393, March 1967.

58. "Liability for Retrolental Fibroplasia," 212 *JAMA* No. 13, page 2343, June 29, 1970.

59. E.g., Hammer v. Polsky, 233 NYS 2d 110, NY 1962; "Physician's Liability for Improper Disclosure," 198 *JAMA* No. 7, page 331, November 14, 1966; "Disclosure of Confidential Information," 216 *JAMA* No. 2, page 385, April 12, 1971.

60. Mich Stats Ann, Section 338.53.

61. Maniaci v. Marquette University, 184 NW 2d 168, Wisc 1971; but *see, contra,* Morris v. Rousos, 397 SW 2d 504, Tex 1965; Tarasoff v. Board of Regents, 529 P 2d 553, Cal 1974.

62. E.g., Iverson v. Frandsen, 237 F 2d 898, CCA 10, 1956.

63. For a general discussion of the issue of disclosure of records, see E. Hayt and J. Hayt, *Legal Aspects of Medical Records,* Berwin, Ill, Physicians' Record Co., 1964, Ch 5, "Release of Medical Information"; George J. Annas, *The Rights of Hospital Patients,* New York, Avon Books, 1975, Ch 10, "Hospital Records," Ch 11, " Confidentiality and Privacy."

64. E.g., Berry v. Moench, 331 P 2d 814, Utah 1958; Smith v. DiCara, 329 F Supp 439, DC NY 1971.

65. Vigil v. Rice, 397 P 2d 719, NM 1964.

66. E.g., Everest v. McKenny, 162 NW 277, Mich 1917; Kenney v. Gurley, 95 So 34, Ala 1923.

67. Van Allen v. McCleary, 211 NYS 2d 501, NY 1961.

CHAPTER VIII

THE PEDIATRICIAN

AND

THE COURTS

In the course of a pediatric practice the physician may deal with a number of legal issues other than those in which he may be directly participating, such as a malpractice case involving his patients. The most frequent areas in which a pediatrician may play a role include adoptions, custody cases, child abuse cases, and evaluation or medical treatment of a child who is a juvenile offender or suspected of delinquency. This chapter will attempt to provide the pediatrician with sufficient background knowledge of these areas of law and his own potential liability exposure in each to enable him to function with some degree of confidence. It should, however, be understood that particularly in these areas of the legal system, state statutes usually control and these statutes vary enormously. Therefore, any physician who is actively involved in any specific situations in these areas should obtain legal advice from his attorney.

ADOPTION

Since adoption was unknown in common law, all adoptions in this country are decreed under the authority of the specific statute on the subject in the state that has jurisdiction of the matter.[1] The first adoption statute in the country was the Massachusetts law enacted in 1851, and until 1953 there was a great diversity among state statutes. In 1953 the first Uniform Adoption Act was drafted, and the revised Uniform Adoption Act was approved by the National Conference of Commissioners on Uniform State Laws in 1969.[2] The legislative development of recent adoption statutes in some states has been affected by this statute, but very few states have ratified it in the form suggested by the commissioners.

There are three types of adoptions. One is the adoption of a child by a step-parent or other relative, which is usually not subjected to the same judicial scrutiny as is an adoption of a child by strangers. Second, independent, or private placement, adoptions are those made by the natural parents either directly to the adopting parents or through an intermediary such as a physician or a lawyer. Third, agency adoptions are those made by licensed private adoption agencies or an official state bureau established for that purpose. These agencies are also the ones who receive children after they have been judicially declared abandoned or parental rights have been terminated in some form of court proceeding. In all of these situations the physician may be called on to assist with the adoption.

Private Placement

Physicians are often confronted with situations in which either an unwed mother or prospective adoptive parents, usually those who cannot obtain a child through an agency, ask him to serve as intermediary in an adoption and facilitate finding a home for the baby or finding a child for the couple. Private placement adoptions probably cannot be eliminated entirely even by strict statutory prohibitions. Whatever the defects of the system of independent placement, the shortage of workers in adoption agencies who are available to help with agency placements, particularly in rural areas where there may be no adoption agencies available at all, may preclude their becoming the sole means of child placement. It may well be that the physician in this situation is the only agent who can help all persons concerned, but he must be extremely wary of the legal pitfalls that may occur.

Statutory restrictions.   Some states absolutely forbid private adoptions. For example, in Florida arrangement of adoptions by anyone who is not connected with a licensed agency and who receives any fee whatever for those arrangements is a violation of criminal law. Criminal proceedings brought under these statutes against attorneys and physicians are by no means unknown.[3]

The District of Columbia adoption statute known as the "Baby Brokers Law" forbids independent placement of infants or children for adoption. An attorney was convicted of violating the law. He represented a woman who was separated from her husband and was being divorced on the ground of adultery. She was pregnant by another man at the time the divorce was final. She asked her attorney to find someone who would provide a good home for her child and adopt him. He advised her to go to an adoption agency. She rejected this advice. The client phoned him persistently at his home and office several times a week to find out if he was making any effort to find a home for her child. Finally, when she was about seven months pregnant, he told her he had learned of a couple who were interested in adopting the child and he would have them contact her. She refused to meet them and asked him to act as intermediary. It was eventually agreed that the lawyer would come to the hospital after the child was born and arrange for the transfer. The attorney took the release agreement to the hospital and the mother signed it after the child was born. At the time she was discharged the attorney took the child from her and physically delivered it to the adopting father who was waiting at another door of the hospital. The couple adopted the child. The attorney charged the mother nothing in the divorce case and refused to accept any fee for his services in connection with the placement of the child for adoption. He did, however, accept a small sum above the figure that he collected from the adoptive couple to cover the mother's medical expenses. The woman later changed her mind and sought his service in regaining custody of the child. He refused and she filed a complaint with the Bureau of Public Welfare on the ground that he had placed the child without having a license to place children for adoption. This complaint resulted in criminal prosecution. In upholding his conviction the court held that the "appellant did these things without compensation, that he was animated by the most humane motives, that he was perhaps imposed upon by the mother and yielded in sheer pity to her cries of distress, all this we may concede. All this appeals to our sympathy for him, but it cannot justify us in holding that his actions were within the law."[4]

This case indicates the perils of attempting to be helpful in a private adoption situation unless it is clear that independent placements are legal within the state. Some statutes prohibit not only the placement of children except by an agency but also assistance in arranging for the placement, which is usually construed to prohibit unauthorized persons, such as attorneys and physicians, from assisting natural parents and legal guardians who legally may make such a placement.[5]

Some states' statutes prohibit private placement but exempt placements with relatives from normal adoption procedures.[6] Some states allow private placement as long as the appropriate court exercises its authority to have the placement reviewed by an independent agency before the decree is granted. There are actually very few criminal prosecutions even in those states where private placements are strictly prohibited.[7] According to Department of Health, Education and Welfare statistics, in 1971, 17,400 children were adopted in independent placements.[8] Profit-making placements, "black-market adoptions," are clearly against the law in all states. Furthermore, in some states payment of the mother's medical expenses, much less any greater financial reward for placement of a child, is likely to affect the validity of the release for adoption.[9]

If a physician is inclined to act in the capacity of a child-placement expert, he must be careful to do so only after consultations with an attorney as to both the legality of a private placement in his state and the statutory provisions that must be followed in order to prevent his being caught in a dispute between the natural parent or parents and the adopting parents later, if there is an attempt to revoke consent.

Revocation of consent. The most frequent source of litigation involving the validity of adoptions is an attempt by the natural mother to regain custody of the child after she changes her mind and decides that her release of the child for adoption was a mistake. The consent of a natural mother of an illegitimate child is normally sufficient to release the child for adoption without the consent of the father and in fact is usually upheld over his objections, although in some situations he has the right to be heard prior to termination of his rights.[10] Most courts have held that as long as the unmarried mother is alive she alone has the right to make the decision to release her child or children for adoption, and the father, unless he is or has been married to her and the children are legitimate or unless the relationship between the parties is one in which a clear common-law marriage existed, has no ground on which to stop such an adoption.[11] If the mother has abandoned the children or has died and they are in the physical custody of their natural father, who is providing them with a fit home in which they have not been neglected, he has been held by the United States Supreme Court to have a primary right of custody as against a state agency that wishes to remove the children, terminate his rights to them, and place them for adoption.[12]

Even though the law on this subject might appear to be simple, it is fraught with dangerous complexities in determining the validity of a consent to release a child for adoption. Any attempt to argue with an unmarried mother and persuade her to release her child for adoption may well involve a later claim of duress. This is particularly true where the person who is attempting to counsel her about the advantages of giving up her child is the physician who delivers the baby. Courts recognize that she is under unusual constraints and is unusually vulnerable in this situation when dealing with her obstetrician.[13] Therefore, it is clearly advisable that even though the physician may be responsible for the private placement of the child, he should under *no* circumstances be the person who negotiates the release with the natural mother.

Some states prohibit execution of releases of children for adoption prior to birth, in which case any such release is automatically invalidated.[14] Even where the release has been signed after the child is born, however, particularly if it is during the period where the mother is still in the hospital, any consent to release the child for adoption that is either negotiated or witnessed by her obstetrician is likely to be held invalid. In all cases, if the consent is held invalid for reasons of fraud or duress, courts invariably uphold the right of the natural mother to reclaim custody of the child if she changes her mind within a reasonable period of time.[15]

An unmarried pregnant woman's physician recommended an adoption agency. She went to the agency once and never went back. At her next visit to him when she reported that she was not willing to proceed through the agency, he told her that he knew of a couple who were willing to adopt the child. She authorized the physician to inform the couple that he had an unmarried mother in his care but also told him that she was not sure whether or not she would release the child for adoption. During this period, the father of the child adamantly rejected her request to support the child after its birth. She decided, finally, to release the child for adoption. After the baby was born the physician made the physical arrangements, transferring the baby to its adoptive parents. The attorney for the adopting parents prepared the consents and both natural parents signed them in the presence of a notary public. A few months later, the natural mother sent the physician the child's birth certificate with the request that the baby's parents notify the officials of the child's first name. At the time the adopting couple went to court for the final proceeding, the natural mother made her first attempt to recover the child by filing a petition to have the child returned to her on the ground that the physician had exerted undue pressure on her to surrender the baby. The trial court ordered the adopting parents to return the child to its natural mother and they appealed. The appellate court said that parental rights of the natural parent could not be cut off by statute unless the parent had forsaken legal obligations to the child and criticized the physician's wisdom in participating in the arrangements for placing the child, but rejected the concept that he exerted "undue pressure." The trial court's decision was reversed and the case was remanded to complete the adoption. It should be noted, however, that a substantial lapse of time occurred between the mother's release from the hospital and her attempt to regain custody of the child. If she had acted promptly to regain the child under the same circumstances and alleged undue and continuing influence by the physician, it is overwhelmingly probable that she would have succeeded.[16]

A physician arranged an adoption. The natural mother gave the baby to him and also gave him her consent in a letter. He placed the child with a couple who instituted appropriate adoption proceedings. The natural mother revoked her consent the day before the adoption hearing. The court held that she was entitled to regain custody of her child because the statute in that particular state made a consent binding before the adoption decree only if it had been given to a licensed agency.[17]

Thus, the inherent difficulties in attempting to be of service in negotiating adoption releases should always be borne in mind by the physician and should be avoided whenever possible. Even if the physician is not violating the law in any private placement situation he is taking upon himself serious responsibilities for the selection of proper parents without the investigative resources available to agencies. Furthermore, he may later find himself caught in a lawsuit between the adoptive parents and the natural mother. The best practice is for physicians to refer the unmarried mother patient and their patients who wish to adopt children to an appropriate agency. At the minimum, however, any attempt to assist in these matters, for altruistic or other reasons, must be done in close connection with an attorney who is well versed in the adoption law of the particular state.

Agency Adoptions

Even if the physician has no direct part in arranging an independent adoption he may be called on to examine a baby prior to placement by a licensed agency or to evaluate the physical or mental health of either the natural mother or the adoptive parents. In cases where there is any serious contest about the health of the natural mother or the adopting parents, courts may call on physicians to act as independent authorities on behalf of the court to evaluate the situation. In most states release of a child to a placement agency is held irrevocable in the absence of a showing of fraud, duress, mistake, or incapacity in the release.[18]

The famous "Baby Lenore case" is an example of the circumstances that can result if adoption surrenders are not negotiated with extreme regard for the rights of the natural mother. Baby Lenore was born to an unmarried 32-year-old woman who had come from her native Colombia to have her baby in New York. She was a college graduate and had gone to college in this country. Four days after the birth of the baby she placed her for board and care with an adoption agency, and ten days later when the child was two weeks old, she executed a surrender document. Five days later she changed her mind and requested that the child be returned to her. After several unsuccessful attempts to regain her child, the mother began a *habeas corpus* proceeding. The court held that the status of the natural parent is so important in determining the best interests of the child that it may counterbalance or even outweigh superior material and cultural advantages that may be afforded by the adopting parents and held that the mother's timely request for the return of her child, only five days after the prospective adoptive parents had gained custody, indicated that the child should be returned.[19] In this case, however, Baby Lenore's adoptive parents fled from New York with the baby, initiated adoption proceedings in Florida, and prevailed on the Florida court not to give full recognition to the New York decree. As far as is known, Baby Lenore and her adoptive parents remain in Florida.[20]

Examination of the child.   If the physician is acting as the agent of either the adopting parents or the agency in evaluating the condition of the child, he may be liable for malpractice if he fails to discover a condition that would be material to the parental decision to adopt and that is a condition the reasonably prudent physician would have discovered at the time the child was examined. It is quite possible that if a child is suffering from a severe defect at the time he is examined for placement and the defect is not discovered, the result may be not only a suit for malpractice against the examining physician but in some situations a suit for fraud as well.

A husband and wife sought to adopt a baby through private placement. They asked the delivering physician about the health of the child. He assured them that the baby was healthy. The physician also told them that they should seek the service of an attorney and go through the proper procedure for adoption. The couple then took possession of the child. Shortly thereafter the couple took the child to another physician for further examination, and it was determined that the child had hydrocephalus and would probably die within a fairly short time. The would-be adoptors then placed the baby in a home for sick children, where it died. After the baby's death, suit was filed against the physician for fraudulently representing the child to be in good health. The court found that since the couple had stopped adoption proceedings as soon as they discovered the child's illness, they had no standing to sue the physician. They were neither natural nor adoptive parents of the child. It is very clear from that opinion, however, that the court would have protected the right of the parents to bring a suit if they had discovered the child's condition after the adoption was concluded.[21]

A physician failed to discover a congenital defect in a baby prior to its adoption. The adoptive parents sued him for malpractice. The court held that no physician-patient relationship had existed between the parents and the physician at the time of the examination since they were not then in possession of the child. The court held, however, that a contractual relationship had existed and that if they had sued for breach of contract they would have had a cause of action.[22]

Annulment of Adoptions

Even in the absence of fraud, a serious error in diagnosis of the condition of a baby where the defect is such that a reasonable person would find it material in determining whether or not to adopt the baby may engender a malpractice suit. It is very clear that misstatements with intent to deceive an adoptive parent as to the condition or the background of the child may invalidate an adoption and in some cases allow the parents to abrogate the adoption altogether, thereby making the child a person without any family at all.

A couple applied to a county welfare department for a child, and a girl apparently about six years of age was placed with them. They were assured by the social worker that she was healthy, intellectually normal, and of an acceptable family background. In fact, the agency's records indicated, and the social workers knew, that the child had been diagnosed as retarded, the father was in a penitentiary for incest with his oldest daughter, and the mother's sexual history was bizarre. All the child's older siblings were retarded and several were then in institutions for delinquents. The court awarded the adopting couple damages for fraud and in a most unusual decree also annulled the adoption.[23]

In most cases, however, although the couple may recover damages for either fraud or misdiagnosis, they cannot annul the adoption once the final decree has been granted.[24] Courts usually hold that in the absence of specific statutory authority to annul a completed adoption, there is no right to do so since the result would leave the child with no parents.

An adoption agency placed a three-year-old girl with the plaintiffs, and the adoption was finalized about the time of her fourth birthday. Soon after, behavioral problems began to occur, and by the time she was six the degree of her retardation was so severe that institutionalization became necessary. After she was placed in a home for retarded children, the parents sued the agency for damages for fraud and also asked the court to annul the adoption. In addition to determining that there was no judicial authority to set aside the decree, the court concluded that there was no evidence of fraud by the agency. There was evidence that the child's behavior before placement should have alerted a careful caseworker that something was wrong, and the child should have at least been examined by an appropriate physician, but no action to obtain any examination had been taken. The court found that the agency had been guilty of gross carelessness but not of fraud.[25]

An 11-year-old girl who had been adopted through an agency developed severe mental disturbances shortly after the adoption proceedings were complete. Her parents sought to annul the adoption. The court held that the only grounds for annulment of an adoption are fraud and unavoidable accident or mistake, and that even where those factors may be present, the best interests of the child should prevail. In this case, the court refused to annul the adoption because the child would have become a public charge.[26]

It would appear to be fraud as a matter of law for a physician or agency not to reveal known problems about a child to prospective parents. Most of the cases, however, involve situations that are probably not discoverable at birth and that may not become manifest for many months and perhaps years after placement of an infant. In this case, it is unlikely that any agency or physician would be subject to a suit for fraud or negligence. The court would in fact be justified in pointing out to the adoptive parents who wished to annul their relationship with the child or sue the physician that natural parents also do not receive guarantees with their babies.

In other cases, where a couple's fitness to adopt is in question, the physician may be asked to present testimony on their behalf or to serve as an independent medical expert on behalf of the court. If there is serious evidence of physical disease or psychological maladjustment arrived at after a duly careful diagnosis, a trial court is clearly entitled to refuse to permit adoption, although a past history of psychiatric treatment for nonserious difficulties is certainly not grounds for refusal to allow a would-be parent to adopt.[27] If a physician is appointed as an independent expert on behalf of the court, no physician-patient relationship is established with the person who is examined. The parties examined may not object to admission of the testimony evaluating their physical or mental health and probably cannot sue for malpractice if the independent expert has not been grossly negligent.[28] In most cases, state statutes provide that physicians who examine parties as independent medical experts and then report directly to the court are immune from suit even though they may have made a good faith error of judgment.[29]

CHILD ABUSE

The problem of child abuse in this country has grown markedly in terms of awareness if not in incidence in the past few years.[30] Most abused children are very young and are literally "battered babies." In one study in Denver, for example, 33.7 percent of the children abused were under one year of age, 56 percent were under three, 68 percent were under five, and 32 percent were between six and thirteen.[31]

Penalties

In addition to proceedings that declare the child to be neglected or dependent for the purpose of removing him from the custody of his parents and placing him in a foster home, the abusive parent may also be charged with violation of criminal law. If the child recovers from the injury, the usual charge, in the absence of a specific statute providing penalties for child abuse, is assault and battery. If the child dies, most prosecutions seem to be for manslaughter[32] as opposed to murder, but first-degree murder convictions are not unknown.[33] Jail sentences in these cases are quite common, although most courts try to provide supportive psychological counseling for the parents at least for a trial period after the incident.

Some studies show that jailing a parent is not likely to produce reform.[34] One group of authors cited the example that one mother, after serving a jail sentence for child abuse, committed three similar offenses. A second mother who served a jail sentence stood a good chance of getting her child back, despite numerous social work and medical opinions against return of the child. These authors conclude that, in general, prosecution and punishment when used alone serve only to increase the child's time in the psychological limbo of foster homes and do nothing to help clarify the child's future status in regard to adequate parental care.[35]

Most authorities now emphasize the importance of a treatment plan in the initial stages of working with an abused child and his family. Many feel that unless the first incidence of abuse was a serious threat to life, the appropriate approach in these cases is to make the child a ward of the juvenile court and allow him to return to his parents while certain safeguards are employed.[36] The parents should be required to undergo a few months' diagnostic trial of psychological assistance. The safeguards for the child should include "almost daily" checks of the child by community health social workers and educational personnel in an effort to see if the parents can be induced to work through their problems. If they cannot, termination of rights should follow. Most authorities on child development take the position that removal of a child from his home to a foster home while the parents are treated is an unsatisfactory solution because the child himself is more disrupted and the stress is removed from the abusive parents, who come to feel that they have changed but who may resume their former behavior when the child is returned to them. In most communities, however, the realities of the situation may require removal of the child. Practically no juvenile court has a sufficient staff to permit "almost daily" home visits to check on the safety of an abused child, and a case-worker dealing with child abuse cases may have such a large case load that home visits occur infrequently, if at all.

Furthermore, a judge who permits a child to remain at home after he has been injured sufficiently to create a charge of abuse has to take the risk that the next incident may result in death. One authority has said: "No task is more difficult than predicting the recurrence of misbehavior and this balancing of interests is made even more difficult when a judge, who is considering whether to take a child from his father and mother, is faced with evidence that leaves it unclear whether the parents were the actual perpetrators of the abuse. Nevertheless, the chance taken by refusal to suspend parental custody of a child who bears the marks of unusual injuries, marks which suggest that the injuries were intentionally inflicted, is a chance taken with the child's life."[37]

For this reason and because of the shortage of staff to supervise the parents, the actual practice may be immediate removal of the child to a foster home with long-term treatment plans devised later. However unsatisfactory this may be in terms of psychological trauma, it at least protects the child from further physical harm. If and when juvenile courts have adequate financial support to provide sufficient staff to manage these cases properly, the practice will doubtless more nearly approach the theory.

Statutory Reporting Requirements

Almost all states have child abuse reporting statutes. Most of those statutes make it mandatory for a physician who is aware of an incident of child abuse to report it to the appropriate authority, which is now usually a social service agency rather than the police department. It is clear that prior to passage of these statutes, many physicians failed to report child abuse cases, treated the child, and sent him home. In some instances this failure to report seemed to be the result of a fear of civil or criminal liability. Others regarded reporting as a breach of the confidential physician-patient relationship, and others simply felt like meddlers. A mandatory reporting requirement in most states means that a physician himself, at least hypothetically, could be charged with a violation of criminal law for his failure to report a known case of child abuse, although prosecution on this ground is unknown as far as can be determined. Failure to report a case of child abuse, furthermore, may make the physician liable for civil damages in a malpractice case.

There have been several decisions, many of them quite old, in which it was held that failure to comply with a reporting statute constitutes conclusive evidence of medical negligence.

In one very old case a physician failed to comply with the state statute that required him to report cases of smallpox. One of his patients had smallpox, unknown to his neighbor. The neighbor went to visit him, since the patient was not quarantined, exposed himself to the disease, and died. The widow brought a wrongful death action against the physician, and it was held that the physician's failure to comply with the contagious disease reporting statute was the cause of the decedent's death.[38]

Other cases have held that failure of physicians who delivered babies to comply with the statutory duty to report cases of eye disease was negligence. Since violation of these statutes was criminally punishable, the doctor's failure to report was adjudged to be evidence of negligence in itself without the necessity of further proof.[39] Other cases, however, usually from the 1920s, indicate that failure to report contagious diseases such as typhoid is not to be considered evidence of negligence in a later malpractice suit unless the person who contracted the disease and brings the suit can prove that he would not have been exposed if the statutory requirements had been met. The plaintiff therefore must be able to prove that there is a causal connection between the failure to report the disease and his illness.[40]

Failure to Report as Malpractice

It is at least arguable that if a child is damaged again after a physician is, or should have been, aware that the child had been abused but makes no report, the physician's failure is the proximate cause of judicial failure to remove the child to a safe place, and the physician is therefore legally responsible for subsequent injuries to the child.[41] One recent case imposed liability in this situation, and it was noted in the opinion that it was a case of first impression in the United States.

An 11-month-old girl was brought to an emergency room with a fracture of the leg. The type of fracture was such that a reasonably careful physician would have assumed that an investigation of abuse was indicated. The child was treated and released and was readmitted to the hospital a short while later with serious and permanent injuries that were obviously related to child abuse. After she was removed from her parents, an action was brought on her behalf against the physicians in the emergency room who had seen and treated her at the first visit. The court held that her guardian stated a cause of action against the physicians. They were not liable for negligence in failing to diagnose child abuse but rather for failure to report a suspected case to the proper authorities for a more extensive investigation than they were capable of making in the emergency room. A cause of action thus existed against them for the injuries inflicted on the child in the second beating.[42]

Any agency that places a child in a foster or adoptive home without adequate investigation is also presumably liable for any brutality against the child.

A county welfare department placed two children in a foster home. One, a four-year-old, was dead on arrival at the hospital. The examining physician testified that she had died of a beating and that there was medical evidence of other assaults. The other child also gave physical indication of beatings. At the trial of the foster parents, witnesses testified that they had seen them beating both children with a stick while all were working in a berry field. The jury found both foster parents guilty of manslaughter, and convictions were upheld on appeal. No discussion was given to the civil liability of the agency or the employees who had placed the children in this environment, but if a suit had been filed, it is clear that the agency would have been liable.[43]

All state statutes provide that the physician who in good faith reports a suspected case of child abuse is immune from any suit for negligence or defamation if he is mistaken. Even in the absence of such a provision, as long as the reasonably prudent physician would have thought the child's injuries indicated some form of abuse, he would not be liable in any action brought by the parents under common-law principles.[44]

The extreme youth of most of these children and their resulting defenselessness mean that any physician encountering one of these cases who does not report it or make other reasonable attempts to protect the child from further abuse must live with the moral consequences, even though he is not the defendant in a suit.

Confidentiality

Physician-patient confidentiality does not apply in these cases. The child, not the parent, is the physician's patient, and even if he has also been treating the parents, all courts hold that no physician-patient privilege exists in a child abuse case.[45] Therefore, the report does not violate a confidential relationship between the parent and the physician. If a child abuse case is dealt with by a juvenile court with an order to the parents to consult a psychiatrist, psychologist, or some other physician or social worker for therapy in addition to, or instead of, a criminal sentence, the treating professional normally reports periodically to the court on the progress made by the parents. It should therefore be pointed out to these patients that reports will be made available to the juvenile court, if this is the condition of the court's disposition of the case, and that the normal rules of physician-patient confidentiality do not apply.

In no case, even if the physician feels certain that the parents will go to jail for their abuse of their child, should he fail to report out of misguided sympathy for them any case that he has reason to believe involves a "battered baby." The physician is the first person, and usually the only adult outside the family, who encounters these young children, and therefore he may well be the only protector the battered child will have.

CHILD CUSTODY

Custody proceedings involve placement of children after a divorce or disputes among family members after the death of one or both parents by grandparents or other relatives as well as in some other situations. Arguments among well-meaning family members over the physical control of a child are among the most difficult decisions for any judge to resolve.

The physician's involvement in a custody case may arise in one of several ways. He may have treated the parent, or he may be appointed by the court during a divorce proceeding to make an examination of one or both parents of the child and report his findings to the court. Except where child abuse is alleged as the ground for change of custody or acquisition, very few custody cases involve the mental or physical health of the child. Where this is the case, however, the rules of testimony are similar to that of a physician who testifies in any other case, meaning that he is subject to subpoena and to cross-examination at the hearing.[46]

Mental Health of the Parent

The usual point at which a physician becomes involved in a custody case is where the ground for the suit is allegation of mental illness by one parent against the other.[47] Allegations of mental disturbance are very frequent in custody disputes, since custody is invariably determined on the ground of the best interests of the child,[48] and obviously the court is likely to rule that a parent who is mentally ill cannot give a child a sufficiently stable environment to allow him or her to receive custody. A physician who is involved in a custody case should be aware that these may be the most bitterly fought, hostile, and emotionally charged cases that appear before the courts. In many cases the parent who is attempting to get the child away from the other may be far more motivated by hostility to the spouse than he or she is by concern for the child. Using the child as a pawn or weapon for revenge in protracted, bitter litigation usually is sufficiently damaging to all persons concerned, including the child, to raise serious questions of how the best interests of the child can be served by the proceedings, regardless of the outcome.[49]

An active psychotic or a parent who is in a mental hospital at the time of the custody hearing is most unlikely to receive custody.[50] On the other hand, the fact that one parent has been hospitalized for mental illness at some prior time but has made a good recovery would certainly not preclude a court from giving that parent custody of the children as long as he or she is presently able to care for them.[51]

The criterion used by the courts to determine the effect of a history of mental difficulty on custody is not the degree of difficulty that exists but the effects it will have on the child.[52] In short, if the child is adversely affected, minor emotional problems might eliminate custody, whereas a more serious one that did not involve the child might be overlooked.[53] For example, neurotically overprotective parents who refuse to let their children play outside for fear of germs are likely to be deprived of custody.[54] Alcoholism or drug abuse is usually considered sufficient to deprive a parent of custody.[55] When a parent who has recovered from mental illness or some sort of emotional problem is given custody of a child, the court may properly order him or her to have periodic appointments with a psychiatrist or social welfare agency in order to provide supervision and reports to the court that things are continuing to go well.[56]

Unlike other types of court orders, custody awards are never final. All courts empowered to award custody retain their jurisdiction over the child until he is grown, precisely to make sure that his best interests are preserved, and custody may always be changed if circumstances or personalities change. After a child has adapted to the life of one parent and one environment he will not be transferred to the other without just cause, particularly if there is a geographical distance between the two, but if necessary it can always be done.

Confidentiality

The physician who has examined or treated a parent for emotional problems at any time may be a prominent figure in any custody case. In most situations, once a judge has issued a subpoena for the physician's testimony at the request of the other parent, courts hold that the physician-patient privilege does not apply in custody cases. The right of the parent patient to physician-patient confidentiality is considered less important than establishing the facts in order to protect the best interests of the child. Most cases have held that the patient's right to privilege must yield to the paramount rights of the child and the court's duty to protect those rights. However, subpoenas are not issued without "just cause shown," and in no situation should a physician testify about a patient or reveal any information without the patient's consent unless a subpoena has been served.[57]

In general, courts hold that if a psychotherapist or other physician believes that the condition of his patient would seriously impair his ability to care for a child, he may disclose such information in chambers to the judge, at which point the privilege is dropped.[58] If the physician is not currently treating the patient who is a party to the custody action, the parent who wishes to have the physician's testimony admitted must bear the burden of proof that there is a relationship between the past and present medical condition. If substantial time has elapsed since treatment terminated, it is very unlikely, unless it is clear that the parent was actively psychotic, that the testimony or records of a psychiatrist would be subject to subpoena.[59] Furthermore, the privilege is not generally considered to be waived in any action for temporary, as opposed to permanent, custody.[60]

Orders for medical testimony are considered to be within the discretion of the court. Therefore, in unusual circumstances trial judges have the power to order testimony about a patient in any custody case where they feel it is necessary.[61] In some rare situations the report from a psychiatrist made at the direction of the court may be admitted into evidence without the right of cross-examination.[62] It should be noted that a trial court's refusal to order a parent to submit to a psychiatric examination is also generally within its discretion.[63] The court may also order an examination of the child by a physician or psychiatrist.[64]

In any case where a physician testifies as an independent medical expert appointed by the court, his testimony is not covered by physician-patient privilege because he is not considered a treating physician for purposes of confidentiality or privilege statutes. Therefore, his role is as an "arm of the court" to investigate those matters that are within his professional expertise and not to represent the interests of any party to the action.[65] Divorce actions where no children's rights are involved and in which their custody is not at issue generally do not constitute an exception to the rules of physician-patient privilege, and a psychiatrist usually cannot be forced to testify simply because his patient is a party to a divorce case.[66]

Failure to wait to transfer information about a patient until one has been ordered to do so by a court may, however, subject the physician to a malpractice suit.

In a child custody case the mother had been in psychotherapy for a substantial time during her marriage and following separation from her husband. The attorney for her husband asked her psychiatrist to make an affidavit divulging information he had received while treating her and to give his opinion on her fitness to be the custodial parent. The psychiatrist agreed to do so, made the affidavit, and delivered it to the attorney. The woman lost custody and sued the psychiatrist for malpractice. The trial court decided in favor of the physician, but this finding was reversed on appeal. The appellate court found that a physician-patient relationship had existed at the time the psychiatrist acquired the information and that the contention of the psychiatrist that he would have had to testify to the same material on the witness stand was irrelevant. The court said that it was not concerned with what the psychiatrist might have been compelled to disclose as a witness, because his affidavit was first given to an attorney as the result of a simple request and not to a court as the result of a court order. The court held that the interests of the children would have been adequately protected by the psychiatrist from the witness stand under subpoena.[67]

This case would appear to establish a sensible rule. If an attorney for either party in a custody dispute consults a physician about his treatment of either the child or a parent, the physician should never disclose any information without the consent of his patient, or, if his patient is the child, the parent who had actual physical possession of the child at the time he saw the child and from whom he had obtained consent to treat the child. If the parent is his patient, no information whatever should be given out without the consent of the patient. If his testimony is needed in the case, the trial judge will subpoena him and in that case the physician must testify. It is clear, however, that except under subpoena no information should be given without the consent of the person with whom the physician-patient relationship was established. Gratuitous discussions of information bearing on the child or the parent with anyone, including other relatives, attorneys, or social workers, except where a child abuse report has been made or neglect is suspected, is a clear breach of confidentiality and of the physician's ethical, moral, and, usually, legal obligations.

THE CHILD AS AN OFFENDER

The theory of the juvenile court system has been that a child who has committed an offense should be treated or rehabilitated in some therapeutic sense and not punished as an adult offender. The juvenile courts in this country are considered to be civil not criminal courts.[68] As an unfortunate result, however, until the Supreme Court decision of *In re Gault,*[69] a child was effectively denied all of the benefits of the Bill of Rights and other constitutional and legal safeguards that were required prior to imprisonment of an adult offender.[70] With that decision, the Supreme Court of the United States established that important constitutional rights apply to children who are before a juvenile court and ushered in a new era of legal safeguards to protect the child who has been charged with an offense.

Due Process in the Juvenile Court

Juvenile courts have two types of jurisdiction over allegedly delinquent children. The first type of jurisdiction applies to children who are considered incorrigible. These children have not broken any criminal law; they are truants, runaways, or in some way difficult to handle and considered in need of supervision.[71] The penalties for these semioffenses can be incarceration in a juvenile institution. The second type of juvenile offender is the child charged with an offense that would be considered criminal if committed by an adult, such as murder, arson, burglary, car theft, or the like. The procedures within the court are, however, the same for both. There is substantial doubt that a child charged with being "in danger of leading an idle life"[72] or "disorderly" should in fact be dealt with as if he were a criminal, but thus far these statutes have not been successfully challenged. Most commentators on the subject acknowledge that juvenile delinquency statutes are so far ranging, including such behavior as "smoking cigarettes in a public place," that almost every child in the country could be adjudicated a delinquent.[73]

The consequences to the child of arrest as a delinquent, either for behavior that is normally considered criminal or for behavior that irritates a parent, may very well be incarceration in an institution. In many cases he may be incarcerated for misbehavior that in no way endangers anyone or anything. As a result, following the *Gault* case, other courts began to hold that certain basic rights of due process of law do apply to a child. For example, he has the right to know the nature and cause of the accusation against him,[74] the right to counsel,[75] and the right to bail.[76] In most juvenile court situations the child is rarely held in jail prior to trial unless he is likely to run away or he presents a serious threat to the public safety. Thus, theoretically, his family's financial ability or inability to provide bail should be irrelevant. The child also has the right to a speedy trial.[77] It has, however, been held that a child does not have the right to a trial by jury, since the theory of the juvenile court is to make the disposition of the child's case amenable to personal and idiosyncratic factors.[78] Evidence that is inadmissible in an ordinary criminal case generally cannot be used in a juvenile court against a child.[79]

Both state and federal courts have frequently found confessions by minors to be involuntary. The Supreme Court held in one case: "But a 14-year-old boy, no matter how sophisticated, is unlikely to have any conception of what will confront him when he is made accessible only to the police. That is to say, we deal with a person who is not equal to the police in knowledge and understanding of the consequences of the questions and answers being recorded and he is unable to know how to protect his own interests or how to get the benefits from his constitutional rights."[80]

Examinations of Detained Juveniles

The self-incrimination privilege is the one most likely to confront a physician in his professional relationships with a juvenile court. In most large cities, children who are picked up and held in detention prior to trial for any reason, even briefly, are examined by a physician. It should be very clear that no questions about the offense should be asked of the child unless those questions are somehow necessary to the physical examination and are related to a reasonable evaluation of the young person's medical condition. If, for example, he has been injured in the course of a struggle during arrest, it will be necessary to know exactly what happened. It would not, however, be necessary in most cases for the physician to know about the circumstances that preceded the arrest.

A physician who is employed by the juvenile court to examine a child is not considered the child's treating physician. Therefore, the normal rules of physician-patient privilege do not apply. If the child is asked by the physician, either alone or in the presence of police officers, to make any statement whatever or to discuss in any way the acts with which he has been charged, the child's privilege against self-incrimination has been violated.[81] The child and his parents must be told that he does not have to make a statement about the alleged offense unless his attorney is present.[82] Any attempts to discuss the matter with the child without advising him of his right to have counsel present may well result in a reversal of a juvenile court's finding that the child is in fact guilty. The physician should, in fact, advise the child that he will not preserve confidentiality if the child initiates a discussion of his criminal activities. A frightened young person held in detention and surrounded by law enforcement personnel may very well look to the physician as a person he can trust to help him and thus be very forthcoming with information. The physician who listens, draws the child out, and "gets the whole story," which he then reveals to the police or to a judge, is essentially in the same position as if he had assisted in questioning the child directly, and in either case the child's right to refrain from incriminating himself is destroyed. One judge characterized the use of such a statement made to a court officer whom the child knew well and trusted as "a violation of fundamental fairness and a breach of trust."[83]

In most juvenile courts there is an attempt to make a social investigation of the child, including an evaluation of the severity of the acts proved, prior to disposition of the case. Such dispositions must be determined on the basic facts of the case. If a young person, for example, is charged with stealing a car, no matter how antisocial, neurotic, psychotic, or in need of medical treatment he may be, if he is not guilty of stealing the car he has a right to freedom. All social investigations and other such inquiries should be made only after the child's case has been dealt with on a basis of a judicial determination of guilt. Only after that finding has been made are the social history, the medical history, or other such information relevant to a determination of sentence.

The evaluation report of the juvenile justice system of the city of New York in 1960 stated the following:

> Before deciding upon a disposition, the judge ordinarily adjourns the case for two to three weeks or longer to allow the probation department to complete its investigation and report, and, if necessary to permit medical or psychiatric studies to be made. As helpful as such studies might have been to the judge in making a finding, denial of due process might be alleged if he used them before adjudication, since both the letter and the spirit of the Act creating the court require that a finding relate to the petition and nothing else. The fact that a child before the court is seriously disturbed, for example, does not justify the court's assuming jurisdiction over him if evidence of the alleged act of delinquency is insufficient or conflicting.[84]

If a physician is asked to participate in an evaluation of a child who has been brought before a juvenile court, he should thus be quite sure that the child has already been found guilty at a proper hearing and that he, the physician, is not being asked to evaluate a child who may or may not have committed the offense charged. The only purpose of a pretrial examination should be to determine if the child is in need of immediate medical treatment.[85] He may well have a venereal disease or some other contagious condition that makes it dangerous to hold him in the facility with other children. He may also have serious physical conditions that have never been diagnosed. He may be acutely mentally ill and in need of emergency hospitalization. In all of these situations, of course, immediate treatment is necessary. What should be postponed until after a finding of guilt, however, is any medical or psychiatric examination that goes to the question of the ultimate disposition of the case, as opposed to treatment of immediate medical problems.

Failure to diagnose a serious condition in these pretrial examinations can create serious problems for the young person. The medical attention available to children in reformatories is limited in most cases. If the child enters a reformatory without having a proper examination and is suffering from a serious, undiscovered condition, the examining physician must usually assume that it will not be discovered after he gets there.

The Juvenile After Conviction

It has been established as a constitutional right that a child or adult offender who is institutionalized as mentally ill in lieu of a term of imprisonment has a right to treatment.[86] The same right applies to a prisoner who is physically ill. These rights have been specifically applied to juvenile offenders.[87] As a matter of due process of law, the right of a sick child to receive medical treatment instead of custodial care is no longer a subject of argument.[88] The fact that a state does not have adequate funds is no defense to the fact that mentally or physically ill children are held without proper medical attention.[89] A number of courts have held that juveniles who are institutionalized by a state have a constitutional right to rehabilitative treatment according to "minimally acceptable standards of care and treatment for juveniles and a right to individualized care and treatment."[90]

Behavior modification.   In an attempt to alleviate antisocial behavior, some institutions have begun use of such techniques as behavior modification treatment, aversive therapy, and use of tranquilizers and other medications on inmates.[91] It should be noted that any physician involved in these treatment processes may be violating the constitutional rights of the juvenile inmates in his charge.

A state mental hospital used apomorphine to induce vomiting in patients for violation of rules. The evidence showed that apomorphine was injected for such behavior as not getting up, getting a cigarette from others, talking, swearing, or lying. Patients were given an injection and then exercised. Vomiting began with 15 minutes and lasted from 15 to 60 minutes. A staff physician testified that this aversion therapy was based on Pavlovian conditioning. The court held that it was cruel and unusual punishment, in violation of rights of the inmates under the Eighth Amendment. The court enjoined the use of the medication in treatment of patients except under the following conditions: (1) a written and informed consent must be obtained from each patient; (2) the consent may be revoked at any time after it is given; and (3) each injection had to be authorized by a physician and administered by a physician or a nurse, not by a trustee corpsman.[92]

The same issues have been raised in institutions designed to confine juvenile delinquents.[93]

The Indiana boys' reformatory housed 400 boys from 12 to 18 years of age, one-third of whom were "noncriminal offenders." A class action suit was brought to enjoin the school officials from beating the inmates as punishment and from using intramuscular injections of promazine and chlorpromazine hydrochloride prescribed by a registered nurse or a licensed practical nurse under standing orders of a physician. It was admitted by the reformatory officials that the drugs were not given as a part of a therapeutic program but to control behavior. No physician saw the boys before, during, or after the injections, and one standard dose was to be given to any boy who weighed under 116 pounds, another to those over that weight. The court held that both the beatings and the injections constituted cruel and unusual punishment and, as to the drugs, said, "We do not intend that penal and reform institution physicians cannot prescribe necessary tranquilizing drugs in appropriate cases. Our concern is with actual and potential abuses under policies where juveniles are beaten with an instrument causing serious injuries, and drugs are administered to juveniles intramuscularly by staff, without trying medication short of drugs and without adequate medical guidance and prescription."[94]

Medical care in institutions.   Failure to provide adequate medical treatment for an involuntarily institutionalized inmate who becomes ill is a clear violation of the constitutional prohibition against cruel and unusual punishment. In some states and under the provisions of the federal Tort Claims Act in the federal prison system, prisoners have the same rights to sue for medical malpractice as do any other patients.

The constitutional right of a prisoner to an adequate level of medical care has been established for many years.[95] A suit for violation of any prisoner's basic constitutional right to medical care falls under the federal Civil Rights Act, and it has been held in many decisions that these rights have been violated when prison personnel refused to provide medical care to an obviously sick prisoner.[96] It is not generally considered to be a violation of the guarantees against cruel and unusual punishment to administer proper medical treatment to a prisoner even though he may have religious objections to it.[97]

Once a physician who is responsible for seeing sick prisoners has ordered medication or other treatment, failure of the officials of the institution to comply with such medical orders also constitutes cruel and unusual punishment.[98] In order to violate a prisoner's constitutional rights, improper medical care must be continuing, must not be supported by any competent school of medical practice, and must amount to a complete denial of care.

Negligent treatment that falls short of rights against cruel and unusual punishment may not be sufficient to allow a prisoner to bring a civil rights action. Thus, no treatment at all under circumstances where it is indicated or treatment that is grossly negligent or inadequate constitutes violations of the inmate's civil rights; ordinary malpractice, such as failure to use due care in diagnosis or treatment, does not. Many states deny prisoners any right to bring a civil action for malpractice or for anything else that occurs during his term of imprisonment. Other states, however, permit prisoners to sue as readily as any other patient alleging malpractice.[99] Federal prisoners may also sue for malpractice.[100] Where the action is allowed, however, juries are very reluctant to accept the testimony of a delinquent or an adult prisoner when the adversary party is the prison physician.

A physician who is treating children in an institution for delinquents must be particularly aware of his responsibilities to obtain the informed consent of an inmate's parents to any nonemergency, unusual, or high-risk treatments. Parents of children in these institutions do have the right to be informed of the condition of their child and to consent to or decline proposed medical treatment. They also have the right to refuse to allow their child to take part in any form of biomedical or behavioral research that may be carried out at the institution. Regulations have been proposed by the Department of Health, Education and Welfare that would, if adopted, prohibit any medical research on a minor who is confined to an institution under court order, even though his parents and the minor himself may be willing to consent.[101] Even in the absence of such a regulation, however, it is absolutely necessary that consent be obtained from both the child and the parents.

Most institutions for the incarceration of juvenile offenders are extremely understaffed and very inhumane. If the institution claims to be rehabilitating or treating juvenile offenders, it must make reasonable efforts to show that it is attempting to do so, and it is quite clear that the child does have a right to proper medical treatment.

CONCLUSION

Many situations exist in which the pediatrician, as any other physician, may be involved in litigation on behalf of a child. He may, for example, be a witness in a case involving an automobile accident in which one of his patients was injured. The four areas discussed in this chapter, however, are the ones in which a pediatrician as a pediatrician is peculiarly likely to confront the legal system. Since all states tend to differ in their specific application of various universal legal principles, sound and logical self-protection would indicate that, prior to appearance in court or to making a statement that may be used in court, the physician contact his attorney and discuss the matter with him. It may be of critical importance to himself as well as to his patient that the pediatrician has good legal advice in any specific case involving any of these situations.

NOTES

1. Stephen B. Presser, "The Historical Background of the American Law of Adoption," 11 *J Fam Law* No. 3, page 143, 1972.
2. For a concise but valuable history of American adoption law, see M. G. Paulsen, Walter Wadlington, and J. Goebel, *Domestic Relations: Cases and Materials,* Mineola, NY, University Casebook Series, The Foundation Press, 1974, pages 447–449.

3. E.g., State ex rel Lee v. Buchanan, 191 So 2d 33, Fla 1966.

4. Goodman v. District of Columbia, 50 A 2d 812, DC Mun Ct App 1947.

5. 37 *Opinions of the Wisconsin Attorney General,* 403, 1948, reprinted in C. Foote, R. Levy, and Frank E. A. Sander, *Cases and Materials on Family Law,* 2nd ed., Boston, Little, Brown and Co., 1976, pages 338–340.

6. E.g., NJ Stats Ann, Section 9:3–19; Rogers v. Olander, 286 P 2d 1028, Wash 1955.

7. See "Moppets on the Market," comment, 59 *Yale Law J,* page 715, March 1950; Foote, Levy, and Sander, *op. cit. supra* at 5, pages 342–43.

8. Foote, Levy, and Sander, *supra* at 5, page 344.

9. E.g., A. v. C., 390 SW 2d 116, Ark 1965.

10. E.g., State ex rel Lewis v. Lutheran Social Services, 207 NW 2d 826, Wisc 1973.

11. See, for example, N. Stevenson, "The Legal Rights of Unmarried Fathers: The Impact of Recent Court Decisions," 47 *So Serv Rev,* page 1, 1973; "The Illegitimate and His Father," 216 *JAMA* No. 11, page 1909, June 14, 1971.

12. In re Stanley, 405 US 645, 1972.

13. E.g., State ex rel Nelson v. Whaley, 75 NW 2d 786, Minn 1956; Adoption of McKinzie, 275 SW 2d 365, Mo 1955.

14. E.g., Nev Rev Stats Section 127.070; Mass Gen Laws Ann, c. 210, Section 2.

15. E.g., In re Baby Larson, 91 NW 2d 448, Minn 1958; In re Alsdurf, 133 NW 2d 479, Minn 1965.

16. In re Adoption of a Child, 317 A 2d 382, NJ 1974.

17. Sampson v. Holton, 185 NW 2d 216, Iowa 1971.

18. In re David, 256 A 2d 583, Maine 1969.

19. People ex rel Scarpetta v. Spence Chapin Adoption Service, 269 NE 2d 787, NY 1971, cert den 404 US 805, 1971.

20. Foote, Levy, and Sander, *op. cit. supra* at 5, page 242; "Natural v. Adoptive Parents," note, 57 *Iowa Law Rev,* page 171, 1971; S. N. Katz, "The Adoption of Baby Lenore," 5 *Family Law Quart,* page 405, December 1971.

21. Chappell v. Masten, 255 So 2d 546, Fla 1972.

22. Greenwald v. Grayson, 189 So 2d 204, Fla 1966.

23. County Department of Welfare v. Morningstar, 151 NE 2d 150, Ind 1958.

24. "The Physician and Adoption," 223 *JAMA* No. 8, page 953, February 19, 1973.

25. Allen v. Allen, 330 p 2d 151, Ore 1958.

26. In re McDuffee, 352 SW 2d 23, Mo 1961.

27. E.g., In re Adoption of Schroetter, 67 Cal Reptr 819, Cal 1968.

28. "Appointment of Independent Medical Expert," 216 *JAMA* No. 1, page 207, April 5, 1971.

29. E.g., Carpenter v. City of Rochester, 324 NYS 2d 591, NY 1971; Schanbarger v. Kellogg, 315 NYS 2d 1013, NY 1970.

30. "Child Abuse and the Physician," 222 *JAMA* No. 4, page 517, October 23, 1972.

31. R. E. Helfer, and C. H. Kempe, *The Battered Child,* Chicago, University of Chicago Press, 1968, page 29.

32. E.g., New York v. Henson, 304 NE 2d 358, NY 1973; Minnesota v. Loss, 204 NW 2d 404, Minn 1973; Oregon v. Blocher, 499 P 2d 1346, Ore 1972; North Carolina v. Fredell, 193 SE 2d 587, NC 1972.

33. E.g., California v. Aeschlimann, 104 Cal Rptr 689, Cal 1972.

34. E.g., Lenore C. Terr and Andrew Watson, "The Battered Child Rebrutalized," 124 *Am J Psychiat* No. 10, page 1432, April 1968; C. H. Kempe, "The Battered Child Syndrome," 181 *JAMA,* page 17, 1962. See also Paulsen, Wadlington, and Goebel, *op. cit. supra* at 2, pages 732–751.

35. Terr and Watson, *op. cit. supra* at 34.

36. Monrad G. Paulsen, "The Legal Framework for Child Protection," 66 *Columbia Law Rev,* page 679, 1966.

37. *Ibid.,* page 703.

38. Jones v. Stanko, 160 NE 456, Ohio 1928.

39. E.g., Medlin v. Bloom, 119 NE 773, Mass 1918; Dietsch v. Mayberry, 47 NE 2d 404, Ohio 1942.

40. Davis v. Rodman, 227 SW 612, Ark 1921.

41. Lon B. Isaacson, "Child Abuse Reporting Statutes: The Case for Holding Physicians Civilly Liable for Failing to Report," 12 *San Diego Law Rev* No. 4, page 743, July 1975; Alan Sussman, "Reporting Child Abuse: A Review of the Literature," 8 *Family Law Quart* No. 3, page 245, Fall 1974.

42. Landeros v. Flood, 123 Cal Rptr 713, Cal 1975.

43. State v. Parmenter, 444 P 2d 680, Wash 1968.

44. E.g., Haewsky v. St. John's Hospital, Mich Cir Ct, Wayne Co, June 10, 1970; Sanford N. Katz, R. A. Howe, and Melba McGraft, "Child Neglect Laws in America," 9 *Family Law Quart* No. 1, Spring 1975. This article lists and discusses all relevant child neglect abuse statutes in the United States. It also includes the statutes themselves and is the only such digest available. This article also contains a bibliography of books and articles on the subject of child abuse and is in itself the definitive study of the existing law on this subject.

45. E.g., In re John Children, 306 NYS 2d 797, NY 1969.

46. E.g., Kesseler v. Kesseler, 180 NE 2d 402, 236 NYS 2d 472, NY 1962; Rea v. Rea, 245 P 2d 884, Ore 1952.

47. "Mental Illness and Parental Rights," 216 *JAMA* No. 3, page 575, April 19, 1971.

48. E.g., Painter v. Bannister, 140 NW 2d 152, Iowa 1966.

49. For an excellent, if controversial, discussion of the entire range of legal and psychological problems inherent in child custody cases, see Joseph Goldstein, Anna Freud, and Albert J. Solnit, *Beyond the Best Interests of the Child,* New York, The Free Press, 1973.

50. E.g., Colombo v. Colombo, 162 P 2d 995, Cal 1945; Schultz v. Schultz, 404 P 2d 987, Wash 1965.

51. Commonwealth v. Edinger, 98 A 2d 172, Pa 1953; Commonwealth v. Bender, 178 A 2d 779, Pa 1962; Alden v. Alden, 174 A 2d 793, Md 1961.

52. Nichols v. Nichols, 247 SW 2d 143, Tex 1952; Combs v. Combs, 327 P 2d 164, Cal 1958; Willey v. Willey, 115 NW 2d 833, Iowa 1962.

53. Swanson v. Swanson, 290 NW 908, Neb 1940.

54. Ericson v. Ericson, 195 Pac 234, Wash 1921; Stoll v. Stoll, 68 NW 2d 367, Minn 1955; Atkinson v. Atkinson, 231 P 2d 641, Wash 1951.

55. E.g., Hardman v. Hardman, 214 SW 2d 391, Ky 1948.

56. E.g., Application of Richman, 227 NYS 2d 42, NY 1962; Knapp v. Knapp, 250 NYS 2d 390, NY 1964.

57. D. v. D., 260 A 2d 255, NJ 1969.

58. Usen v. Usen, 269 NE 2d 442, Mass 1971.

59. Application of DoVidio, 288 NYS 2d 21, NY 1968.

60. Gustafson v. Gustafson, 158 SE 2d 619, NC 1968.

61. Commonwealth of Pennsylvania ex rel Romanowicz v. Romanowicz, 248 A 2d 238, Pa 1968; Bender v. Bender, 304 NYS 2d 482, NY 1969.

62. In re Blaine, 282 NYS 2d 359, NY 1967; "Use of Extra-Record Information in Custody Cases," (comment,) 24 *U of Chicago Law Rev* No. 2, page 349, Winter 1957; Lincoln v. Lincoln, 247 NE 2d 659, NY 1969.

63. Stone v. Stone, 431 P 2d 802, Utah 1967.

64. Siegman v. Kraitchman, 294 NYS 2d 1005, NY 1968.

65. See "Appointment of Independent Medical Expert," *supra* at 28.

66. Ellis v. Ellis, 472 SW 2d 741, Tenn 1971.

67. Schaffer v. Spicer, 215 NW 2d 134, SD 1974.

68. E.g., In re Holmes, 109 A 2d 523, Pa 1954, cert den 348 US 973, 1955; M. G. Paulsen, "Juvenile Courts and the Legacy of '67," 43 *Ind Law J,* page 527, 1968.

69. In re Gault, 387 US 1, 1967.

70. Chester J. Antieau, *Modern Constitutional Law,* Rochester, New York, The Lawyers Cooperative Publishing Co., 1969.

71. E.g., In re Mario, 317 NYS 2d 659, NY 1971; David L. Bazelon, "Beyond Control of the Juvenile court," 21 *Juvenile Court J,* page 42, 1970.

72. Deering's Cal Code, Welfare and Institutions, Section 601, cited in Antieau, *op. cit. supra* at 70, Section 6.7.

73. M. G. Paulsen, "Fairness to the Juvenile Offender," 41 *Minn Law Rev* page 555, 1957.

74. In re Gault, 387 US 1, 1967.

75. Powell v. Hocker, 453 F 2d 652, CCA 9, 1971; Kemplen v. Maryland, 428 F 2d 169, CCA 4, 1970.

76. Kinney v. Lenon, 425 F 2d 209, CCA 9, 1970; Trimble v. Stone, 187 F Supp 483, DC DC 1960; Louisiana v. Franklin, 12 So 2d 211, La 1943.

77. "The Right to Bail and the Pre-trial Detention of Juveniles Accused of Crime," note, 18 *Vanderbilt Law Rev,* page 2096, 1965.

78. McKeiver v. Pennsylvania, 403 US 528, 1971.

79. E.g., Ciulla v. Texas, 434 SW 2d 948, Tex 1968; In re Williams, 267 NYS 2d 91, 1966.

80. Gallegos v. Colorado, 370 US 49, 1962.

81. In re Sadleir, 94 P 2d 161, Utah 1939.

82. In re D., 290 NYS 2d 935, NY 1968; Wansley v. Slayton, 487 F 2d 90, CCA 4, 1973.

83. Wansley v. Miller, 353 F Supp 42, DC Va 1973.

84. See "Juvenile Delinquency Evaluation Report of the City of New York," in Jay Katz, and Joseph Goldstein, *The Family and the Law,* New York, The Free Press, 1965, page 969.

85. Tippett v. Maryland, 436 F 2d 1153, CCA 4, 1971; McNeil v. Director, Patuxent Institution, 407 US 245, 1972.

86. "The Right to Treatment," 220 *JAMA* No. 8, page 1165, May 22, 1972; "The Right to Treatment," symposium, 57 *Georgetown Law J,* March 1969; Rouse v. Cameron, 373 F 2d 451, DC CA 1966; Millard v. Cameron, 373 F 2d 468, DC CA 1966; Morton Birnbaum, "The Right to Treatment," 46 *ABAJ,* page 499, May 1960.

87. E.g., Elmore v. Stone, 355 F 2d 841, DC CA 1966; Clayton v. Stone, 358 F 2d 548, DC CA 1956.

88. Martarella v. Kelley, 349 F Supp 575, DC NY 1972; Morales v. Turman, 364 F Supp 166, DC Tex 1973.

89. Wyatt v. Stickney, 325 F Supp 781, DC Ala 1971.

90. Nelson v. Heyne, 491 F 2d 352, CCA 7, 1974, cert den 417 US 976, 1974.

91. See, for one of many cases on this subject, Mackey v. Procunier, 477 F 2d 877, CCA 9, 1973. Dozens of articles on the medical, legal, and ethical issues in behavior modification of prisoners by drugs, psychosurgery, and other means have appeared in the past several years. See *Hastings Center Bibliography* for an extensive list. Two of the most recent articles on the legal aspects involved in these procedures are: Michael L. Shapiro, "Legislating the Control of Behavior Control," 47 *So Cal Law Rev,* page 237, 1974; and J. C. Murphy, "Total Institutions and the Possibility of Consent to Organic Therapies," 5 *Human Rights* No. 1, page 25, Fall 1975.

92. Knecht v. Gillman, 488 F 2d 1136, CCA 8, 1973.

93. E.g., In re Owen, 295 NE 2d 455, Ill 1973.

94. Nelson v. Heyne, 491 F 2d 352, CCA 7, 1974, cert den 417 US 976, 1974.

95. "Prisoner's Right to Medical Treatment," 216 *JAMA* No. 7, page 1253, May 17, 1971; Ramsey v. Ciccone, 310 F Supp 600, DC Mo 1970; Willis v. White, 310 F Supp 205, DC La 1970.

96. McCollum v. Mayfield, 130 F Supp 112, DC Cal 1955; Hirons v. Patuxent Institution, 351 F 2d 613, CCA 4, 1965; Edwards v. Duncan, 355 F 2d 993, CCA 4, 1966; Tolbert v. Eyman, 434 F 2d 625, CCA 9, 1970.

97. Veals v. Ciccone, 281 F Supp 1017, DC Mo 1968.

98. Sawyer v. Sigler, 445 F 2d 818, CCA 8, 1971; Martinez v. Mancusi, 443 F 2d 921, CCA 2, 1970.

99. Barney Sneidman, "Prisoners and Medical Treatment: Their Rights and Remedies," 4 *Crim Law Bull,* page 450, October 1968.

100. United States v. Muniz, 374 US 150, 1963.

101. See 33 *Fed Reg* No. 221, page 31747, November 16, 1973.

CHAPTER IX

THE MINOR

AND

THE PSYCHIATRIST

Although problems peculiar to the relationship between a psychiatrist and a patient may involve patients of any age, the primary source of legal problems involving minors in psychiatric treatment has been adolescent patients. Adolescents are certainly not easy persons with whom a parent can coexist. The inevitable collisions between parents and child during adolescence increase the difficulties that adolescents face as they come to terms with themselves as individuals and begin to develop a sense of their place in society. For this reason, a great many adolescents either want or are given psychiatric help. Although there is a considerable body of legal literature on the psychiatrist's legal responsibility in dealing with adults, there is virtually nothing on the subject of the rights of child or adolescent patients. This chapter examines from the legal viewpoint some of the more obvious problems that have not been discussed by either courts or law journals. Some of these questions are: (1) Does a minor of any age have a right to psychiatric treatment against the wishes of his parents? (2) Does an adolescent whose parents for reasons of their own consider him to be mentally disturbed, when he may merely be behaving in a way normal to his developmental stage, have a right to refuse treatment from a psychiatrist? (3) When, if ever, should a parent be able to commit a child or adolescent to a mental institution without specific legal protection for the child? (4) What limitations exist on confidentiality between psychiatrist and patient in terms of what information the patient's parents should receive? The last is probably the most troublesome question.

Adolescence is a very difficult time for both the child and his parents.[1] The adolescent is emerging into an independent social life, first with his peer group of the same sex and then into dating and other heterosexual behavior. Peer group pressure is strong, and in our current society the peer group may be more effective in determining behavior norms than it may have been in a time when parents were more certain of their moral values and young people emerging into their own identities at least knew precisely what their developmental rebellions were against. Identity crisis is also part of adolescent devel-

237

opment. As Erik Erikson phrases it, the adolescent is "consolidating his social roles." As a result, the values of the peer group, "the only people who understand," become increasingly important to a young person. Erikson points out that although the adolescent is vulnerable to specious ideas, he can put an enormous amount of energy and loyalty at the disposal of any convincing philosophical system, often to the distress of his family.[2] Erikson notes that an ideology, good or bad, gives an adolescent the following:[3]

1. A simplified perspective of the future
2. A strongly felt correspondence between the inner world of ideals and evils and the social world with its goals and dangers
3. An opportunity for uniformity of appearance and behavior
4. An opportunity to collectively experiment with roles
5. An introduction into the ethos of the prevailing technology
6. A geographic-historical world image as a framework of individual identity
7. A rationale for a sexual way of life
8. Submission to leaders who are above the ambivalence of the parent-child relationship

This integration of adolescent social roles can be interfered with in a variety of ways, and given a quantity of sudden drives that may become unmanageable, the adolescent may zoom out of control and become a delinquent. He may become a member of some religious cult such as the Children of God. His parents may feel threatened by an inability to control the young person as they could when the child was six or seven years old. The parents may be embarrassed to have him in jail, becoming a religious fanatic, using drugs, or wearing long hair. As a result of a variety of such tensions—some of which are confined to the family, others of which may spill over into the legal area and involve actions by courts—a psychiatrist may become involved with the young person and his family.

THE RIGHT TO SEEK TREATMENT

In our society psychiatric treatment of any kind is still considered socially unacceptable in many places. A somewhat conservative parent may strenuously object to a child visiting a psychiatrist under circumstances in which the child wishes to have treatment. The child's right to seek such treatment is unclear from the literature, statutes, and case law on the subject.

The Right to Other Forms of Medical Care

As has been discussed, a parent may not deny a physically ill child adequate medical treatment. Under all child neglect statutes, failure to obtain medical care for a child is explicitly or implicitly within the definition of "child abuse." The right to medical care does not vary with the reasons the parent may have had for his refusal to have the child treated. Even if the objection is based on religion, the parent may not, for example, as shown by the many Jehovah's Witnesses cases, refuse to allow the child to have a blood transfusion if such a transfusion is necessary to save the child's life.[4]

Courts in most states in which the issue has been raised are beginning to rule that medical treatment that is highly desirable, even if it is not absolutely necessary to save a child's life, may be ordered by the court under the doctrine of *parens patriae,* the state's authority to protect children, in spite of parental objections based on religious or other reasons.

A 14-year-old boy suffered from a serious neck and face deformity which could be alleviated by surgery. He wished to have the operation so that he would be able to lead a normal life. The mother had no objections to the surgery, but she was a Jehovah's Witness and refused to consent to surgically necessary blood transfusions. The surgeon refused to perform the operation unless he could transfuse the patient. The court held that the child was "neglected" and ordered the surgery performed.[5]

Four young children were removed from their home by court order on grounds of physical neglect and child abuse. Their father refused to allow necessary tonsillecto- mies on religious grounds, but his objection was overruled by the court.[6]

Other courts, however, have taken the position that orders for nonemer- gency care to which a parent objects will be subject to very strict review and will not be automatically granted.[7]

A 14-year-old boy had a cleft palate and a harelip, for which his father had refused to permit surgery on the ground that he believed in "mental healing." The health department of the county petitioned the juvenile court to have the boy declared neglected and to order surgery performed. The boy himself testified to the judge that he did not want to have the operation. The petition was dismissed on the ground that the boy did not have to have surgery if he did not wish to, since he was old enough to give a reasonably informed consent.[8]

An 11-year-old girl had been born with an abnormal growth on her left arm. The arm was useless and was also a menace to her health. The examining physicians who saw her at the request of the welfare department and her school indicated that, although there was a "fair degree of risk to life" involved in the operation, they would uniformly recommend that the arm be amputated. The girl's mother refused to consent because she was afraid that the operation was too dangerous. The trial court ordered surgery performed, and the parents appealed. The Supreme Court of Washington held that the local juvenile court had no statutory authority to order the operation since, under the circumstances, there was no neglect of the child.[9]

Thus, the case law on the right to nonemergency medical treatment of a child over parental objection is not clear. Courts are reluctant to order trivial treatment over parental objections. Serious tonsil and adenoid problems appear to be the bottom line which courts are willing to consider as sufficiently "necessary" medical care to order for the young child as a part of their neglect jurisdiction.

The Right to Psychiatric Care

By analogy, in regard to psychiatric treatment it is quite easy to see that if a child presents acute psychotic symptoms that are noticed by teachers or that have resulted in antisocial behavior to a degree that has come to the attention of a juvenile court or other authority, a judge probably has the same right to order the parent to allow the child to be treated by a psychiatrist as he does to order a blood transfusion for the desperately ill child of a Jehovah's Witness. There are, however, extraordinarily few decisions on this subject.

A boy in his early teens had been referred to a juvenile court after a series of incidents that apparently involved physical assaults on others. His mother had been urged by school personnel to have the child evaluated by a psychiatrist but had failed to do so. From the tone of the opinion, it seems probable that her failure was the result of inertia, not religious or other conviction. In ordering her to take the child to a specified psychiatrist, the trial judge ruled that failure to provide psychiatric care when necessary constituted child neglect.[10]

At the other extreme, however, there may be a young person who simply feels that he would like to discuss his problems with a psychiatrist but whose parents object for some reason. If the child located a prospective guardian or other family member who would agree to file a petition in the local juvenile court requesting that treatment be ordered, there is serious question under those circumstances that a court would require the parent to permit treatment. Without clear indication of psychosis or serious developmental or social difficulties, a judge would probably conclude that in this area of parental-adolescent conflict the law is simply incompetent to deal with the situation.[11]

The problem of the young person's right to seek proper psychiatric treatment is unlikely to involve private psychiatric treatment, since the parent can refuse to pay the bill and in most cases a young person cannot afford to pay for private psychotherapy himself. A more practical question involves an adolescent's right of access to a community mental health facility, a drug treatment center, a counseling center for troubled adolescents, or some other form of crisis-intervention center, such as centers for runaway children. These facilities are normally funded by charitable contributions or public funds. Some may have full-time qualified psychiatrists or well-qualified clinical psychologists on their staff. Others may have back-up consultants in these fields and be able to refer seriously disturbed children to a qualified psychiatrist if necessary. Particularly in drug rehabilitation centers, many of the personnel may themselves be former drug addicts. Although this may be a viable method of treating addiction, it considerably complicates the issue in terms of dealing with the legal rights of the adolescent.

Analogizing again to the law of medical treatment, there have not been any cases in recent years in which a psychiatrist or any other physician or surgeon has been liable for proper, nonnegligent treatment of a minor 15 years old or older without parental consent.[12] In addition, most states have passed minor treatment statutes that allow minors to consent to medical treatment.[13] No case law indicates whether this would include psychotherapy. However, in the absence of a specific restriction to the contrary in any particular statute, it would seem that a psychiatrist who is a licensed physician would also be covered by the treatment statutes. With an increasing number of state legislatures willing to enact these statutes and with the majority of them having done so at the present time, it is likely that this trend will continue. At whatever age specified by the state statute, at the time the minor has the right to consent to "treatment by a qualified physician," the right would presumably apply to all treatment, from acne to surgery to emotional disturbance. Of course, in this situation the psychiatrist assumes the risk that the minor's parents will refuse to pay the bill if the treatment is not considered necessary for the minor's well-being. However, the psychiatrist who is willing to forego payment is also presumably protected from any suit by the parents for good faith medical or psychiatric treatment.

It would therefore seem that if the child has access to a duly qualified physician-psychiatrist he does have the effective right to seek treatment even in the absence of a treating statute as long as he is "an older minor." If a parent wishes to intervene by bringing an action against the psychiatrist for damages or by attempting to obtain an injunction of some sort against further therapy, it is highly unlikely that the parent would prevail as long as the treatment given was standard psychotherapy that would be considered acceptable by a reasonably prudent psychiatrist. Some of the more bizarre forms of therapy, however, are sufficiently repugnant to middle-class Americans so that a parent who objected to a child's being treated by such methods would no doubt have a viable malpractice case. Furthermore, the parent might well have the right to intervene in a situation where a young person is not being treated by a physician but by a guru-type therapist. A practitioner who opened an adolescent counseling center and who was, for example, dedicated to a therapy based on Wilhelm Reich's theories that orgasms are essential to mental health might well be convicted on a charge of contributing to the delinquency of a minor on a warrant signed by an irate parent. Given the tendencies of adolescents to espouse new and "repressed" ideologies, for the reasons Erik Erikson notes, any form of bizarre therapy that holds itself out as presenting philosophical as well as therapeutic value is likely to attract this age group as strongly as the hard-core "Jesus Freak" movement. In those situations a parent would probably have the right to remove a minor from treatment. As is true of medical or surgical treatment, the legal criteria for the selection of a mode of therapy is that it is accepted by at least a "respectable minority" of the profession.[14]

Treatment by Nonphysicians

Under the provisions of the Model Act of the Group for the Advancement of Psychiatry and its revisions, which deal with psychiatrist-patient privilege in relation to court testimony,[15] a distinction is made between unlicensed persons engaging in psychotherapy and physicians or certified clinical psychologists. Social workers, for example, are covered by privilege, if at all, only while acting as the agent of a physician.[16] This is probably a valid differentiation, based on qualifications, to be drawn in the area of consent to psychiatric treatment as well as in the area of privilege. The minor would probably prevail in a conflict between himself and his parents over the right to treatment if conventional psychotherapy is being given by a qualified psychotherapist or clinical psychologist. A parent may, on the other hand, take justified offense at advice given to a child by a social worker, drug addiction counselor, or other person "in authority" whose credentials and qualifications to make valid judgments on the home situation or reasonably valid diagnoses of the child's problem are open to serious question.

For example, many social workers in crisis-counseling centers have a B.A. degree in sociology from a teachers' college and no graduate credentials. In many cases an adolescent comes to a center of this sort and relates a story of considerable parental difficulties and announces his intention to run away from home. These crisis centers have been known to find a residence for the child away from home. The child may be genuinely abused or his complaints of gross mistreatment may have arisen from the fact that he was asked to wash dishes the night before. A parent, it would seem, would have a perfectly legitimate legal action against a well-meaning social worker who has aided and abetted his minor child in finding a place to live other than at home where there is no actual abuse of the child physically or emotionally. The proper recourse in such a situation, in which a social worker is not qualified to make a psychiatric diagnosis, even though there may have been actual abuse, should be a petition to a juvenile court to have the child declared abused or neglected. The court may then proceed with an adjudication on the merits of the case. This is a far more prudent course of action than the social worker's assistance to the young person in leaving the home or supporting other behavior to which a reasonable parent would have legitimate objection.

In the case where such assistance has in fact occurred, a parent might well have a valid criminal action against the social worker or other "therapeutic person" for contributing to the delinquency of a minor, since running away from home is an act of delinquency, even though in some cases it may be a very sensible thing to do. The parent would also undoubtedly have an action for damages against any such counselor.[17]

Thus, it seems that even without the minor treatment statutes now in effect in many states, a young person does have a right to consent to reputable psychiatric treatment as opposed to the right to engage in a form of therapy that is not approved by at least a reasonable minority of reputable members of the medical profession.[18]

The standard community mental health center is probably covered by the normal rules of minor consent that apply to other medical treatment, since those institutions, most of which receive federal funds, must be very careful to comply with requirements of proper credentials for all staff members. In these situations and in other well-run institutions where psychiatric social workers are an important part of the staff, the social worker works directly under the supervision and direction of a qualified psychiatrist; therefore this problem is unlikely to occur. It would seem that the child would have the right to seek out and consent to psychiatric social work intervention in such surroundings.

In terms of other forms of mental health treatment, however, it is unlikely that such a right exists. The wisdom of allowing young people to be treated by well-meaning but untrained personnel in makeshift counseling centers without their parents' knowledge is seriously debatable.

Canon 4 of the Pediatric Bill of Rights specifies the following: "Every person regardless of age will have the right to seek out and to receive psychiatric care and counseling in doctor-patient confidentiality."[19] This, of course, assumes that the counseling is given by or under the supervision of a physician. The Model Act of the American Academy of Pediatrics also provides for a minor's consent to psychiatric treatment by a licensed health professional as a part of the general range of health services to which the minor may consent.[20]

A preteenager is not likely to have knowledge of or access to psychiatric care without parental knowledge. The older minor, on the other hand, may have an after-school job and choose to invest his pay in private psychiatric treatment or know about and have access to clinics. Furthermore, a younger child is more subject to parental control in all aspects of his life as a matter of physical necessity than is an adolescent. It is therefore unlikely, even if the younger child did not want to tell his parents that psychiatric treatment was undertaken, that the treatment would be very successful without notification of the parents, since parental cooperation in family-centered therapy is at this stage of the child's development a most successful means of treating the child's problem. For reasons of sound psychiatric practice there may be a difference between accepting a 16- or a 17-year-old in psychotherapy on an individual basis and without parental knowledge and on the other hand refusing to accept a 12- or 13-year-old, whose problems are so much more entwined with his interactions with his parents that it is useless to attempt to treat him without parental consent.

The parent may, of course, bring an action for malpractice on behalf of the child if the psychiatric treatment is negligent even though the minor has the clear right to consent to proper treatment. Furthermore, advocacy by a psychiatrist of some form of behavior that would constitute an act of delinquency, such as running away, entering into a sexual relationship in which the minor is not already active, or the illegal use of drugs, might well result in a criminal conviction of contributing to the delinquency of the patient. Needless to say, statutory rape is a very serious crime, and it is no defense to allege that sexual intercourse with a minor patient was undertaken with therapeutic intent. In fact, any such claim is likely to result in a revocation of a medical license in addition to a jail sentence.[21]

A teenage girl engaged in very promiscuous sexual activities. Her parents sent her to a psychiatrist, whose treatment consisted of having intercourse with her. He was convicted of statutory rape and his license to practice was revoked. The court held that this particular offense was not only "a crime involving moral turpitude" but also violated the position of trust in which he had placed himself.[22]

To differentiate between the substantive quality of advice or therapy given on the basis of the therapist's license or credentials or to argue that the adolescent's legal right to consent to psychotherapy should depend on these credentials might appear unduly obsequious to "mainline psychiatry." However, licensing laws and the process of residency training in psychiatry and clinical residency guarantee a legally determinable and enforceable standard of due skill, care, and knowledge. These standards do not exist for social workers, drug counselors, or other nonphysician personnel now engaged in various forms of counseling. There may be social workers in private practice who in fact are more adept in working with adolescents than most board-certified psychiatrists. In attempting to set legal policy, however, one must rely on general assumptions, and by analogy, none of the minor treatment statutes gives a minor the right to consent to treatment by a chiropractor. As difficult as it may be to enforce a patient's claim of negligence against a psychiatrist or psychologist, it is virtually impossible to do so against other types of counselors because of the lack of legally established standards of due care. In case of negligent treatment, an adolescent can at least have recourse in law for damages against a psychiatrist or clinical psychologist. It is likely that a court would deem sensible a policy of allowing the adolescent to consent to treatment in proportion to the higher standard of care imposed on physicians and qualified clinical psychologists, since it does not appear equitable in law to hold an adolescent who is troubled enough to want help to the doctrine of assumption of risk if he encounters some unusual or bizarre form of therapy.

THE RIGHT TO REFUSE TREATMENT

Treatment Requested by Parents

Many forms of behavior that may seem perfectly rational to an adolescent can be interpreted by a parent as sufficiently abnormal to warrant psychiatric intervention, at least on an outpatient basis. A parent may object to a child's desire to seek psychiatric treatment because the parent feels embarrassed or threatened by the fact that the child needs help, and having a child see a psychiatrist may make the parent feel that he or she has failed. In many cases this feeling of failure may be sufficient to eliminate the parent's objectivity about the need for treatment. The same emotional forces may also induce the parent to insist that the child see a psychiatrist. The child's behavior, for example, may be a social embarrassment to the parent. An upper-middle-class child who looks as if he came from the depths of the ghetto, unwashed, unkempt, with long hair, and wearing torn blue jeans or who is engaged in some form of sexual activity or the use of marijuana or other drugs may convince the parent, particularly if the parent's moral values are rigid, that the child has gone raving mad. Thus, the child may be taken to a psychiatrist when what his parent really wants to do is to take him to the barber shop. The child's right to refuse treatment in this situation may present a serious issue for a psychiatrist.

An even more serious issue, and one that has not yet been consistently resolved by the courts, is the right of a parent to remove a minor child from the confines of a religious commune, such as those maintained by the Children of God and similar groups, and once the minor has been removed, sometimes by force, to have him either "deprogrammed" or placed in the care of a psychiatrist. Some of these forceable removals have involved cult members who have reached the age of majority, and the parents and those assisting them have, on a few occasions, been charged with kidnapping. However, recapturing a minor even by force is probably within the acceptable limits of parental prerogative, since there is ample evidence that the sanitary and psychological standards prevailing in most of these residences are less than reasonably acceptable. In terms of the scope of this discussion, however, the issue is the right of the parent to subject the child, once recaptured, to treatment to alter the child's religious, political, or philosophical convictions which he adopted while a member of the group. Erikson's analysis of the adolescent's propensities for acceptance of deviant philosophical systems is clearly applicable in these situations, but the problem remains that the child's right to freedom of religious thought is definitely protected, at least in other contexts, by the First Amendment.[23] At present there do not appear to have been any false imprisonment suits brought by minors against psychiatrists who hospitalized them at their parents' request after they were removed from these groups, or any malpractice suits for outpatient treatment under the same circumstances. As the result of the special protection given to religious freedom under our legal system, it is impossible to predict the outcome of cases that may arise in the future involving this situation. Running away to join a "deviant" group that is not involved with religion, however, would appear to constitute such a threat to the child's welfare, as well as being within the legal definition of a delinquent act, that courts would probably hold that the parent has a right to insist that the child have psychiatric treatment on an outpatient basis, although it probably does not constitute grounds for commitment.

By definition, this discussion involves those minors who would be generally considered "normal neurotics" in adult psychiatry. These adolescents are functional and are not engaging in any antisocial behavior of a criminal or dangerous nature. They have not engaged in definitive delinquent behavior and are not dangerous to themselves or others. Their parents simply think that they are "crazy" because they persist in doing things to which the parents object.

Any child who has the right to consent to treatment under the law apparently has the right to refuse treatment. Only one case has arisen specifically under a minor treatment statute involving outpatient medical treatment, and in that case the girl's right to refuse was upheld.

A 16-year-old girl refused to have an abortion. She was pregnant and wanted to marry her boyfriend, but her mother took strenuous exception to the idea and took her to a gynecologist for an abortion. The gynecologist, who was concerned about his potential legal liability, refused to perform the operation without a declaratory judgment or an order from the local juvenile court. The court refused to give the order, the mother appealed, and the Maryland Supreme Court held that since the child had the right to consent to medical treatment under the Maryland statute, she had an equal right to refuse it.[24]

As will be discussed below, several recent decisions indicate as well that a child may have the right to refuse to be committed on his parent's wishes.

As a fact of psychiatric practice, although it might be possible to subdue a teenager physically in order to remove his appendix or administer other medical treatment, it is absolutely impossible to carry out any form of effective psychotherapy by nonorganic means on an unwilling patient.[25] Involuntary visitors to a psychiatrist's office may not want help, may not trust those who are prepared to give it, and, since the treatment is in the long run ineffective anyway if the patient does not want it, it is a futile waste of valuable psychiatrist's time to attempt to treat an unwilling patient in any meaningful way. This discussion, of course, involves a minor who has not been committed to a mental institution and who is seeing a psychiatrist on an outpatient basis. If a psychiatrist undertakes to give a hospitalized child electroshock treatments or if psychosurgery or other therapeutic procedures of some organic nature were to be performed on an institutionalized minor, a court would be likely to hold that the child has a right to refuse the procedure or, on release, that he had a cause of action against the physician who performed it over his objection. These problems of the hospitalized minor are dealt with in the last section of this chapter. To analogize from cases involving mental incompetents who have been allowed the right to refuse treatment of physical problems, it is unlikely that a "normal" 16-year-old should be subjected to an invasion of privacy to the extent necessary to undertake conventional psychotherapy without his consent.[26]

In any case, all the young person has to do to enforce his right of privacy is to refuse to talk to the psychiatrist. Although the psychiatrist may be able to convince him that it would be entirely to his benefit to engage in therapeutic efforts, if the patient is unconvinced, he will not cooperate. The right to refuse treatment is in fact in the minor's hands in this situation far more than it is where he may be subjected to some forms of medical intervention, and hence no court intervention to protect his right is necessary. If, however, the alternative to psychiatric treatment is court intervention—that is, the child is given the choice between seeing a psychiatrist or being sent to reform school—due process and privacy rights should come into play as they do in any other juvenile court proceeding. His rights to equal protection of the law and due process would apparently include, although there are no specific decisions on this subject, the same right to privacy given to adults.[27]

A great deal of attention in recent court decisions and law journal articles has been devoted to discussions of whether the right of privacy—first enunciated by the Supreme Court in *Griswold v. Connecticut,*[28] declaring unconstitutional state statutes forbidding the use of contraceptives, and continued in the abortion cases—applies to minors. All the discussions that can be located on the issue of privacy and the teenager deal with adolescent girls' rights to contraception and abortion. In short, there is no case law at present on the subject of minors' privacy rights as a ground for refusal of psychiatric treatment. Nevertheless, given an increasing trend toward decisions holding that adults, competent and otherwise, have a right of privacy as well as of self-determination, which permits them to refuse treatment, it would be a most unusual court that held that a state had a compelling interest in denying the same privacy rights to minors in this context. Such a differentiation would probably be held to violate the Fourteenth Amendment right of equal protection of the law.[29]

A 16-year-old's privacy may in fact be of considerably more importance to him than privacy is to an adult. Denial of any respect for his dignity and privacy might be far more traumatic because of his developmental needs than it would be for an adult who is asked embarrassing questions in the course of some dealing with an authority figure. Therefore, the child should be legally accorded the same right to refuse psychiatric treatment as is given any adult in this country as long as the child is old enough to understand the nature of the offered treatment and his mental condition is such that an adult with the same problem would not be treated against his will.

Thus, it would not be practical to afford a disturbed 4-year-old the right to refuse treatment where virtually all 16-year-olds, no matter how disturbed, might be considered to have such a right. Since conventional psychotherapy requires, by its nature, a good deal of verbal ability, articulate understanding, and ability to express oneself, it would appear that any child to whom the service is offered with the hope of a reasonable degree of success would be considered capable of refusing to have treatment. In short, if the child is old enough to be engaged in conventional psychotherapeutic verbal treatment, he is old enough to understand that he does not have to be treated if he does not wish to be and therefore has the right to refuse to consent.

Treatment Requested by Other Persons

Although there are no cases discussing a child's right of privacy when the adversary party is his parent, in terms of school relations, several courts have held that children have a basic right of privacy under the Constitution which cannot be infringed by a school administration. These cases have involved such things as dress codes and haircut regulations.[30] The same principle has been applied to the right of pregnant and/or married students to attend public school.[31]

At least one court has held that a school system violates the minor's right of privacy if it sets up a system of routine psychological evaluations in the absence of any evidence of emotional disturbance in a particular student whose behavior indicates a need for treatment.

A junior high school administration undertook to administer a psychological test designed to identify potential drug abusers and to place them in a special program.

Parents were not told of the test nor asked to consent. Questions included many personal questions about the child and his family, including asking if the child was "hugged and kissed" when he was small, if his parents "made him feel unloved," and the like. In addition, students and teachers were asked to report other students who made "unusual or odd remarks," without guidance as to the definition of such remarks. Students whose scores reflected an unsatisfactory result were to be placed in a special compulsory group for potential drug abusers with no evidence required to show that the child had ever in fact used an illicit drug. "Deviancy" was to be defined by the group itself and was to include "not only socially proscribed behavior but any action which violates the group's specific normative system." Sanctions and punishment by the group were permitted. A 13-year-old eighth-grade boy and his mother brought suit to enjoin administration of the tests and implementation of the "deviancy" program on the ground that it violated the student's right of privacy and that of the family unit. The court agreed. The trial judge held that a minor's right to privacy is coextensive with an adult's, at least where the school system, not a parent, is in the adverse position to the child. Furthermore, the court regarded with extreme concern testimony by psychiatrists of the serious damage this information could do to a student in the hands of other students, teachers, or guidance counselors who have no training or qualification in psychological therapy but who confidently label a child as a "potential drug abuser." As an example, the court pointed out that other students accused the minor plaintiff of being a drug user because his mother had objected to his participation in the test.[32]

It appears, therefore, that students have a right of privacy in regard to certain aspects of their lives, and it is not inarguable that the same right of privacy should be extended to the right to refuse psychiatric treatment even at the request of the parents.

CONFIDENTIALITY

General Principles of Confidentiality

Once the problems of consent have been resolved, the child wishes to engage in psychotherapy, and the parent is willing to pay the bill or other arrangements have been made, the next issue that may arise is that of confidentiality. After several sessions the parent may come to the psychiatrist and want to know what the child has told him. What is the psychiatrist's obligation of confidentiality to a minor patient? What comment there has been in both case law and legal discussions on the subject of confidentiality involves either physician-patient privilege as it applies to testimony in court or any right the patient—medical, surgical, or psychiatric—has to confidentiality as to information revealed to employers, schools, insurance companies, or others outside his family. There is no legal ruling at present on the confidentiality problem in regard to any right a minor may have to keep his statements to physicians protected from invasion by parental curiosity.

In the practice of pediatrics, however, the physician-patient relationship exists between the physician and the child even though the parent pays the bill. Therefore, there is a considerable body of case law to the effect that a pediatrician, even where not protected by statute, who reports a child abuse case to the proper authorities has not violated the physician-patient privilege because his patient is the child.[33]

Breach of confidence is a well-recognized cause of action against any physician, particularly a psychiatrist.[34] In some states, in fact, statutes provide that a physician may lose his license for unjustified dissemination of confidential information,[35] and it is a criminal offense in the state of Michigan.[36]

Reporting to one spouse information concerning the mental or physical condition of the other, however, is usually not considered a breach of confidence even if the physician has reason to believe that the information would be used against the patient in a future action to dissolve the marriage or in an action such as a child custody case. In one situation involving a couple who were, to the physician's knowledge, separated but not yet divorced, the wife sued the physician for divulging information to her husband, but the court held that the husband had "the right to know."[37] In another case a physician specifically knew that the information he gave a husband involving his wife, the patient, would be used in a pending divorce action, but the court held that the patient's rights had not been violated.[38] Both decisions involved a physician who was treating the patient for a medical problem.

Within the past few years several decisions have held that a married woman does not have to obtain her husband's consent to have an abortion, and that in fact she is not even obligated to tell him that she plans to undergo the procedure.[39] All the confidentiality decisions involving conflicts between spouses predate the Supreme Court's abortion decisions. These decisions are currently being construed in a variety of contexts as creating a right of privacy for the woman even in relation to her husband. In the future it is probable that courts will apply the same rights of spousal confidentiality to the physician-patient relationship in all aspects of medical and psychiatric treatment as is now being applied to abortions. In fact, the only recent intraspousal confidentiality case involved a psychiatrist.

A woman was awarded custody of her three small children at the time she was divorced from her husband. After she obtained custody, however, by private agreement she and her former husband decided that the children would live with their father for a period of several months. At the end of the period to which they had agreed, when the mother wanted the children returned, their father refused to do so. She filed suit to obtain physical possession of the children. At the time the mother attempted to regain possession of the children, she was seeing a private psychiatrist. She had been a voluntary patient in a mental hospital at some time during the marriage. She had also been in outpatient psychotherapy most of the time for several years prior to the divorce. The husband's attorney contacted the psychiatrist, and the psychiatrist voluntarily gave the attorney an eight-page affidavit, which included his opinion that the mother was unfit to have custody. He also disclosed factual information about her life that had not been known to the former husband. The affidavit was given without the knowledge of the patient, and at no time did she consent to the release of the information. As a result of the affidavit's admission into evidence, her former husband was allowed to keep the children. The woman sued the psychiatrist for malpractice. The trial court awarded a summary judgment for the defendant on the ground that confidentiality does not apply in custody cases because the best interests of the child prevail over any parental rights. The appellate court, however, reversed the decision. It held that in some circumstances psychiatrists can be subpoenaed to testify about the condition of a party to a custody case but that there is an absolute privilege in the absence of subpoena. In this case the psychiatrist had volunteered the information to the attorney, and therefore it was held that the former patient did have a cause of action against him for so doing.[40]

This rule is the norm in any medical treatment situation involving public disclosures. Although there is considerable confusion in the law of privilege under subpoena, it is clear that the physician who aids the adverse party prior to the trial of a case involving treatment he has given is guilty of a breach of confidentiality.[41] For example, if an orthopedist has treated a patient who had been in an automobile accident and the patient has filed suit against the other driver, since the condition of the patient is the subject of the litigation the orthopedist probably has to testify at the trial. If, however, prior to trial, in an effort to obtain a settlement, counsel for the other driver comes to the orthopedist and wants "the lowdown" on the patient and the orthopedist cooperates, the patient has a cause of action against him.[42] In a parent-child conflict, the parent and child may in fact be genuinely adverse parties due to the nature of their relationship, and the psychiatrist should assume in most cases that anything he tells the parent will be used against the child.

Disclosure to Parents

The psychiatrist, of course, generally knows more about what his patient thinks about many people and what he is doing than does a physician or a surgeon who treats the same patient for a medical problem. In the case of a minor in psychotherapy the young person may have given the psychiatrist a great deal of factual information about his parents and siblings as well as revealing what he thinks of them. This factual information may be true, some of it may be fantasy, and some of it may be lies, either deliberate or related in good faith about a situation the young person misunderstood. A parent may feel threatened by the idea of the child telling a perfect stranger what he thinks of everyone in the household. This may be extremely frightening to a parent who feels insecure himself, and therefore he may simply be eager to inquire about information "just to know what's going on." Second, the parent may be genuinely concerned about the child's behavior and may seek information from the psychiatrist since most adolescents tend to be uncommunicative to their parents. For example, if a teenage girl is seeing a psychiatrist because she is "sexually permissive," the parents may be extremely concerned for very realistic reasons about the possibility of pregnancy but to be unable to persuade the girl to tell them whether or not she is continuing sexual contacts. The parents may therefore wish to obtain the information for what they believe to be the child's own good.

The most detailed book on the subject of privilege and confidentiality in the psychotherapeutic relationship does not discuss parent-child conflicts at any point.[43] In fact, these authors say:

> Child therapy can never be a strictly two person arrangement. . . . Therapeutic gains with the child will often be short-lived unless the parents are also able to change. . . . The psychiatrist may also find sensitive teachers who may be able, in consultation with the psychiatrist, to contribute effectively to the child's treatment through the teacher-pupil relationship. The broad treatment approach, however, does not, as is commonly understood, forsake confidentiality. The psychiatrist, as a matter of good practice, makes clear to both child (if he is old enough) and his parents the type of rapport he will have with each. Confidentiality, viewed realistically, is maintained. There is no publication to the world. The psychiatrist in this situation is working with persons who are directly responsible for the patient and who can assist in the treatment. Parents, after all, are legally responsible for their children.[44]

Disclosure to Other Persons

In other words, these authorities seem to take the position that a psychiatrist is perfectly free to, and in fact probably should, discuss anything he chooses with the parents of a minor patient and, moreover, discuss the situation with the child's teacher. This is a total violation of the child's right of privacy and as a matter of logic may be of questionable psychiatric practice. Particularly where such outside persons as teachers are involved, merely telling the teacher that the child is under psychiatric treatment may result in a total change in her attitude toward the child for the worse and may cause entry of the fact of treatment on the child's permanent school record for anyone to see. As a great deal of educational research shows, a teacher's estimation of the child's ability may, for good or ill, become a self-fulfilling prophesy.[45] If a teacher knows that a child is undergoing psychotherapy, she may thereafter view the child as aberrant. Once a teacher thinks that there is something seriously wrong with the child, the child may be at serious risk of becoming "difficult," since by placing him in therapy the parents have told him the same thing.

As a matter of any reasonable comprehension of the workings of a school, it would seem that the very last person who should be made aware that the child has been petitioned to a juvenile court or taken to a psychiatrist is his teacher. If his behavior in her presence is so disturbed that he cannot function or is seriously disturbing to others, it is the teacher's responsibility to attempt to institute alleviation of his problems. At that point in a conference with the parents, the parents may choose to reveal that the child is in therapy. If the teacher has no reason to suspect that the child is disturbed, not only is it none of her business that the child is in therapy but also that knowledge may be actively harmful to the child.

It would seem that a minor should have the same right of confidentiality as an adult patient, including protection from disclosures solicited by his parents. In many cases the young person is seeing the psychiatrist in the first place because there is some difficulty in his relationship with the parents. If the patient discovers that his parents have been told what he has said to the psychiatrist, it is highly improbable that he will tell the psychiatrist anything else of any value. The trust and transference necessary for the therapeutic relationship to go forward will be shattered forever, and being dealt with in this fashion by the psychiatrist will probably make the child feel even more rejected than he may already feel.

Confidentiality and College Students

A considerable body of writing exists on the subject of confidentiality problems confronting college psychiatrists.[46] One authoritative work discusses the role of a college psychiatrist at great length, using the fairly obvious principle that a university mental health service should not tell anyone at the school that the student is in fact being treated unless the student's permission is obtained or there is a problem involving suicide, potential homicide, or some other type of extremely serious danger. The authors note:

> Some university health services quite appropriately notify students of exceptions to confidentiality in the following situations: where the student's mental condition is such that immediate action must be taken to protect the student or others from serious consequences of his illness; and when a student is referred for evaluation and an opinion or recommendation is requested.

This rule would appear to apply equally to parental inquiries, and if a parent discovers that his or her child is being seen at a university student mental health center, the psychiatrist would seem to be violating the patient's right of confidentiality to discuss the case with the parent in any way. In continuing their discussion of college students, however, the same authors maintain:

> What should parents know? Parents are legally responsible for their children and consequently they have a right to know about them. Under the law a person is regarded as a minor until he is 21 [this book precedes the ratification of the amendment giving 18-year-olds the right to vote] and until that time (unless he is emancipated) the parents are legally responsible for his care and in some states his misdemeanors. In psychotherapy, however, psychological age and the condition of the patient rather than chronological age must determine the approach the therapist will have to take in dealing with the parents.[47]

Except in cases where the psychiatrist is or should be convinced that the college student, adolescent, or younger child will do harm to himself or others, the minor should have the right of confidentiality across the board in any psychotherapeutic relationship. It is not a parent's business to know everything that a child does however young the child may be. If the psychiatrist feels that the child's parents should know nonemergency information, for example, reports of sexual activities as a result of which the psychiatrist feels that he should urge the patient to ask her parents to take her to a physician to obtain contraceptive pills, the legal system should provide the following:

1. That no information should be revealed without the child's consent.
2. That if the psychiatrist thinks that the parents should be aware of some information he must specifically obtain the child's consent to disclose it to them. If the child refuses to consent to the disclosures, the psychiatrist should abide by that refusal.
3. If the child refuses to consent to transmission of the information and the psychiatrist insists that the child's parents be told, the child should have the right to withdraw from treatment and the information allowed to remain confidential, since the child is at that time no longer a patient of the psychiatrist.

What constitutes an emergency for justified revelation to a parent or other person is, in the last analysis, a matter of professional judgment.

A college student told a university psychologist that he intended to kill his former girlfriend who had terminated her relationship with him. The psychologist was convinced that the student meant what he said and consulted two psychiatrists on the faculty. The three agreed that the boy should be hospitalized. He was picked up by the campus police, but the chairman of the Mental Health Service ordered his immediate release. Some two months later he killed the girl. Her parents brought an action against the university for having failed to warn her and thereby protect her from a reasonably foreseeable harm. The Supreme Court of California held that there may be a duty to warn of the threat of violence if it is likely that such a threat would be carried out.[48]

A parent's right to know should be less restricted than any "right to know" of a third person such as a teacher, particularly if the minor lives with his parents. If the child is threatening suicide or injury to another person, the psychiatrist's decision to report the information to the parents should be based on a far less stringent prediction of probability than would be necessary to believe that information should be divulged to the police, the threatened victim, or some nonfamily member.

By analogy, cases involving contagious diseases hold that a physician has a duty to warn family members in close contact with a person who has a contagious disease.[49] He is not obliged and in fact is not at liberty to tell those more remotely connected to the patient about the patient's problem. The obvious reason for this distinction is that the patient's family is more likely to contract the disease than anyone else. The same principle should be applied in psychiatry. Parents probably should know if there is any risk at all that a child may be dangerous to himself or others, even though the psychiatrist thinks that such conduct is unlikely. A young person who is suicidal or threatening suicide needs not only to be watched but should have extra support at home during the period of crisis. In that instance, telling the parents, if the situation is presented properly, may lead them to try to provide a more supportive, understanding, warmer atmosphere for the child.

Except in cases of threats of violence, however, a child should have the same right to sue for damages for disclosure of confidential information to his parents that an adult patient may have for disclosure of confidential information to a former spouse or other person. The assumption seems to have been made throughout the legal system, however, that parents have an ethical and legal right to total disclosure. The Buckley Amendment, for example, gives the parent, not the child, the right to inspect the school records of a student under 18.[50] An adolescent should have a greater right to know what evaluations have been written in his school file than his parents do. The parents' right of inspection should be limited in the absence of their child's consent to files of children who are too young to realize the implications of the statements contained therein. There is, however, no currently declared legal right of minors to enforce confidentiality of any type against a parent.

Disclosure to persons other than the parents, such as teachers or school administrators, is clearly actionable if it results in any damage to the minor. Never under these circumstances should any information, including acknowledgment of the fact that the minor is or has been a psychiatric patient, be disclosed without the consent of both the minor and his parents or, if the child is quite young, the parents.[51]

COMMITMENT OF CHILDREN AND ADOLESCENTS TO MENTAL HOSPITALS BY THEIR PARENTS

Commitment Statutes

There are two distinct standards for commitment of adult patients to mental institutions. Voluntary commitment takes place in most states where the patient and his physician agree that he would benefit from treatment. The voluntary patient is in short considered in need of help. Involuntary commitment of adults, at least theoretically, is reserved for those persons who are "dangerous to themselves or others."

Children, however, fall into an altogether different category. By statute most states allow "voluntary" commitment of a child by his parents.[52] A minor who is committed as a "voluntary" patient at the parents' behest is in a less legally protected situation than is an adult patient who is committed involuntarily. An adult voluntary patient in a mental hospital can leave at will unless he is deemed after his arrival at the hospital to fall within the acceptable category of "dangerousness" applied to involuntary patients, at which time he must be civilly committed and thus has the right to a judicial hearing. Barring a hearing he has the right to go home. An involuntary patient, on the other hand, has a right to a judicial hearing at the time he is admitted to the hospital and the right to release at the point when he is no longer dangerous to himself or others.[53] Most states, however, provide that a minor may not leave a mental hospital without the approval of his parents. If they choose not to have him returned home, he cannot legally leave the hospital. Thus, on a standard of reasonable due process of law, a hospitalized minor is in a far worse legal position than an adult.[54]

Unjustified Commitments

If all families were healthy, happy families, unjustified commitment would not constitute a serious problem. Unfortunately, however, parents sometimes commit their children because the children's behavior embarrasses them. One author says in regard to treatment of adolescents in mental hospitals:

> The move toward "freedom, love and peace" has incurred anti-social acting-out including increasing use of marijuana and psyche-delic drugs. Consequently, emotionally disturbed young men who are acting in a way that directly conflicts with their parents' stan-dards are being hospitalized in increasing numbers. In this sort of situation whose right to treatment do the advocates of this concept wish to guarantee? That of the parent to commit his rebellious son as mentally ill or that of the child to defy his parents without being subjected to quasi-medical penalties?[55]

Several cases indicate that some parents commit "embarrassingly peculiar" adolescents to mental hospitals without any serious attempt by the admitting psychiatrist to discover whether or not the child is actually mentally ill to the same extent that would justify involuntary commitment of an adult.[56] In conflicts within the parent-child relationship, society and the legal system apparently give the parent an almost irrebutable presumption of good faith. Parental power is allowed by the judicial system to extend to all areas of the child's life other than situations in which there is some authoritatively ex-pressed public policy to the contrary; and as one example of abuse of this power, parents do in fact "dump" their children in mental hospitals because their presence in the family is a source of annoyance or inconvenience.[57] The case law indicates that there are numerous situations in which parents have sought to incarcerate their children in mental hospitals for idiosyncratic rea-sons having nothing to do with the child's needs.

If the child refuses to conform to behavior standards imposed by the parent, society by and large apparently concludes that the child, not the parent, is the one who has the problem. This is not necessarily true. In many cases courts have found that parents were "railroading" their child into a mental hospital when his behavior embarrassed or irritated them.

There may be no question that the young person in these situations does have emotional problems. As has been noted by many writers, the adolescent's revolt against parental authority is normal developmentally, but for a success-ful outcome in the conflict it is important that the breaks and disruptions of attachment should come exclusively from his side and not be imposed on him by any form of abandonment or rejection on the parents' side.[58] Any child who is sufficiently rejected to be brought to a mental hospital for admission by his parents in the first place has very good reasons to feel traumatized, whether he had anything wrong with him prior to that time or not, and it is reasonable to suppose in most cases that the commitment is the final step in a protracted conflict. The question is, however, whether a mental hospital is the proper place for the young person to receive treatment.[59] Several cases indicate the propensity of parents to commit children solely on the basis of differing life styles.

A 26-year-old man's parents were divorced. His mother had remarried. At 19 he had begun to "act like a hippie." He had dropped in and out of several colleges, worked only sporadically, smoked marijuana, had been entirely supported by either his father or his mother and stepfather and had developed into a "flower child." He had gone to New York to live with his father, had an argument with him, returned to Florida, and moved in with his mother and stepfather. There were apparently continual arguments, more typical of midteenage conflicts than with 26-year-olds. One night his mother and stepfather were out, came home, and found him with a date in the house. The girl he was dating was black. The mother's response was to proceed the next morning to the appropriate authorities to file commitment papers. He was admitted to the Florida State Hospital, where he remained for 59 days. After release he filed suit to have his commitment erased from the records. Two psychiatrists at the hospital had diagnosed him as schizophrenic, but he provided expert testimony from three psychiatrists that he was not. At no point was it alleged that he had ever injured himself or been violent in any way to any person. The court held that the "strange philosophies" of the "flower child persuasion" were not conclusive evidence of mental incompetence and neither was dating a black girl. The court found that he had embarrassed his mother but she had continued to support him and made the explicit statement that a great deal of the trouble was her own fault, since if she had ceased to support him he probably would have gone to work and behaved himself. The final decision was that simply being an embarrassment was not evidence of mental incompetency. Although the patient in this case was 26, it is very probable that the same reason has been applied in many attempts to commit younger persons.[60]

A mother tried to commit her 17-year-old daughter to a mental hospital. At the commitment hearing a man introduced himself as a lawyer and friend of the mother's and announced to the court that he wished to represent the daughter's interests as well. The daughter, however, had obtained a lawyer from the local legal services society. Testimony was given by a social worker that the physician who had discussed the girl's problems with her had recommended commitment and had disclosed extremely personal information to the social worker without notifying or obtaining permission from the girl. The mother's claim was that since the girl was a minor, her parent was the proper person to waive physician-patient privilege and to consent to admission as evidence of the statements made by the physician to the social worker. The court objected and held that the physician-patient relationship privilege applied. It held that the physician himself would not be allowed to testify about the information related by the patient over her objection. Much less, the court said, could the social worker testify as to her conversation with the physician, since this was clearly hearsay evidence as well as breach of confidentiality. On the merits, the court ruled that if the mother was an adversary party, as was quite obvious in this case, the minor herself had a right to be heard and to be represented by independent counsel. The court found that the problems that the mother alleged indicated mental illness on the part of the daughter were well within the limits of normal adolescent behavior and reversed the order of commitment.[61]

A 16-year-old boy had an argument with his mother during which he apparently slapped her face but had never at any other time done any violence to her or to anyone else. He also stayed out later at night than she allowed, and he refused to tell her where he was going when he went out. She undertook to have him brought to the juvenile court, declared mentally incompetent, and committed. The juvenile court did so and the boy appealed. The appellate court refused to allow the commitment and in an exhaustive discussion of the facts concluded that the parent-child difficulties were primarily the mother's fault and that evidence to that effect should have been admitted at the commitment hearing.[62]

A 10-year-old boy had been placed in a foster home after he had been abandoned by his natural parents. When New York State enacted a statute providing for subsidy payments to foster parents who adopted their foster children, his foster parents applied for adoption and were granted the decree. He began thereafter to exhibit very troublesome behavior. He allegedly set nine fires, although the court found no realistic evidence that he had in fact done so, and he admittedly beat his dog to death. He was diagnosed as schizophrenic. The now-adoptive parents, confronted with these behavioral difficulties, tried to annul the adoption. When that was refused, they tried to have him committed. The court held that what was wrong with the child was perfectly evident from the transcripts of the adoptive parents' testimony, in which they admitted that they did not want the child and actually loathed him. The court found that the child had had no affection and no love and was simply trying to get attention. Not only did the court refuse to commit him, but the judge ordered the welfare department to remove him from his adoptive parents' home and place him in another foster home.[63]

These cases demonstrate that the assumption that a parent really has the best interests of the child at heart cannot always be made when commitment proceedings are undertaken. Therefore, it seems to be a legal anomaly that a parent can simply drive a child to the door of a mental hospital and have him admitted whenever he feels inclined, which in effect is what happens in some cases.

The Courts' Response

As the concern within the judicial system for all aspects of children's rights continues, there have been several cases in recent years indicating that children do have certain minimal rights of due process of law before being committed to a mental institution. Several lower-court decisions have indicated further that children do have a right to be released from a mental hospital or an institution for the retarded on constitutional grounds if they have been denied a fair hearing and representation by counsel.[64] In a case dealing with "voluntary" admission by their parents of retarded children to the state institution, a three-judge federal panel found unconstitutional the Tennessee statute authorizing the superintendent of a mental hospital to admit minors solely on the application of their parents or guardians.[65]

Two recent appellate cases have held that children do have a right to legal protection from unjustified and unnecessary commitment to a mental hospital.

A 15-year-old Connecticut boy had been signed in as a "voluntary" patient to a private psychiatric institution at his parents' request. Two years later, at age 17, he decided that he wished to leave, but his parents objected to his discharge. He brought a suit. The court held that as a result of Connecticut's statutory adoption of the "Patient's Bill of Rights"—which specifies that anyone 16 years of age or older can be admitted to a mental hospital as a voluntary patient on his own application, not that of his parents—it was only logical to assume that under the statute involved the same person could leave at will. Thus, the child had the right to refuse at least inpatient psychiatric treatment.[66]

A 15-year-old boy was committed by his mother as a "voluntary" patient to the state mental hospital in North Carolina. He applied for a writ of *habeas corpus* and discharge. The court held that the parent has the legal right to adopt such child-raising practices as he chooses, within reason, but that the parent's wish to commit a child may come from a variety of factors that have nothing to do with the child's best interests. Pointing out that there is ample evidence that persons who apply for admission voluntarily or involuntarily to mental hospitals are overdiagnosed, the court further held that the psychiatrist is likely to identify with the parent and to accept the parent's version of the facts. In recognition of the practical necessities of a speedy admission of a minor to a mental hospital under some emergency circumstances, the court held nonetheless that due process rights would apply. It permitted the admission of the child at the request of the parent but held that a due process hearing, with counsel appointed for the minor, must be allowed at the earliest possible time after admission to the hospital, and in no case might such a hearing be delayed for more than 72 hours.[67]

The problem arises about placement for the minor after discharge. It may be assumed that if a parent wants to get rid of a child badly enough to commit him to a mental institution with all the stigmas attached to hospitalization, the parent does not want the child to live at home. Given that logical assumption, it seems very unhealthy for the troubled young person to return there. Any child who is unwanted to that extent, if he is not already suffering from genuine emotional problems, will in due course develop them. Therefore, in addition to the normal procedural rights required in commitment hearings for involuntary adult patients and now increasingly required for minors, all minors committed to a mental institution by their parents should have a hearing that includes a report by an independent psychiatrist appointed by the court. This hearing should not only determine if the child is in fact mentally ill by normal involuntary commitment standards but also suggest a less detrimental alternative placement if he is not and if the minor is too young to leave home and establish an independent existence. By the time a parent wishes to commit a child, it seems that courts should make the assumption that the conflict is so pronounced that counseling either or both parties will be futile, at least on an immediate basis. Therefore, in the best interests of the child, courts should, as a part of their general jurisdiction over minors, be prepared to provide alternative placement as a matter of right. The child may very well belong neither at home nor in a mental hospital. If a state concludes that it will allow institutionalization of a child at the behest of his parents without stringent, objective examinations of the parents' motives, the child should have a right to alternative placement in a foster home or other institution.

Malpractice Liability

Malicious commitment is, of course, an actionable wrong as is false imprisonment. There are literally dozens of cases in which adult plaintiffs who have been committed by their relatives to mental hospitals for improper or malicious reasons have obtained substantial damages for false imprisonment and malicious commitment from both the relatives and the physicians who signed the commitment papers without actually examining the patient.[68] If this is a wrong for which an adult may be compensated, it is an even more grievous wrong to a child when his parents, the authority figures in his life, have done the same thing. By any reasonable definition of child abuse and neglect, an attempted improper commitment meets the accepted standard of provable harm. With the increasing number of states that allow intrafamily tort suits, it is likely that the minor may have a cause of action in tort for damages against his parents and presumably against any physician who signed commitment papers without making a thorough examination of the child.

For purposes of treatment, the presumption may be that the child's behavior that is bothering his parents may be "wrong," but such behavior should not be considered sufficiently deviant to result in commitment to a mental institution.[69]

Most adolescents exhibiting bizarre but nonviolent behavior which their parents believe indicates mental illness will in the normal developmental process outgrow it. As has been noted by many authorities, the same sorts of behavior that induce parents to commit children also result in many attempts by parents to place children within the jurisdiction of juvenile courts for punitive or allegedly rehabilitative purposes. A great deal of juvenile court intake work involving petitions signed by parents indeed involve acts that are totally trivial. As a committee of the California Assembly observed: "Well adjusted youths who need no help whatever from the courts typically at some time or other while growing up get drunk, stay out late, have sex, cut school, others rebel against parental authority. If left alone most survive and become normal adults."[70]

Most adolescent behavior that alarms or embarrasses parents and for which the parents then consult either a juvenile court or a mental hospital amounts to nothing more than a transitional acting-out hardly indicative of a lifelong commitment to criminal behavior or borderline psychosis. It remains obvious, however, that the number of these children being committed by their parents has increased markedly in the years since adolescents began to become involved with a freer life style.[71]

Thus, in terms of the physician's responsibility for the decision to sign commitment papers, a minor should not be committed to a mental institution by a parent for any less cause than would be required for the involuntary commitment of an adult; in other words, that the child is, under recognized standards of psychiatric practice, dangerous to himself or others. It should be at least as difficult, if not more so, considering the stigmatizing effects of hospitalization, to commit a minor to a mental institution than it is to commit an adult.

The same law of malicious commitment and false imprisonment that applies to adult patients would be applied to children in appropriate cases. A physician would be liable if he failed to comply with the state's statutory requirements and signed a commitment of a child he had not seen. Damages in these cases may be very substantial, and due care in diagnosis is absolutely necessary.

A 16-year-old freshman in college was very unhappy and discussed with her parents her desire to leave school. They urged her to return to school and promised her that if she still did not enjoy it she would be free to leave and come home. After several weeks she decided that she wished to withdraw and notified the dean of women. The dean did not ask the student if her parents knew she was going to withdraw, so the student did not tell the dean that she had parental permission for this move. When her parents could not be immediately located by telephone, the dean called in the school physician. The dean and the physician tricked the student into accompanying them to a mental hospital, where she was placed in a locked ward. After several hours of confinement she managed to make contact with a friend of her family's. He came to the hospital, talked to her, and then notified her parents, who demanded her immediate release. She was not, however, released until the next morning. The judgment against the school, the dean, and the college physician for abuse of process was upheld on appeal.[72]

Thus, although statutes in most states permit parents to commit their children virtually at will, serious questions of due process of law are involved. If a child resists hospitalization, he should have the same right to a fair hearing at which he is represented by counsel that an adult patient already has. Any physician who attempts to short-circuit the minor's constitutional right in this regard may well be faced with serious difficulties as a defendant in an action for substantial damages.

The issues involved in parental commitments of minors to mental hospitals may be resolved in the very near future. The Supreme Court of the United States has agreed to review a case from Pennsylvania in which the lower courts had held that the child did have the same procedural rights before commitment as an adult patient.[73] When this decision is handed down the issues will be clarified, and the child's rights in this situation will be much easier to enforce.

NOTES

1. See, for example, Group for the Advancement of Psychiatry, *Normal Adolescence,* New York, Charles Scribner's Sons, 1968.

2. Richard I. Evans, *Dialogue with Erik Erikson,* New York, E. P. Dutton and Co., 1969, page 34.

3. Erik Erikson, *Identity: Youth and Crisis,* New York, W. W. Norton and Co., 1968, pages 187–188.

4. E.g., Hoener v. Bertinato, 171 A 2d 140, NJ 1961; People ex rel Wallace v. Labrenz, 104 NE 2d 769, Ill 1952; State v. Perricone, 181 A 2d 751, NJ 1962; In re Clark, 185 NE 2d 128, Ohio 1962.

5. In re Sampson, 317 NYS 2d 641, NY 1970.

6. In re Karwath, 199 NW 2d 147, Iowa 1972.

7. James A. Baker, "Court Ordered Non-emergency Medical Care for Infants," 18 *Cleveland-Marshall Law Rev* No. 2, page 296, May 1969.

8. In the Matter of Seiforth, 127 NE 2d 820, NY 1955.

9. In re Hudson, 126 P 2d 765, Wash 1942.

10. In re Carstairs, 115 NYS 2d 314, NY 1952.

11. See, for example, Joseph Goldstein, Anna Freud, and Albert J. Solnit, *Beyond the Best Interests of the Child,* New York, The Free Press, 1973, pages 49–52.

12. Crawford Morris and Alan Moritz, *Doctor and Patient and the Law* 5th ed., St. Louis, The C. V. Mosby Co., 1971, pages 163–166; Angela R. Holder, *Medical Malpractice Law,* New York, John Wiley and Sons, 1975, pages 24–28; Harriet F. Pilpel, "Minor's Right to Medical Care," 36 *Albany Law Rev,* page 462, 1972; Walter Wadlington, "Minors and Health Care: The Age of Consent," 11 *Osgoode Hall Law J,* page 115, 1973; Younts v. St. Frances Hospital, 469 P 2d 330, Kans 1970; Lacey v. Laird, 139 NE 2d 25, Ohio 1956.

13. See Chapter V within this work and Lawrence P. Wilkins, "Children's Rights: Removing the Parental Consent Barrier," 1975 *Arizona State Law J* No. 1, page 31 for a full table of minor treatment statutes as of the date of publication.

14. E.g., McHugh v. Audet, 72 F Supp 394, DC Pa 1947; Hodgson v. Bigelow, 7 A 2d 338, Pa 1939; "Alternative Medical Procedures," 212 *JAMA* No. 2, page 385, April 13, 1970.

15. Abraham S. Goldstein and Jay Katz, "Psychiatrist-Patient Privilege: The GAP Proposal and the Connecticut Statute," 118 *Am J Psychiat,* page 733, 1962.

16. Ralph Slovenko, *Psychiatry and the Law,* Boston, Little, Brown and Co., 1973, pages 63 and 355; "Underprivileged Communications: Extension of the Psychotherapist-Patient Privilege to Patients of Psychiatric Social Workers," comment, 61 *Cal Law Rev,* page 1050, 1973.

17. E.g., "Counseling the Counselors: Legal Implications of Counseling Minors Without Parental Consent," note, 31 *Md Law Rev* No. 4, page 332, 1971.

18. E.g., Browning v. Hoffman, 103 SE 484, W Va 1920; Foxluger v. New York, 203 NYS 2d 985, NY 1960.

19. The Pediatric Bill of Rights Adopted by the Board of Trustees of the National Association of Children's Hospitals on February 25, 1974, is set forth in full and discussed in G. Emmett Raitt, "The Minor's Right to Consent to Medical Treatment," 48 *So Cal Law Rev,* page 1417, 1975.

20. American Academy of Pediatrics, Model Act, 51 *Pediatrics* No. 2, page 293, February 1973.

21. Cadilla v. Board of Medical Examiners, 103 Cal Rptr 455, Cal 1972.

22. Bernstein v. Board of Medical Examiners, 22 Cal Rptr 419, Cal 1962.

23. See, for example, Angela Holder, "The School Prayer Cases and the Right to Privacy," 12 *J Church State* No. 2, page 289, Spring 1970.

24. In re Smith, 295 A 2d 238, Md 1972.

25. Jay Katz, "The Right to Treatment: An Enchanting Legal Fiction?" 36 *U of Chicago Law Rev,* page 755, 1969.

26. In re Maida Yetter, 62 Pa D & C 2d 619, Pa 1973; Petition of Nemser, 273 NYS 2d 624, NY 1966; Palm Springs General Hospital v. Martinez, Fla Cir Ct, Dade Co, 1971.

27. See, for example, McNeil v. Director, Pautuxent Institution, 407 US 245, 1972, in which the Supreme Court held that cooperation with psychiatrists who wished to evaluate a prisoner could not be made a condition of release from a penal institution once the prisoner had served the term provided by law for his offense.

28. Griswold v. Connecticut, 381 US 479, 1965.

29. See Chapter X.

30. E.g., Breen v. Kahl, 419 F 2d 1034, CCA 7, 1969; Cordova v. Chonko, 315 F Supp 953, DC Ohio 1970; Meyers v. Arcata Union High School District, 75 Cal Rptr 68, Cal 1969; Massie v. Henry, 455 F 2d 779, CCA 4, 1972.

31. E.g., Perry v. Grenada Municipal School District, 300 F Supp 748, DC Miss 1969; Estay v. LaFourche Parish School Board, 230 So 2d 443, La 1969; Ordway v. Hargraves, 323 F Supp 1155, DC Mass 1971; Shull v. Columbus Municipal School District, 338 F Supp 1376, DC Miss 1972.

32. Merriken v. Cressman, 364 F Supp 913, DC Pa 1973. For a further discussion of the legal aspects of these testing programs, see Charles W. Sheerer and Ronald A. Roston, "Some Legal and Psychological Concerns About Personality Testing in Public Schools," 30 *Fed Bar J* No. 2, page 111, Spring 1971.

33. "Child Abuse and the Physician," 222 *JAMA* No. 4, page 517, October 23, 1972.

34. E.g., Boyd v. Wynn, 150 SW 2d 648, Ky 1941; New York v. Leyra, 98 NE 2d 553, rev'd on other grounds, 347 US 556, 1954; Berry v. Moench, 331 P 2d 814, Utah 1958; "Keeping the Patient's Secrets," 195 *JAMA* No. 5, page 227, January 31, 1966; "Physician's Liability for Improper Disclosure," 198 *JAMA* No. 7, page 331, November 14, 1966; "Disclosure of Confidential Information," 216 *JAMA* No. 2, page 385, April 12, 1971.

35. E.g., McPheeters v. Board of Medical Examiners, 284 Pac 938, Cal 1930.

36. Mich Stats Ann, Section 338.53.

37. Pennison v. Provident Life Insurance Co., 154 So 2d 617, La 1963.

38. Curry v. Corn, 277 NYS 2d 470, NY 1966.

39. E.g., Poe v. Gerstein, 517 F 2d 787, CCA 5, 1975; see also Chapter X on the minor's right to abortion without parental knowledge.

40. Schaffer v. Spicer, 215 NW 2d 134, SD 1974.

41. Angela Holder, "How Much Would You Tell a Lawyer?" 2 *Prism* No. 6, page 52, June 1974; Hammonds v. Aetna Casualty and Surety Co., 243 F Supp 793, DC Ohio 1965.

42. Alexander v. Knight, 177 A 2d 142, Pa 1962.

43. Ralph Slovenko and Gene Usdin, *Psychotherapy, Confidentiality, and Privileged Communication,* Springfield, Ill, Charles C Thomas Publisher, 1966.

44. *Ibid.,* page 57 et seq.

45. See, for judicial comment on this research, Merriken v. Cressman, *supra* at 32, and Hobson v. Hansen, 269 F Supp 401, DC DC, 1967.

46. Thomas S. Szasz, "The Psychiatrist as Double Agent," *Transaction,* pages 16–24, October 1967.

47. Slovenko and Usdin, *op. cit. supra* at 43, page 68 et seq.

48. Tarasoff v. Regents of the University of California, 118 Cal Rptr 129, Cal 1974.

49. E.g., Hofmann v. Blackmon, 241 So 2d 752, Fla 1970; Golia v. Greater New York Health Insurance Plan, 166 NYS 2d 889, NY 1957.

50. Buckley Amendment, 20 USCA, Section 1232g.

51. See the discussion on confidentiality as to inquiries from school personnel in Chapter VII.

52. The applicable statutes and procedures for commitments of minors and exhaustive discussions of both may be found in two recent and excellent law review articles: James W. Ellis, "Volunteering Children: Parental Commitment of Minors to Mental Institutions," 62 *Cal Law Rev,* page 840, 1974; and Louis Lessem, "On the Voluntary Admission of Minors," 8 *U of Mich J of Law Reform* No. 1, page 189, Fall 1974.

53. "Right to Release from Mental Hospital," 220 *JAMA* No. 10, page 1405, June 5, 1972.

54. See discussions in the articles in 52 *supra,* and the cases cited in this section.

55. Thomas S. Szasz, "The Right to Health," 57 *Georgetown Law J,* page 746, 1969.

56. Andrew J. Kleinfield, "The Balance of Power Among Infants, Their Parents, and the State," 4 *Family Law Quart,* page 410, 1970.

57. E.g., Lessem, *op. cit. supra* at 52, page 210.

58. Goldstein, Freud, and Solnit, *op. cit. supra* at 11, page 34.

59. See, generally, "Analysis of Legal and Medical Considerations in Commitment of the Mentally Ill," note, 56 *Yale Law J,* page 1178, 1947.

60. In re Sealy, 218 So 2d 765, Fla 1969.

61. In re Sippy, 97 A 2d 455, DC Mun Ct App 1953.

62. In re G., 104 Cal Rptr 585, Cal 1972.

63. In re Anonymous, 248 NYS 2d 608, NY 1964.

64. In re Lee, 6 *Clearinghouse Rev,* page 284, August 1972 and page 575, January 1973.

65. Saville v. Treadway, 8 *Clearinghouse Rev,* page 119, June 1974.

66. Melville v. Sabbatino, 313 A 2d 886, Conn 1973.

67. In re Long, 214 SE 2d 626, NC 1975.

68. See, for example, Holder, *op. cit. supra* at 12, and cases cited at pages 284–290 therein.

69. Aidan R. Gough, "The Beyond-Control Child and the Right to Treatment: An Exercise in the Synthesis of Paradox," 16 *St. Louis Law J,* page 182, Winter 1971. This article discusses parental recourse to juvenile courts for removal of "troublesome" children to reform schools, but the motivations and resultant problems for the minor are the same.

70. Report of the California Assembly Interim Committee on Criminal Procedure, Juvenile Justice Processes 7, 1971.

71. See statistical data on the numbers of children committed by parents in Lessem, *op. cit. supra* at 52, pages 191–192.

72. Maniaci v. Marquette University, 184 NW 2d 168, Wisc 1971.

73. Bartley v. Kremens, 402 F Supp 1039, DC Pa, cert granted 424 US 000, 47 L Ed 2d 731, 1976.

CHAPTER X

MINORS,

CONTRACEPTION,

AND

ABORTION

Nothing in the parent-child relationship during adolescence is more likely to produce serious conflict than sexual activity by the minor. The potential for serious disruption of the parent-child relationship is such that this issue may be among the most difficult with which the physician is called on to deal. What is his legal responsibility if a teenage girl requests contraceptives? Does a minor require parental consent for abortion? Are there any circumstances under which a sexually active minor may be surgically sterilized at the parent's request? These issues involve some of the most hotly debated ethical, medical, and legal subjects in the area of adolescent medicine, and this chapter attempts to give the physician some guidelines to follow when confronted with one of these situations.

CONTRACEPTION

The Supreme Court of the United States in 1965 declared that a state statute forbidding the prescription of contraceptives to a married adult violated marital privacy.[1] In that case, *Griswold v. Connecticut,* the Supreme Court for the first time held that a constitutional right of privacy existed. This right was held to be derivative from other specific guarantees in the Bill of Rights, and the Court held that it applied to sexual relations between spouses. In 1972 the Supreme Court held that the right of privacy also gave a constitutional right to access to contraceptives to unmarried adults.[2] The Court held that to "condemn the unmarried" to risks of pregnancy, which had already been declared unconstitutional, if the state required married people to assume them, was a violation of the unmarried adult's right to equal protection of the law under the Fourteenth Amendment. The Court specifically held in that case that the state could not show a compelling interest requiring it to regulate an adult's sexual activity.

In both of these cases the plaintiffs were adults. Thus, the question of a minor's legal right of access to contraception has never been the subject of a decision by the Supreme Court. All authorities in the field, however, seem to agree that the public interest in holding down the costs of welfare as well as the interests of the individual teenage girls requires that "something be done" about the number of girls in their early teens who have babies. One author reports that in 1970, 350,000 babies were born to unmarried minors in this country.[3] According to the 1968 Report of the Family Law Section of the American Bar Association, 1 out of every 19 babies born in 1967 was illegitimate.[4] More than 40 percent of those mothers were under 19 years of age and a "substantial number" were under 15.

After an exhaustive study, the section report concluded that refusal of a teenager's request for contraceptives is far more likely to result in her becoming pregnant than it is in her becoming abstinent. The report concluded:

> In view of the impulsiveness of the adolescent as well as the lack of foresight and trust-to-luck against pregnancy observed among sexually mature teenagers, the availability of birth control cannot be thought to be determinant of whether or not they engage in sexual relations. The development of a youthful standard of sexual morality is a matter for the home, church and the community; it cannot be maintained through ignorance of the availability of birth control.

The same position has been taken by many medical organizations. Canon 2 of the Pediatric Bill of Rights states the following:

> Every person regardless of his age shall have the right to seek out and to receive information concerning medically accepted contraceptive devices and birth control services in doctor-patient confidentiality. Every person, regardless of age, shall have the right to receive medically prescribed contraceptive devices in doctor-patient confidentiality.[5]

Other professional organizations have strongly advised that the individual physician should have the discretion to give contraceptives to minors. The American Medical Association recommends the following:

> Consistent with responsible preventive medicine and in the interest of reducing the incidence of teenage pregnancy . . . the teenage girl whose sexual behavior exposes her to possible conception should have access to medical consultation and the most effective con-

traceptive advice and methods consistent with her physical and emotional needs.[6]

Similar statements have been made by the American Academy of Pediatrics, the American Academy of General Practice, and the American College of Obstetrics and Gynecology.[7]

The American Medical Association suggested to its members that those physicians who chose to provide birth control to a teenager should, of course, attempt to obtain parental consent, consider the case history—which would, of course, include a determination that the minor is in fact already sexually active—reflect in the medical records for their own protection that the hazards of pregnancy—medical, social, legal, and psychological—would be greater than those inherent in administration of the contraceptive measures, and require the patient's signature on written consent forms.[8]

On the other side of this controversy are those who take the position that allowing teenage girls to receive prescribed birth control devices or medication will, first, increase immoral sexual activity and, second, destroy parental control of the adolescent girl. The Rockefeller Commission on Population strongly recommended in its report that teenagers be given free access to contraceptive information. This report was specifically rejected by Richard Nixon, then President, on the grounds that it would result in an increase in immoral activities and destroy parental control of the child.[9] When a statute was passed by the California legislature specifically granting teenagers the right of access to medically prescribed contraceptives, it was vetoed by Governor Ronald Reagan, who said, "Birth control should begin with—prior to marriage—saying no."[10] Thus, both deterrence of fornication and parental control are asserted as legitimate state purposes for legal restrictions on the availability of contraception to minors. For example, Governor Reagan continued in his veto message that the bill "represented the unwarranted intrusion into the prerogatives of parents . . . and would endanger the traditional vital role of the family structure in our society. . . . If this bill were to become law I believe it could establish yet another opening wedge into the ultimate removal of parental authority and prerogatives in any number of areas."[11]

The legal concept on which a right to obtain contraceptives can be based is that of the right to privacy. There has yet been no ruling on the minor's right of privacy where the conflicting interest is that of his parents and not the state. An increasing number of cases hold that the minor does have a right of privacy that prevents unwarranted state intrusion into his personal life. For example, children have the right to engage in peaceable demonstrations on political issues at public schools.[12]

A minor's mother brought a suit to enjoin the use of psychological test questionnaires asking very personal questions about family life in an attempt to identify potential drug abusers. The court granted the injunction and held that the child's right of privacy forbade such interference by the school.[13] Twenty-five years ago the Supreme Court began to hold that sectarian religious observances in public schools violated the parental rights of privacy in that area of their children's education.[14]

In all of the litigated situations, however, the parent and child were of a common mind, in opposition to the position adopted by some state official. Very little litigation has attempted to establish the boundaries of the parent's control of the child where the conflict is between the parent and the child and the state is not involved.

It is clear, however, that an increasing number of courts are recognizing some elements of the right of sexual privacy for adolescents. For example, a federal district judge recently declared unconstitutional a New York statute forbidding sale of nonprescription contraceptives to those under 16.[15] The judge held that minors have the same right to privacy in this regard as do adults and pointed out that there was no evidence that sexual activity increases when contraceptives are available. Only one decision has indicated a contrary position in this context, but it has been effectively abrogated.

A 16-year-old unmarried girl sued the Planned Parenthood Association of Utah, which had regulations forbidding acceptance of minors as patients for contraceptive services without parental consent. The Supreme Court of Utah upheld this position and noted that the right of privacy which gave adults the right to obtain contraceptives was "not intended to make strumpets or streetwalkers out of school girls." The trial judge had ruled that the girl's right of privacy had been invaded. On this point the Supreme Court of Utah held that the parents had a duty to instruct children and that the availability of contraception was more likely to induce the plaintiff to commit fornication and pointed out that since the court did not consider single minors to fall into the same category as married people, the regulation was not a denial of equal protection of the laws.[16]

The Department of Health, Education and Welfare has issued regulations applicable to all family planning projects that receive federal funds.[17] These regulations require that "services will be made available without regard to religion, creed, age, sex, parity, or marital status." Thus, in such clinics, parental consent requirements would seem to be prohibited.

This interpretation prevailed when a federal trial court in Utah held that the regulations that prohibited Planned Parenthood from providing contraceptive assistance to minors without parental consent conflicted with the Social Security Act and violated the minor's right to privacy, thus for all practical purposes abrogating the earlier decision of the Supreme Court of Utah discussed above.

A 15-year-old member of a family receiving Aid to Families with Dependent Children sought to obtain contraception from the Utah Planned Parenthood Association. Since she refused to attempt to obtain permission from her parents, Planned Parenthood denied her the services. She then sued the association. A three-judge federal court panel held that this regulation was illegal. The court held that states wishing to receive Aid to Families with Dependent Children funds from the federal government must have their plans for family planning programs approved by the Department of Health, Education and Welfare, and any plan that excludes persons eligible under federal regulations violated the Social Security Act and was therefore invalid. The only condition allowed under federal regulations is that sexually active minors must voluntarily request family planning assistance and may not be required to have it as a condition of receiving welfare assistance. Medicaid regulations also require that medical assistance be provided to all eligible persons. The court thus held that the parental consent requirement in the Utah system conflicted with the federal requirements and was therefore unconstitutional, at least as to a minor receiving federal assistance. The court also ruled that the parental consent requirement violated the minor's right of privacy, and thus the enforcement of the regulation was enjoined.[18]

It is argued by some that a physician who gave contraceptives to a minor without parental consent might be criminally liable for "contributing to the delinquency of a minor."[19] There have been, however, no prosecutions on this basis. The Ohio Supreme Court decided in 1965 that the "contributing" statute did not apply to the mother of a 16-year-old girl who was arrested for instructing her daughter in the use of contraceptives instead of requiring her to be abstinent.[20] The woman's conviction on that ground was reversed because it was held to violate the mother's freedom of speech. This case appears to be the only one in which any attempt has been made to bring criminal charges against anyone, physician or otherwise, for giving contraceptive advice to minors.

In terms of civil liability in the form of a suit by the parents, the result of any such case is likely to be a finding that the physician had the right to prescribe such drugs or other forms of contraceptives as long as the minor was already sexually active at the time that she asked for the drugs. It is extremely unlikely that a teenager will come to a physician prior to engaging in sexual activity, since most teenage sexual activity tends to be spontaneous and only after it is undertaken at fairly frequent intervals is the attempt made to obtain contraceptives. That being the case, some authors have argued that contraceptive services may be considered, in view of the alternatives, as emergency treatment: "On the basis of the recent developments in the law, it would seem then that there are many tenable rationales available to a physician who, after weighing all the circumstances, responsibly prescribes contraception to a sexually active minor. Certainly the trend seems to be in favor of his doing what his professional obligation requires."[21]

The authors of this statement suggest, however, that when dealing with a minor the following practices should be observed:

1. Inquiry should always be made as to the feasibility of parental consent.
2. A full case history, including preexisting sexual activity, should be obtained and maintained, and it should demonstrate that the physician has considered the "total situation" of the patient.
3. A record should be kept of "emergency" need and a judgment by the physician that pregnancy would constitute a serious health hazard, one more serious than the possible disadvantages of the prescription.
4. The minor should be clearly aware of the problems presented and the nature and consequences of the procedures suggested, including very specific discussions of the side effects of contraceptive pills if those are to be prescribed. She should be required to sign a consent form so indicating.
5. Where follow-up care is indicated, it should be insisted upon.

Thus, prior to a determination of the constitutionality of the right to contraception for minors, it is very unlikely that a physician would be found liable if he were sued by parents for giving contraceptives without their consent. In terms of the preservation of the family unit argued by opponents of this concept, it should be noted that by the time a girl wants contraception, is sexually active, and her parents do not know about it, breakdown in family communication is already at hand. Forbidding the procurement of contraceptives is unlikely to be a successful method of restoring the parent-child relationship to an ideal level.

The teenage girl who gives birth to a child out of wedlock is considered emancipated for the purpose of having the legal authority to release the child for adoption.[22] As long as the girl is considered emancipated for that purpose, it defies rational logic to believe that she should not be considered emancipated for purposes of preventing the conception of the same child.

If a court assumes that the parent has the right to control this decision and the parent's objection to contraception is specifically based on religious grounds, enforcement of the parent's beliefs by state law means that the parent's religious views are upheld at the expense of the minor's. It is at least arguable that the minor's right of freedom of religion under the First Amendment has been violated. One author has put it in the following way:

> There is a basic tension that inheres in the family structure between the adolescent's struggle for independence and the guardianship exercised by his parents. Resolution of that tension as the adolescent

progresses towards independence depends upon the complex interaction of the personalities of family members and the gradual transfer of responsibility from parents to child. Conditioning access to contraceptives on state-supported parental fiat rather than on the relative effectiveness of parent and minor in persuading each other to respect the other's values can unnecessarily upset the delicate workings of the family. In families where the parent retains most decisionmaking functions or where the parent automatically consents to the decisions of the child, the parental consent requirement may have no significance. But where the minor has developed a sense of responsibility and autonomy, or where the family has established an effective informal pattern of resolving conflicts, state-imposed consent requirements may undermine viable dispute resolution techniques. They may, for example, force the minor to discuss his activities at what is a particularly inopportune time from the adolescent's perspective. . . . Of course, the result of eliminating the parental consent requirement will be that in some instances minors will simply obtain contraceptives without informing their parents. But it is difficult to see why the state should attempt to compensate for such breakdowns in parent-child relations by reinforcing parental authority, especially since the practical consequences of withholding contraceptives are so much more serious than those of permitting access unguided by parents.[23]

If a parent refuses to allow contraception and the girl remains sexually active, it is at least arguable that the parent is guilty of child neglect. If one assumes parental knowledge of continuing sexual activities by a teenage girl and if whatever arguments or discipline the disapproving parents can muster are ineffective and the sexual activity continues, a good hypothetical case could be made that the parent is guilty of neglect if the girl is not provided with contraception arranged by the parent forthwith. Failure to provide necessary medical care constitutes neglect, as numerous cases have indicated. Considering the high risk of medical, sociological, and psychological problems occasioned by teenage pregnancy, it can be argued that the risk of pregnancy is just as serious as that of untreated appendicitis, and failure to obtain medical care for appendicitis would clearly constitute neglect. No court has yet discussed this possibility, but it would seem hard to dispute.

Therefore, the consensus among the authorities on this subject seems to be that the physician's first concern should be the welfare of his patient. If he determines that the use of contraceptives will serve her best interests, it is highly unlikely that he would be found legally liable for acting on his belief.[24]

If contraceptive pills are prescribed, as with any other drug with potentially serious side effects, the physician must disclose all reasonable risks to the patient and allow her to make the choice of contraceptive method. If the girl has an adverse reaction there would be no possibility of justifying a failure to inform her at the time the physician first prescribed the pills. Since the medication is elective, therapeutic privilege does not apply, and he could not claim she was incompetent to understand what he otherwise would have told her, because implicit in the physician's agreement to treat any minor without parental consent is a statement that he believes the minor to be capable of giving a valid consent.

In the last analysis, the imminent likelihood of pregnancy would appear to be the ultimate act of emancipation and at that point, attempting to protect the girl, her morals, or enforcement of the right of parental guidance by a court seems to become an exercise in "locking the barn door" after the horse has been stolen.

Thus, a physician who wishes to provide minors with contraceptive services may do so without undue fear of a suit by the parents for failing to obtain their consent or of prosecution for contributing to his patient's delinquency. Equally, unless the physician is practicing in a publicly supported clinic, he has the right to refuse to treat the patient if he feels that he would rather not. His objections may be based on moral, religious, medical, or other reasons, but in any case a physician in private practice cannot be required to accept any individual as a new patient if he does not wish to do so.[25] In this context, even if the physician is the regular physician of the adolescent girl, failure to comply with her request for contraceptives undoubtedly would not constitute abandonment if he can show that his medical judgment indicated that denying such services would be to her benefit. Since there is, however, an increasing sentiment that the patient does have a right of access to contraceptives, an appropriate course of action in the continuing care situation would be to advise the girl where she may obtain such help and make appropriate referrals, as the same physician would do in any other case where referral is indicated.

STERILIZATION

Surgical sterilization of a minor raises far different issues than those that arise in the case of contraception.

Eugenic Sterilization

The question of requiring eugenic sterilization of the mentally retarded or mentally ill has remained an ongoing legal, medical, and moral issue for decades. Around the turn of the century, many states enacted statutes that provided for the compulsory sterilization of "mental defectives," and at the present time 24 states still have eugenic sterilization statutes.[26] These statutes have been criticized as resting on unscientific assumptions as well as being unconstitutional, but at present there is no consistent judicial position that they are unconstitutional. In fact, in 1927 the United States Supreme Court upheld as constitutional state statutes providing for compulsory sterilization of the retarded, in a decision that included the famous sentence, "Three generations of imbeciles are enough,"[27] and the Court has not accepted a case on the subject for review since that time. Numerous state court decisions of the same era approved the statutes as necessary in the public interest.[28]

Recently, the number of decisions involving compulsory sterilization has declined sharply, but these statutes have been upheld as valid in some states within the past few years.

A retarded woman had eight children. She was confined to a state institution for the mentally deficient. Sterilization was made a prerequisite of her release. The constitutional attack on the statute brought by her attorney failed when the state supreme court upheld it as a valid exercise of the state police power. It further pointed out that whereas there is a natural right to have children, no individual's right to do so is superior to the common good. The court also held that the state did not have to demonstrate that the children the woman might have if she were not sterilized would inherit her retardation.[29]

A procedure to request involuntary sterilization may be commenced in 19 states by an application from a superintendent of an institution where the patient is confined.[30] Courts in states that provide for compulsory sterilization at the behest of a superintendent of a mental institution or other state official have, however, held that constitutional guarantees of due process of law mandate that the would-be patient receive notice, a guardian must be appointed, and a judicial hearing must be provided.[31]

Most, but not all, statutes provide that involuntary sterilization cannot be performed on a person who is not a resident of an institution for the mentally retarded.

A 13-year-old girl was declared a ward of the court as a result of a protracted series of indiscriminate and impulsive sexual involvements. She was placed in foster homes, a detention home, a state hospital, and a state school. Four years later, a petition for sterilization was filed with the Board of Social Protection as provided under Oregon law. The board allowed sterilization. In the judgment of the majority, childbirth by the girl would produce "a child or children who would become neglected or dependent because of the girl's inability by reason of mental illness or mental retardation to provide adequate care for them." The board specifically found that in all probability the girl's condition would never improve. The appellate court upheld the ruling on the theory that the law referred to the prevention of the birth of children who would become "dependent and neglected" because of the parent's inability to provide adequate care.[32]

Courts increasingly require very strict standards of proof of the necessity of the operation and have virtually halted the unfettered discretion of superintendents of mental institutions in these matters. For example, one federal judge has already held that before involuntary sterilization surgery can be performed on an inmate of an institution for the retarded, temporary birth control measures must be found inadequate.[33] Furthermore, inmates to be sterilized must be over 21 and must give an informed consent in writing after the director of the institution provides complete information concerning the nature and consequences of sterilization. The director must also prepare a report evaluating the inmate's understanding of the proposed sterilization. If the inmate is unable to consent, a judicial determination must be made that sterilization is in the best interest of the resident. Furthermore, prior approval of a review committee must be obtained. This committee must include a physician and an attorney, and at least two of the committee members must be women and two from minority groups. The committee must interview the inmate and concerned relatives, review appropriate medical, social, and psychological information concerning the resident, and determine whether he has given his informed consent for sterilization. The ruling also guaranteed the right to counsel throughout these procedures and specifically stated that consent cannot be made a condition for receiving public assistance or any other social services.

In spite of the fact that involuntary sterilization statutes are still on the books and are still used in some states, their constitutionality is subject to serious question. In view of the abortion decisions, it is probable that at some point in the future the Supreme Court will rule that since a woman who wants an abortion has a right not to bear a child, the woman who might be compulsorily sterilized is equally able to have as many children as she wants, in view of the fact that the right to privacy has now been elevated to a constitutional right that specifically includes the right to bear children.

In any situation involving involuntary sterilization under a court order a physician is well advised, both in terms of possible professional disciplinary action and civil suits by patients, to consult local counsel and to make absolutely certain that the patient's legal rights have been protected and that the court order is specifically authorized by a state statute. If the hearing was improper, a liability suit is likely, and an order that exceeds the statutory authority of a court to issue it will not be sufficient to make the physician immune from suit.

A 17-year-old girl had been brought before a juvenile court for sexual delinquency on three separate occasions. As a result, the judge ordered that she be sterilized, and pursuant to the court order a gynecologist performed a hysterectomy. The young woman filed a conspiracy suit against the judge, the gynecologist, and others, and claimed that sterilization had deprived her of her constitutional and civil rights. The court held that there had been no statutory authority under which the judge could have issued a valid order. Since the order was invalid, the gynecologist as well as the other defendants were not protected from suit, and thus the matter was ordered to trial against all defendants.[34]

Punitive sterilization for purposes of dealing with criminal offenders has long been declared unconstitutional.[35] Sterilization as an alternative for imprisonment for those convicted of a sex crime is clearly unconstitutional, and no physician should perform one even under a court order. Even if the offender consented, the coercion implicit in the choice between freedom with sterilization and long-term incarceration would serve to invalidate his agreement.

After disclosures were made that minor girls being treated at federally supported health facilities were sterilized without valid consent of their parents, Congress authorized a restriction on any attempt at involuntary sterilization under Medicaid and Aid to Families of Dependent Children programs. Under this mandate the Department of Health, Education and Welfare issued new guidelines restricting the circumstances under which clinics or other agencies that were recipients of federal family planning funds could allow performance of sterilization operations. These regulations required that both legally competent adults and minors were required to give informed consent to the sterilization and that affirmative assurances be made that continued assistance was not contingent on consent to sterilization. A special review committee of independent persons from the community was required to review a minor's consent. Any sterilization of a legally incompetent minor and/or a mental incompetent of any age was required under these guidelines to be sanctioned by both the review committee and an appropriate court. Personal consent was not required in these cases.[36]

These guidelines were challenged immediately on constitutional grounds and were found to be unreasonable and a violation of congressional intent. The trial judge held that the guidelines were insufficient to protect a minor or an incompetent. The court concluded that in federally assisted family planning programs, sterilization was permissible only with the voluntary, uncoerced consent of persons competent to give their consent. In its order the court declared that the Department of Health, Education and Welfare regulations were unreasonable and ordered the department to amend them promptly. The court further enjoined the department from providing funds for the sterilization of any mental incompetents or minors.[37]

As a result, in any program funded by the federal government, sterilizations can only be performed at the voluntary request of the would-be patient, who must be capable of giving "legally effective informed consent." The regulation continues:

(d) "Informed consent" means the voluntary, knowing assent from the individual on whom any sterilization is to be performed after he had been given, as evidenced by a document executed by such individual:

(1) A fair explanation of the procedures to be followed;

(2) A description of the attendant discomforts and risks;

(3) A description of the benefits to be expected;

(4) An explanation concerning appropriate alternative methods of family planning and the effect and impact of the proposed sterilization, including the fact that it must be considered to be an irreversible procedure;

(5) An offer to answer any inquiries concerning the procedures; and

(6) An instruction that the individual is free to withhold or withdraw his or her consent to the procedure at any time prior to the sterilization without prejudicing his or her future care and without loss of other project or program benefits to which the patient might otherwise be entitled.

(7) The documentation referred to in this section shall be provided by one of the following methods:

(i) Provision of a written consent document detailing all of the basic elements of informed consent (paragraphs (d)(1) through (d)(6) of this section).

(ii) Provision of a short form written consent document indicating that the basic elements of informed consent have been presented orally to the patient. The short form document must be supplemented by a written summary of the oral presentation. The short form document must be signed by the patient and by an auditor-witness to the oral presentation. The written summary shall be signed by the person obtaining the consent and by the auditor-witness. The auditor-witness shall be designated by the patient.

(iii) Each consent document shall display the following legend printed prominently at the top:

NOTICE: Your decision at any time not to be sterilized will not result in the withdrawal or withholding of any benefits provided by programs or projects.[38]

Sterilization at the Parent's Request

The usual situation involving sterilization of a mentally incompetent is an attempt by a parent or guardian to have a mentally retarded but sexually capable minor or adult sterilized as an alternative to institutionalization. In many states the parent or legal guardian has the right under a special sterilization statute to obtain such a ruling from an appropriate court and to give consent for sterilization on the same basis as he or she may consent to any other surgical procedure that is in the interest of the retarded person. However, if there is no such statute, no such judicial authority exists, since the incompetent, by the nature of the incompetency, cannot give his or her own consent to this procedure and it is not one that is necessary for treatment of an illness.

The mother of a 13-year-old asked a juvenile court to approve a hysterectomy on her daughter. The child's father was divorced from the mother, but he had also filed his approval of sterilization. At the hearing, it was established that the girl had an IQ of about 50; she had severe learning problems and was unable to care for herself. Although the juvenile court approved, the appellate court refused to allow the juvenile judge to authorize the procedure. It held that although the juvenile code was to be liberally construed to provide "care necessary for the child's welfare," it could not give a court power that had not been conferred on it by statute. Since no section of the state's juvenile code allowed a juvenile judge to authorize sterilization, and in fact no statute existed to permit any court in the state to order an involuntary sterilization, the appellate court held that no such power existed. The opinion distinguished the request from one for authorization of ordinary medical treatment or for surgery to preserve the life of the child.[39]

The mother of a retarded adult petitioned the court to have her sterilized. The daughter already had two children who were solely her mother's responsibility. The court denied the request, holding that in the absence of a statute permitting such a procedure, an incompetent ward did not have the legal capacity to give a valid consent and her guardian equally had no authority.[40]

A father petitioned a probate court seeking appointment as guardian of his retarded adult daughter and for authority to consent to therapeutic sterilization for her. He proved that he had been informed by experienced medical practitioners that the daughter was capable of engaging in sexual activities but was mentally unable to understand the results and implications of such activities. The trial court found that the woman's health would be severely impaired if she became pregnant, that the use of an IUD was medically contraindicated and that birth control pills which had been prescribed had had an adverse affect on her health. The probate court authorized the father, as her guardian, to consent to the performance of sterilization. The daughter appealed. The appellate court held that there was no statute conferring such authority on a probate court; thus, the court could not authorize such a procedure.[41]

A 15-year-old boy had been hit by a car when he was a young child and had sustained permanent brain damage. His IQ had been tested at 83 and he was in a special education class. Psychiatric evidence indicated that he would probably be able to earn his own livelihood. He began to want to date and have a girlfriend, and his mother petitioned a court to authorize a vasectomy. The court refused and the refusal was upheld on appeal. The appellate decision indicated that such an order would be invalid in the absence of specific statutory authority and further that there was no common-law power in parents to consent to such procedures since they are not medically necessary.[42]

Thus, even if the guardian or parent of a retarded individual requests sterilization, a physician should not undertake to perform this procedure without a court order granted after a full hearing on the question of the necessity of the procedure and its relevance to the best interests of the retarded person. The right to procreate is a basic one[43] and should not be denied, if at all, on the grounds of anything less than total incapacity to comprehend the meaning of parenthood. The eugenic sterilization program undertaken by the Nazis in concentration camps should serve forever as a reminder of the extreme lengths to which some systems will go in defining the word "eugenic." For his own protection the physician should be very careful not to undertake any such procedures under any condition without advice of his own counsel that a state statute permits it, the protection of a court order and consent of the guardian *ad litem* appointed by the court to defend the retarded person's interest, and the written consent of the parent or natural guardian who wishes the procedure to be performed. In the absence of a state statute that specifically allows such procedures, the physician is well advised not to do it at all.[44]

ABORTION

In January 1973, the United States Supreme Court declared that statutory restrictions on abortions during the first trimester of pregnancy were unconstitutional insofar as they exceeded the requirement that they be performed by a licensed medical practitioner. During the second trimester the state might require, if it saw fit to do so, that abortions be performed in a hospital or clinic with emergency facilities. During the last trimester, the Court held, the state did have the right to prohibit abortion except where the mother's life or health might be endangered by a continuation of the pregnancy.[45]

The Supreme Court based its decisions on the concept that the woman's right to privacy and control over her body gave her the right to decide whether or not to bear a child without interference by the state, except insofar as was in conformity with the limits on state action imposed in those decisions. All of the plaintiffs involved in the two abortion cases were adult women, thus the obvious question unanswered by the Court was whether or not a minor girl could consent to have an abortion without parental knowledge or consent.

The Minor's Right to Consent

Since the Supreme Court's decisions several lower courts have ruled on this problem. Most of them have held that a minor has the same right to privacy, and therefore to an abortion, as an adult woman. Several of these decisions also note that if a parent refuses permission for a minor girl to have an abortion when the girl wishes to do so, the minor, not the parent, is legally responsible for the support of that child after its birth and for providing it with a suitable environment. In almost all cases a grandparent is not legally liable for the support of a grandchild unless the grandparent has been awarded legal custody.[46]

On the other hand, the issue of parental control of the pregnant minor is again raised in this situation. There is, also, of course, the possibility that the minor may be so immature and so distressed by her unwanted pregnancy that there may be legitimate concern about her capacity to give a genuinely informed consent to the procedure.[47]

Prior to the Supreme Court decisions, the state of California and the District of Columbia had provided very permissive atmospheres for abortion. In both jurisdictions the abortion statutes were far more liberal than those obtaining in most other states. In each of them, decisions had indicated that "older minors" of 18 and 20, respectively, have a right to abortions without the consent of their parents and also without specific statutory authority permitting them to consent to the procedure.[48] In both those jurisdictions, however, statutes had been enacted permitting minors over 15 to consent to medical treatment of any type without parental consent, and thus the court held that abortions were no more nor less than ordinary medical treatment. The courts simply concluded, in both cases, that the minor treatment statutes emancipated unmarried pregnant minors for the purpose of obtaining abortions without parental consent.[49]

Since *Roe v. Wade* and *Doe v. Bolton,* the principal problem in dealing with minors' abortion rights is that the decisions were based on the right of privacy; that is, that decisions as to procreation should be made without intermeddling of outside agencies such as the states. The same right of privacy has been discussed for many years in cases involving protection of the family unit from outside interference by such entities as the public school system.[50] Since all prior cases involving privacy rights for the family have protected the parent-child relationship from interference from outsiders, little, if any, consideration has been given to the respective rights of privacy that may arise in conflicts within the family unit. Therefore, almost no case law is available on any right of privacy where interests of parent and child conflict.

However, almost immediately after the *Doe* and *Roe* decisions, lower courts began to make decisions on a minor's rights in this context, and in most cases the minor has been allowed to consent to the abortion.

A 16-year-old girl was living in an orphanage. Her mother had deserted the family and her whereabouts were unknown. Her father had not been able to care for his daughter and had brought her to the orphanage at the age of nine, although he remained in close contact with her. When the girl became pregnant, she asked for an abortion. The orphanage notified her father who consented at first but after talking with his priest withdrew his consent. The welfare department petitioned the court to appoint a guardian for purposes of consent. The court noted that since by statute in Delaware a minor over 12 could consent to medical treatment, the appointment of a guardian was therefore unnecessary and the girl had the right to consent to an abortion herself.[51]

The first case in a federal court arose in Florida. The Florida legislature revamped its abortion statutes after the Supreme Court's rulings. The new statutes required the husband's consent for the abortion of a married woman and parental consent for the abortion of a minor. Several gynecologists and obstetricians filed a suit testing the constitutionality of these statutes, and two pregnant women, one 18 years old and the other a married woman whose husband refused to consent, joined in the action challenging the Florida statute. The trial court found these provisions unconstitutional. After pointing out the fact that the *Roe* and *Doe* cases did not discuss the issues of the interest of the husband or the parents of unmarried minors, the district judge in Florida wrote:

> We are persuaded that if the state cannot interfere to protect the fetus' interest in its potential life until the compelling point of viability is reached, neither can it interfere on behalf of husbands or parents to protect their interest in that potential life until the fetus becomes viable. . . . If the State could demonstrate that the third-party interests sought to be protected by this decision attach at the moment of conception and are interests which fall completely outside the category of protection of maternal health and potential life, *Roe v. Wade* would not be controlling and the provisions would withstand constitutional attack. . . .
>
> We recognize further that the interest of parents within a family unit is qualitatively different, at least in part, from the interest which a pregnant minor daughter may have in her maternal health and the interest which the viable fetus may have in its potential life. The State of Florida has urged persuasively that the family unit is, except by positive provision of state law to the contrary, a self-governing entity and that the traditional and primary obligation for the custody, care, control and nurture of minor children resides in their parents.
>
> But while these paternal and parental interests may be compelling and may in fact exist at the moment of conception, it is apparent that not all paternal or parental interests fall outside the category of protection of maternal health and potential life. We cannot avoid the conclusion that at least a portion of the interests which husbands and parents have in their pregnant wives or minor daughters may

> be reasonably related to the protection of maternal health and pro-
> tection of potential life. . . . If [the Florida statute] allows the parent
> or husband to withhold consent out of concern for maternal health
> or the potential life of a fetus in addition to other compelling reasons
> they may have for doing so. . . . It follows inescapably that the State
> cannot statutorily delegate to the husband or parents authority the
> State itself does not possess. . . .
>
> A state which has no power to regulate abortions in certain areas
> simply cannot constitutionally grant power to husbands and parents
> to regulate in those areas. Therefore, husbands and parents cannot
> look to the state to prosecute and punish the physician or other
> participants who perform an abortion against the wishes of a hus-
> band or parents.[52]

This conclusion was affirmed on appeal by the Fifth Circuit Court of Appeals.[53] In the appellate decision the Court of Appeals held that minors do
have a constitutional right to privacy and that all criteria of *Roe v. Wade*
should apply to unwed teenagers even more than to adults in view of the more
serious consequences of pregnancy to a teenager's health. The Circuit Court
also pointed out that the ability of the parent to improve the quality of an
abortion decision reached by a minor is questionable, since the minor is required to be legally responsible for the care and nurture of the child if her
parents veto her decision and she has her baby. The court also answered the
objection that to allow minors the unrestricted right of abortion would destroy
parental control, by pointing out that by the time the teenage girl is pregnant,
effective parental control within the family has already broken down and that
the right to veto an abortion will not restore family unity. Other cases have
agreed with this view.

A 16-year-old girl with a five-month-old illegitimate child became pregnant again, and
her mother refused for religious reasons to consent to an abortion. The girl brought
suit to have the Colorado statute requiring parental consent declared unconstitutional.
The court found that she had been adequately counseled and informed and had made
an intelligent decision in favor of abortion. The court further held that the right to
privacy encompasses abortion and that although the state has a special interest in the
welfare of minors, many constitutional rights are being extended to them, of which
the right of privacy is one. The court held finally that the right to consent to abortion
should not be different from the right to consent to any other medical procedure and
pointed out that earlier cases that upheld parental control in matters of privacy had
been cases involving state intrusion and not parent-child conflicts.[54]

The same conclusion has been reached in Kentucky[55] and Pennsylvania.[56]
Most state statutes that require parental consent to a minor's abortion have

made failure to obtain that consent a criminal offense if a physician performs an abortion without consulting the parents. The Supreme Court of the state of Washington has recently held such a criminal statute to be unconstitutional.

A 16-year-old girl became pregnant and her parents refused to consent to an abortion. The girl petitioned a juvenile court to permit the procedure and the judge complied, although her parents and the Catholic Children's Services, which was her legal guardian, refused to consent. Her parents appealed and the appellate court issued a stay of the order pending determination of the issues. The physician performed the abortion in spite of the ruling and was found in contempt. He appealed on the ground that the statute requiring consent was unconstitutional. The supreme court of the state agreed with him. It held that the statute unjustifiably discriminated among groups of pregnant females and that parental consent requirements violated the privacy rights of the minor. The court said: "*Prima facie* the constitutional rights of minors, including privacy, are coextensive with those of adults. Where minors' rights have been held subject to curtailment by the state in excess of that permissible in the case of adults, it has been because some peculiar state interest existed in the regulation and protection of children, not because the rights are of some inferior kind. Parental prerogatives must yield to fundamental rights of the child. In the circumstances there seems to be little parental control left for the parents." The court held finally that any conclusive presumption that the parents' judgment is better than the pregnant girl's cannot withstand constitutional scrutiny and held that the age of fertility was the age of capacity to consent to abortion.[57]

The problem inherent in requiring parental consent is exemplified by a case that arose in Massachusetts which was then appealed to the Supreme Court of the United States.

The Massachusetts legislature enacted a statute making it a criminal offense to perform an abortion on a minor without the consent of both parents. The father of a 16-year-old girl told her after one of her friends became pregnant that he would throw her out of the house and kill the boy who was responsible if she ever became pregnant. When she became pregnant she was afraid to tell her parents and brought suit to have the state statute declared unconstitutional. The court found as a fact that she had an adequate capacity to consent and noted that many parents are unsympathetic and unsupportive and that communication with their adolescent children is very bad. Other children may not wish to tell their parents of their pregnancies because of the distress it would cause their parents. The court found that a significant number of minors are capable of giving a valid consent to abortion and held that the right of privacy does not have to depend on age. Since the girl's parents do not have to bear the child, the court held that in the case of adverse interests the pregnant girl should prevail.[58]

Only one case has held that spousal and parental consent requirements are constitutional. In that decision the court found that state interest is vital in protecting the marital relationship and in upholding the authority of the family. The court also held that a minor cannot as a matter of law give a valid consent to abortion.[59] The Supreme Court also agreed to hear an appeal in this case.

Courts, both state and federal, at all levels are apparently issuing consistent rulings, with that one exception, and are deciding that minors have the same rights as adults to abortion as long as the minor understands the nature and consequences of the operation.

A 17-year-old unmarried girl who was between eight and ten weeks pregnant appealed to the juvenile court in the District of Columbia for permission to have an abortion after her parents refused to consent. Her mother was a licensed and ordained minister who was opposed to abortion on religious grounds. The girl already had one illegitimate child because her parents refused to give permission for abortion when she became pregnant at 14 years of age, although she had wanted an abortion at that time. The court said that the girl had gone to an abortion clinic for counseling and was fully aware of the nature of the operation and further held that she was entitled to an abortion on either of two grounds: first, because she would suffer great and immediate harm to her physical and mental health if the pregnancy continued and, second, because rights guaranteed by the Constitution and the Bill of Rights, including the right to abortion, apply to juveniles as well as to adults.[60]

The consequences of refusal to perform an abortion on a minor may be very serious, since a girl who is intent on abortion is quite likely, if denied one by a physician, to turn to an illegal abortionist or attempt to abort herself. Either action may have serious, possibly life-threatening effects. To allow a parent to veto abortion without a concomitant requirement in law that the parent must assume total financial and parenthood responsibilities for the grandchild when born would appear to place the girl in a totally untenable position. Ideally, of course, in situations of such far-reaching consequences the girl should have her parent's understanding, sympathy, and support, but in an unfortunate number of cases parents do not behave in a supportive fashion. The extent of the problem and the number of girls who may need adequate medical attention for an unwanted pregnancy may be best reflected in a news report of September 14, 1974, that the Children's Hospital Medical Center in Boston had recently opened an entire pediatric abortion unit solely for girls aged 11 to 17 years.[61]

Some physicians have apparently concluded that the malpractice liability in these cases may be very high if the parent is not asked to consent. In one article, for example, a physician alleges that the minor does not have the right to consent to medical treatment and that "therefore as a general proposition it must be held that in the absence of a bona fide emergency the consent of the parent or guardian remains necessary for the operation on a child that carries some considerable risk to her life and well-being."[62] This view entirely overlooks not only the specific cases that have upheld the child's right to obtain an abortion in many states but also the general provision incorporated in the concept that a mature minor has the right to consent to medical treatment even in the absence of a specific statute to that effect. Furthermore, this view also overlooks the provisions of the *Restatement of Torts,* [63] which deals with the legal capacity of an unemancipated minor to consent to ordinary surgery. The *Restatement* provides: "If the child is capable of appreciating the nature, extent, and consequences of the invasion of his body, his assent prevents the invasion from creating a liability even though the assent of the parents is expressly refused."

The Pediatric Bill of Rights and the Model Act of the American Academy of Pediatrics adopt diametrically opposing views on this issue. Canon 4 of the Bill of Rights provides as follows:[64] "Every person, regardless of age, shall have the right to seek out and to accept, in doctor-patient confidentiality, the diagnosis and treatment of any medical condition related to pregnancy. Every person, regardless of age, shall have the right to adequate and objective counseling relating to pregnancy and abortion in doctor-patient confidentiality; and every person, regardless of age, shall have the right to request and to receive medically accepted treatment which will result in abortion in doctor-patient confidentiality." In contrast, Section 6 of the Model Act provides, "Self-consent of minors shall not apply to sterilization or abortion."[65] The Model Act was, however, drafted before the Supreme Court's abortion decisions, and revisions will no doubt take those decisions into account.

The Minor's Right to Refuse

The converse problem will arise where a girl wishes to have her baby but her parents refuse to allow this and want her to have an abortion. There has been only one case since the Supreme Court's abortion decisions in which a girl was required by her mother to present herself to a gynecologist for an abortion. In view of the likelihood that there are a fair number of these situations, it appears extraordinary that only one of them has been litigated.

A 16-year-old high-school student was pregnant. The father of her unborn child was also a high-school student. They wanted to get married, set up housekeeping, and raise the child. The girl's father was dead and her mother took exception to this plan and insisted that the girl have an abortion. The mother took her daughter to a gynecologist and asked him to perform the operation. In view of the girl's vehement objections to the entire procedure, the gynecologist refused, and in order to protect his own legal interests told the mother that he would not perform the abortion without an order of the appropriate juvenile court. The juvenile court held that the mother could not force the girl to have an abortion. The mother appealed and this conclusion was upheld by the Supreme Court of Maryland. The state statute gave a minor over the age of 15 years the right to consent to general medical treatment without specific regard to the nature of such treatment. The statute did not mention abortion. The court held in an extremely brief opinion that if a minor has the right to consent to treatment, that same minor has the right to refuse treatment, and therefore the girl had the right to have her baby if she wished.[66]

Any physician who would perform an abortion at parental request on a minor who objects runs a fairly high risk of being sued for assault and battery when the minor comes of age. Therefore, prudence indicates that any physician in this situation should tell the parent that he will not perform the abortion without a court order clearly authorizing him to do so. If no appeal is taken from the order allowing the abortion, the physician may assume that such an order will protect him from later liability from assault and battery, but under no circumstances should he proceed without one.

As was indicated in relation to the involuntary sterilization cases, if a court issues an order for compulsory medical treatment but exceeds its statutory jurisdictional authority in doing so, the physician is not protected from a suit for assault and battery on the ground that he performed the operation under that order. For this reason, in a situation in which adolescent girl objects to having an abortion at the request of her parents, the physician should either require an order from the highest court of the state, not merely a local juvenile judge, or include in the girl's file written opinion from his own counsel that the juvenile judge is explicitly empowered to issue such an order, and that if the girl does not appeal the judge's order within the normal time for filing appeals, that ruling cannot be overturned on grounds of lack of jurisdiction by a higher court when she reaches majority.

Since the Supreme Court's abortion decisions, various malpractice suits have dealt with abortion procedures, all of which have involved adult patients. Some have claimed that the woman was not actually pregnant at the time the abortion was performed.[67] Others have charged negligence in the method of abortion with the result that the patient's uterus was perforated or other damage was inflicted.[68] In some cases it has been proved that the abortion was unsuccessful, but the physician did not realize that the woman was still pregnant until too late for a legal abortion to be performed.[69] In all of these cases the standard of care required is that of the reasonably prudent medical practitioner who performs these procedures.[70] Considering the number of abortions performed every year in this country, however, there are extraordinarily few malpractice cases brought as the result of medical negligence during the procedures. The chief concern of a physician dealing with minors should be the consent problem, not any substantial concern about a negligence suit brought by the minor upon obtaining majority.

On July 1, 1976, the Supreme Court gave at least a partial answer to the questions of a minor's rights to abortion in the case of parental opposition or her refusal to divulge her pregnancy to her parents.[71] The Missouri abortion statute had specifically mandated that first trimester abortions required consent of the husband if the patient was married, apparently without regard to actual paternity, and of one parent if the patient was under 18 and unmarried. The Court found these provisions to be unconstitutional.

The majority opinion, written by Justice Blackmun, indicated that a husband's veto of a woman's right to abort would in effect have given him a state power that the state could not exercise under the rulings of the earlier abortion decisions. The opinion noted that, "The obvious fact is that when the wife and husband disagree on this decision, the view of only one of the two marriage partners can prevail. Since it is the woman who physically bears the child and who is the more directly and immediately affected by the pregnancy, as between the two the balance weighs in her favor."

Using the same principles as a guide, the Court also held that the state does not have the authority to give to a third party, a parent, a veto over a minor's right to abortion. The Court found that the interest of the parent is no more weighty than the right of "the competent minor mature enough to have become pregnant." The Court also noted that the veto power was designed to enhance parental authority but was in fact unlikely to do so in a situation where the girl's pregnancy has already fractured the family structure. Having thus indicated that any girl of normal intelligence who is old enough to get pregnant is old enough to consent to abortion, the Court then continued, without further amplification, to note that, "We emphasize that our holding does not suggest that every minor, regardless of age or maturity may give effective consent for termination of her pregnancy."

It thus appears that the Court was implicitly adopting the "mature minor rule" which, as was discussed in Chapter V, has been applied to situations involving other forms of medical intervention. The decision does appear to indicate that very young pregnant girls probably could not give effective consent as they cannot to other forms of surgery, whereas older girls would presumed to be able to do so. Pending further litigation on this subject, which now appears inevitable, it seems that consent can be negotiated for abortion on the same basis as it may be for other interventions, that is, on the basis of the actual degree of comprehension shown by the individual patient in discussion of any nonemergency procedure. In case of doubt, however, the girl should always be urged to discuss her pregnancy with her parents and obtain their consent wherever possible. Further, the Missouri statute dealt only with first trimester abortions and the Supreme Court decision quite clearly was limited to discussion of those cases. The right of a minor to consent to a procedure later in her pregnancy should not be assumed from this decision, and in general the same standards of comprehension required for an acceptable consent from a minor to a major surgical procedure should be adopted.

In a companion case decided on the same day[72] in which the Court remanded a Massachusetts statute requiring consent of both parents or a court
order permitting abortion of a minor back to state court for further definition,
it seems that the Supreme Court is willing in future cases to allow parents some
voice in the abortion decision of their minor daughter as long as their control
of that decision is not absolute. By implication, if the girl has the right to obtain
a court order or an alternative recourse if parental permission is refused, the
Court will not necessarily strike down some appropriate statute requiring such
permission if it is presented at a later time.

Thus, in spite of the recent ruling, the issues of consent to abortion remain
unclear at least in terms of the physician's civil liability in the event of a suit
by the parents. The statutes involved in both of these decisions were criminal
statutes, allowing prosecution of physicians for performing abortions without
parental consent and, in the Missouri statute, subjecting them to revocation
of their medical licenses. To date, no such civil action has been reported at the
appellate level, but it is certainly not impossible that one will eventually be
filed.

NOTES

1. Griswold v. Connecticut, 381 US 479, 1965.

2. Eisenstadt v. Baird, 405 US 438, 1972.

3. Robert P. Cavenaugh, "Minors and Contraception: The Physician's Right to Assist Unmarried Minors in California," 23 *Hastings Law J*, page 1486, May 1972.

4. "Family Planning and the Law," report, 1 *Family Law Quart*, pages 103–108, December
   1967.

5. See G. Emmett Raitt, "The Minor's Right to Consent to Medical Treatment," 48 *So Cal
   Law Rev*, page 1417, 1975.

6. *Proceedings of the AMA House of Delegates* 5556, June 20–24, 1971, quoted in Elizabeth
   Jordan, "A Minor's Right to Contraceptives," 7 *U of Cal at Davis Law Rev*, page 270, 1974.

7. *Ibid.*, page 290. Adele D. Hofmann and Harriet F. Pilpel, "The Legal Rights of Minors,"
   20 *Pediat Clin N Am* No. 4, page 1001, November 1973.

8. "Minors and Contraception," 216 *JAMA* No. 12, page 2059, June 21, 1971.

9. Nixon's statement is quoted in Judith Blake, "The Teenage Birth Control Dilemma and
   Public Opinion," 180 *Science*, page 708, May 18, 1973.

10. Neil Bodine, "Minors and Contraceptives: A Constitutional Issue," 3 *Ecology Law Quart*,
    page 859, 1973.

11. Ibid., page 860.

12. Tinker v. Des Moines School District, 393 US 503, 1969.

13. Merriken v. Cressman, 364 F Supp 913, DC Pa 1973.

14. McCollum v. Board of Education, 333 US 203, 1948; Zorach v. Clauson, 343 US 306, 1952;
    Abington Township v. Schempp, 374 US 203, 1963; Engel v. Vitale, 370 US 421, 1962;

Angela Holder, "The School Prayer Cases and the Right of Privacy," 12 *J Church State* No. 2, page 289, Spring 1970.

15. Population Services International v. Wilson, 398 F Supp 321, DC NY 1975.

16. Doe v. Planned Parenthood Association of Utah, 510 P 2d 75, Utah 1973.

17. 42 CFR, Section 59.5(2).

18. T. H. v. Jones, F Supp (unpublished), DC Utah July 23, 1975, 32 *Citation,* No. 8, pages 93–94, cert den 424 US 000, 48 L Ed 2d 811, May 24, 1976.

19. Cavenaugh, *op. cit. supra* at 3.

20. Ohio v. McLaughlin, 212 NE 2d 635, Ohio 1965.

21. Harriet F. Pilpel and Nancy F. Wechsler, "Birth Control, Teenagers and the Law," 1 *Family Planning Perspectives,* page 29, 1969.

22. E.g., In re Brock, 25 So 2d 659, Fla 1946; Petition of Gonzales, 46 NW 2d 453, Mich 1951; Matter of Presler, 171 Misc 559, NY 1939.

23. "Parental Consent Requirements and Privacy Rights of Minors: The Contraceptive Controversy," note, 88 *Harvard Law Rev* No. 5, pages 1018–1019, March 1975.

24. E.g., "Minors and Contraception," *supra* at 8.

25. For a discussion of the right of physicians to refuse to accept persons as new patients, see Angela R. Holder *Medical Malpractice Law,* New York, John Wiley and Sons, 1975, Ch 1.

26. Rex Dunn, "Eugenic Sterilization Statutes: A Constitutional Re-evaluation," 14 *J Family Law* No. 2, page 280, 1975. This article contains an appendix which includes tables of all current state eugenic sterilization statutes.

27. Buck v. Bell, 274 US 200, 1927.

28. State ex rel Smith v. Schaffer, 270 Pac 604, Kans 1928; State v. Troutman, 299 Pac 668, Idaho 1931; In re Clayton, 234 NW 630, Neb 1931; In re Main, 19 P 2d 153, Okla 1933.

29. In re Cavitt, 157 NW 2d 171, Neb 1968.

30. Samuel J. Brakel and Ronald S. Rock, *The Mentally Disabled and the Law,* rev. ed., Chicago, University of Chicago Press, 1971, Ch 6, "Eugenic Sterilization." This book is generally considered to be the preeminent authority on the subject of laws concerning the rights of the mentally ill or mentally retarded. The chapter mentioned has a table of all eugenic sterilization statutes in effect as of its date of publication.

31. State ex rel Smith v. Schaffer, *supra* at 28; In re Opinion of the Justices, 162 So 123, Ala 1935; In re Hendrickson, 123 P 2d 322, Wash 1942; Brewer v. Valk, 167 SE 638, NC 1933.

32. Cook v. Oregon, 495 P 2d 768, Ore 1972.

33. Wyatt v. Aderholt, 368 F Supp 1383, DC Ala 1974.

34. Wade v. Bethesda Hospital, 356 F Supp 380, DC Ohio 1973.

35. Skinner v. Oklahoma, 316 US 535, 1942.

36. 38 *Fed Reg,* page 20930, August 3, 1973.

37. Relf v. Weinberger, 372 F Supp 1196, DC DC 1974.

38. 42 *CFR,* Section 50.202.

39. In the Interest of M.K.R., 515 SW 2d 467, Mo 1974.

40. Frazier v. Levi, 440 SW 2d 393, Tex 1969.

41. In re Estate of Kemp, 118 Cal Rptr 64, Cal 1974.

42. A. L. v. G. R. H., 325 NE 2d 501, Ind 1975.

43. Loving v. Virginia, 388 US 1, 1967.

44. "Compulsory Sterilization," 221 *JAMA* No. 2, page 229, July 10, 1972.

45. Roe v. Wade, 410 US 113, 1973; Doe v. Bolton 410 US 179, 1973. For the most comprehensive discussion available of the theoretical bases for these cases, see Laurence H. Tribe, "Toward a Model of Roles in the Due Process of Life and Law," 87 *Harvard Law Rev* No. 1, page 1, November 1973.

46. See, for example, "The Minor's Right to Abortion and the Requirement of Parental Consent," comment 60 *Va Law Rev* No. 2, page 305, 1974; Harriet Pilpel and Nancy Zuckerman, "Abortion and the Rights of Minors," in *Abortion and the Law,* Cleveland, Case-Western Reserve Press, 1973, pages 275–309.

47. Richard Wasserman, "Implications of the Abortion Decisions," 74 *Columbia Law Rev,* page 247, March 1974.

48. In re Boe, 322 F Supp 872, DC DC 1971; Ballard v. Anderson, 484 P 2d 1345, Cal 1971.

49. Pilpel and Zuckerman, op. cit. *supra* at 46, page 280.

50. E.g., Meyer v. Nebraska, 262 US 390, 1923; Pierce v. Society of Sisters, 268 US 510, 1925; Wisconsin v. Yoder, 406 US 205, 1972.

51. In re Diane, 318 A 2d 629, Del 1974.

52. Coe v. Gerstein, 376 F Supp 695, DC Fla 1974, pages 697–699.

53. Poe v. Gerstein, 517 F 2d 787, CCA 5, 1975.

54. Foe v. Vanderhoof, 389 F Supp 947, DC Colo 1975.

55. Wolfe v. Schroering, 388 F Supp 631, DC Ky 1974.

56. Planned Parenthood Association v. Fitzpatrick, 401 F Supp 554 Pa 1975.

57. Washington v. Koome, 530 P 2d 260, Wash 1975, page 263.

58. Baird v. Bellotti, 393 F Supp 847, DC Mass 1975.

59. Planned Parenthood Association v. Danforth, 392 F Supp 1362, DC Mo 1975.

60. In the Matter of P. J., Sup Ct of DC, Family Div, February 6, 1973, discussed in 2 *Family Planning-Population Reporter* No. 3, page 57, June 1973.

61. *National Observer,* September 14, 1974, page 1.

62. Richard S. Gibbs, "Therapeutic Abortion and the Minor," 1 *J Leg Med* No. 1, page 36, March-April 1973.

63. *Restatement of Torts* 2d, St. Paul, ALI Publishers, Section 59.

64. Raitt, *op. cit. supra* at 5, page 1444.

65. Model Act, 51 *Pediatrics* No. 2, page 295, February 1973.

66. In re Smith, 295 A 2d 238, Md 1972.

67. E.g., Meyer v. Kaiser Foundation Hospital, Cal Sup Ct 1975, 32 *Citation* No. 10, page 112, March 1, 1976.

68. E.g., Bryant v. Inglewood Hospital, Cal Sup Ct, June 11, 1975, 31 *Citation* No. 12, page 136, October 1, 1975; Foster v. Birge, Cal Sup Ct 1974, 30 *Citation* No. 8, page 122, February 1, 1975.

69. E.g., Mechikoff v. Humphreys, Cal Sup Ct, 1975, 32 *Citation* No. 11, pages 125–126, March 15, 1976.

70. Michigan v. Nixon, 201 NW 2d 635, Mich 1972.

71. Planned Parenthood Association v. Danforth, 424 US 000, 49 L Ed 2d 788, 1976.

72. Bellotti v. Baird, 424 US 000, 49 L Ed 2d 844, 1976.

CASES

A. v. C., 390 SW 2d 116, Ark 1965. Ch 1, n 17; Ch 8, n 9.

People ex rel Abajian v. Dennett, 184 NYS 2d 178, NY 1958. Ch 1, n 40.

Abington Township v. Schempp, 374 US 203, 1963. Ch 3, n 77; Ch 10, n 14.

Agnew v. Larson, 185 P 2d 851, Cal 1947. Ch 7, n 53.

Alden v. Alden, 174 A 2d 793, Md 1961. Ch 8, n 51.

Alden v. Providence Hospital, 382 F 2d 163, DC CA 1967. Ch 7, n 8.

Alexander v. Knight, 177 A 2d 142, Pa 1962. Ch 9, n 42.

Allen v. Allen, 330 P 2d 151, Ore 1958. Ch 8, n 25.

In re Alsdurf, 133 NW 2d 479, Minn 1965. Ch 8, n 15.

Adoption of Anderson, 50 NW 2d 278, Minn 1951. Ch 3, n 101.

In re Anonymous, 248 NYS 2d 608, NY 1964. Ch 9, n 63.

In re Adoption of Anonymous, 345 NYS 2d 430, NY 1973. Ch 1, n 42.

Aronoff v. Snider, 292 So 2d 418, Fla 1974. Ch 1, n 78.

Adoption of Ashton, 97 A 2d 368, Pa 1953. Ch 1, n 20.

Atkinson v. Atkinson, 231 P 2d 641, Wash 1951. Ch 8, n 54.

Austin v. Collins, 200 SW 2d 666, Tex 1947. Ch 3, n 101.

Bach v. Long Island Jewish Hospital, 267 NYS 2d 289, NY 1966. Ch 5, n 10.

Baird v. Bellotti, 393 F Supp 847, DC Mass 1975. Ch 10, n 58.

Baker v. Owen, 423 US 907, 1975. Ch 6, n 30.

Baldor v. Rogers, 81 So 2d 658, Fla 1955. Ch 6, n 18.

Baldwin v. Butcher, 184 SE 2d 428, W Va 1971. Ch 3, n 17, n 18.

Ballard v. Anderson, 484 P 2d 1345, Cal 1971. Ch 3, n 100; Ch 10, n 48.

Bartley v. Kremens, 402 F Supp 1039, DC Pa, cert granted 424 US 000, 47 L Ed 2d 731, 1976. Ch 9, n 73.

Barwin v. Reidy, 307 P 2d 175, NM 1957. Ch 1, n 21.

Battistella v. Society of the New York Hospital, 191 NYS 2d 626, NY 1959. Ch 2, n 51; Ch 7, n 26.

Beadling v. Sirotta, 176 A 2d 546, NJ 1961. Ch 2, n 53; Ch 7, n 27.

Bellman v. San Francisco High School District, 81 P 2d 894, Cal 1938. Ch 7, n 22.

Bellotti v. Baird, 424 US 000, 49 L Ed 2d 844, 1976. Ch 10, n 72.

Bender v. Bender, 304 NYS 2d 482, NY 1969. Ch 8, n 61.

Benson v. Dean, 133 NE 125, NY 1921. Ch 2, n 15; Ch 7, n 17.

Bernstein v. Board of Medical Examiners, 22 Cal Rptr 419, Cal 1962. Ch 9, n 22.

Berry v. Moench, 331 P 2d 814, Utah, 1958. Ch 7, n 64; Ch 9, n 34.

In re Blaine, 282 NYS 2d 359, NY 1967. Ch 8, n 62.

Block v. McVay, 126 NW 2d 808, SD 1964. Ch 7, n 32.

Board of Education v. Homer, 362 NYS 2d 798, NY 1974. Ch 7, n 24.

In re Boe, 322 F Supp 872, DC DC 1971. Ch 3, n 100; Ch 10, n 48.

Bonbrest v. Kotz, 65 F Supp 138, DC DC 1946. Ch 3, n 12.

Bonner v. Moran, 126 F 2d 121, CA DC 1941. Ch 5, n 9; Ch 6, n 53.

Booth v. United States, 155 F Supp 235 (Ct Cl), 1957. Ch 7, n 8.

Bowers v. Talmage, 159 So 2d 888, Fla 1963. Ch 2, n 59.

Boyd v. Wynn, 150 SW 2d 648, Ky 1941. Ch 9, n 34.

Breen v. Kahl, 419 F 2d 1034, CCA 7, 1969. Ch 9, n 30.

Brewer v. Valk, 167 SE 638, NC 1933. Ch 2, n 92; Ch 10, n 31.

Briere v. Briere, 224 A 2d 588, NH 1966. Ch 1, n 75.

Britt v. Sears, 277 NE 2d 20, Ind 1971. Ch 3, n 17.

In re Brock, 25 So 2d 659, Fla 1946. Ch 10, n 22.

Brooks v. Serrano, 209 So 2d 279, Fla 1968. Ch 3, n 15.

Brown v. Board of Education, 347 US 483, 1954. Ch 3, n 73; Ch 7, n 42.

Brown v. Hughes, 30 P 2d 259, Colo 1934. Ch 1, n 29.

Browning v. Hoffman, 103 SE 484, W Va 1920. Ch 9, n 18.

Brune v. Belinkoff, 235 NE 2d 793, Mass 1968. Ch 2, n 21.

Bryant v. Inglewood Hospital, Cal Sup Ct, June 11, 1975, 31 *Citation* No. 12, page 136, October 1, 1975. Ch 10, n 68.

Buchanan v. Buchanan, 197 SE 426, Va 1938. Ch 6, n 33.

Buck v. Bell, 274 US 200, 1927. Ch 2, n 89; Ch 10, n 27.

Burge v. City and County of San Francisco, 262 P 2d 6, Cal 1953. Ch 5, n 5.

Burke v. Burke, 75 A 2d 42, Conn 1950. Ch 6, n 33.

Burns v. Alcala, 420 US 575, 1975. Ch 3, n 34.

Cadilla v. Board of Medical Examiners, 103 Cal Rptr 455, Cal 1972. Ch 9, n 21.

California v. Aeschlimann, 104 Cal Rptr 689, Cal 1972. Ch 8, n 33.

Callahan v. Longwood Hospital, 208 NE 2d 247, Mass 1965. Ch 2, n 31.

Campbell v. Campbell, 441 SW 2d 658, Tex 1969. Ch 5, n 5.

Campbell v. Wainwright, 416 F 2d 949, CCA 5, 1969. Ch 1, n 55.

Canterbury v. Spence, 464 F 2d 772, CA DC 1972. Ch 2, n 25; Ch 5, n 30; n 33; Ch 6, n 2.

Capelouto v. Kaiser Foundation Hospitals, 500 P 2d 880, Cal 1972. Ch 3, n 25.

Capuano v. Jacobs, 305 NYS 2d 837, NY 1969. Ch 2, n 32.

Carpenter v. City of Rochester, 324 NYS 2d 591, NY 1971. Ch 8, n 29.

Carroll v. Richardson, 110 SE 2d 193, Va 1959. Ch 2, n 49.

In re Carstairs, 115 NYS 2d 314, NY 1952. Ch 9, n 10.

In re Cavitt, 157 NW 2d 171, Neb 1968. Ch 2, n 91; Ch 10, n 29.

Chappell v. Masten, 255 So 2d 546, Fla 1971. Ch 8, n 21.

In re Adoption of a Child, 317 A 2d 382, NJ 1974. Ch 8, n 16.

Chrisafogeorgis v. Brandenburg, 304 NE 2d 88, Ill 1973. Ch 3, n 17.

Christy v. Saliterman, 179 NW 2d 288, Minn 1970. Ch 2, n 21.

Cidis v. White, 336 NYS 2d 362, NY 1972. Ch 5, n 24.

Cirillo v. Milwaukee, 150 NW 2d 460, Wisc 1967. Ch 7, n 22.

Ciulla v. Texas, 434 SW 2d 948, Texas 1968. Ch 8, n 79.

In re Clark, 185 NE 2d 128, Ohio 1962. Ch 4, n 18; Ch 9, n 4.

Clark v. Board of Education, 107 NYS 2d 582, NY 1951. Ch 7, n 22.

Clark v. United States, 402 F 2d 950, CCA 4, 1968. Ch 2, n 19; Ch 7, n 12.

In re Clayton, 234 NW 630, Neb 1931. Ch 10, n 28.

Clayton v. Stone, 358 F 2d 548, DC CA 1966. Ch 8, n 87.

Cobbs v. Grant, 502 P 2d 1, Cal 1972. Ch 5, n 32; Ch 6, n 2.

Coe v. Gerstein, 376 F Supp 695, DC Fla 1974. Ch 1, n 58; Ch 3, n 87; Ch 10, n 52.

Coffee v. McDonnell-Douglas Corp., 503 P 2d 1366, Cal 1972. Ch 2, n 54; Ch 7, n 27.

Coleman v. Garrison, 281 A 2d 616, Del 1971. Ch 1, n 70.

Colombo v. Colombo, 162 P 2d 995, Cal 1945. Ch 8, n 50.

Combs v. Combs, 327 P 2d 164, Cal 1958. Ch 8, n 52.

Commonwealth v. Bender, 178 A 2d 779, Pa 1962. Ch 8, n 51.

Commonwealth v. Edinger, 98 A 2d 172, Pa 1953. Ch 8, n 51.

Cook v. Oregon, 495 P 2d 768, Ore 1972. Ch 2, n 91; Ch 10, n 32.

Cordova v. Chonko, 315 F Supp 953, DC Ohio 1970. Ch 9, n 30.

County Department of Welfare v. Morningstar, 151 NE 2d 150, Ind 1958. Ch 1, n 22; Ch 8, n 23.

Craig v. State, 155 A 2d 684, Md 1959. Ch 4, n 25.

Cramer v. Hoffman, 390 F 2d 19, CCA 2, 1968, Ch 7, n 25.

Crovella v. Cochrane, 102 So 2d 307, Fla 1958. Ch 7, n 16.

Cullen v. Grove Press, Inc, 276 F Supp 727, DC NY 1967. Ch 2, n 103.

Curry v. Corn, 277 NYS 2d 470, NY 1966. Ch 2, n 45; Ch 5, n 37; Ch 9, n 38.

Custodio v. Bauer, 59 Cal Rptr 463, Cal 1967. Ch 1, n 69.

In re D., 290 NYS 2d 935, NY 1968. Ch 8, n 82.

D. v. D., 260 A 2d 255, NJ 1969. Ch 8, n 57.

Darrah v. Kite, 301 NYS 2d 286, NY 1969. Ch 5, n 28; Ch 6, n 40.

In re David, 256 A 2d 583, Me 1969. Ch 8, n 18.

Davis v. Rodman, 227 SW 612, Ark 1921. Ch 8, n 40.

Davis v. Wilson, 143 SE 2d 107, NC 1965. Ch 2, n 31.

In re Diane, 318 A 2d 629, Del 1974. Ch 10, n 51.

Dietrich v. Northhampton, 138 Mass 14, 1884. Ch 3, n 11.

Dietsch v. Mayberry, 47 NE 2d 404, Ohio 1942. Ch 8, n 39.

Dietze v. King, 184 F Supp 944, DC Va 1960. Ch 5, n 29.

Di Filippo v. Preston, 173 A 2d 333, Del 1961. Ch 5, n 29.

DiMartini v. Alexandria Sanitarium, 13 Cal Rptr 564, Cal 1961. Ch 2, n 22.

Dinner v. Thorp, 338 P 2d 137, Wash 1959. Ch 3, n 13.

Doe v. Bolton, 410 US 179, 1973. Ch 1, n 57; Ch 2, n 86; Ch 3, n 3; Ch 10, n 45.

Doe v. Doe, 314 NE 2d 128, Mass 1974. Ch 1, n 58; Ch 3, n 87.

Doe v. Planned Parenthood Association of Utah, 510 P 2d 75, Utah 1973. Ch 10, n 16.

Doe v. Rampton, 366 F Supp 189, DC Utah 1973. Ch 1, n 58.

Doerr v. Villate, 220 NE 2d 767, Ill 1966. Ch 1, n 68.

Domina v. Pratt, 13 A 2d 198, Vt 1940. Ch 7, n 11, n 49.

Application of DoVidio, 288 NYS 2d 21, NY 1968. Ch 8, n 59.

Dunham v. Wright, 423 F 2d 940, CCA 3, 1970. Ch 2, n 25.

Durfee v. Durfee, 87 NYS 2d 275, NY 1949. Ch 4, n 51; Ch 5, n 6.

Eaglen v. State, 231 NE 2d 147, Ind 1967. Ch 4, n 25.

Edwards v. Duncan, 355 F 2d 993, CCA 4, 1966. Ch 8, n 96.

Eich v. Town of Gulf Shores, 300 So 2d 354, Ala 1974. Ch 3, n 17.

Eisenstadt v. Baird, 405 US 438, 1972. Ch 2, n 83; Ch 10, n 2.

Ellis v. Ellis, 472 SW 2d 741, Tenn 1971. Ch 8, n 66.

Elmore v. Stone, 355 F 2d 841, DC CA 1966. Ch 8, n 87.

Endresz v. Friedberg, 248 NE 2d 901, NY 1969. Ch 3, n 23.

Engel v. Vitale, 370 US 421, 1962. Ch 3, n 77; Ch 10, n 14.

Ericson v. Ericson, 195 Pac 234, Wash 1921. Ch 8, n 54.

Estay v. Lafourche Parish School Board, 230 So 2d 443, La 1969. Ch 9, n 31.

Everest v. McKenny, 162 NW 277, Mich 1917. Ch 7, n 66.

Favalora v. Aetna Casualty Co., 144 So 2d 544, La 1962. Ch 2, n 20.

Fiorentino v. Wenger, 227 NE 2d 296, NY 1967. Ch 1, n 30; Ch 3, n 99; Ch 6, n 1.

Foe v. Vanderhoof, 389 F Supp 947, DC Colo 1975. Ch 10, n 54.

Fortner v. Koch, 261 NW 762, Mich 1935. Ch 1, n 29.

Foster v. Birge, Cal Sup Ct 1974, 30 *Citation* No. 8, page 122, February 1, 1975. Ch 10, n 68.

Fowler v. Woodward, 138 SE 2d 42, SC 1964. Ch 3, n 17, n 18.

Foxluger v. New York, 203 NYS 2d 985, NY 1960. Ch 9, n 18.

Frazier v. Levi, 440 SW 2d 393, Tex 1969. Ch 2, n 93; Ch 10, n 40.

Frederic v. United States, 246 F Supp 368, DC La 1965. Ch 2, n 22.

Funke v. Fieldman, 512 P 2d 539, Kan 1973. Ch 2, n 58.

In re G., 104 Cal Rptr 585, Cal 1972. Ch 9, n 62.

Gallegos v. Colorado, 370 US 49, 1962. Ch 8, n 80.

Gardner v. State, 22 NE 2d 344, NY 1939. Ch 7, n 22.

Gluckstein v. Lipsett, 209 P 2d 98, Cal 1949. Ch 2, n 26.

Golia v. Greater New York Health Insurance Plan, 166 NYS 2d 889, NY 1957. Ch 5, n 41; Ch 9, n 49.

Petition of Gonzales, 46 NW 2d 453, Mich 1951. Ch 10, n 22.

Goodman v. District of Columbia, 50 A 2d 812, DC Mun Ct App, 1947. Ch 8, n 4.

Gottsdanker v. Cutter Laboratories, 6 Cal Rptr 320, Cal 1960. Ch 2, n 100.

In re Green, 292 A 2d 387, Pa 1972. Ch 4, n 59.

Greenwald v. Grayson, 189 So 2d 204, Fla 1966. Ch 8, n 22.

Griswold v. Connecticut, 381 US 479, 1965. Ch 2, n 82; Ch 9, n 28; Ch 10, n 1.

Gursky v. Gursky, 242 NYS 2d 406, NY 1963. Ch 1, n 40.

Gustafson v. Gustafson, 158 SE 2d 619, NC 1968. Ch 8, n 60.

T. H. v. Jones, F Supp (unpublished), DC Utah, July 23, 1975, 32 *Citation* No. 8, pages 93–94, *cert den* 424 US 000, 48 L Ed 2d 811, May 24, 1976. Ch 10, n 18.

Haewsky v. St. John's Hospital, Mich Cir Ct Wayne Co, June 10, 1970. Ch 8, n 44.

Hale v. Manion, 368 P 2d 1, Kans 1962. Ch 3, n 17.

Hall v. United States, 381 F Supp 224, DC SC 1974. Ch 5, n 42.

Hammer v. Polsky, 233 NYS 2d 110, NY 1962. Ch 7, n 59.

Hammonds v. Aetna Casualty and Surety Co., 243 F Supp 793, DC Ohio 1965. Ch 9, n 41.

Hardman v. Hardman, 214 SW 2d 391, Ky 1948. Ch 8, n 55.

Hart v. Brown, 289 A 2d 386, Conn 1972. Ch 6, n 45, n 54, n 58.

Harvey v. Silber, 2 NW 2d 483, Mich 1942. Ch 2, n 28.

Harwick v. Harris, 166 So 2d 912, Fla 1964. Ch 7, n 14.

Hatala v. Markiewicz, 224 A 2d 406, Conn 1966. Ch 3, n 17.

Hathaway v. Worcester City Hospital, 475 F 2d 701, CCA 1, 1973. Ch 2, n 85.

Henderson v. National Drug Co., 23 A 2d 743, Pa 1942. Ch 7, n 53.

In re Hendrickson, 123 P 2d 322, Wash 1942. Ch 2, n 92; Ch 10, n 31.

Hendrix v. Hunter, 110 SE 2d 35, Ga 1959. Ch 1, n 16.

Hendry v. United States, 280 F Supp 27, DC NY 1968. Ch 7, n 15.

Hewellette v. George, 9 So 885, Miss 1891. Ch 1, n 74.

Hinkle v. Hargens, 81 NW 2d 888, SD 1957. Ch 5, n 25.

Hirons v. Director, Patuxent Institution, 351 F 2d 613, CCA 4, 1965. Ch 8, n 96.

Hobson v. Hansen, 269 F Supp 401, DC Cir, 1967, 408 F 2d 175, CA DC, 1969. Ch 7, n 5, n 20; Ch 9, n 45.

Hoder v. Sayet, 196 So 2d 205, Fla 1967. Ch 1, n 50.

Hodgson v. Bigelow, 7 A 2d 338, Pa 1939. Ch 9, n 14.

Hoener v. Bertinato, 171 A 2d 140, NJ 1961. Ch 4, n 18; Ch 9, n 4.

Hoffman v. Tracy, 406 P 2d 323, Wash 1965. Ch 1, n 76.

Hofmann v. Blackmon, 241 So 2d 752, Fla 1970. Ch 5, n 41; Ch 9, n 49.

Holland v. Metalious, 198 A 2d 654, NH 1964. Ch 3, n 44.

In re Holmes, 109 A 2d 523, Pa 1954, cert den 348 US 973, 1955. Ch 8, n 68.

Holmes v. Powers, 439 SW 2d 579, Ky 1968. Ch 2, n 93.

In re Hudson, 126 P 2d 765, Wash 1942. Ch 4, n 22; Ch 9, n 9.

Hundley v. Martinez, 158 SE 2d 159, W Va 1967. Ch 2, n 21.

Hutchins v. Blood Services of Montana, 506 P 2d 449, Mont 1973. Ch 1, n 50.

Hyman v. Jewish Chronic Disease Hospital, 206 NE 2d 338, NY 1965. Ch 6, n 38.

Incollingo v. Ewing, 282 A 2d 206, Pa 1971. Ch 2, n 18, n 20.

Ison v. Florida Sanitarium and Benevolent Association, 302 So 2d 200, Fla 1974. Ch 5, n 23.

Iverson v. Frandsen, 237 F 2d 898, CCA 10, 1956. Ch 7, n 62.

In the Matter of P. J., Sup Ct of DC, February 6, 1973, discussed in 2 *Family Planning Population Reporter* No. 3, page 57, June 1973. Ch 10, n 60.

Jackson v. Rupp, 228 So 2d 916, Fla 1969. Ch 3, n 56.

Jarboe v. Harting, 397 SW 2d 775, Ky 1965. Ch 3, n 22.

Jeanes v. Milner, 428 F 2d 598, CCA 8, 1970. Ch 2, n 32.

Jessin v. County of Shasta, 79 Cal Rptr 359, Cal 1969. Ch 2, n 84.

Jines v. General Electric Corp., 303 F 2d 76, CCA 9, 1962. Ch 2, n 51; Ch 7, n 26.

In re John Children, 306 NYS 2d 797, NY 1969. Ch 8, n 45.

Johnson v. St. Paul Mercury Insurance Co., 219 So 2d 524, La 1969. Ch 7, n 10.

Johnston v. Brother, 12 Cal Rptr 23, Cal 1961. Ch 7, n 55.

Jones v. Smith, 278 So 2d 339, Fla 1973. Ch 1, n 58.

Jones v. Stanko, 160 NE 456, Ohio 1928. Ch 8, n 38.

Jones v. United States, 308 F 2d 307, CA DC 1962. Ch 4, n 35.

Jorgensen v. Meade Johnson Laboratories, 483 F 2d 237, CCA 10, 1973. Ch 1, n 61.

Kaiser v. Suburban Transportation Co., 398 P 2d 14, Wash 1965. Ch 7, n 56.

Karp v. Cooley, 493 F 2d 408, CCA 5, 1974. Ch 1, n 29, n 62; Ch 3, n 88; Ch 6, n 19.

In re Karwath, 199 NW 2d 147, Iowa 1972. Ch 4, n 20; Ch 9, n 6.

Keesee v. Board of Education, 235 NYS 2d 300, NY 1962. Ch 7, n 22.

In re Estate of Kemp, 118 Cal Rptr 64, Cal 1974. Ch 10, n 41.

Kemplen v. Maryland, 428 F 2d 169, CCA 4, 1970. Ch 8, n 75.

Kenney v. Gurley, 95 So 34, Ala 1923. Ch 7, n 66.

Kern v. Kogan, 226 A 2d 186, NJ 1967. Ch 2, n 29.

Kesseler v. Kesseler, 180 NE 2d 402, 236 NYS 2d 472, NY 1962. Ch 8, n 46.

Keyes v. Construction Service, 165 NE 2d 912, Mass 1960. Ch 3, n 23.

Kinney v. Lenon, 425 F 2d 209, CCA 9, 1970. Ch 8, n 76.

Knapp v. Knapp 250 NYS 2d 390, NY 1964. Ch 8, n 56.

Knecht v. Gillman, 488 F 2d 1136, CCA 8, 1973. Ch 8, n 92.

Korman v. Hagen, 206 NW 650, Minn 1925. Ch 3, n 15.

Koury v. Follo, 158 SE 2d 548, NC 1968. Ch 6, n 6.

Kwaterski v. State Farm Mutual Automobile Insurance Co., 148 NW 2d 107, Wisc 1967. Ch 3, n 17.

A. L. v. G. R. H., 325 NE 2d 501, Ind 1975. Ch 10, n 42.

Lacey v. Laird, 139 NE 2d 25, Ohio 1956. Ch 5, n 19; Ch 9, n 12.

Landeros v. Flood, 123 Cal Rptr 713, Cal 1975. Ch 8, n 42.

Larrabee v. United States, 254 F Supp 613, DC Cal 1966. Ch 3, n 26.

Larry P. v. Riles, 343 F Supp 1306, DC Cal 1972. Ch 7, n 6.

In re Baby Larson, 91 NW 2d 448, Minn 1958. Ch 8, n 15.

Larson v. Chase, 50 NW 238, Minn 1891. Ch 3, n 56.

Lau v. Nichols, 412 US 938, 1973. Ch 7, n 1.

In re Lee, 6 *Clearinghouse Review* 284, 575, August 1972, January 1973. Ch 9, n 64.

State ex Rel Lee v. Buchanan, 191 So 2d 33, Fla 1966. Ch 8, n 3.

Leithold v. Plass, 413 SW 2d 698, Tex 1967. Ch 5, n 5.

State ex rel Lewis v. Lutheran Social Services, 207 NW 2d 826, Wisc 1973. Ch 8, n 10.

Libbee v. Permanente Clinic, 518 P 2d 636, Ore 1974. Ch 3, n 17, n 19.

Lincoln v. Lincoln, 247 NE 2d 659, NY 1969. Ch 8, n 62.

Logan v. Field, 75 Mo App 594, Mo 1898. Ch 2, n 15; Ch 7, n 17.

In re Long, 214 SE 2d 626, NC 1975. Ch 9, n 67.

Lotspeich v. Chance-Vought Aircraft Co., 369 SW 2d 705, Tex 1963. Ch 2, n 52.

Louisiana v. Franklin, 12 So 2d 211, La 1943. Ch 8, n 76.

Love v. Wolf, 58 Cal Rptr 42, Cal 1967. Ch 2, n 18.

Loving v. Virginia, 388 US 1, 1967. Ch 2, n 87, n 88; Ch 10, n 43.

Luka v. Lowrie, 136 NW 1106, Mich 1912. Ch 5, n 8.

Lundahl v. Rockford Memorial Hospital Association, 235 NE 2d 671, Ill 1968. Ch 2, n 20.

Lundberg v. Bay View Hospital, 191 NE 2d 821, Ohio 1963. Ch 2, n 27.

Mackey v. Procunier, 477 F 2d 877, CCA 9, 1973. Ch 8, n 91.

Maertins v. Kaiser Foundation Hospitals, 328 P 2d 494, Cal 1958. Ch 2, n 35.

Magee v. Wyeth Laboratories, 29 Cal Rptr 322, Cal 1963. Ch 2, n 100.

In re Main, 19 P 2d 153, Okla 1933. Ch 10, n 28.

Maniaci v. Marquette University, 184 NW 2d 168, Wisc 1971. Ch 7, n 61; Ch 9, n 72.

Manion v. Tweedy, 100 NW 2d 124, Minn 1959. Ch 2, n 16; Ch 7, n 18.

Marchese v. Monaco, 145 A 2d 809, NJ 1958. Ch 7, n 53.

In re Mario, 317 NYS 2d 659, NY 1971. Ch 8, n 71.

Martarella v. Kelley, 349 F Supp 575, DC NY 1972. Ch 8, n 88.

Martinez v. Mancusi, 443 F 2d 921, CCA 2, 1970. Ch 8, n 98.

Massachusetts v. Wiseman, 249 NE 2d 610, Mass 1969. Ch 2, n 103.

Massie v. Henry 455 F 2d 779, CCA 4, 1972. Ch 9, n 30.

McCartney v. Austin, 298 NYS 2d 26, NY 1969. Ch 4, n 19.

McCollum v. Board of Education, 333 US 203, 1948. Ch 3, n 77; Ch 10, n 14.

McCollum v. Mayfield, 130 F Supp 112, DC Cal 1955. Ch 8, n 96.

In re McDuffee, 352 SW 2d 23, Mo 1961. Ch 8, n 26.

McHugh v. Audet, 72 F Supp 394, DC Pa 1947. Ch 1, n 29; Ch 9, n 14.

McKeiver v. Pennsylvania, 403 US 528, 1971. Ch 8, n 78.

McKinnon v. First National Bank of Pensacola, 82 So 748, Fla 1919. Ch 6, n 15.

Adoption of McKinzie, 275 SW 2d 365, Mo 1955. Ch 1, n 19; Ch 8, n 13.

McNeil v. Director, Patuxent Institution, 407 US 245, 1972. Ch 8, n 85; Ch 9, n 27.

McPheeters v. Board of Medical Examiners, 284 Pac 938, Cal 1930. Ch 9, n 35.

Mechikoff v. Humphreys, Cal Sup Ct, 1975, 32 *Citation* No. 11, pages 125–126, March 15, 1976. Ch 10, n 69.

Medlin v. Bloom, 119 NE 773, Mass 1918. Ch 8, n 39.

Melville v. Sabbatino, 313 A 2d 886, Conn 1973. Ch 4, n 61; Ch 5, n 35; Ch 9, n 66.

Memorial Hospital v. Maricopa County, 415 US 250, 1974. Ch 5, n 1.

Merriken v. Cressman, 364 F Supp 913, DC Pa 1973. Ch 7, n 20; Ch 9, n 32, n 45; Ch 10, n 13.

Metropolitan Life Insurance Co. v. Evans, 184 So 426, Miss 1938. Ch 2, n 51; Ch 7, n 26.

Meyer v. Kaiser Foundation Hospital, Cal Sup Ct 1975, 32 *Citation* No. 10, page 112, March 1, 1976. Ch 10, n 67.

Meyer v. Nebraska, 262 US 390, 1923. Ch 10, n 50.

Meyer v. Ritterbush, 92 NYS 2d 595, NY 1949. Ch 1, n 76.

Meyers v. Arcata Union High School District, 75 Cal Rptr 68, Cal 1969. Ch 9, n 30.

Michigan v. Bricker, 208 NW 2d 172, Mich 1973. Ch 3, n 36.

Michigan v. Nixon, 201 NW 2d 635, Mich 1972. Ch 10, n 70.

Millard v. Cameron, 373 F 2d 468, DC CA 1966. Ch 8, n 86.

Mills v. Board of Education, 348 F Supp 866, DC DC 1972. Ch 2, n 94, n 97; Ch 3, n 74; Ch 7, n 2.

Minnesota v. Loss, 204 NW 2d 404, Minn 1973. Ch 8, n 32.

Mississippi Baptist Hospital v. Holmes, 55 So 2d 142, Miss 1951. Ch 2, n 31.

Mitchell v. Couch, 285 SW 2d 901, KY 1955. Ch 3, n 17.

Mitchell v. Robinson, 334 SW 2d 11, Mo 1960. Ch 5, n 27.

Morales v. Turman, 364 F Supp 166, DC Tex 1973. Ch 8, n 88.

Morgan v. Sheppard, 188 NE 2d 808, Ohio 1963. Ch 2, n 20.

Morris v. Rousos, 397 SW 2d 504, Tex 1965. Ch 7, n 61.

Mueller v. Mueller, 221 NW 2d 39, SD 1974. Ch 6, n 4.

Mulder v. Parke-Davis and Co., 181 NW 2d 882, Minn 1970. Ch 2, n 18; Ch 6, n 6.

Mull v. Emory University, 150 SE 2d 276, Ga 1966. Ch 7, n 32.

Naccarato v. Grob, 180 NW 2d 788, Mich 1970. Ch 2, n 21; Ch 4, n 44; Ch 7, n 9.

Natanson v. Kline, 350 P 2d 1093, 354 P 2d 670, Kans 1960. Ch 5, n 27.

National Homeopathic Hospital v. Phillips, 181 F 2d 293, CA DC 1950. Ch 2, n 31.

Neilson v. Regents of the University of California, 665-047, Sup Ct of Cal, County of San Francisco, 1973. Ch 6, n 31.

Nelson v. Heyne, 491 F 2d 352, CCA 7, 1974, cert den 417 US 976, 1974. Ch 8, n 90, n 94.

State ex rel Nelson v. Whaley, 75 NW 2d 786, Minn 1956. Ch 8, n 13.

Petition of Nemser, 273 NYS 2d 624, NY 1966. Ch 4, n 52; Ch 9, n 26.

New Jersey v. Haren, 307 A 2d 644, NJ 1973. Ch 3, n 36.

New York v. Henson, 304 NE 2d 358, NY 1973. Ch 8, n 32.

New York v. Leyra, 98 NE 2d 553, rev'd on other grounds, 347 US 556, 1954. Ch 9, n 34.

Nichols v. Nichols, 247 SW 2d 143, Tex 1952. Ch 8, n 52.

Nishi v. Hartwell, 473 P 2d 116, Hawaii 1970. Ch 3, n 88.

North Carolina v. Fredell, 193 SE 2d 587, NC 1972. Ch 8, n 32.

O'Beirne v. Sup Ct, Cal, Santa Clara Co, December 7, 1967. Ch 1, n 59

State ex rel Odham v. Sherman, 198 A 2d 71, Md 1964. Ch 3, n 17.

Ohio v. McLaughlin, 212 NE 2d 635, Ohio 1965. Ch 6, n 28; Ch 10, n 20.

O'Neill v. Morse, 188 NW 2d 785, Mich 1971. Ch 3, n 17.

In re Opinion of the Justices, 162 So 123, Ala 1935. Ch 10, n 31.

Ordway v. Hargraves, 323 F Supp 1155, DC Mass 1971. Ch 9, n 31.

Oregon v. Blocher, 499 P 2d 1346, Ore 1972. Ch 8, n 32.

Orford v. Orford, 58 DLR 251, 1921. Ch 1, n 39.

In re Owen, 295 NE 2d 455, Ill 1973. Ch 8, n 93.

Painter v. Bannister, 140 NW 2d 152, Iowa 1966. Ch 8, n 48.

Palm Springs General Hospital v. Martinez, Fla Cir Ct, Dade Co, 1971. Ch 4, n 52; Ch 9, n 26.

Panagopoulous v. Martin, 295 F Supp 220, DC W Va 1969. Ch 3, n 27.

Park v. Nissen, Cal Sup Ct, Orange Co, Docket 190033, December 13, 1974, reported in 31 *Citation,* OG Counsel, AMA, No. 4, page 38, June 1, 1975. Ch 2, n 14.

Parker v. Rampton, 497 P 2d 848, Utah 1972. Ch 2, n 84.

Pearce v. United States, 236 F Supp 431, DC Okla 1964. Ch 7, n 8.

Pearson v. Sav-on Drugs, 108 Cal Rptr 307, 1974. Ch 1, n 71.

Pennison v. Provident Life Insurance Co., 154 So 2d 617, La 1963. Ch 2, n 45; Ch 5, n 37; Ch 9, n 37.

Pennsylvania Association for Retarded Children v. Pennsylvania, 343 F Supp 279, DC Pa 1972. Ch 2, n 94, n 97; Ch 7, n 3.

People v. Edwards, 249 NYS 2d 325, NY 1964. Ch 4, n 25.

People v. Jackson, 319 NYS 2d 331, NY 1971. Ch 7, n 43.

People v. Montecino, 152 P 2d 5, Cal 1944. Ch 4, n 35.

People v. Pierson, 68 NE 243, NY 1903. Ch 4, n 25.

People v. Sorensen, 437 P 2d 495, Cal 1968. Ch 1, n 35, n 41.

Perry v. Grenada Municipal School District, 300 F Supp 748, DC Miss 1969. Ch 9, n 31.

In re Pescinski, 226 NW 2d 180, Wisc 1975. Ch 6, n 50, n 56.

Pierce v. Society of Sisters, 268 US 510, 1925. Ch 10, n 50.

Planned Parenthood Association v. Danforth, 392 F Supp 1362, DC Mo 1975. Ch 10, n 59.

Planned Parenthood Association v. Danforth, 424 US 000, 49 L Ed 2d 788, 1976. Ch 10, n 71.

Planned Parenthood Association v. Fitzpatrick, 401 F Supp 544, Pa 1975. Ch 10, n 56.

Poe v. Gerstein, 517 F 2d 787, CCA 5, 1975. Ch 9, n 39; Ch 10, n 53.

Poliquin v. MacDonald, 135 A 2d 249, NH 1957. Ch 3, n 17.

Population Services International v. Wilson, 398 F Supp 321, DC NY 1975. Ch 10, n 15.

Porter v. Lassiter, 87 SE 2d 100, Ga 1955. Ch 3, n 17, n 28.

Poudre Valley Hospital District v. Heckart, 491 P 2d 984, Colo 1971. Ch 5, n 22.

Powell v. Hocker, 453 F 2d 652, CCA 9, 1971. Ch 8, n 75.

Pratt v. Davis, 79 NE 562, Ill 1906. Ch 5, n 26.

Matter of Presler, 171 Misc 559, NY 1939. Ch 10, n 22.

Price v. Neyland, 320 F 2d 674, CA DC 1963. Ch 2, n 29; Ch 4, n 45; Ch 7, n 16.

Prince v. Massachusetts, 321 US 158, 1944. Ch 4, n 31; Ch 6, n 32.

Pugh v. Swiontek, 253 NE 2nd 3, Ill 1969. Ch 3, n 22.

In the Interests of M. K. R., 515 SW 2d 467, Mo 1974. Ch 10, n 39.

Rainey v. Horn, 72 So 2d 434, Miss 1954. Ch 3, n 17.

Raleigh-Fitkin Memorial Hospital v. Anderson, 201 A 2d 537, NJ 1964. Ch 3, n 85.

Ramsey v. Ciccone, 310 F Supp 600, DC Mo 1970. Ch 8, n 95.

Rea v. Rea, 245 P 2d 884, Ore 1952. Ch 8, n 46.

Reed v. Church, 8 SE 2d 285, Va 1940. Ch 2, n 18; Ch 7, n 51.

Redding v. United States, 196 F Supp 871, DC Ark 1961. Ch 2, n 31.

Relf v. Weinberger, 372 F Supp 1196, DC DC 1974. Ch 10, n 37.

Rewis v. United States, 369 F 2d 595, CCA 5, 1966. Ch 7, n 10.

In re Richardson, 284 So 2d 185, La 1973. Ch 6, n 49, n 55.

Application of Richman, 227 NYS 2d 42, NY 1962. Ch 8, n 56.

Rieck v. Medical Protective Co. of Fort Wayne, 219 NW 2d 242, Wisc 1974. Ch 1, n 67.

Riste v. General Electric Co., 289 P 2d 338, Wash 1955. Ch 2, n 51; Ch 7, n 26.

Rockhill v. Pollard, 485 P 2d 28, Ore 1971. Ch 7, n 30.

Roe v. Wade, 410 US 113, 1973. Ch 1, n 56; Ch 2, n 86; Ch 3, n 3; Ch 10, n 45.

Rogers v. Olander, 286 P 2d 1028, Wash 1955. Ch 8, n 6.

Roller v. Roller, 79 Pac 788, Wash 1905. Ch 1, n 73.

Pennsylvania ex rel Romanowicz v. Romanowicz, 248 A 2d 238, Pa 1968. Ch 8, n 61.

Ross v. Sher, 483 SW 2d 297, Tex 1972. Ch 7, n 14.

Rotan v. Greenbaum, 273 F 2d 830, CA DC 1959. Ch 7, n 55.

Rouse v. Cameron, 373 F 2d 451, DC CA 1966. Ch 8, n 86.

In re Sadleir, 94 P 2d 161, Utah 1939. Ch 8, n 81.

Salgo v. Leland Stanford Board of Trustees, 317 P 2d 170, Cal 1957. Ch 6, n 40.

In re Sampson, 317 NYS 2d 641, 328 NYS 686, NY 1972. Ch 4, n 21; Ch 9, n 5.

Sampson v. Holton, 185 NW 2d 216, Iowa 1971. Ch 8, n 17.

Saville v. Treadway, 8 *Clearinghouse Review* 119, June 1974. Ch 9, n 65.

Sawyer v. Sigler, 445 F 2d 818, CCA 8, 1971. Ch 8, n 98.

People ex rel Scarpetta v. Spence-Chapin Adoption Service, 269 NE 2d 787, NY 1971, cert den 404 US 805, 1971. Ch 8, n 19.

Schaffer v. Spicer, 215 NW 2d 134, SD 1974. Ch 5, n 38, n 39, n 40; Ch 8, n 67; Ch 9, n 40.

Schanbarger v. Kellogg, 315 NYS 2d 1013, NY 1970. Ch 8, n 29.

Schloendorff v. Society of New York Hospital, 105 NE 92, NY 1914. Ch 5, n 26.

In re Adoption of Schroetter, 67 Cal Rptr 819, Cal 1968. Ch 8, n 27.

Schultz v. Schultz, 404 P 2d 987, Wash 1965. Ch 8, n 50.

Schwartz v. United States, 226 F Supp 84, DC DC 1964. Ch 2, n 22.

Scott v. McPheeters, 92 P 2d 678, Cal 1939. Ch 3, n 15.

In re Sealy, 218 So 2d 765, Fla 1969. Ch 9, n 60.

In the Matter of Seiferth, 127 NE 2d 820, NY 1955. Ch 4, n 23, n 58; Ch 9, n 8.

Shapiro v. Howard, 78 Atl 58, Md 1910. Ch 3, n 29.

Sharpe v. Pugh, 155 SE 2d 108, NC 1967. Ch 2, n 18.

Shull v. Columbus Municipal School District, 338 F Supp 1376, DC Miss 1972. Ch 9, n 31.

Siegman v. Kraitchman, 294 NYS 2d 1005, NY 1968. Ch 8, n 64.

Simmons v. Howard University, 323 F Supp 529, DC DC 1971. Ch 3, n 17.

Simonsen v. Swenson, 177 NW 831, Neb 1920. Ch 2, n 43; Ch 5, n 41.

In re Sippy, 97 A 2d 455, DC Mun Ct App 1953. Ch 9, n 61.

Skinner v. Oklahoma, 316 US 535, 1942. Ch 2, n 90; Ch 10, n 35.

In re Smith, 295 A 2d 238, Md 1972. Ch 1, n 58; Ch 4, n 60; Ch 5, n 34; Ch 9, n 24; Ch 10, n 66.

Smith v. DiCara, 329 F Supp 439, DC NY 1971. Ch 2, n 102; Ch 7, n 64.

State ex rel Smith v. Schaffer, 270 Pac 604, Kans 1928. Ch 2, n 92; Ch 10, n 28, n 31.

Smith v. Wright, 305 P 2d 810, Kans 1957. Ch 3, n 22.

Smith v. Yohe, 194 A 2d 167, Pa 1963. Ch 7, n 12.

Spears v. Mississippi, 278 So 2d 443, Miss 1973. Ch 3, n 36.

In re Stanley, 405 US 645, 1972. Ch 8, n 12.

State v. Clark, 261 A 2d 294, Conn 1969. Ch 4, n 25.

State v. Lowe, 68 NW 1094, Minn 1896. Ch 4, n 35.

State v. Parmenter, 444 P 2d 680, Wash 1968. Ch 8, n 43.

State v. Perricone, 181 A 2d 751, NJ 1962. Ch 4, n 18; Ch 9, n 4.

State v. Troutman, 299 Pac 668, Idaho 1931. Ch 10, n 28.

Stidam v. Ashmore, 167 NE 2d 106, Ohio 1959. Ch 3, n 17.

Stoll v. Stoll, 68 NW 2d 367, Minn 1955. Ch 8, n 54.

Stone v. Stone, 431 P 2d 802, Utah 1967. Ch 8, n 63.

Stottlemire v. Cawood, 213 F Supp 897, DC DC 1963. Ch 2, n 18.

Strnad v. Strnad, 78 NYS 2d 390, NY 1948. Ch 1, n 40.

Strunk v. Strunk, 445 SW 2d 145, Ky 1969. Ch 6, n 48, n 58.

Sullivan v. Montgomery, 279 NYS 575, NY 1935. Ch 5, n 8.

Swanson v. Swanson, 290 NW 908, Neb 1940. Ch 8, n 53.

Swenson v. Swenson, 227 SW 2d 103, Mo 1950. Ch 5, n 11.

Sylvia v. Gobeille, 220 A 2d 222, RI 1966. Ch 1, n 60; Ch 3, n 15.

Tarasoff v. Board of Regents, 529 P 2d 553, Cal 1974. Ch 7, n 61; Ch 9, n 48.

Tessier v. United States, 164 F Supp 779, DC Mass 1958. Ch 2, n 28.

Thompson v. Brent, 245 So 2d 751, La 1971. Ch 2, n 30.

Tinker v. Des Moines School District, 393 US 503, 1969. Ch 10, n 12.

Tippett v. Maryland, 436 F 2d 1153, CCA 4, 1971. Ch 8, n 85.

Tolbert v. Eyman, 434 F 2d 625, CCA 9, 1970. Ch 8, n 96.

Toth v. Community Hospital at Glen Cove, 239 NE 2d 368, NY 1968. Ch 7, n 16.

Trimble v. Stone, 187 F Supp 483, DC DC 1960. Ch 8, n 76.

Troppi v. Scarf, 187 NW 2d 511, Mich 1971. Ch 1, n 65.

In re Tuttendario, 21 Pa Dist 561, Pa 1912. Ch 4, n 24.

Union Carbide and Carbon Co. v. Stapleton, 237 F 2d 229, CCA 6, 1956. Ch 2, n 53; Ch 7, n 27.

United States v. Muniz, 374 US 150, 1963. Ch 8, n 100.

United States v. Repouille, 165 F 2d 152, CCA 2, 1947. Ch 4, n 30.

Valdez v. Percy, 217 P 2d 422, Cal 1950. Ch 2, n 28.

Valence v. Louisiana Power and Light Co., 50 So 2d 847, La 1951. Ch 3, n 14, n 17.

Van Allen v. McCleary, 211 NYS 2d 501, NY 1961. Ch 7, n 67.

Veals v. Ciccone, 281 F Supp 1017, DC Mo 1968. Ch 8, n 97.

Verkennes v. Corniea, 38 NW 2d 838, Minn 1949. Ch 3, n 16, n 17.

Vigil v. Rice, 397 P 2d 719, NM 1964. Ch 7, n 65.

Wade v. Bethesda Hospital, 356 F Supp 380, DC Ohio 1973. Ch 2, n 93; Ch 10, n 34.

People ex rel Wallace v. Labrenz, 104 NE 2d 769, Ill 1952. Ch 4, n 18; Ch 9, n 4.

Wansley v. Miller, 353 F Supp 42, DC Va 1973. Ch 8, n 83.

Wansley v. Slayton, 487 F 2d 90, CCA 4, 1973. Ch 8, n 82.

Washington v. Koome, 530 P 2d 260, Wash 1975. Ch 10, n 57.

Welch v. Dunsmuir High School, 326 P 2d 633, Cal 1958. Ch 7, n 31.

Welch v. Frisbie Memorial Hospital, 9 A 2d 761, NH 1939. Ch 2, n 32.

Wheatley v. Heideman, 102 NW 2d 343, Iowa 1960. Ch 7, n 8, n 46.

White v. Yup, 458 P 2d 617, Nev 1969. Ch 3, n 17.

Whitfield v. Daniel Construction Co., 83 SE 2d 460, SC 1954. Ch 7, n 56.

Willey v. Willey, 115 NW 2d 833, Iowa 1962. Ch 8, n 52.

In re Williams, 267 NYS 2d 91, NY 1966. Ch 8, n 79.

Williams v. Menehan, 379 P 2d 292, Kans 1963. Ch 5, n 29.

CASES BY

JURISDICTION

Foreign Case

Orford v. Orford, 58 DLR 251, 1921. Ch 1, n 39.

Alabama

Eich v. Town of Gulf Shores, 300 So 2d 354, Ala 1974. Ch 3, n 17.

Kenney v. Gurley, 95 So 34, Ala 1923. Ch 7, n 66.

In re Opinion of the Justices, 162 So 123, Ala 1935. Ch 10, n 31.

Arkansas

A. v. C., 390 SW 2d 116, Ark 1965. Ch 1, n 17; Ch 8, n 9.

Davis v. Rodman, 227 SW 612, Ark 1921. Ch 8, n 40.

California

Agnew v. Larson, 185 P 2d 851, Cal 1947. Ch 7, n 53.

Ballard v. Anderson, 484 P 2d 1345, Cal 1971. Ch 3, n 100; Ch 10, n 48.

Bellman v. San Francisco High School District, 81 P 2d 894, Cal 1938. Ch 7, n 22.

Bernstein v. Board of Medical Examiners, 22 Cal Rptr 419, Cal 1962. Ch 9, n 22.

Bryant v. Inglewood Hospital, Cal Sup Ct, June 11, 1975, 31 *Citation* No. 12, page 136, October 1, 1975. Ch 10, n 68.

Burge v. City and County of San Francisco, 262 P 2d 6, Cal 1953. Ch 5, n 5.

Cadilla v. Board of Medical Examiners, 103 Cal Rptr 455, Cal 1972. Ch 9, n 21.

California v. Aeschlimann, 104 Cal Rptr 689, Cal 1972. Ch 8, n 33.

Capelouto v. Kaiser Foundation Hospital, 500 P 2d 880 Cal 1972. Ch 3, n 25.

Cobbs v. Grant, 502 P 2d 1, Cal 1972. Ch 5, n 32; Ch 6, n 2.

Coffee v. McDonnell-Douglas Corp., 503 P 2d 1366, Cal 1972. Ch 2, n 54; Ch 7, n 27.

Colombo v. Colombo, 162 P 2d 995, Cal 1945. Ch 8, n 50.

Combs v. Combs, 327 P 2d 164, Cal 1958. Ch 8, n 52.

Custodio v. Bauer, 59 Cal Rptr 463, Cal 1967. Ch 1, n 69.

DiMartini v. Alexandria Sanitarium, 13 Cal Rptr 564, Cal 1961. Ch 2, n 22.

Foster v. Birge, Cal Sup Ct 1974, 30 *Citation* No. 8, page 122, February 1, 1975. Ch 10, n 68.

In re G., 104 Cal Rptr 585, Cal 1972. Ch 9, n 62.

Gluckstein v. Lipsett, 209 P 2d 98, Cal 1949. Ch 2, n 26.

Gottsdanker v. Cutter Laboratories, 6 Cal Rptr 320, Cal 1960. Ch 2, n 100.

Jessin v. County of Shasta, 79 Cal Rptr 359, Cal 1969. Ch 2, n 84.

Johnston v. Brother, 12 Cal Rptr 23, Cal 1961. Ch 7, n 55.

In re Estate of Kemp, 118 Cal Rptr 64, Cal 1974. Ch 10, n 41.

Landeros v. Flood, 123 Cal Rptr 713, Cal 1975. Ch 8, n 42.

Love v. Wolf, 58 Cal Rptr 42, Cal 1967. Ch 2, n 18.

Maertins v. Kaiser Foundation Hospitals, 328 P 2d 494, Cal 1958. Ch 2, n 35.

Magee v. Wyeth Laboratories, 29 Cal Rptr 322, Cal 1963. Ch 2, n 100.

McPheeters v. Board of Medical Examiners, 284 Pac 938, Cal 1930. Ch 9, n 35.

Mechikoff v. Humphreys, Cal Sup Ct 1975, 32 *Citation* No. 11, pages 125–126, March 15, 1976. Ch 10, n 69.

Meyer v. Kaiser Foundation Hospital, Cal Sup Ct 1975, 32 *Citation* No. 10, page 112, March 1, 1976. Ch 10, n 67.

Meyers v. Arcata Union High School District, 75 Cal Rptr 68, Cal 1969. Ch 9, n 30.

Neilson v. Regents of the University of California, 665-047, Sup Ct of Cal, County of San Francisco, 1973. Ch 6, n 31.

O'Beirne v. Sup. Ct, Cal, Santa Clara Co, December 7, 1967. Ch 1, n 59.

Park v. Nissen, Cal Sup Ct, Orange County, Docket 190033, December 13, 1974, 31 *Citation,* OG Counsel, AMA, No. 4, page 38, June 1, 1975. Ch 2, n 14.

Pearson v. Sav-on Drugs, 108 Cal Rptr 307, 1974. Ch 1, n 71.

People v. Montecino, 152 P 2d 5, Cal 1944. Ch 4, n 35.

People v. Sorensen, 437 P 2d 495, Cal 1968. Ch 1, n 35, n 41.

Salgo v. Leland Stanford Board of Trustees, 317 P 2d 170, Cal 1957. Ch 6, n 40.

In re Adoption of Schroetter, 67 Cal Rptr 819, Cal 1968. Ch 8, n 27.

Scott v. McPheeters, 92 P 2d 678, Cal 1939. Ch 3, n 15.

Tarasoff v. Board of Regents, 529 P 2d 553, Cal 1974. Ch 7, n 61; Ch 9, n 48.

Valdez v. Percy, 217 P 2d 422, Cal 1950. Ch 2, n 28.

Welch v. Dunsmuir High School, 326 P 2d 633, Cal 1958. Ch 7, n 31.

Colorado

Brown v. Hughes, 30 P 2d 259, Colo 1934. Ch 1, n 29.

Poudre Valley Hospital District v. Heckart, 491 P 2d 984, Colo 1971. Ch 5, n 22.

Connecticut

Burke v. Burke, 75 A 2d 42, Conn 1950. Ch 6, n 33.

Hart v. Brown, 289 A 2d 386, Conn 1972. Ch 6, n 45, n 54; n 58, n 61.

Hatala v. Markiewicz, 224 A 2d 406, Conn 1966. Ch 3, n 17.

Melville v. Sabbatino, 313 A 2d 886, Conn 1973. Ch 4, n 61; Ch 5, n 35; Ch 9, n 66.

State v. Clark, 261 A 2d 294, Conn 1969. Ch 4, n 25.

Delaware

Coleman v. Garrison, 281 A 2d 616, Del 1971. Ch 1, n 70.

In re Diane, 318 A 2d 629, Del 1974. Ch 10, n 51.

Di Filippo v. Preston, 173 A 2d 333, Del 1961. Ch 5, n 29.

Worgan v. Greggo and Ferrara, Inc., 128 A 2d 557, Del 1956. Ch 3, n 17.

District of Columbia

Alden v. Providence Hospital, 382 F 2d 163, DC CA 1967. Ch 7, n 8.

In re Boe, 322 F Supp 872, DC DC 1971. Ch 3, n 100; Ch 10, n 48.

Bonbrest v. Kotz, 65 F Supp 138, DC DC 1946. Ch 3, n 12.

Bonner v. Moran, 126 F 2d 121, CA DC 1941. Ch 5, n 9; Ch 6, n 53.

Booth v. United States, 155 F Supp 235 (Ct Ct), 1957. Ch 7, n 8.

Canterbury v. Spence, 464 F 2d 772, CA DC 1972. Ch 2, n 25; Ch 5, n 30, n 33; Ch 6, n 2.

Clayton v. Stone, 358 F 2d 548, DC CA 1966. Ch 8, n 87.

Elmore v. Stone, 355 F 2d 841, DC CA 1966. Ch 8, n 87.

Goodman v. District of Columbia, 50 A 2d 812, DC Mun Ct App 1947. Ch 8, n 4.

Hobson v. Hansen, 269 F Supp 401, DC Cir 1967, 408 F 2d 175, CA DC 1969. Ch 7, n 5, n 20.

In the Matter of P. J., Sup Ct of DC, February 6, 1973, 2 *Family Planning Population Reporter* No. 3, page 57, June 1973. Ch 10, n 60.

Jones v. United States 308 F 2d 307, CA DC 1962. Ch 4, n 35.

Millard v. Cameron, 373 F 2d 468, DC CA 1966. Ch 8, n 86.

Mills v. Board of Education, 348 F Supp 866, DC DC 1972. Ch 2, n 94, n 97; Ch 3, n 74; Ch 7, n 2.

National Homeopathic Hospital v. Phillips, 181 F 2d 293, CA DC 1950. Ch 2, n 31.

Price v. Neyland, 320 F 2d 674, CA DC 1963. Ch 2, n 29; Ch 4, n 45; Ch 7, n 16.

Relf v. Weinberger, 372 F Supp 1196, DC DC 1974. Ch 10, n 37.

Rotan v. Greenbaum, 273 F 2d 830, CA DC 1959. Ch 7, n 55.

Rouse v. Cameron, 373 F 2d 451, DC CA 1966. Ch 8, n 86.

Schwartz v. United States, 226 F Supp 84, DC DC 1964. Ch 2, n 22.

Simmons v. Howard University, 323 F Supp 529, DC DC 1971. Ch 3, n 17.

In re Sippy, 97 A 2d 455, DC Mun Ct App 1953. Ch 9, n 61.

Stottlemire v. Cawood, 213 F Supp 897, DC DC 1963. Ch 2, n 18.

Trimble v. Stone, 187 F Supp 483, DC DC 1960. Ch 8, n 76.

Florida

Aronoff v. Snider, 292 So 2d 418, Fla 1974. Ch 1, n 78.

Baldor v. Rogers, 81 So 2d 658, Fla 1955. Ch 6, n 18.

Bowers v. Talmage, 159 So 2d 888, Fla 1963. Ch 2, n 59.

In re Brock, 25 So 2d 659, Fla 1946. Ch 10, n 22.

Brooks v. Serrano, 209 So 2d 279, Fla 1968. Ch 3, n 15.

Chappell v. Masten, 255 So 2d 546, Fla 1971. Ch 8, n 21.

Crovella v. Cochrane, 102 So 2d 307, Fla 1958. Ch 7, n 16.

Greenwald v. Grayson, 189 So 2d 204, Fla 1966. Ch 8, n 22.

Harwick v. Harris, 166 So 2d 912, Fla 1964. Ch 7, n 14.

Hoder v. Sayet, 196 So 2d 205, Fla 1967. Ch 1, n 50.

Hofmann v. Blackmon, 241 So 2d 752, Fla 1970. Ch 5, n 41; Ch 9, n 49.

Ison v. Florida Sanitarium and Benevolent Association, 302 So 2d 200, Fla 1974. Ch 5, n 23.

Jackson v. Rupp, 228 So 2d 916, Fla 1969. Ch 3, n 56.

Jones v. Smith, 278 So 2d 339, Fla 1973. Ch 1, n 58.

State ex rel Lee v. Buchanan, 191 So 2d 33, Fla 1966. Ch 8, n 3.

McKinnon v. First National Bank of Pensacola, 82 So 748, Fla 1919. Ch 6, n 15.

Palm Springs General Hospital v. Martinez, Fla Cir Ct, Dade Co, 1971. Ch 4, n 52; Ch 9, n 26.

In re Sealy, 218 So 2d 765, Fla 1969. Ch 9, n 60.

Georgia

Hendrix v. Hunter, 110 SE 2d 35, Ga 1959. Ch 1, n 16.

Mull v. Emory University, 150 SE 2d 276, Ga 1966. Ch 7, n 32.

Porter v. Lassiter, 87 SE 2d 100, Ga 1955. Ch 3, n 17, n 28.

Wright v. Wright, 70 SE 2d 152, Ga 1952. Ch 1, n 76.

Hawaii

Nishi v. Hartwell, 473 P 2d 116, Hawaii 1970. Ch 3, n 88.

Idaho

State v. Troutman, 299 Pac 668, Idaho 1931. Ch 10, n 28.

Illinois

Chrisafogeorgis v. Brandenburg, 304 NE 2d 88, Ill 1974. Ch 3, n 17.

Doerr v. Villate, 220 NE 2d 767, Ill 1966. Ch 1, n 68.

In re Lee, 6 *Clearinghouse Review,* 284, 575, August 1972, January, 1973. Ch 9, n 64.

Lundahl v. Rockford Memorial Hospital Association, 235 NE 2d 671, Ill 1968. Ch 2, n 20.

In re Owen, 295 NE 2d 455, Ill 1973. Ch 8, n 93.

Pratt v. Davis, 79 NE 562, Ill 1906. Ch 5, n 26.

Pugh v. Swiontek, 253 NE 2d 3, Ill 1969. Ch 3, n 22.

People ex rel Wallace v. Labrenz, 104 NE 2d 769, Ill 1952. Ch 4, n 18; Ch 9, n 4.

Zepeda v. Zepeda, 190 NE 2d 849, Ill 1963. Ch 1, n 63.

Indiana

Britt v. Sears, 277 NE 2d 20, Ind 1971. Ch 3, n 17.

County Department of Welfare v. Morningstar, 151 NE 2d 150, Ind 1958. Ch 1, n 22; Ch 8, n 23.

Eaglen v. State, 231 NE 2d 147, Ind 1967. Ch 4, n 25.

A. L. v. G. R. H., 325 NE 2d 501, Ind 1975. Ch 10, n 42.

Iowa

In re Karwath, 199 NW 2d 147, Iowa 1972. Ch 4, n 20; Ch 9, n 6.

Painter v. Bannister, 140 NW 2d 152, Iowa 1966. Ch 8, n 48.

Sampson v. Holton, 185 NW 2d 216, Iowa 1971. Ch 8, n 17.

Wheatley v. Heideman, 102 NW 2d 343, Iowa 1960. Ch 7, n 8, n 46.

Willey v. Willey, 115 NW 2d 833, Iowa 1962. Ch 8, n 52.

Kansas

Funke v. Fieldman, 512 P 2d 539, Kans 1973. Ch 2, n 58.

Hale v. Manion, 368 P 2d 1, Kans 1962. Ch 3, n 17.

Natanson v. Kline, 350 P 2d 1093, 354 P 2d 670, Kans 1960. Ch 5, n 27.

State ex rel Smith v. Schaffer, 270 Pac 604, Kans 1928. Ch 2, n 92; Ch 10, n 28, n 31.

Smith v. Wright, 305 P 2d 810, Kans 1957. Ch 3, n 22.

Williams v. Menehan, 379 P 2d 292, Kans 1963. Ch 5, n 29.

Younts v. St. Frances Hospital, 469 P 2d 330, Kans 1970. Ch 5, n 18; Ch 9, n 12.

Kentucky

Boyd v. Wynn, 150 SW 2d 648, Ky 1941. Ch 9, n 34.

Hardman v. Hardman, 214 SW 2d 391, Ky 1948. Ch 8, n 55.

Holmes v. Powers, 439 SW 2d 579, Ky 1968. Ch 2, n 93.

Jarboe v. Harting, 397 SW 2d 775, Ky 1965. Ch 3, n 22.

Mitchell v. Couch, 285 SW 2d 901, Ky 1955. Ch 3, n 17.

Strunk v. Strunk, 445 SW 2d 145, Ky 1969. Ch 6, n 48, n 58.

Louisiana

Estay v. Lafourche Parish School Board, 230 So 2d 443, La 1969. Ch 9, n 31.

Favalora v. Aetna Casualty Co., 144 So 2d 544, La 1962. Ch 2, n 20.

Johnson v. St. Paul Mercury Insurance Co., 219 So 2d 524, La 1969. Ch 7, n 10.

Louisiana v. Franklin, 12 So 2d 211, La 1943. Ch 8, n 76.

Pennison v. Provident Life Insurance Co., 154 So 2d 617, La 1963. Ch 2, n 45; Ch 5, n 37; Ch 9, n 37.

In re Richardson, 284 So 2d 185, La 1973. Ch 6, n 49, n 55.

Thompson v. Brent, 245 So 2d 751, La 1971. Ch 2, n 30.

Valence v. Louisiana Power and Light Co., 50 So 2d 847, La 1951. Ch 3, n 14, n 17.

Maine

In re David, 256 A 2d 583, Me 1969. Ch 8, n 18.

Maryland

Alden v. Alden, 174 A 2d 793, Md 1961. Ch 8, n 51.

Craig v. State, 155 A 2d 684, Md 1959. Ch 4, n 25.

Shapiro v. Howard 78 Atl 58, Md 1910. Ch 3, n 29.

State ex rel Odham v. Sherman, 198 A 2d 71, Md 1964. Ch 3, n 17.

In re Smith, 295 A 2d 238, Md 1972. Ch 1, n 58; Ch 4, n 60; Ch 5, n 34; Ch 9, n 24; Ch 10, n 66.

Massachusetts

Brune v. Belinkoff, 235 NE 2d 793, Mass 1968. Ch 2, n 21.

Callahan v. Longwood Hospital, 208 NE 2d 247, Mass 1965. Ch 2, n 31.

Dietrich v. Northhampton, 138 Mass 14, 1884. Ch 3, n 11.

Doe v. Doe, 314 NE 2d 128, Mass 1974. Ch 1, n 58; Ch 3, n 87.

Keyes v. Construction Service, 165 NE 2d 912, Mass 1960. Ch 3, n 23.

Massachusetts v. Wiseman, 249 NE 2d 610, Mass 1969. Ch 2, n 103.

Medlin v. Bloom, 119 NE 773, Mass 1918. Ch 8, n 39.

Michigan

Everest v. McKenny, 162 NW 277, Mich 1917. Ch 7, n 66.

Fortner v. Koch, 261 NW 762, Mich 1935. Ch 1, n 29.

Petition of Gonzales, 46 NW 2d 453, Mich 1951. Ch 10, n 22.

Haewsky v. St. John's Hospital, Mich Cir Ct, Wayne Co., June 10, 1970. Ch 8, n 44.

Harvey v. Silber, 2 NW 2d 483, Mich 1942, Ch 2, n 28.

Luka v. Lowrie, 136 NW 1106, Mich 1912. Ch 5, n 8.

Michigan v. Bricker, 208 NW 2d 172, Mich 1973. Ch 3, n 36.

Michigan v. Nixon, 201 NW 2d 635, Mich 1972. Ch 10, n 70.

Naccarato v. Grob, 180 NW 2d 788, Mich 1970. Ch 2, n 21; Ch 4, n 44; Ch 7, n 9.

O'Neill v. Morse, 188 NW 2d 785, Mich 1971. Ch 3, n 17.

Troppi v. Scarf, 187 NW 2d 511, Mich 1971. Ch 1, n 65.

Minnesota

In re Alsdurf, 133 NW 2d 479, Minn 1965. Ch 8, n 15.

Adoption of Anderson, 50 NW 2d 278, Minn 1951. Ch 3, n 101.

Christy v. Saliterman, 179 NW 2d 288, Minn 1970. Ch 2, n 21.

Korman v. Hagen, 206 NW 650, Minn 1925. Ch 3, n 15.

In re Baby Larson, 91 NW 2d 448, Minn 1958. Ch 8, n 15.

Larson v. Chase, 50 NW 238, Minn 1891. Ch 3, n 56.

Manion v. Tweedy, 100 NW 2d 124, Minn 1959. Ch 2, n 16; Ch 7, n 18.

Minnesota v. Loss, 204 NW 2d 404, Minn 1973. Ch 8, n 32.

Mulder v. Parke-Davis and Co., 181 NW 2d 882, Minn 1970. Ch 2, n 18; Ch 6, n 6.

State ex rel Nelson v. Whaley, 75 NW 2d 786, Minn 1956. Ch 8, n 13.

State v. Lowe, 68 NW 1094, Minn 1896. Ch 4, n 35.

Stoll v. Stoll, 68 NW 2d 367, Minn 1955. Ch 8, n 54.

Verkennes v. Corniea, 38 NW 2d 838, Minn 1949. Ch 3, n 16, n 17.

Mississippi

Hewellette v. George, 9 So 885, Miss 1891. Ch 1, n 74.

Metropolitan Life Insurance Co. v. Evans, 184 So 426, Miss 1938. Ch 2, n 51; Ch 7, n 26.

Mississippi Baptist Hospital v. Holmes, 55 So 2d 142, Miss 1951. Ch 2, n 31.

Rainey v. Horn, 72 So 2d 434, Miss 1954. Ch 3, n 17.

Spears v. Mississippi, 278 So 2d 443, Miss 1973. Ch 3, n 36.

Missouri

Logan v. Field, 75 Mo App 594, Mo 1898. Ch 2, n 15; Ch 7, n 17.

In re McDuffee, 352 SW 2d 23, Mo 1961. Ch 8, n 26.

Adoption of McKinzie, 275 SW 2d 365, Mo 1955. Ch 1, n 19; Ch 8, n 13.

Mitchell v. Robinson, 334 SW 2d 11, Mo 1960. Ch 5, n 27.

In the Interests of M. K. R., 515 SW 2d 467, Mo 1974. Ch 10, n 39.

Swenson v. Swenson, 227 SW 2d 103, Mo 1950. Ch 5, n 11.

Montana

Hutchins v. Blood Services of Montana, 506 P 2d 449, Mont 1973. Ch 1, n 50.

Nebraska

In re Cavitt, 157 NW 2d 171, Neb 1968. Ch 2, n 91; Ch 10, n 29.

In re Clayton, 234 NW 630, Neb 1931. Ch 10, n 28.

Simonsen v. Swenson, 177 NW 831, Neb 1920. Ch 2, n 43; Ch 5, n 41.

Swanson v. Swanson, 290 NW 908, Neb 1940. Ch 8, n 53.

Nevada

White v. Yup, 458 P 2d 617, Nev 1969. Ch 3, n 17.

New Hampshire

Briere v. Briere, 224 A 2d 588, NH 1966. Ch 1, n 75.

Holland v. Metalious, 198 A 2d 654, NH 1964. Ch 3, n 44.

Poliquin v. MacDonald, 135 A 2d 249, NH 1957. Ch 3, n 17.

Welch v. Frisbie Memorial Hospital, 9 A 2d 761, NH 1939. Ch 2, n 32.

New Jersey

Beadling v. Sirotta, 176 A 2d 546, NJ 1961. Ch 2, n 53; Ch 7, n 27.

In re Adoption of a Child, 317 A 2d 382, NJ 1974. Ch 8, n 16.

D. v. D., 260 A 2d 255, NJ 1969. Ch 8, n 57.

Hoener v. Bertinato, 171 A 2d 140, NJ 1961. Ch 4, n 18; Ch 9, n 4.

Kern v. Kogan, 226 A 2d 186, NJ 1967. Ch 2, n 29.

Marchese v. Monaco, 145 A 2d 809, NJ 1958. Ch 7, n 53.

New Jersey v. Haren, 307 A 2d 644, NJ 1973. Ch 3, n 36.

Raleigh-Fitkin Memorial Hospital v. Anderson, 201 A 2d 537, NJ 1964. Ch 3, n 85.

State v. Perricone, 181 A 2d 751, NJ 1962. Ch 4, n 18; Ch 9, n 4.

New Mexico

Barwin v. Reidy, 307 P 2d 175, NM 1957. Ch 1, n 21.

Vigil v. Rice, 397 P 2d 719, NM 1964. Ch 7, n 65.

Woods v. Brumlop, 377 P 2d 520, NM 1962. Ch 2, n 59.

New York

People ex Rel Abajian v. Dennett, 184 NYS 2d 178, NY 1958. Ch 1, n 40.

In re Anonymous, 248 NYS 2d 608, NY 1964. Ch 9, n 63.

In re Adoption of Anonymous, 345 NYS 2d 430, NY 1973. Ch 1, n 42.

Bach v. Long Island Jewish Hospital, 267 NYS 2d 289, NY 1966. Ch 5, n 10.

Battistella v. Society of the New York Hospital, 191 NYS 2d 626, NY 1959. Ch 2, n 51; Ch 7, n 26.

Bender v. Bender, 304 NYS 2d 482, NY 1969. Ch 8, n 61.

Benson v. Dean, 133 NE 125, NY 1921. Ch 2, n 15; Ch 7, n 17.

In re Blaine, 282 NYS 2d 359, NY 1967. Ch 8, n 62.

Board of Education v. Homer, 362 NYS 2d 798, NY 1974. Ch 7, n 24.

Capuano v. Jacobs, 305 NYS 2d 837, NY 1969. Ch 2, n 32.

Carpenter v. City of Rochester, 324 NYS 2d 591, NY 1971. Ch 8, n 29.

In re Carstairs, 115 NYS 2d 314, NY 1952. Ch 9, n 10.

Cidis v. White, 336 NYS 2d 362, NY 1972. Ch 5, n 24.

Clark v. Board of Education, 107 NYS 2d 582, NY 1951. Ch 7, n 22.

Curry v. Corn, 277 NYS 2d 470, NY 1966. Ch 2, n 45; Ch 5, n 37; Ch 9, n 38.

In re D., 290 NYS 2d 935, NY 1968. Ch 8, n 82.

Darrah v. Kite, 301 NYS 2d 286, NY 1969. Ch 5, n 28; Ch 6, n 40.

Application of DoVidio, 288 NYS 2d 21, NY 1968. Ch 8, n 59.

Durfee v. Durfee, 87 NYS 2d 275, NY 1949. Ch 4, n 51; Ch 5, n 6.

Endresz v. Friedberg, 248 NE 2d 901, NY 1969. Ch 3, n 23.

Fiorentino v. Wenger, 227 NE 2d 296, NY 1967. Ch 1, n 30; Ch 3, n 99; Ch 6, n 1.

Foxluger v. New York, 203 NYS 2d 985, NY 1960. Ch 9, n 18.

Gardner v. State, 22 NE 2d 344, NY 1939. Ch 7, n 22.

Golia v. Greater New York Health Insurance Plan, 166 NYS 2d 889, NY 1957. Ch 5, n 41; Ch 9, n 49.

Gursky v. Gursky, 242 NYS 2d 406, NY 1963. Ch 1, n 40.

Hammer v. Polsky, 233 NYS 2d 110, NY 1962. Ch 7, n 59.

Hyman v. Jewish Chronic Disease Hospital, 206 NE 2d 338, NY 1965. Ch 6, n 38.

In re John Children, 306 NYS 2d 797, NY 1969. Ch 8, n 45.

Keesee v. Board of Education, 235 NYS 2d 300, NY 1962. Ch 7, n 22.

Kesseler v. Kesseler, 180 NE 2d 402, 236 NYS 2d 472, NY 1962. Ch 8, n 46.

Knapp v. Knapp, 250 NYS 2d 390, NY 1964. Ch 8, n 56.

Lincoln v. Lincoln, 247 NE 2d 659, NY 1969. Ch 8, n 62.

In re Mario, 317 NYS 2d 659, NY 1971. Ch 8, n 71.

McCartney v. Austin, 298 NYS 2d 26, NY 1969. Ch 4, n 19.

Meyer v. Ritterbush, 92 NYS 2d 595, NY 1949. Ch 1, n 76.

Petition of Nemser, 273 NYS 2d 624, NY 1966. Ch 4, n 52; Ch 9, n 26.

New York v. Henson, 304 NE 2d 358, NY 1973. Ch 8, n 32.

People v. Edwards, 249 NYS 2d 325, NY 1964. Ch 4, n 25.

People v. Jackson, 319 NYS 2d 331, NY 1971. Ch 7, n 43.

People v. Pierson, 68 NE 243, NY 1903. Ch 4, n 25.

Matter of Presler, 171 Misc 559, NY 1939. Ch 10, n 22.

Application of Richman, 227 NYS 2d 42, NY 1962. Ch 8, n 56.

In re Sampson, 317 NYS 2d 641, 328 NYS 2d 686, NY 1972. Ch 4, n 21; Ch 9, n 5.

People ex rel Scarpetta v. Spence-Chapin Adoption Service, 269 NE 2d 787, NY 1971, cert den 404 US 805, 1971. Ch 8, n 19.

Schanbarger v. Kellogg, 315 NYS 2d 1013, NY 1970. Ch 8, n 29.

Schloendorff v. Society of New York Hospital, 105 NE 92, NY 1914. Ch 5, n 26.

In the Matter of Seiforth, 127 NE 2d 20, NY 1955. Ch 4, n 23, n 58; Ch 9, n 8.

Siegman v. Kraitchman, 294 NYS 2d 1005, NY 1968. Ch 8, n 64.

Strnad v. Strnad, 78 NYS 2d 390, NY 1948. Ch 1, n 40.

Sullivan v. Montgomery, 279 NYS 575, NY 1935. Ch 5, n 8.

Toth v. Community Hospital at Glen Cove, 239 NE 2d 368, NY 1968. Ch 7, n 16.

Van Allen v. McCleary, 211 NYS 2d 501, NY 1961. Ch 7, n 67.

In re Williams, 267 NYS 2d 91, NY 1966. Ch 8, n 79.

Williams v. New York, 223 NE 2d 343, NY 1966. Ch 1, n 64.

Zeleznik v. Jewish Chronic Disease Hospital, 366 NYS 2d 163, NY 1975. Ch 5, n 31.

Ziemba v. Sternberg, 357 NYS 2d 265, NY 1974. Ch 1, n 66.

North Carolina

Brewer v. Valk, 167 SE 638, NC 1933. Ch 2, n 92; Ch 10, n 31.

Davis v. Wilson, 143 SE 2d 107, NC 1965. Ch 2, n 31.

Gustafson v. Gustafson, 158 SE 2d 619, NC 1968. Ch 8, n 60.

Koury v. Follo, 158 SE 2d 548, NC 1968. Ch 6, n 6.

In re Long, 214 SE 2d 626, NC 1975. Ch 9, n 67.

North Carolina v. Fredell, 193 SE 2d 587, NC 1972. Ch 8, n 32.

Sharpe v. Pugh, 155 SE 2d 108, NC 1967. Ch 2, n 18.

Ohio

In re Clark, 185 NE 2d 128, Ohio 1962. Ch 4, n 18; Ch 9, n 4.

Dietsch v. Mayberry, 47 NE 2d 404, Ohio 1942. Ch 8, n 39.

Jones v. Stanko, 160 NE 456, Ohio 1928. Ch 8, n 38.

Lacey v. Laird, 139 NE 2d 25, Ohio 1956. Ch 5, n 19; Ch 9, n 12.

Lundberg v. Bay View Hospital, 191 NE 2d 821, Ohio 1963. Ch 2, n 27.

Morgan v. Sheppard, 188 NE 2d 808, Ohio 1963. Ch 2, n 20.

Ohio v. McLaughlin, 212 NE 2d 635, Ohio 1965. Ch 6, n 28; Ch 10, n 20.

Stidam v. Ashmore, 167 NE 2d 106, Ohio 1959. Ch 3, n 17.

Oklahoma

In re Main, 19 P 2d 153, Okla 1933. Ch 10, n 28.

Oregon

Allen v. Allen, 330 P 2d 151, Ore 1958. Ch 8, n 25.

Cook v. Oregon, 495 P 2d 768, Ore 1972. Ch 2, n 91; Ch 10, n 32.

Libbee v. Permanente Clinic, 518 P 2d 636, Ore 1974. Ch 3, n 17, n 19.

Oregon v. Blocher, 499 P 2d 1346, Ore 1972. Ch 8, n 32.

Rea v. Rea 245 P 2d 884, Ore 1952. Ch 8, n 46.

Rockhill v. Pollard, 485 P 2d 28, Ore 1971. Ch 7, n 30.

Pennsylvania

Alexander v. Knight, 177 A 2d 142, Pa 1962. Ch 9, n 42.

Adoption of Ashton, 97 A 2d 368, Pa 1953. Ch 1, n 20.

Commonwealth v. Bender, 178 A 2d 779, Pa 1962. Ch 8, n 51.

Commonwealth v. Edinger, 98 A 2d 172, Pa 1953. Ch 8, n 51.

In re Green, 292 A 2d 387, Pa 1972. Ch 4, n 59.

Henderson v. National Drug Co., 23 A 2d 743, Pa 1942. Ch 7, n 53.

Hodgson v. Bigelow, 7 A 2d 338, Pa 1939. Ch 9, n 14.

In re Holmes, 109 A 2d 523, Pa 1954, cert den 348 US 973, 1955. Ch 8, n 68.

Incollingo v. Ewing, 282 A 2d 206, Pa 1971. Ch 2, n 18; Ch 2, n 20.

Pennsylvania ex rel Romanowicz v. Romanowicz, 248 A 2d 238, Pa 1968. Ch 8, n 61.

Smith v. Yohe, 194 A 2d 167, Pa 1963. Ch 7, n 12.

In re Tuttendario, 21 Pa Dist 561, Pa 1912. Ch 4, n 24.

Wohlert v. Seibert, 23 Pa Sup Ct 213, 1903. Ch 7, n 18.

In re Maida Yetter, 62 Pa D & C 2d 619, Pa 1973. Ch 4, n 52; Ch 9, n 26.

Zaman v. Schultz, 19 Pa D & C 309, 1933. Ch 5, n 3.

Rhode Island

Sylvia v. Gobeille, 220 A 2d 222, RI 1966. Ch 1, n 60; Ch 3, n 15.

South Carolina

Fowler v. Woodward, 138 SE 2d 42, SC 1964. Ch 3, n 17, n 18.

Whitfield v. Daniel Construction Co., 83 SE 2d 460, SC 1954. Ch 7, n 56.

South Dakota

Block v. McVay, 126 NW 2d 808, SD 1964. Ch 7, n 32.

Hinkle v. Hargens, 81 NW 2d 888, SD 1957. Ch 5, n 25.

Mueller v. Mueller, 221 NW 2d 39, SD 1974. Ch 6, n 4.

Schaffer v. Spicer, 215 NW 2d 134, SD 1974. Ch 5, n 38, n 39; n 40; Ch 8, n 67; Ch 9, n 40.

Tennessee

Ellis v. Ellis, 472 SW 2d 741, Tenn 1971. Ch 8, n 66.

Saville v. Treadway, 8 *Clearinghouse Rev,* 119, June 1974. Ch 9, n 65.

Texas

Austin v. Collins, 200 SW 2d 666, Tex 1947. Ch 3, n 101.

Campbell v. Campbell, 441 SW 2d 658, Tex 1969. Ch 5, n 5.

Ciulla v. Texas, 434 SW2d 948, Tex 1968. Ch 8, n 79.

Frazier v. Levi, 440 SW 2d 393, Tex 1969. Ch 2, n 93; Ch 10, n 40.

Leithold v. Plass, 413 SW 2d 698, Tex 1967. Ch 5, n 5.

Lotspeich v. Chance-Vought Aircraft Co., 369 SW 2d 705, Tex 1963. Ch 2, n 52.

Morris v. Rousos, 397 SW 2d 504, Tex 1965. Ch 7, n 61.

Nichols v. Nichols, 247 SW 2d 143, Tex 1952. Ch 8, n 52.

Ross v. Sher, 483 SW 2d 297, Tex 1972. Ch 7, n 14.

Utah

Berry v. Moench, 331 P 2d 814, Utah 1958. Ch 7, n 64; Ch 9, n 34.

Doe v. Planned Parenthood Association of Utah, 510 P 2d 75, Utah 1973. Ch 10, n 16.

Parker v. Rampton, 497 P 2d 848, Utah 1972. Ch 2, n 84.

In re Sadleir, 94 P 2d 161, Utah 1939. Ch 8, n 81.

Stone v. Stone, 431 P 2d 802, Utah 1967. Ch 8, n 63.

Vermont

Domina v. Pratt, 13 A 2d 198, Vt 1940. Ch 7, n 11, n 49.

Virginia

Buchanan v. Buchanan, 197 SE 426, Va 1938. Ch 6, n 33.

Carroll v. Richardson, 110 SE 2d 193, Va 1959. Ch 2, n 49.

Reed v. Church, 8 SE 2d 285, Va 1940. Ch 2, n 18; Ch 7, n 51.

Washington

Atkinson v. Atkinson, 231 P 2d 641, Wash 1951. Ch 8, n 54.

Dinner v. Thorp, 338 P 2d 137, Wash 1959. Ch 3, n 13.

Ericson v. Ericson, 195 Pac 234, Wash 1921. Ch 8, n 54.

In re Hendrickson, 123 P 2d 322, Wash 1942. Ch 2, n 92; Ch 10, n 31.

Hoffman v. Tracy, 406 P 2d 323, Wash 1965. Ch 1, n 76.

In re Hudson, 126 P 2d 765, Wash 1942. Ch 4, n 22; Ch 9, n 9.

Kaiser v. Suburban Transportation Co., 398 P 2d 14, Wash 1965. Ch 7, n 56.

Riste v. General Electric Corp., 289 P 2d 338, Wash 1955. Ch 2, n 51; Ch 7, n 26.

Rogers v. Olander, 286 P 2d 1028, Wash 1955. Ch 8, n 6.

Roller v. Roller, 79 Pac 788, Wash 1905. Ch 1, n 73.

Schultz v. Schultz, 404 P 2d 987, Wash 1965. Ch 8, n 50.

State v. Parmenter, 444 P 2d 680, Wash 1968. Ch 8, n 43.

Washington v. Koome, 530 P 2d 260, Wash 1975. Ch 10, n 57.

West Virginia

Baldwin v. Butcher, 184 SE 2d 428, W Va 1971. Ch 3, n 17, n 18.

Browning v. Hoffman, 103 SE 484, W Va 1920. Ch 9, n 18.

Hundley v. Martinez, 158 SE 2d 159, W Va 1967. Ch 2, n 21.

Wisconsin

Cirillo v. Milwaukee, 150 NW 2d 460, Wisc 1967. Ch 7, n 22.

Kwaterski v. State Farm Mutual Automobile Insurance Co., 148 NW 2d 107, Wisc 1967. Ch 3, n 17.

State ex rel Lewis v. Lutheran Social Services, 207 NW 2d 826, Wisc 1973. Ch 8, n 10.

Maniaci v. Marquette University, 184 NW 2d 168, Wisc 1971. Ch 7, n 61; Ch 9, n 72.

In re Pescinski, 226 NW 2d 180, Wisc 1975. Ch 6, n 50, n 56.

Rieck v. Medical Protective Co. of Fort Wayne, 219 NW 2d 242, Wisc 1974. Ch 1, n 67.

United States District Courts
(Excluding the District of Columbia)

Baird v. Bellotti, 393 F Supp 847, DC Mass 1975. Ch 10, n 58.

Coe v. Gerstein, 376 F Supp 695, DC Fla, 1974. Ch 1, n 58; Ch 3, n 87; Ch 10, n 52.

Cordova v. Chonko, 315 F Supp 953, DC Ohio 1970. Ch 9, n 30.

Cullen v. Grove Press, Inc., 276 F Supp 727, DC NY 1967. Ch 2, n 103.

Dietze v. King, 187 F Supp 944, DC Va 1960. Ch 5, n 29.

Doe v. Rampton, 366 F Supp 189, DC Utah 1973. Ch 1, n 58.

Foe v. Vanderhoof, 389 F Supp 947, DC Colo 1975. Ch 10, n 54.

Frederic v. United States, 246 F Supp 368, DC La 1965. Ch 2, n 22.

T. H. v. Jones, F Supp (unpublished), DC Utah, July 23, 1975, cert den, 424 US 000, 48 L Ed 2d 811, May 24, 1976. 32 *Citation* No. 8, pages 93–94. Ch 10, n 18.

Hall v. United States, 381 F Supp 224, DC SC 1974. Ch 5, n 42.

Hammonds v. Aetna Casualty and Surety Co., 243 F Supp 793, DC Ohio, 1965. Ch 9, n 41.

Hendry v. United States, 280 F Supp 27, DC NY 1968. Ch 7, n 15.

Larrabee v. United States, 254 F Supp 613, DC Cal 1966. Ch 3, n 26.

Larry P. v. Riles, 343 F Supp 1306, DC Cal 1972. Ch 7, n 6.

Martarella v. Kelley, 349 F Supp 575, DC NY 1972. Ch 8, n 88.

McCollum v. Mayfield, 130 F Supp 112, DC Cal 1955. Ch 8, n 96.

McHugh v. Audet, 72 F Supp 394, DC Pa 1947. Ch 1, n 29; Ch 9, n 14.

Merriken v. Cressman, 364 F Supp 913, DC Pa 1973. Ch 7, n 20; Ch 9, n 32, n 45; Ch 10, n 13.

Morales v. Turman, 364 F Supp 166, DC Tex 1973. Ch 8, n 88.

Ordway v. Hargraves, 323 F Supp 1155, DC Mass 1971. Ch 9, n 31.

Panagopoulous v. Martin, 295 F Supp 220, DC W Va, 1969. Ch 3, n 27.

Pearce v. United States, 236 F Supp 431, DC Okla, 1964. Ch 7, n 8.

Pennsylvania Association for Retarded Children v. Pennsylvania, 343 F Supp 279, DC Pa 1972. Ch 2, n 94, n 97; Ch 7, n 3.

Perry v. Grenada Municipal School District, 300 F Supp 748, DC Miss 1969. Ch 9, n 31.

Planned Parenthood Association v. Danforth, 392 F Supp 1362, DC Mo 1975. Ch 10, n 59.

Planned Parenthood Association v. Fitzpatrick, 401 F Supp 554, DC Pa 1975. Ch 10, n 56.

Population Services International v. Wilson, 398 F Supp 321, DC NY 1975. Ch 10, n 15.

Ramsey v. Ciccone, 310 F Supp 600, DC Mo 1970. Ch 8, n 95.

Redding v. United States, 196 F Supp 871, DC Ark 1961. Ch 2, n 31.

Shull v. Columbus Municipal School District, 338 F Supp 1376, DC Miss 1972. Ch 9, n 31.

Smith v. DiCara, 329 F Supp 439, DC NY 1971. Ch 2, n 102; Ch 7, n 64.

Tessier v. United States, 164 F Supp 779, DC Mass 1958. Ch 2, n 28.

Veals v. Ciccone, 281 F Supp 1017, DC Mo 1968. Ch 8, n 97.

Wade v. Bethesda Hospital, 356 F Supp 380, DC Ohio 1973. Ch 2, n 93; Ch 10, n 34.

Wansley v. Miller, 353 F Supp 42, DC Va 1973. Ch 8, n 83.

Willis v. White, 310 F Supp 205, DC La 1970. Ch 8, n 95.

Wolfe v. Schroering, 388 F Supp 631, DC Ky 1974. Ch 10, n 55.

Wyatt v. Aderholt, 368 F Supp 1383, DC Ala 1974. Ch 10, n 33.

Wyatt v. Stickney, 325 F Supp 781, DC Ala 1971. Ch 2, n 96; Ch 8, n 89.

United States Circuit Courts of Appeal
(Excluding the District of Columbia)

Breen v. Kahl, 419 F 2d 1034, CCA 7, 1969. Ch 9, n 30.

Campbell v. Wainwright, 416 F 2d 949, CCA 5, 1969. Ch 1, n 55.

Clark v. United States, 402 F 2d 950, CCA 4, 1968. Ch 2, n 19; Ch 7, n 12.

Cramer v. Hoffman, 390 F 2d 19, CCA 2, 1968. Ch 7, n 25.

Dunham v. Wright, 423 F 2d 940, CCA 3, 1970. Ch 2, n 25.

Edwards v. Duncan, 355 F 2d 993, CCA 4, 1966. Ch 8, n 96.

Hathaway v. Worcester City Hospital, 475 F 2d 701, CCA 1, 1973. Ch 2, n 85.

Hirons v. Patuxent Institution, 351 F 2d 613, CCA 4, 1965. Ch 8, n 96.

Iverson v. Frandsen, 237 F 2d 898, CCA 10, 1956. Ch 7, n 62.

Jeanes v. Milner, 428 F 2d 598, CCA 8, 1970. Ch 2, n 32.

Jines v. General Electric Corp., 303 F 2d 76, CCA 9, 1962. Ch 2, n 51; Ch 7, n 26.

Jorgensen v. Meade Johnson Laboratories, 483 F 2d 237, CCA 10, 1973. Ch 1, n 61.

Karp v. Cooley, 493 F 2d 408, CCA 5, 1974. Ch 1, n 29, n 62; Ch 3, n 88; Ch 6, n 19.

Kemplen v. Maryland, 428 F 2d 169, CCA 4, 1970. Ch 8, n 75.

Kinney v. Lenon, 425 F 2d 209, CCA 9, 1970. Ch 8, n 76.

Knecht v. Gillman, 488 F 2d 1136, CCA 8, 1973. Ch 8, n 92.

Mackey v. Procunier, 477 F 2d 877, CCA 9, 1973. Ch 8, n 91.

Martinez v. Mancusi, 443 F 2d 921, CCA 2, 1970. Ch 8, n 98.

Massie v. Henry, 455 F 2d 779, CCA 4, 1972. Ch 9, n 30.

Nelson v. Heyne, 491 F 2d 352, CCA 7, 1974, cert den 417 US 976, 1974. Ch 8, n 90, n 94.

Poe v. Gerstein, 517 F 2d 787, CCA 5, 1975. Ch 9, n 39; Ch 10, n 53.

Powell v. Hocker, 453 F 2d 652, CCA 9, 1971. Ch 8, n 75.

Rewis v. United States, 369 F 2d 595, CCA 5, 1966. Ch 7, n 10.

Sawyer v. Sigler, 445 F 2d 818, CCA 8, 1971. Ch 8, n 98.

Tippett v. Maryland, 436 F 2d 1153, CCA 4, 1971. Ch 8, n 85.

Tolbert v. Eyman, 434 F 2d 625, CCA 9, 1970. Ch 8, n 96.

Union Carbide and Carbon Co. v. Stapleton, 237 F 2d 229, CCA 6, 1956. Ch 2, n 53; Ch 7, n 27.

United States v. Repouille, 165 F 2d 152, CCA 2, 1947. Ch 4, n 30.

Wansley v. Slayton, 487 F 2d 90, CCA 4, 1973. Ch 8, n 82.

Winters v. Travia, 495 F 2d 839, CCA 2, 1974. Ch 7, n 45.

United States Supreme Court

Abington Township v. Schempp, 374 US 203, 1963. Ch 3, n 77; Ch 10, n 14.

Baker v. Owen, 423 US 907, 1975. Ch 6, n 30.

Bartley v. Kremens, 402 F Supp 1039, cert granted 424 US 000, 47 L Ed 2d 731. Ch 9, n 73.

Bellotti v. Baird, 424 US 000, 49 L Ed 2d 844, 1976. Ch 10, n 72.

Brown v. Board of Education, 347 US 483, 1954. Ch 3, n 73; Ch 7, n 42.

Buck v. Bell, 274 US 200, 1927. Ch 2, n 89; Ch 10, n 27.

Burns v. Alcala, 420 US 575, 1975. Ch 3, n 34.

Doe v. Bolton, 410 US 179, 1973. Ch 1, n 57; Ch 2, n 86; Ch 3, n 3; Ch 10, n 45.

Eisenstadt v. Baird, 405 US 438, 1972. Ch 2, n 83; Ch 10, n 2.

Engel v. Vitale, 370 US 421, 1962. Ch 3, n 77; Ch 10, n 14.

Gallegos v. Colorado, 370 US 49, 1962. Ch 8, n 80.

Griswold v. Connecticut, 381 US 479, 1965. Ch 2, n 82; Ch 9, n 28; Ch 10, n 1.

Lau v. Nichols, 412 US 938, 1973. Ch 7, n 1.

Loving v. Virginia, 388 US 1, 1967. Ch 2, n 87, n 88; Ch 10, n 43.

McCollum v. Board of Education, 333 US 203, 1948. Ch 3, n 77; Ch 10, n 14.

McKeiver v. Pennsylvania, 403 US 528, 1971. Ch 8, n 78.

McNeil v. Director, Patuxent Institution, 407 US 245, 1972. Ch 8, n 85; Ch 9, n 27.

Memorial Hospital v. Maricopa County, 415 US 250, 1974. Ch 5, n 1.

Meyer v. Nebraska, 262 US 390, 1923. Ch 10, n 50.

New York v. Leyra, 98 NE 2d 553, rev'd on other grounds, 347 US 556, 1954. Ch 9, n 34.

Pierce v. Society of Sisters, 268 US 510, 1925. Ch 10, n 50.

Planned Parenthood Association v. Danforth, 424 US 000, 49 L Ed 2d 788, 1976. Ch 10, n 71.

Prince v. Massachusetts, 321 US 158, 1944. Ch 4, n 31; Ch 6, n 32.

Roe v. Wade, 410 US 113, 1973. Ch 1, n 56; Ch 2, n 86; Ch 3, n 3; Ch 10, n 45.

Skinner v. Oklahoma, 316 US 535, 1942. Ch 2, n 90; Ch 10, n 35.

In re Stanley, 405 US 645, 1972. Ch 8, n 12.

Tinker v. Des Moines School District, 393 US 503, 1969. Ch 10, n 12.

United States v. Muniz, 374 US 150, 1963. Ch 8, n 100.

Wisconsin v. Yoder, 406 US 205, 1972. Ch 4, n 32; Ch 6, n 29; Ch 10, n 50.

Yarborough v. Yarborough, 290 US 202, 1933. Ch 5, n 7.

Zorach v. Clauson, 343 US 306, 1952. Ch 3, n 77; Ch 10, n 14.

OTHER

REFERENCES

"Law and Medicine" Series,
Journal of the American Medical Association

"Alternative Medical Procedures," 212 *JAMA* No. 2, page 385, April 13, 1970. Ch 9, n 14.

"Appointment of Independent Medical Expert," 216 *JAMA* No. 1, page 207, April 5, 1971. Ch 8, n 28, n 65.

"Authorization for Autopsies," 203 *JAMA* No. 5, page 199, January 29, 1968. Ch 3, n 54.

"Birth Injuries," 219 *JAMA* No. 1, page 129, January 3, 1972. Ch 3, n 21.

"Child Abuse and the Physician," 222 *JAMA* No. 4, page 517, October 23, 1972. Ch 8, n 30; Ch 9, n 33.

"Compulsory Sterilization," 221 *JAMA* No. 2, page 229, July 10, 1972. Ch 2, n 91; Ch 10, n 44.

"Consent in Clinical Investigation," 203 *JAMA* No. 7, page 281, February 12, 1968. Ch 1, n 29.

"Criminal Prosecution for Patient's Death," 222 *JAMA* No. 10, page 1341, December 4, 1972, Ch 4, n 34.

"Critical Areas in Clinical Investigation," 203 *JAMA* No. 8, page 241, February 19, 1968, Ch 3, n 99.

"Disclosure of Confidential Information," 216 *JAMA* No. 2, page 385, April 12, 1971. Ch 7, n 59; Ch 9, n 34.

"Duty to Consult," 226 *JAMA* No. 1, page 111, October 1, 1973. Ch 4, n 47.

"Duty to Refer to Larger Hospital," 224 *JAMA* No. 12, page 1687, June 18, 1973. Ch 2, n 17.

"Duty to Refer Patient to a Medical Specialist," 204 *JAMA* No. 8, page 281, May 20, 1968. Ch 2, n 15; Ch 7, n 17.

"Failure to Make Diagnostic Tests," 210 *JAMA* No. 1, page 213, October 6, 1969. Ch 7, n 12.

"Failure to Take Medical History," 226 *JAMA* No. 4, page 509, October 22, 1973. Ch 7, n 48.

"The Illegitimate and His Father," 216 *JAMA* No. 11, page 1909, June 14, 1971. Ch 8, n 11.

"Keeping the Patient's Secrets," 195 *JAMA* No. 5, page 227, January 31, 1966. Ch 9, n 34.

"Legal Implications of Photographing Surgical Operations," 198 *JAMA* No. 13, page 221, December 26, 1966. Ch 2, n 65.

"Liability for Mental Anguish," 217 *JAMA* No. 6, page 869, August 9, 1971. Ch 2, n 101.

"Liability for Obstetrical Injuries," 217 *JAMA* No. 7, page 1015, August 16, 1971. Ch 3, n 21.

"Liability of Referring Physician," 204 *JAMA* No. 3, page 273, April 15, 1968. Ch 7, n 13.

"Liability for Retrolental Fibroplasia," 212 *JAMA* No. 13, page 2343, June 29, 1970. Ch 7, n 58.

"Liability for Transfusion Hepatitis," 211 *JAMA* No. 8, page 1431, February 23, 1970, Ch 1, n 50.

"Mental Illness and Parental Rights," 216 *JAMA* No. 3, page 575, April 19, 1971. Ch 6, n 27; Ch 8, n 47.

"Minors and Contraception," 216 *JAMA* No. 12, page 2059, June 21, 1971. Ch 10, n 8, n 24.

"Misdiagnosis of Tuberculosis," 219 *JAMA* No. 4, page 561, January 24, 1972. Ch 2, n 99.

"Misdiagnosis Without Fault": I. 219 *JAMA* No. 7, page 967, February 14, 1972; II. 219 *JAMA* No. 8, page 1127, February 21, 1972. Ch. 7, n 47.

"Mother's Right to Consent," 213 *JAMA* No. 8, page 1393, August 24, 1970. Ch 5, n 4.

"Organ Donation by Incompetent," 213 *JAMA* No. 3, page 513, July 20, 1970. Ch 6, n 73.

"Package Inserts as Evidence," 208 *JAMA* No. 3, page 589, April 21, 1969. Ch 6, n 7; Ch 7, n 52.

"The Physician and Adoption," 223 *JAMA* No. 8, page 953, February 19, 1973. Ch 8, n 24.

"Physician's Liability for Drug Reactions," 213 *JAMA* No. 12, page 2143, September 21, 1970. Ch 7, n 50.

"Physician's Liability for Improper Disclosure," 198 *JAMA* No. 7, page 331, November 14, 1966. Ch 7, n 59; Ch 9, n 34.

"Prenatal Injuries," 214 *JAMA* No. 11, page 2105, December 14, 1970. Ch 1, n 60; Ch 3, n 12.

"Prisoner's Right to Medical Treatment," 216 *JAMA* No. 7, page 1253, May 17, 1971. Ch 8, n 95.

"Recent Decisions on Transfusion Hepatitis," 228 *JAMA* No. 6, page 786, May 6, 1974. Ch 1, n 50.

"Referral to a Specialist," 211 *JAMA* No. 11, page 1911, March 16, 1970. Ch 2, n 15; Ch 7, n 17.

"Right to Release from Mental Hospital," 220 *JAMA* No. 10, page 1405, June 5, 1972. Ch 9, n 53.

"The Right to Sterilization," 226 *JAMA* No. 9, page 1151, November 26, 1973. Ch 2, n 84.

"The Right to Treatment," 220 *JAMA* No. 8, page 1165, May 22, 1972. Ch 2, n 96; Ch 8, n 86.

"Transplant Problems," 223 *JAMA* No. 11, page 1315, March 12, 1973. Ch 6, n 52.

"Treating a Minor for Venereal Disease," 214 *JAMA* No. 10, page 1949, December 7, 1970. Ch 5, n 13.

"Unauthorized Autopsies," 214 *JAMA* No. 5, page 967, November 2, 1970. Ch 3, n 54.

"The United States Supreme Court and Abortions": I. 225 *JAMA* No. 2, page 215, July 9, 1973; II. 225 *JAMA* No. 3, page 343, July 16, 1973; III. 225 *JAMA* No. 4, page 447, July 23, 1973. Ch 3, n 8.

"Voluntary Sterilization," 225 *JAMA* No. 13, page 1743, September 24, 1973. Ch 2, n 84.

**Medical Journals and
Other Medical Publications**

AMA *News,* April 17, 1967, page 4. Ch 5, n 14.

"Bedside Ethics for the Hopeless Case," editorial, 289 *New Engl J Med,* page 914, October 25, 1973. Ch 4, n 10.

Bentovin, Arnon, "Emotional Disturbances of Handicapped Preschool Children," 3 *Brit Med J,* page 579, 1972. Ch 4, n 8.

Bernstein, D. M., and Simmons, R. G., "The Adolescent Kidney Donor: The Right to Give," 131 *Am J Psychiat* No. 12, page 1338, December 1974. Ch 6, n 67.

"The Birth of an Abnormal Child: Telling the Parents," editorial, *Lancet,* November 13, 1971, page 1075. Ch 4, n 8.

1 *Brit Med J,* page 523, 1970. Ch 2, n 11.

Campbell, A. G. M., "Infants, Children and Informed Consent," 3 *Brit Med J,* page 334, 1974. Ch 6, n 21.

Capron, Alexander, "Legal Considerations Affecting Clinical Pharmacological Studies in Children," *Clin Res,* page 146, February 1973. Ch 6, n 14, n 21, n 36.

Chalkley, Donald T., *Medical World News,* June 8, 1973, page 41. Ch 6, n 25.

Conners, C. K., Eisenberg, L., and Barcai, A., "Effects of Dextroamphetamine on Children," 17 *Arch Gen Psychiat,* page 478, October 1967. Ch 7, n 54.

Curran, William J., "Kidney Transplantation in Identical Twin Minors: Justice Is Done in Connecticut," 287 *New Engl J Med,* page 26, July 6, 1972. Ch 2, n 62.

Curran, William J., and Beecher, Henry K., "Experimentation in Children," 210 *JAMA* No. 1, page 77, October 6, 1969. Ch 6, n 21, n 23.

"Drug Testing in Children: FDA Regulations," 43 *Pediatrics* No. 3, page 463, March 1969. Ch 6, n 8.

Duff, Raymond, and Campbell, A. G. M., "Moral and Ethical Dilemmas in the Special-Care Nursery," 289 *New Engl J Med,* page 890, October 1973. Ch 4, n 7.

Eckhart, Walter, "Genetic Disease Modification of Cells by Viruses," 21 *Bioscience,* page 171, 1971. Ch 2, n 104.

Editorial, 128 *Am J Diseases Children* No. 3, page 295. Ch 3, n 37.

Fantel, Alan G., and Shepard, Thomas H., "Legislative Threats to Research on Human Congenital Defects," 38 *Conn Med* No. 10, page 535, October 1974. Ch 3, n 39.

Fish, Barbara, "Drug Use in Psychiatric Disorders of Children," 124 *Am J Psychiat* No. 8, page 31, February 1968. Ch 7, n 54.

Freeman, John M., "To Treat or Not to Treat, Ethical Dilemmas of Treating the Infant with a Myelomeningocele," 20 *Clin Neurol,* page 135. Ch 4, n 2, n 12, n 48.

Gaylin, Willard, editorial, 286 *New Engl J Med,* page 1361, 1972. Ch 2, n 34.

Gerbie, A. B., and Nadler, H. L. "Amniocentesis in Genetic Counseling," 109 *Am J Obstet Gynecol,* page 766, 1971. Ch 2, n 10.

Goldby, Stephen, "Experiments at the Willowbrook State School," 1 *Lancet,* page 749, 1971. Ch 6, n 10.

Goldstein, Abraham S., and Katz, Jay, "Psychiatrist-Patient Privilege: The GAP Proposal and the Connecticut Statute," 118 *Am J Psychiat,* page 733, 1962. Ch 9, n 15.

Gordon, Hymie, "Genetic Counseling," 217 *JAMA* No. 9, page 1215, August 30, 1971. Ch 2, n 98.

Gustafson, James M., "Mongolism, Parental Desires, and the Right to Life," *Perspectives Biol Med,* page 529, Summer 1973. Ch 4, n 14, n 15.

Hofmann, Adele D., and Pilpel, Harriet F., "The Legal Rights of Minors," 20 *Pediat Clin N Am* No. 4, page 1001, November 1973. Ch 10, n 7.

Holder, Angela, "How Much Would You Tell a Lawyer?" 2 *Prism* No. 6, page 52, June 1974. Ch 9, n 41.

"Is There a Right to Die Quickly?" editorial, 80 *J Pediat,* page 904, 1972. Ch 4, n 13.

Kempe, C. H., "The Battered Child Syndrome," 181 *JAMA* No. 1, page 17, 1962. Ch 8, n 34.

Krugman, S., Giles, J. P., Hammond, Jack, "Viral Hepatitis, Type B (MS-2 Strain): Studies on Active Immunization," 217 *JAMA,* page 41, 1971. Ch 6, n 11

Lappé, Marc, "Mass Genetic Screening Programs," *Med Dimensions,* February 1973. Ch 2, n 72.

Letter, 221 *JAMA* No. 4, page 408, July 24, 1972. Ch 2, n 36.

Letter, *Lancet,* page 728, September 29, 1973. Ch 1, n 4.

Letter from Edward J. Rourke, Assistant General Counsel, DHEW, 211 *JAMA* No. 2, page 301, January 12, 1970. Ch 6, n 21, n 22.

Levine, M. D., Camitta, B. M., Nathan, D., and Curran, W. J. "The Medical Ethics of Bone Marrow Transplantation in Childhood," 86 *J Pediat* No. 1, page 145, January 1975. Ch 6, n 47, n 59, n 63, n 65, n 69, n 70.

Littlefield, John W., "The Pregnancy at Risk for Genetic Disorder," 282 *New Engl J Med* No. 11, page 627, 1970. Ch 2, n 13, n 40.

"Live Abortus Research Raises Hackles of Some, Hopes of Others," *Medical World News,* October 5, 1973, page 32. Ch 3, n 80, n 81.

Lockhart, Jean D., "The Information Gap in Pediatric Drug Therapy," *Mod Med,* page 56, November 16, 1970. Ch 6, n 9.

Lorber, J., "Results of Treatment of Myelomeningocele," 13 *Develop Med Child Neurol,* page 279, 1971. Ch 4, n 2, n 5, n 36, n 37.

Lowe, C. U., Alexander, D., and Mishkin, B., "Nontherapeutic Research on Children: An Ethical Dilemma," 84 *J Pediat* No. 4, page 472, April 1974. Ch 6, n 14.

Lynch, Henry et al., "Genetic Counseling," 211 *JAMA* No. 4, page 647, January 26, 1970. Ch 2, n 98.

MacIntyre, R. "Chromosome Problems and Intrauterine Diagnosis," 7 *Birth Defects* No. 5, page 11, 1971, Ch 2, n 12.

McCormick, Richard A., "Proxy Consent in the Experimental Situation," 18 *Perspectives Biol Med* No. 1, page 2, Autumn 1974. Ch 6, n 20, n 21, n 24, n 25, n 37.

McCormick, Richard A., "To Save or Let Die: The Dilemma of Modern Medicine," 229 *JAMA* No. 2, page 172, July 8, 1974. Ch 4, n 15, n 38, n 42, n 43.

Menees, T. O., Miller, J. D., and Holly L. E., "Amniography," 24 *Am J Roentgenol,* page 363, 1930, Ch 2, n 6.

Menkes, M., Rowe, J., and Menkes, J., "A Twenty-five Year Follow-up Study on the Hyperkinetic Child with Minimal Brain Dysfunction," 39 *Pediat* No. 3, page 393, March 1967. Ch 7, n 57.

Millichap, J. Gordon, "Drugs in Management of Hyperkinetic and Perceptually Handicapped Children," 206 *JAMA* No. 7, page 1527, November 11, 1968. Ch 7, n 40, n 54.

Milunsky, Aubrey et al., "Prenatal Genetic Diagnosis," 283 *New Engl J Med* No. 25, page 1370, December 17, 1970; No. 26, page 1441, December 24, 1970; No. 27, page 1498, December 31, 1970. Ch 2, n 8, n 9.

Mitchell, Ross G., "The Child and Experimental Medicine," 1964 *Brit Med J* No. 1, page 721. Ch 6, n 26.

Model Act, 51 *Pediatrics* No. 2, page 293, February 1973. Ch 5, n 15, n 36; Ch 9, n 20; Ch 10, n 65.

Osmundsen, John, "We Are All Mutants: Preventive Genetic Medicine," *Med Dimensions,* page 26, February 1973. Ch 2, n 2, n 3.

Peel Report, (summary), 38 *Conn Med* No. 10, page 539, October 1974. Ch 3, n 78.

Pinkerton, Philip, "Parental Acceptance of the Handicapped Child," 12 *Develop Med Child Neurol,* page 207, 1970. Ch 4, n 8.

Pipel, Harriet F., and Wechsler, Nancy F., "Birth Control, Teenagers and the Law," 1 *Family Planning Perspectives,* page 29, 1969. Ch 10, n 21.

Proceedings of the AMA House of Delegates 5556, June 20–24, 1971. Ch 10, n 6.

"Regulations and Legislation Concerning Abortus Research," commentary, *JAMA* No. 10, page 1303, September 2, 1974. Ch 3, n 38, n 39.

Research Group, Institute of Society, Ethics and The Life Sciences, "Ethical and Social Issues in Screening for Genetic Disease," 286 *New Engl J Med,* page 1129, May 25, 1972. Ch 2, n 71, n 72.

"Research Investigations and the Fetus," symposium, *Brit Med J,* page 464, May 26, 1973. Ch 3, n 78.

Rickham, Peter, "The Ethics of Surgery in Newborn Infants," 8 *Clin Pediat* 251, 1969. Ch 4, n 17, n 40.

Schowalter, John, Ferholt, Julian, and Mann, Nancy, "The Adolescent Patient's Decision to Die," 51 *Pediatrics* No. 1, page 97, January 1973. Ch 4, n 55, n 57.

Schroeder, Leila, "New Life: Person or Property?" 131 *Am J Psychiat* No. 5, page 541, May 1974. Ch 1, n 79.

Shaw, Anthony, "Informed Consent in Children," 289 *New Engl J Med* No. 885, page 889, 1973. Ch 4, n 3, n 46.

Shirkey, Harry, "Therapeutic Orphans," 72 *J Pediat* No. 1, page 119, January 1968. Ch 6, n 9.

Schwartz, A. Herbert, "Children's Concepts of Research Hospitalization," 287 *New Engl J Med* No. 12, page 589, September 1972. Ch 6, n 17.

"Studies with Children Backed on Medical, Ethical Grounds," 8 *Medical Tribune,* February 20, 1967, page 23. Ch 6, n 13.

Sulzbacher, Stephen I., "The Learning-Disabled or Hyperactive Child," 234 *JAMA* No. 9, page 938, December 1975. Ch 7, n 40.

Terr, Lenore C., and Watson, Andrew, "The Battered Child Rebrutalized," 124 *Am J Psychiat* No. 10, page 1432, April 1968. Ch 8, n 34, n 35.

Toch, Rudolph, "Management of the Child with a Fatal Disease," 3 *Clin Pediat* No. 7, page 423, July 1964. Ch 4, n 54, n 56.

Vernick, Joel, and Karon, Myron, "Who's Afraid of Death on a Leukemia Ward?" 109 *Am J Diseases Children,* 393, May 1965. Ch 4, n 56.

Whitten, Charles F., "Sickle Cell Programming," 288 *New Engl J Med,* page 318, 1973. Ch 2, n 62.

Zuk, G. H., "The Religious Factor and the Role of Guilt in Parental Acceptance of the Retarded Child," 64 *Am J Mental Deficiency,* page 139. Ch 4, n 8.

Legal Journals

"Abortion: The Father's Rights," note, 42 *U Cinn Law Rev,* page 441, 1973. Ch 1, n 58.

"Analysis of Legal and Medical Considerations in Commitment of the Mentally Ill," note, 56 *Yale Law J,* page 1178, 1947. Ch 9, n 59.

Baker, James A., "Court-Ordered Non-emergency Medical Care for Infants," 18 *Cleveland-Marshall Law Rev* No. 2, page 296, May 1969. Ch 9, n 7.

Barnett, F. J., "Liability for Adverse Drug Reactions," 1 *J Legal Med* No. 2, page 47, May/June 1973. Ch 7, n 52.

Baron, C. H., Botsford, M., and Cole, G. F., "Live Organ and Tissue Transplants from Minor Donors in Massachusetts," 55 *Boston U Law Rev,* page 169, 1975. Ch 6, n 34, n 44, n 46, n 47, n 57, n 63, n 64, n 66.

Bazelon, David L., "Beyond Control of the Juvenile Court," 21 *Juvenile Court J* page 42, 1970. Ch 8, n 71.

Birnbaum, Morton, "The Right to Treatment," 46 *ABAJ,* page 499, May 1960. Ch 8, n 86.

Bodine, Neil, "Minors and Contraceptives: A Constitutional Issue," 3 *Ecology Law Quart,* page 843, 1973. Ch 10, n 10, n 11.

Capron, Alexander M., "Informed Decisionmaking in Genetic Counseling: A Dissent to the Wrongful Life Debate," 48 *Ind Law J,* page 581, 1973. Ch 2, n 50, n 55, n 56, n 57.

Cavenaugh, Robert P., "Minors and Contraception: The Physician's Right to Assist Unmarried Minors in California," 23 *Hastings Law J,* page 1486, May 1972. Ch 10, n 3, n 19.

"Counseling the Counselors: Legal Implications of Counseling Minors without Parental Consent," note, 31 *Md Law Rev* No. 4, page 332, 1971. Ch 9, n 17.

"Criminal Law: Attempted Suicide," note, 40 *NC Law Rev,* page 323, 1962. Ch 1, n 52.

Curran, William J., "A Problem of Consent: Kidney Transplantation in Minors," 34 *NYU Law Rev,* page 891, May 1959, Ch 6, n 43, n 51, n 60, n 64, n 71.

"Damages for the Wrongful Death of a Fetus," comment, 51 *Chicago Kent Law Rev,* page 227, 1974, Ch 3, n 17.

Dukenminier, Jesse, "Supplying Organs for Transplantation," 68 *Mich Law Rev,* page 811, 1970, Ch 1, n 51.

Dunn, Rex, "Eugenic Sterilization Statutes: A Constitutional Re-Evaluation," 14 *J Family Law* No. 2, page 280, 1975. Ch 10, n 26.

Ellis, James W., "Volunteering Children: Parental Commitment of Minors to Mental Institutions," 62 *Cal Law Rev,* page 840, 1974. Ch 9, n 52.

Ely, John, "The Wages of Crying Wolf: A Comment on *Roe v. Wade,*" 82 *Yale Law J,* page 920, 1973, Ch 2, n 38, n 39.

Epstein, Charles J., "Legal Implications of Recent Advances in Medical Genetics," 21 *Hasting Law J,* page 35, 1969. Ch 2, n 40.

"Family Planning and the Law," Report of the ABA Family Law Section, 1 *Family Law Quart,* page 103, Winter 1967. Ch 10, n 4.

Forbes, Peter, "Voluntary Sterilization of Woman as a Right," 18 *DePaul Law Rev,* No. 2–3, page 560, Summer 1969. Ch 2, n 84.

Friedman, Jane M., "Legal Implications of Amniocentesis," 123 *U Pa Law Rev,* page 92, 1974. Ch 2, n 1, n 23, n 24, n 38, n 44, n 48.

Gibbs, Richard S., "Therapeutic Abortion and the Minor," 1 *J Legal Med* No. 1, page 36, March–April 1973. Ch 10, n 62.

Gough, Aidan R., "The Beyond-Control Child and the Right to Treatment: An Exercise in the Synthesis of Paradox," 16 *St. Louis Law J,* page 182, Winter 1971. Ch 9, n 69.

Holder, Angela, "The School Prayer Cases and the Right to Privacy," 12 *J Church State* No. 2, page 289, Spring 1970. Ch 3, n 77; Ch 9, n 23; Ch 10, n 14.

Holder, James B., "Serum Hepatitis," 6 *Lawyers' Med J,* page 79, May 1970. Ch 1, n 49.

Hudock, George A., "Gene Therapy and Genetic Engineering," 48 *Ind Law J,* page 533, 1973. Ch 1, n 72.

Isaacson, Lon B., "Child Abuse Reporting Statutes: The Case for Holding Physicians Civilly Liable for Failing to Report," 12 *San Diego Law Rev* No. 4, page 743, July 1975. Ch 8, n 41.

Jordan, Elizabeth, "A Minor's Right to Contraceptives," 7 *U Cal at Davis Law Rev,* page 270, 1974. Ch 10, n 6, n 7.

Kamisar, Yale, "Some Non-religious Views Against Proposed Mercy-Killing Legislation," 42 *Minn Law Rev* No. 6, page 969, May 1958. Ch 4, n 27, n 28, n 29.

Katz, Jay, "The Right to Treatment: An Enchanting Legal Fiction," 36 *U Chicago Law Rev,* page 755, 1969. Ch 9, n 25.

Katz, Sanford N., "The Adoption of Baby Lenore," 5 *Family Law Quart,* page 405, Winter 1971. Ch 8, n 20.

Katz, Sanford N., Howe, R. A., and McGraft, Melba, "Child Neglect Laws," 9 *Family Law Quart* No. 1, Spring 1975. Ch 8, n 44.

Kirp, David L., "Schools as Sorters," 121 *U Pa Law Rev,* page 705, April 1973. Ch 7, n 1, n 4.

Kleinfield, Andrew J., "The Balance of Power Among Infants, Their Parents and the State," 4 *Family Law Quart,* page 410, 1970. Ch 9, n 56.

Leach, W. B., "Perpetuities in the Atomic Age: The Sperm Bank and the Fertile Decedent," 48 *ABAJ,* page 942, 1962. Ch 1, n 45.

"The Legal Consequences of Artificial Insemination in New York," note, 19 *Syracuse Law Rev* 1009, 1968. Ch 1, n 38.

Lessem, Louis, "On the Voluntary Admission of Minors," 8 *U Mich J Law Reform* No. 1, page 189, Fall 1974. Ch 9, n 52, n 57, n 71.

Louisell, David, "Abortion, the Practice of Medicine and the Due Process of Law," 16 *UCLA Law Rev* page 233, 1969. Ch 3, n 33.

"The Minor's Right to Abortion and the Requirement of Parental Consent," comment, 60 *Va Law Rev* No. 2, page 305, 1974. Ch 10, n 46.

Morris, Crawford, "Doctors and the Sporting Life," 39 *Ins Counsel J* 283, July 1972. Ch 7, n 21.

"Moppets on the Market," comment, 59 *Yale Law J,* page 715, March 1950. Ch 8, n 7.

Murphy, J. C., "Total Institutions and the Possibility of Consent to Organic Therapies," 5 *Human Rights* No. 1, page 25, Fall 1975. Ch 8, n 91.

"Natural v. Adoptive Parents," note, 57 *Iowa Law Rev,* page 171, 1971. Ch 8, n 20.

Note, 4 *Texas Tech Law Rev,* page 244, 1972. Ch 6, n 62.

Oakley, Mary Ann B., "Test Tube Babies," 8 *Family Law Quart,* page 385, Winter 1974. Ch 1, n 31.

"Parental Consent Requirements and Privacy Rights of Minors: The Contraceptive Controversy," note, 88 *Harvard Law Rev* No. 5, page 1001, March 1975. Ch 10, n 23.

Paulsen, M. G., "Fairness to the Juvenile Offender," 41 *Minn Law Rev,* page 547, 1957. Ch 8, n 73.

"Paulsen, M. G., "The Legal Framework for Child Protection," 66 *Columbia Law Rev,* page 679, 1966. Ch 8, n 36, n 37.

Pilpel, Harriet F., "Minors' Right to Medical Care," 36 *Albany Law Rev,* page 462, 1972. Ch 5, n 12, n 17; Ch 9, n 12.

Presser, Stephen B., "The Historical Background of the American Law of Adoption," 11 *J Family Law* No. 3, page 43, 1972. Ch 8, n 1.

Raitt, G. Emmett, "The Minor's Right to Consent to Medical Treatment," 48 *So Cal Law Rev,* page 1417, 1975. Ch 5, n 16; Ch 9, n 19; Ch 10, n 5, n 64.

Reback, Gary E., "Fetal Experimentation: Moral, Legal and Medical Implications," 26 *Stanford Law Rev,* page 1191, 1974. Ch 3, n 10.

"Revocation of Parental Consent to Adoption," note, 28 *U Chicago Law Rev,* page 564, 1961. Ch 1, n 19.

"The Right to Bail and the Pre-Trial Detention of Juveniles Accused of Crime," note, 18 *Vanderbilt Law Rev,* page 2096, 1965. Ch 8, n 77.

"The Right to Treatment," symposium, 57 *Georgetown Law J,* March 1969. Ch 8, n 86.

Riley, Phillip, "Sickle Cell Anemia Legislation": I. 1 *J Leg Med* No. 4, page 39, September 1973; II. 1 *J Leg Med* No. 5, page 36, October 1973. Ch 2, n 61, n 63.

Robertson, John A., "Involuntary Euthanasia of Defective Newborns: A Legal Analysis," 27 *Stanford Law Rev,* page 213, 1975. Ch 4, n 6, n 33, n 39.

"The Sale of Human Body Parts," comment, 72 *Mich Law Rev,* page 1196, May 1974. Ch 1, n 51; Ch 6, n 68.

Shapiro, Michael L., "Legislating the Control of Behavior Control," 47 *So Cal Law Rev,* page 237, 1974. Ch 8, n 91.

Sheerer, Charles W., and Roston, Ronald A., "Some Legal and Psychological Concerns About Personality Testing in Public Schools," 30 *Fed Bar J* No. 2, page 111, Spring 1971. Ch 9, n 32.

Smith, George P., "Through a Test-Tube Darkly: Artificial Insemination and the Law," 67 *Mich Law Rev,* page 127, 1968. Ch 1, n 47.

Sneidman, Barney, "Prisoners and Medical Treatment: Their Rights and Remedies," 4 *Crim Law Bull,* page 450, October 1968. Ch 8, n 99.

Sussman, Alan, "Reporting Child Abuse: A Review of the Literature," 8 *Fam Law Quart,* page 245, Fall 1974. Ch 8, n 41.

Szasz, Thomas S., "The Right to Health," 57 *Georgetown Law J,* page 734, 1969. Ch 9, n 55.

Tribe, Laurence H., "Toward a Model of Roles in the Due Process of Life and Law," 87 *Harvard Law Rev* No. 1, page 1, November 1973. Ch 10, n 45.

"Underprivileged Communications: Extension of the Psychotherapist-Patient Privilege to Patients of Psychiatric Social Workers," comment, 61 *Cal Law Rev,* page 1050, 1973. Ch 9, n 16.

"Use of Extra-Record Information in Custody Cases," comment, 24 *U Chicago Law Rev* No. 2, page 349, Winter 1957. Ch 8, n 62.

Wadlington, Walter, "Artificial Insemination: The Dangers of a Poorly Kept Secret," 64 *Northwestern Law Rev* No. 6, page 777, January 1970. Ch 1, n 47.

Wadlington, Walter, "Minors and Health Care: The Age of Consent," 11 *Osgoode Hall Law J,* page 115, 1973. Ch 5, n 21; Ch 9, n 12.

Waltz, Jon R., and Thigpen, Carol R., "Genetic Screening and Counseling, the Legal and Ethical Issues," 68 *Northwestern Law Rev.* No. 4, page 696, 1974. Ch 2, n 60, n 64, n 66, n 95.

Wasserman, Richard, "Implications of the Abortion Decisions," 74 *Columbia Law Rev,* page 237, March 1974. Ch 10, n 47.

Wells, William W., "Drug Control of School Children: The Child's Right to Choose," 46 *So Cal Law Rev,* page 585, 1973. Ch 7, n 38, n 41, n 44.

Wilkins, Lawrence P., "Children's Rights: Removing the Parental Consent Barrier," 1975 *Ariz State Law J* No. 1, page 31. Ch 5, n 12; Ch 9, n 13.

**Other Journals, Newspapers
and Popular Periodicals**

Blake, Judith, "The Teenage Birth Control Dilemma and Public Opinion," 180 *Science,* page 708, May 18, 1973. Ch 10, n 9.

"Case Studies in Bioethics: On the Birth of a Severely Handicapped Infant," *Hastings Center Report,* page 10, September 1973. Ch 4, n 49.

Charlotte Observer, July 15, 1973. Ch 3, n 35. July 17, 1975, page 8A. Ch 1, n 48.

Cohen, Pauline, "Impact of the Handicapped Child on the Family," 43 *Social Casework,* page 137, 1962. Ch 4, n 8.

Culliton, Barbara, "Grave Robbing: Charges Against Four from Boston City Hospital," 186 *Science,* page 420, 1974. Ch 3, n 53.

Culliton, Barbara, "Sickle Cell Anemia: National Program Raises Problems as Well as Hopes," 178 *Science,* page 283, October 1972. Ch 2, n 77.

Danielli, James F., "Industry, Society and Genetic Engineering," *Hastings Center Report,* page 5, December 1972. Ch 2, n 104.

Davis, Bernard D., "Prospects for Genetic Intervention in Man," 170 *Science,* page 1279, December 18, 1970. Ch 2, n 104.

Duff, Raymond, "Interview," *Hastings Center Report,* page 7, April 1975. Ch 4, n 11.

Edwards, R. G., and Fowler, Ruth E., "Human Embryos in the Laboratory," 223 *Scientific American* No. 6, page 44, December 1970. Ch 1, n 2, n 23.

Eisenberg, Leon, "Role of Drugs in Treating Disturbed Children," 2 *Children* No. 5, page 167, September/October 1964. Ch 7, n 40.

"Facing Death," symposium, 2 *Hastings Center Studies* No. 2, May 1974. Ch 4, n 53.

Fletcher, John, "Attitudes Toward Defective Newborns," 2 *Hastings Center Studies* No. 1, page 21, January 1974. Ch 4, n 8, n 9.

Fletcher, John, "The Brink: The Parent-Child Bond in the Genetic Revolution," 33 *Theological Studies,* page 459, September 1972. Ch 2, n 7, n 41.

Friedmann, Theodore, "Prenatal Diagnosis of Genetic Disease," 225 *Scientific American,* page 37, November 1971. Ch 2, n 5.

Friedmann, Theodore, and Roblin, Richard, "Gene Therapy for Human Genetic Disease," 175 *Science,* page 949, March 1972. Ch 2, n 104.

"Genes Are Held Able to Cure Disease," *New York Times,* October 22, 1967, page 67, Col. 1. Ch 2, n 104.

"Genetic Counseling," editorial, 184 *Science,* page 751, May 17, 1974. Ch 2, n 33.

Grinspoon, Lester, and Singer, Susan B. "Amphetamines in the Treatment of Hyperkinetic Children," 43 *Harvard Educational Rev* No. 4, page 515, November 1973. Ch 7, n 33, n 38.

Grossman, Edward, "The Obsolescent Mother," 227 *Atlantic* No. 5, page 39, May 1974. Ch 1, n 13.

Grunberg, Frederick, "Who Lives and Dies?" *New York Times,* April 22, 1974, page 35, Col. 2. Ch 4, n 41.

Hemphill, Michael, "Pretesting for Huntington's Disease," *Hastings Center Report,* page 12, June 1973. Ch 2, n 74.

Ireland, Roderick L., and Dimond, Paul R., "Drugs and Hyperactivity: Process Is Due," 9 *Inequality in Education,* page 19, 1971. Ch 7, n 44.

Kass, Leon R., "Making Babies: The New Biology and the Old Morality," 26 *Public Interest,* page 31, Winter 1972. Ch 1, n 24.

Ladd, Edward T., "Pills for Classroom Peace," 53 *Saturday Review* No. 47, page 66, November 21, 1970. Ch 7, n 34, n 38.

Lappé, Marc, "The Genetic Counselor: Responsible to Whom?" 1 *Hastings Center Report* No. 2, page 6, September 1971. Ch 2, n 44.

McCormick, Richard, 5 *Hastings Center Report* No. 3, page 28, June 1975. Ch 3, n 91.

Murray, Robert F., "Problems Behind the Promise: Ethical Issues and Mass Genetic Screening," 2 *Hastings Center Report* No. 2, page 10, April 1972. Ch 2, n 75, n 76.

National Observer, September 14, 1974, page 1. Ch 10, n 61.

New York Times, February 27, 1970, page 8, Col. 3. Ch 1, n 14. October 17, 1971, page 65. Ch 1, n 44. July 16, 1974, page 8, Col. 3. Ch 1, n 6. July 17, 1974, page 14, Col. 4. Ch 1, n 7. July 19, 1974, page 31, Col. 1, Ch 1, n 8. August 20, 1974, page 39, Col. 6. Ch 1, n 26. June 20, 1975, page 36c. Ch 2, n 73. June 24, 1975. Ch 2, n 78.

Powledge, Tabitha M., "The New Ghetto Hustle," *Saturday Review,* February 1973, page 38. Ch 2, n 61, n 64, n 77.

Powledge, Tabitha M., "New Trends in Genetic Legislation," *Hastings Center Report,* page 6, December 1973. Ch 2, n 66, n 70.

Recommendations of the Commission, 5 *Hastings Center Report* No. 3, page 45, June 1975. Ch 3, n 84, n 95.

Report of the Conference on Hyperkinesis, 9 *Inequality in Education,* page 14, 1971. Ch 7, n 35, n 36, n 37, n 39.

Rorvick, David, "The Embryo Sweepstakes," *New York Times* (magazine section), September 15, 1974, page 17 et seq. Ch 1, n 10, n 11, n 13, n 27.

Rorvick, David, "Embryo Transplants," *Good Housekeeping,* page 78, June 1975. Ch 1, n 12, n 28.

Schafer, "Programmed for Social Class: Tracking in High School," *Transaction,* October 1970, page 39. Ch 7, n 4.

151 *Science,* page 663, 1963. Ch 6, n 39.

186 *Science,* page 715, November 22, 1974. Ch 2, n 73.

Seigel, Seymour, 5 *Hastings Center Report* No. 3, page 25, June 1975. Ch 3, n 90.

Shaw, Anthony, "Doctor, Do We Have a Choice?" *New York Times Magazine,* January 30, 1972, page 50. Ch 4, n 1.

Shettles, Landrum B., letter, 229 *Nature,* page 343, January 29, 1971. Ch 1, n 3.

Smith, David H., "On Letting Some Babies Die," *Hastings Center Studies* No. 2, page 37, May 1974, Ch 4, n 6.

Stevenson, N., "The Legal Rights of Unmarried Fathers: The Impact of Recent Court Decisions," 47 *So Serv Rev,* page 1, 1973. Ch 8, n 11.

Szasz, Thomas S., "The Psychiatrist as Double Agent," *Transaction,* October 1967. Ch 9, n 46.

Toulmin, Stephen, "Exploring the Moderate Consensus," 5 *Hastings Report* No. 3, page 31, June 1975. Ch 3, n 40.

Veatch, Robert M., "The Unexpected Chromosome," 2 *Hastings Center Report* No. 1, page 8, February 1972. Ch 2, n 33.

Walters, Leroy, 5 *Hastings Center Report* No. 3, page 15, June 1975. Ch 3, n 89.

Washington Post, March 3, 1970. Ch 1, n 25. April 13, 1973, page A1. Ch 3, n 1, n 4. February 25, 1974, page A-1. Ch 4, n 16.

Witler, Charles, "Drugging and Schooling," *Transaction,* page 31, July/August 1971. Ch 7, n 34.

Books

Anderson, W. French, "Genetic Therapy," in *The New Genetics and the Future of Man,* Grand Rapids, Mich, Wm. B. Eerdmans Publishing Co., 1972. Ch 2, n 46.

53 *Am Jur* 2 d, "Mayhem." Ch 1, n 54.

20 *Am Jur Trials,* "Trials of Wrongful Death Actions." Ch 3, n 24.

Annas, George J., *The Rights of Hospital Patients,* New York, Avon Books, 1975. Ch 7, n 63.

Antieau, Chester J., *Modern Constitutional Law,* Rochester, NY, The Lawyers Co-operative Publishing Co., 1969. Ch 8, n 70, n 72.

Blackstone, *Commentaries,* Book I, Philadelphia, J. B. Lippincott Co., 1913. Ch 3, n 28.

Brakel, Samuel J., and Rock, Ronald S., *The Mentally Disabled and the Law,* rev. ed., Chicago, University of Chicago Press, 1971. Ch 10, n 30.

Chayet, Neil L., *Legal Implications of Emergency Care,* New York, Appleton-Century-Crofts, 1969. Ch 7, n 28, n 29.

Daube, David, "Transplantation Acceptability of Procedures and the Required Legal Sanctions," in *Ethics in Medical Progress,* Boston, Little, Brown and Co., 1966. Ch 6, n 68.

Erikson, Erik, *Identity: Youth and Crisis,* New York, W. W. Norton and Co., 1968. Ch 9, n 3.

Evans, Richard I., *Dialogue with Erik Erikson,* New York, E. P. Dutton and Co., 1969. Ch 9, n 2.

Fletcher, Joseph, *The Ethics of Genetic Control,* New York, Anchor Press, Doubleday and Co., 1974. Ch 2, n 81; Ch 3, n 10.

Foote, C., Levy, R., and Sander, Frank E. A., *Cases and Materials on Family Law,* 2nd ed., Boston, Little, Brown and Co., 1976. Ch 1, n 18, n 20; Ch 8, n 5, n 7, n 8.

Francouer, Robert T., *Utopian Motherhood,* New York, A. S. Barnes and Co., 1973. Ch 1, n 1, n 15, n 32; Ch 2, n 4.

Gelfand, Leo, "Modern Concepts of Property in a Dead Body," in C. H. Wecht, ed., *Legal Medicine Annual,* New York, Appleton-Century-Crofts, 1971. Ch 3, n 55.

Goldberg, Passow, and Justman, *The Effects of Ability Grouping,* New York, Teachers College Press, 1966. Ch 7, n 4.

Goldstein, Joseph, Freud, Anna, and Solnit, Albert J., *Beyond the Best Interests of the Child,* New York, The Free Press, 1973. Ch 8, n 49; Ch 9, n 11, n 58.

Group for the Advancement of Psychiatry, *Normal Adolescence,* New York, Charles Scribner's Sons, 1968. Ch 9, n 1.

Guttmacher, M. S., "The Legal Status of Therapeutic Abortions," in Harold Rosen, ed., *Abortion in America,* Boston, Beacon Press, 1967. Ch 3, n 8, n 86.

Hayt, E., and Hayt, J., *Legal Aspects of Medical Records,* Berwin, Ill, Physicians' Record Co., 1964. Ch 2, n 65; Ch 7, n 63.

Helfer, R. E., and Kempe, C. H., *The Battered Child,* Chicago, University of Chicago Press, 1968. Ch 8, n 31.

Holder, Angela R., *Medical Malpractice Law,* New York, John Wiley and Sons, 1975. Ch 1, n 50; Ch 2, n 27, n 37; Ch 4, n 50; Ch 7, n 23; Ch 9, n 12, n 68; Ch 10, n 25.

Hollings, Ernest F., *Hunger in America,* New York, Cowles Press, 1970. Ch 2, n 80.

"Juvenile Delinquency Evaluation Report of the City of New York," in Jay Katz and Joseph Goldstein, eds., *The Family and the Law,* New York, The Free Press, 1965. Ch 8, n 84.

Katz, Jay, *Experimentation with Human Beings,* New York, Russell Sage Foundation, 1972. Ch 2, n 34; Ch 4, n 53.

Kirp, David L., and Yudof, Mark G., *Educational Policy and the Law,* Berkeley, Cal, McCutchan Publishing Corp., 1974. Ch 7, n 1.

Leach, Gerald, *The Biocrats: Ethics and the New Medicine,* Baltimore, Penguin Books, 1972. Ch 1, n 43; Ch 2, n 79; Ch 4, n 4.

Lippman, Leopold, and Goldberg, I. L., *Right to Education,* New York, Teachers College Press, 1973. Ch 3, n 74.

Louisell, David and Williams, Harold, *Medical Malpractice*, New York, Matthew Bender and Co., 1960 and annual supplements. Ch 5, n 25.

Morris, Crawford, and Moritz, Alan, *Doctor and Patient and the Law*, 5th ed., St. Louis, The C. V. Mosby Co., 1971. Ch 9, n 12.

Page on Wills, Cincinnati, The W. H. Anderson Co., 1960, Section 17.4. Ch 3, n 30.

Paulsen, M. G., Wadlington, Walter, and Goebel, J., *Domestic Relations: Cases and Materials*, University Casebook Series, Mineola, NY, The Foundation Press, 1974. Ch 8, n 2, n 34.

Pilpel, Harriet, and Zuckerman, Nancy, "Abortion and the Rights of Minors," in *Abortion, Society and the Law*, Cleveland, Case Western Reserve Press, 1973, pages 275–309. Ch 10, n 46, n 49.

Pitmas, Carl, *The Gift Relationship*, New York, Vintage Books, Random House, 1971. Ch 1, n 50.

Prosser, William L., *Torts*, 4th ed., St. Paul, West Publishing Co., 1971. Ch 1, n 77.

Ramsey, Paul, *The Ethics of Fetal Research*, New Haven, Conn, Yale University Press, 1975. Ch 3, n 79, n 92.

Ramsey, Paul, *The Patient as Person*, New Haven, Conn, Yale University Press, 1974. Ch 4, n 53; Ch 6, n 12, n 13, n 20.

Ramsey, Paul, "Screening: An Ethicist's View," in *Ethical Issues in Human Genetics*, New York: Plenum Publishing Corp., 1973, page 157. Ch 2, n 40.

Report of WHO Scientific Group, *Paediatric Research*, WHO Tech. Rep. Series, No. 400 Geneva, 1968. Ch 6, n 41.

Restatement of Torts 2 d, St. Paul, ALI Publishers, Section 59. Ch 10, n 63.

Scott, W. Austin, *Scott on Trusts*, 3rd ed., Sections 112.1 and 112.2, "Unborn Children," Boston, Little, Brown and Co., 1967. Ch 3, n 31, n 32.

Sexton, Patricia C., *Education and Income*, New York, The Viking Press, 1961. Ch 7, n 5.

Shartel, Burke, and Plant, Marcus, *The Law of Medical Practice*, Springfield, Ill, Charles C Thomas Publisher, 1959. Ch 5, n 20.

Simes and Smith, *Future Interests*, St. Paul, West Publishing Co., 1956, Section 227 et seq. Ch 3, n 30.

Slovenko, Ralph, *Psychiatry and the Law*, Boston, Little, Brown and Co., 1973. Ch 9, n 16.

Slovenko, Ralph, and Usdin, Gene, *Psychotherapy, Confidentiality and Privileged Communications*, Springfield, Ill, Charles C. Thomas Publisher, 1966. Ch 9, n 43, n 44, n 47.

Solnit, Albert J., and Green, Morris, "Pediatric Management of the Dying Child: Part II, The Child's Reaction to the Fear of Dying," in *Modern Perspectives in Child Development*, New York, International Universities Press, 1963. Ch 4, n 56.

Sorgen, M. S., Duffy, P. S., Kaplan, W. A., and Margolin, E., *State, School and Family*, New York, Matthew Bender and Co., 1973. Ch 7, n 1.

Wasmuth, C. E., and Wasmuth, C. E., Jr., *Law and the Surgical Team*, Baltimore, The Williams and Wilkins Co., 1969. Ch 6, n 42.

Williams, Glanville, *The Sanctity of Life and the Criminal Law*, New York, Alfred A. Knopf, 1957. Ch 4, n 26.

Federal Statutes, Regulations, and Publications

Buckley Amendment, 20 USCA, Section 1232g. Ch 7, n 19; Ch 9, n 50.

42 *CFR*, Section 50.202. Ch 10, n 38. Section 59.5(2). Ch 10, n 17.

33 *Fed Reg*, No. 221, page 31747, November 16, 1973. Ch 6, n 16, n 35; Ch 8, n 101.

38 *Fed Reg,* page 20930, August 3, 1973. Ch 10, n 36

40 *Fed Reg,* pages 33526–33552, August 8, 1975. Ch 3, n 102.

Kefauver-Harris Act, 21 USC, Section 355. Ch 6, n 3.

National Sickle Cell Anemia Control Act, 42 USCA, Section 300b–300b(5). Ch 2, n 47.

OPRR (NIH, PHS, DHEW) *Reports,* February 1976. Ch 6, n 31.

PL 93-348, 93rd Congress, July 12, 1974. Ch 3, n 5. Section 202(b). Ch 3, n 82. Section 202(3)(b). Ch 3, n 6, n 7. Section 213. Ch 3, n 83.

Report and Appendix to the *Report on Fetal Research* of the Commission for the Protection of Human Subjects of Biomedical and Behavioral Research. Ch 3, n 41, n 95.

Report Prepared for the Subcommittee on Science, Research and Development of the Committee on Science and Astronautics, U.S. House of Representatives, 93rd Congress, 2nd Session, by the Science Policy Research Division of the Congressional Research Service, December 1974, U.S.G.P.O., Washington, D.C., 1974, page 17. Ch 1, n 5, n 9.

Report of Professor Alexander M. Capron to the Commission for the Protection of Human Subjects, Appendix to the Report on Fetal Research. Ch 3, n 45, n 96, n 97, n 98.

Transcript of Public Hearings of the National Commission for the Protection of Human Subjects of Biomedical and Behavioral Research, February 14, 1975, page 130c. Ch 3, n 2, n 93, n 94.

State Executive Orders, Legislative Reports and Statutes

Cal Evidence Code, Section 621. Ch 1, n 36.

Cal Health and Safety Code, Section 25956. Ch 3, n 51. Section 25960. Ch 3, n 57.

Cal Welfare and Institutions Code, Section 601. Ch 8, n 72.

Report of the California Assembly Interim Committee on Criminal Procedure, Juvenile Justice Processes 7, 1971. Ch 9, n 70.

Conn Gen Stats Ann, Section 53 (a)–56. Ch 1, n 53.

Ga Code Ann, Sections 74.101.1 and 74-9904. Ch 1, n 33. Section 88-1201.1. Ch 2, n 68.

Ill Crim Code, Title 38, Section 81 (26). Ch 3, n 47, n 58.

Ind Code, Section 10-112. Ch 3, n 46, n 72.

Kans Stats Ann, Section 23:128–30. Ch 1, n 47.

Ky Crim Code, Section 436.026. Ch 3, n 59.

La Rev Stats Ann, Section 13:1569–70. Ch 3, n 98. Section 14:87.2. Ch 3, n 60.

Me Rev Stats, Title 22, Sections 1574–1576. Ch 3, n 61.

Md Code Ann, Art 43, Section 33a(H). Ch 2, n 69.

Mass Gen Laws, Ch 112, Section 12J as Amended by Ch 421, Mass Ann Laws, 1974, 257. Ch 3, n 48, n 62.

Mass Gen Laws Ann, c. 210, Section 2. Ch 1, n 18; Ch 8, n 14.

Mich Stats, Section 701.19(b) "Kidney Transplant, Donor's Qualifications; Procedure." Ch 6, n 72.

Mich Stats Ann, Section 338.53. Ch 7, n 60; Ch 9, n 36.

Minn Public Health Laws, Section 145.38. Ch 3, n 52.

Mo Gen Laws, Section 188.035. Ch 3, n 64. Section 188.040. Ch 3, n 98.

Mont Rev Stats Ann, Section 94-5-6 (17). Ch 3, n 65. Section 94-5-617 (2) (b). Ch 3, n 98.

Neb Rev Stats, Section 28-4 161. Ch 3, n 66.

Nev Rev Stats, Section 127.070. Ch 1, n 18; Ch 8, n 14.

NJ Stats Ann, Section 9:3–19. Ch 8, n 6.

New York City Health Code, Art 21. Ch 1, n 38.

NY Dom Rel Code, Section 13-aa. Ch 2, n 67.

NY Pub Health Code, Section 4164. Ch 3, n 67.

Ohio Rev Code Ann, Section 2919.14. Ch 3, n 49, n 68.

Okla Stats Ann, Title 10, Sections 551–553. Ch 1, n 34.

Pa Stats Ann, Title 35, Section 6605. Ch 3, n 69.

SD Compiled Laws Ann, Section 34-23A-17. Ch 3, n 17, n 50.

37 *Opinions of the Wisconsin Attorney General* 403, 1948. Ch 8, n 5.

Uniform Anatomical Gift Act, Section 1B. Ch 3, n 42. Section 2B. Ch 3, n 43; Ch 6, n 74.

Utah Code Ann, Section 76-7-312. Ch 3, n 71.

Vt Stats Ann, Title 27, Section 501. Ch 1, n 46.

Foreign Statute

British Adoption Act of 1958. Ch 1, n 18.

INDEX